TRACKING DISCOURSES

Tracking Discourses

Politics, Identity and Social Change

Edited by
Annika Egan Sjölander
&
Jenny Gunnarsson Payne

NORDIC ACADEMIC PRESS

Nordic Academic Press
P.O. Box 1206
SE-221 05 Lund, Sweden
info@nordicacademicpress.com
www.nordicacademicpress.com

© Nordic Academic Press and the authors 2011
Typesetting: Frederic Täckström, www.sbmolle.com
Cover: Lönegård & Co
Coverphoto: Istockphoto.com
Print: ScandBook AB, Falun, Sweden 2011
ISBN: 978-91-85509-39-3

Contents

Preface

It is such a pleasure to finally write the very first words of *Tracking Discourses*. As is often said, the end marks a new beginning, and as authors we are all excited to hear about our readers' responses to our joint attempt at gaining a better grasp of the complexities involved in investigating how discourses can be understood, and more importantly, analysed *in practice*. Even though the research presented in this book is primarily conducted within a variety of Swedish contexts, in which a range of different discourses are explored and scrutinised, the contributions deal with more general problems that transcend its geographical scope. These main issues that the book addresses are summarised in its subtitle: politics, identity and social change.

The discourse analytical perspectives dealt with in this book have gained increased attention in the last decades among Scandinavian scholars of various disciplines; however, such applications are not yet substantially reflected in English-language or other international scholarly literature. This multidisciplinary collection is therefore an attempt to fill a gap in the existing body of literature. The contributions are from a wide range of disciplines in the social sciences and the humanities such as political science, sociology, social work, media and communication studies, ethnology and linguistics. We hope to present the reader with an insight into the ways in which discourse analytical perspectives have been received and re-worked in Swedish academia. The emphasis lies on the empirical use of various theoretical perspectives; a subject that has engaged many discourse analytical scholars around the world during the last decade.

This point in time would not have arrived without the thorough support of many people and institutions along the way. First of all we want to thank all the invited guest lecturers to the Ph.D. course 'Perspectives on Discourse Analysis: Democracy, Politics and Social Change' for their generous contributions and willingness to take part in a (self-)reflective dialogue in relation to the research traditions of discourse theory (DT) and critical discourse analysis (CDA). We could not have hoped for a better outcome when the initial idea to study these popular traditions together was firstly formulated in the summer of 2006. We were also imbued with energy when it was discovered that everyone we approached was interested in taking part in the project. Apart from the project initiators and editors, Dr Annika Egan Sjölander, senior lecturer at Umeå University, Sweden and Dr Jenny Gunnarsson Payne, lecturer and researcher at Södertörn University, Sweden, the guest teachers have included the CDA scholars Dr Michał Krzyżanowski, senior research fellow at Lancaster University, UK, and Dr Peter Berglez, associate professor at Örebro University, Sweden, and two DT scholars from the University of Essex, UK: Dr Aletta Norval, reader and director of the Ph.D. programme in Ideology and Discourse Analysis, and Dr Jason Glynos, senior lecturer. We would also like to express our gratitude to Professor Ruth Wodak, distinguished professor in discourse studies at Lancaster University, Professor Lilie Chouliaraki, professor from the London School of Economics and Political Science, and Dr David Howarth, reader and co-director of the Centre for Theoretical Studies, for showing interest and support in the initial planning process of the project. One of the authors in this book, David Payne, is enrolled in the IDA Ph.D. programme at the University of Essex and gave a lecture about the Marxist influence on discourse analysis.

The focus on the exchange of thoughts between leading representatives of these two traditions was a rather unusual exercise at the time. Since then, similar types of meetings between scholars of DT and CDA have been set up by others, and their aims have also been to investigate the similarities and differences between these (and other) influential schools within the field of discourse studies (cf. Glynos et al. 2009).[1] These meeting points continue to constitute important places of discovery, and there are several strands of thought that need to be investigated in more depth – if not to identify common features and possible points of cross-fertilisation, then to flesh out variations in more detail. The atmosphere and dialogue during our talks can be summarised mainly as a manifestation of commonalities between the two approaches. The different kinds of overlaps that were discussed and how distinctions were articulated will be presented in the following Introduction.

Apart from the curiosity and substantial commitment from the doctoral students who took part in the Ph.D. course 'Perspectives on Discourse Analysis: Democracy, Politics and Social Change' – many of whom have contributed to this volume – there is one person in particular who has made the 'book dream' a reality; namely, our publisher Annika Olsson from Nordic Academic Press, Lund. Of crucial importance for completing the book was also our editor Magnus Ingvarsson, whose expertise as well as helpful and positive attitude carried us through the final stages of publication. In addition, our warmest thanks go to Adrián Groglopo, Ph.D. student from the Sociology Department at Umeå University, who came up with the main title for the book: *Tracking Discourses*. Dr Martin Shaw, our English language editor from Språkcentrum (also at Umeå University), has been a wonder of patience to work with and we are very grateful for his help. Our former librarian at the Umeå University Library, the late Ludmila Andersson, also deserves to be mentioned and especially remembered for making sure that all the course books, including suggested reference literature, were easily available. Her professional service enabled us to improve the library's body of literature in this vibrant field of research, and this will be of great benefit for future users. During the work with this book, one of the editors (Egan Sjölander) also had the privilege of taking part in the lively seminars of the Language-Ideology-Power group at Lancaster University, led by Ruth Wodak. These encounters provided important levels of input to the project, especially regarding the understanding of CDA and its many varieties. Two other individuals have steadfastedly supported the whole project and helped out along the way by encouraging us to be innovative and to find alternative ways to secure the funding that has been required to row this relatively ambitious project ashore. The first person is Dr Bo Nilsson, the former head of the Department of Culture and Media Studies, Umeå University, who encouraged us to pursue our ideas from the very beginning, and the second is the current head of department, Dr Kerstin Engström, who also provided vital support at the very end of the working process regarding practical administrative matters. Thanks also to Ulla Westermark, who worked diligently for several years on the administration of the projects and took care of the financial accounts.

We have been fortunate to receive essential financial support from several external and internal institutions. The Swedish Foundation for International Cooperation in Research and Higher Education (STINT) contributed with a generous grant in relation to the Ph.D. course. The Royal Swedish Academy of Letters, History and Antiquities (Kungliga Vitterhetsakademien) and the Letterstedska Association (Letterstedska föreningen) helped in meeting the costs of guest lecturers. Riksbankens Jubileumsfond (RJ) contributed with substantial funding covering the expenses for meetings and building up the contact network necessary for carrying through this project. Besides the financial support from the Department of Culture and Media Studies regarding some overhead costs, the Faculty of Arts and the Faculty of Social Sciences, including the Graduate School in Population Dynamics and Public Policy, all contributed to covering the costs associated with both the Ph.D. course and the consequent book production. The central administration at Umeå University also catered for some of the essential 'fika' breaks during this intellectual endeavour. Many thanks to all.

Annika Egan Sjölander, on behalf of the editors

Notes

1 Two such examples are the project 'Discourse Analysis Network', which was supported during 2008/2009 by the UK Economic Social Research Council's National Centre for Research Methods Networks for Methodological Innovation, and a Ph.D. course that was arranged by Roskilde University at the end of 2009 called 'Applying Discourse Theory and CDA in the study of media, images and film'. Both editors had the advantage of participating in the final closing workshop of the UK network in Essex in April 2009 and to present and discuss our respective discourse analytical research with a diverse group of researchers (Egan Sjölander 2009; Gunnarsson Payne 2009).

References

Egan Sjölander, A., 2009. Rare and Fruitful – The Concrete Use of Foucault's Discourse Theory in Media and Communication Research. Paper presented at the ESRC Networks for Methodological Innovation's Conference in Discourse Analysis held at the University of Essex, UK, April 2009.

Glynos, J., Howarth, D., Norval, A. & Speed, E., 2009. *Discourse Analysis: Varieties and Methods.* ESRC National Centre for Research Methods Review Paper. ESRC National Centre for Research Methods. NCRM/014. August 2009.

Gunnarsson Payne, J., 2009. Beyond Different Wave-Lengths in the Study of Feminist Media. Paper presented at the ESRC Networks for Methodological Innovation's Conference in Discourse Analysis held at the University of Essex, UK, April 2009.

CHAPTER I

Introduction

Comparing Critical Discourse Analysis and Discourse Theory

Annika Egan Sjölander

Ever since the linguistic turn, the study of 'discourse' has become increasingly popular in a wide range of disciplines within the humanities and social sciences (Howarth 2007, p. 10; Wodak & Krzyżanowski 2008, p. 1).[1] As Aletta Norval (1999, p. 1) writes, the linguistic turn in the social sciences and humanities not only indicated a renewed interest in language as such, but also implied a realisation that language is at least partly constitutive of the world, rather than merely a mirror of it, as was previously the predominant view (cf. Alvesson & Kärreman 2000, p. 137).[2] As a consequence of this widespread activity in the discourse analytical field, the notion of 'discourse' has come to include not only analysis of text in the strict sense of the word, but is also frequently used to interpret wider cultural and socio-political processes. The meaning of politics, formations of identities and the possibilities of social change are all issues that capture the interest of the authors in this volume, as well as discourse analytical scholars all around the world.

In *Discourse in Late Modernity: Rethinking Critical Discourse Analysis*, Lilie Chouliaraki and Norman Fairclough (1999, p. 4) argue that there is room, and a great need for, 'critical analysis of discourse as a fundamental element in the critical theorisation and analysis of late modernity'. Several of the case studies presented in this volume deal with contemporary issues and living conditions in the early twenty-first century, such as the meaning of an ageing population (Chapter 11 by Lundgren) or the discrimination of immigrants (Chapter 5 by Ngeh). In Chouliaraki and Fairclough's (1999) frequently referred to book, the authors embark on a 'transdisciplinary' expedition with various theorists about social life, critical research on social change, and contemporary conditions in late modern societies.[3] Their aims are to establish a better theoretical basis for critical discourse analysis, as well as to show the tradition's contribution regarding the analysis of language and discourse, which has become all the more important in critical social science in general (Chouliaraki & Fairclough 1999, p. 4). Since then, Fairclough (2003) has himself continued this pedagogic ambition by attempting to provide scholars in the social sciences and humanities with a useable framework for analysing spoken and written language.[4]

In the introduction to *Discourse Theory and Political Analysis: Identities, Hegemonies and Social Change*, David Howarth and Yannis Stavrakakis (2000, p. 1) point out the need for political analysis from different discourse analytical perspectives. The authors stress the importance of conducting more research focused on 'key *political issues*', such as populist and nationalist ideologies, new social movements and diverse forms of hegemonic struggles, which they claim have been missing. Analyses of this type were subsequently presented in Howarth et al. (2000), and build on the research programme of discourse theory that was originally formulated by Ernesto Laclau and Chantal Mouffe (1985/2001) in their 'modern classic' *Hegemony and Socialist Strategy: Towards a Radical Democratic Politics*. Several of the authors in *Tracking Discourses* also devote their attention to what could be classified as key political issues. One example is an analysis of the controversial issue of paternity leave, inspired by Michel Foucault's (1993/1971) understanding of discourse(s) (Chapter 6 by Sylwan). Others apply central concepts within discourse theory, and not only from Laclau's and Mouffe's respective writings (cf. Chapter 3 by Carlbaum), but also from the 'logics approach' that has been developed by Jason Glynos and David Howarth (2007) in *Logics of Critical Explanation in Social and Political Theory* (cf. Chapter 10 by Sjöstedt Landén). Here, Glynos and Howarth (2007, p. 4) strive to 'develop an approach that respects the self-interpretations of social actors, while not reducing explanations to their subjective viewpoints alone', and to search for 'a type of explanation that admits of a certain generality, provides space for critique, and yet respects the specificity of the case under investigation'. Building on Laclau's previous work, the authors formulate a poststructuralist alternative to what they define as dominant paradigms in social science, such as positivism and hermeneutics. Based on their particular ontological and epistemological standpoints, Glynos and Howarth (2007, pp. 11, 28) also contest what Roy Bhaskar and his critical realist followers (cf. Archer et al. 1998) suggest as an alternative to positivism.[5]

Purpose

The aim of this introduction is threefold. The first purpose is to discuss the motives for the study of critical discourse analysis (henceforth CDA) and discourse theory (henceforth DT) in parallel. This is partly in order to gain a better understanding of the reasons behind the previous lack of dialogue between the perspectives. It is also motivated by the need within the field to further clarify unarticulated understandings of key concepts such as 'critical' and 'discourse' (including their relation to the 'non-discursive'). These unexplained viewpoints tend to generate confusion and obscure significant differences in standpoints between researchers.

The second purpose is to explore some of the crucial similarities and differences between the traditions that have been revealed, and especially in relation to the common themes that are dealt with in this book: politics, identity and social change. I will do so by discussing literature and by 'narrating' or 'documenting' parts of the dialogue that took place between leading representatives of CDA and DT during a roundtable discussion on these issues held in October 2008.[6] Part of our overall ambition with the whole project was to create this meeting point between the two perspectives.

A third purpose is to provide some background, as well as to introduce the structure and the collection of contributions presented in *Tracking Discourses*. As is the case in any research activity, it is meaningful to understand the context within which a project unfolds. In essence, I would argue, that is the meaning behind the idea of knowledge being 'socially constructed' (Berger & Luckmann 1991/1966; Burr 2003).

In what follows I will describe the focus of our joint project and the rationale for undertaking it. Thereafter, I will share a few thoughts from the editors' point of view regarding this comparison and present some of my own discourse analytical research. I will then sketch important influences and features in each of the studied 'schools', including work of its main representatives, and how the authors in this book have made use of their respective perspectives. In the next section I will discuss crucial similarities and differences between CDA and DT. Finally, I will introduce the overall aim and structure of the book, including the different contributions to *Tracking Discourses*.

Focus and motives

CDA and DT represent two highly influential traditions within the discourse analytical field as a whole. Both schools have been of great importance and they continue to inspire researchers, also in Scandinavia.[7] This is one important reason why the two schools have been our main focus in the Ph.D. course 'Perspectives on Discourse Analysis: Democracy, Politics and Social Change' and when conducting the empirical research that is presented here. However, despite this shared interest in CDA and DT, some authors have found it more relevant to explore and apply other variations within the discourse analytical field. Mediated discourse analysis (henceforth MDA), which was developed by Ron Scollon, Suzie Scollon, Sigrid Norris and others, is one such example, and has been used in the analysis of blogging practices (Chapter 8 by Faye Hendrick).[8] Another important motive for us to focus on CDA and DT has been these traditions' strong commitments to discuss, and to explore in depth, issues relating to democracy, politics and social change. These focal points overlap with our own common knowledge interests. Even though one can easily identify commonalities between the two schools, such as a poststructuralist influence combined with a conflict theoretical perspective, in the main they do appear to have developed separately from each other. This in itself constitutes a third reason motivating us to study both perspectives in parallel. We have been curious to learn more about the reasons why dialogue between the two has been so rare until relatively recently. Given the degree of similar research interests and common intellectual 'herit-age', this scarcity of dialogue seems puzzling, at a glance.[9] In order to gain a better grasp of each tradition, the curriculum of the Ph.D. course focused on ontological and epistemological presuppositions, 'classic' texts, as well as key concepts within CDA and DT. We also looked at more recent theoretical developments and methodological strategies, and studied their contributions to contemporary debates on democracy, politics and social change.

The author's position

It is indeed a challenge to capture these multifaceted traditions in a sensible way. This task is made all the more difficult as I have not conducted research specifically within any of the studied discourse analytical schools before and could therefore be viewed as somewhat of an outsider to both. This might on the other hand be seen as an advantage from the comparative point of view, because I have not previously invested heavily in either of the perspectives.[10] Readers also ought to keep in mind what has been stated many times: most discourse analytical perspectives are diverse in and of themselves (Winther Jørgensen & Phillips 1999, pp. 72, 121; Glynos et al. 2009).[11] According to Jacob Torfing (2005, p. 5), there are many traditions that internally 'vary both according to their understand-ing of discourse and their understanding of the imbrication of lan-guage and political power struggles'. Furthermore, as reinforced by the panel participants during the roundtable discussion, different researchers tend to develop their own interpretations and speciali-ties within each school. In my understanding of CDA and DT, the former seems to be more internally diverse than the latter. One crucial factor that produces this diversity within CDA consists of the eclectic approaches that are nurtured through the strong multi-disciplinary, interdisciplinary and transdisciplinary commitment of several of its scholars (cf. Weiss & Wodak 2003; Wodak & Chilton 2005; Chouliaraki & Fairclough 1999).[12]

In my thesis, *Kärnproblem* (Sjölander 2004), the societal handling of highly radioactive and long-lived nuclear waste from power production was studied. The thesis had a particular focus on the sense-making process regarding the long-term management of the localisation and storage problems that all countries using nuclear power struggle with; that is what I call 'the nuclear waste discourse'. This particular environmental problem constitutes one of the unwanted side effects of the production of wealth in what Ulrich Beck (1992) calls the risk society. Opinion formation and various public communication initiatives came to play a pivotal role in the evolving decision-making process in the Swedish local community that I studied. In short, 'information' was seen by all the involved stakeholders as a vital source for reaching a legitimate decision. The entire process from the industry's first proposal to conduct a pre-study in the municipality, to the local referendum that was held at the end, and which resulted in a 'no' to further investigations, took five years in total. This was significantly longer than first predicted.[13] With a large amount of empirical material to deal with (over a thousand published news articles, and so on) I was in good need of a theoretical base and perspective that could be of help in the selection process for the analysis, both regarding which research questions to prioritise and which phenomena to focus on in the practical text/content analysis.

The close integration of theory and method in most discourse analytical perspectives, 'a whole package', as Winther Jørgensen and Phillips (1999, p. 12) describe it, therefore suited this case study very well. In particular, it was the research programme that Michel Foucault (1971/1993; 1981) presents in *The Order of Discourse* that caught my attention. Foucault offers not only relevant definitions of what constitutes discourse(s) and how they 'function', but also points out what to look for as a researcher when studying the exclusionary mechanisms that are always at work, and that control and delimit the content and form of any discourse. This contribution is one important reason why Foucault is often referred to as the very founder of discourse analysis (Fairclough 1992, p. 37). In almost all textbooks about discourse analysis, Foucault's work is mentioned as instrumental, and especially so regarding the understanding of discourse(s) and their productive power, including his innovative conception of power (Mills 1997, p. 7).[14] His writings have clearly influenced both DT and CDA (cf. Fairclough 1992, pp. 37–61; Howarth 2007, pp. 59–89).[15]

Contrary to the widespread reception of this controversial sociologist, historian and philosopher, I found the Foucaultian framework not only more coherent and comprehensive than others, but also more practical to use in the concrete analysis of the nuclear waste discourse (Egan Sjölander 2009). Of course, what was of crucial importance here was that I could subscribe to his ontological and epistemological views, and in particular to his understanding of discourses: for example, however critical as researchers we are of the discourses we study, we are always part of their continuous constitution. Even should we wish to, we cannot escape the power of discourse(s), as Foucault (1981, p. 49) states at the very beginning of his famous inaugural lecture at the Collège de France. However, he also shows that analytical work does at least offer a possibility for resistance to the taken-for-grantedness that discourses (re)produce. Furthermore, Foucault (1971, p. 7; 1981, p. 52) emphasises that discourses must not be understood as something hidden, structural or abstract that are waiting to be discovered or revealed by a researcher; instead, he stresses that they have a 'formidable materiality'.

> We must not imagine that there is a great unsaid or a great un-thought which runs throughout the world and intertwines with all its forms and all its events, and which we would have to articulate or to think at last. Discourses must be treated as discontinuous practices, which cross each other, are sometimes juxtaposed with one another, but can just as well exclude or be unaware of each other. (Foucault 1981, p. 67)

After re-reading *The Order of Discourse* quite a few years after my very first encounter with the text, I decided that it was well worth the attempt to apply his proposal in full instead of creating a 'model' of my own. Therefore, part of the aim of the thesis project was to explore whether Foucault's discourse analytical understanding, which was rooted in the discipline of history and used to describe long time periods, would also make sense when analysing contemporary issues and traditional types of corresponding empirical materials. How it worked out is ultimately up to the readers of *Kärnproblem* to decide, but from my point of view it definitely did. From the

19

very outset, the analysis of the nuclear waste discourse was focused on the external and internal systems of exclusion: firstly, the identification of taboo subjects, the division of madness and the will to truth that were manifested in the talk and institutional setting surrounding the issue; and secondly, the analysis of the role of the author, the commentator, and the organisation of the discourse. All these mechanisms of exclusion had an impact on what was possible to say and by whom in this particular context. I thereafter directed a significant amount of attention to the conditions of possibility upon which these analysed series of events in the nuclear waste discourse depended; like, for example, the complex role of science and expertise in the risk society, the power of the journalistic institution, the crisis of democracy and the lack of legitimacy for traditional political systems in late modern times, including the marginal position of the Samish population in Swedish society, and so on. This genealogical part of the analysis is, according to Foucault, necessary in order to be able to question the regularity of the discourse and the articulated will to truth. I still claim that this Foucaultian framework, even if complicated and contradictory at times, has a great deal to offer that remains unexplored within the broader discourse analytical field (Sjölander 2004; Egan Sjölander 2009). This is also the case when it comes to the 'close analysis of particular texts' that Fairclough and Wodak (1997, p. 261) otherwise note as missing to a large extent in the abstract kind of analysis that Foucault previously has inspired others to pursue. A related type of Foucaultian discourse analysis is undertaken by Mathias Sylwan (Chapter 6) in his historical study of the construction of paternity leave and fatherhood in Swedish television news reports.

Critical discourse analysis

Today, researchers from literally all parts of the world conduct CDA that builds on the work of Teun van Dijk, Norman Fairclough and Ruth Wodak. This trio of researchers have been instrumental for CDA's establishment and are still regarded as its main present-day representatives (Billig 2003, p. 35). van Dijk, Fairclough and Wodak held a workshop in 1991 that is often mentioned in the literature because the research activity expanded dramatically thereafter (Wodak 2001a, p. 4; Chilton & Wodak 2005, pp. xi –xvii; Kendall 2007, p. 3). However, the many historical roots of CDA date back significantly longer than that. Several of the most significant ones have emerged from linguistics, and especially critical linguistics (henceforth CL), which was developed by a research group at the University of East Anglia in the UK from the 1970s and onwards (Fairclough & Wodak 1997, pp. 283–284; Wodak 2001a, p. 3; Chilton & Wodak 2005, p. xi). According to Fairclough (1992, p. 26), 'They tried to marry a method of linguistic text analysis with a social theory of the functioning of language in political and ideological processes'. This attempt to link the social analysis to the linguistic one is very much reflected in Fairclough's own writing. One of the most comprehensive illustrations of how CDA can contribute to social research – based on the argument that language has become more salient and important in a range of contemporary social processes – is articulated in *Discourse in Late Modernity* (Chouliaraki & Fairclough 1999).

Apart from the crucial influence of CL, Wodak and Weiss (2003, p. 11) also mention the importance of classic rhetoric, textlinguistics, socio-linguistics, applied linguistics and pragmatics for the development of CDA. They also include the influence of various sociological approaches that enable the essential analysis of the interrelations between discourse, power and society that is so characteristic of CDA. Alon Lischinsky's (Chapter 9) investigation of the discursive construction of corporate organisations' identities, which consists of a quantitative and qualitative analysis of the linguistic devices used in environmental and corporate social responsibility reports from Swedish multinational companies, is a good example of the linguistic roots of CDA. This disciplinary belonging – which differs for CDA compared to DT, which is more associated with political philosophy – was mentioned several times during the roundtable discussion. It was stated, for example, that the amount of detailed analytical work regularly undertaken at the level of individual texts in CDA is much more than in DT. It was also concluded that the former tradition is 'less theoretical' than the latter.

The different mappings of intellectual influence that I have found regarding CDA reveal a very rich and diverse pattern. The critical theory of the Frankfurt School is among the crucial influences that stand out, and this is partly reflected in the very naming of CDA (Fairclough & Wodak 1997, p. 261; Weiss & Wodak 2003, p. 14).[16] As opposed to other perspectives, such as Emanuel Schlegloff's (1997) descriptive conversational analysis, CDA is framed as a 'critical' type of analysis (Sjölander 2004, p. 43). The term refers to the researchers' radical criticism of the present social order and unequal social relations (Billig 2003, p. 38; Kendall 2007). The problem-oriented commitment to deal with 'everyday' social problems, such as discrimination, exclusion and subordination in society, is widespread among CDA scholars.[17] Furthermore, the will to contribute to social change and to formulate alternative or 'bottom-up' perspectives on language use that establishes and maintains unequal power relations are also common aims for CDA researchers (Fairclough & Wodak 1997, p. 258; Meyer 2001, p. 15; Weiss & Wodak 2003, pp. 14–15).

Michael Billig (2003), who has himself been working within discursive psychology, questions any unreflective use of the term 'critical'. I believe this is a relevant viewpoint, because 'being critical' can imply that the researcher positions himself or herself in a privileged position vis-à-vis both other, so-called non-critical scholars, and in relation to what or who is being studied.[18] Wodak (2001a, p. 9), who has published extensively on the theme of critical research, summarises the meaning as 'having distance to the data, embedding the data in the social, taking a political stance explicitly, and a focus on self-reflection as scholars doing research'.[19] David Payne and Jenny Gunnarsson Payne (Chapter 2) raise fundamental questions regarding the role of criticism in social and political theory and discuss the related and complex issue of emancipation, drawing on the work of Ernesto Laclau, which they conclude manages to leave the Idea of emancipation unharmed.

The two scholars within CDA that we have focused on during the course are Norman Fairclough and Ruth Wodak. We chose them for two main reasons: firstly, they represent two varieties of CDA (Fairclough & Wodak 1997, pp. 264–267) and, secondly, because both have had a significant impact on the Scandinavian research landscape in the period during which discourse analytical approaches have grown in popularity. However, there is only room for a small sample of their key contributions here. Jonathan Ngeh's (Chapter 5) analysis of the structural/institutional discrimination of Cameroonian students in higher education in Sweden is anchored in the writings of both Fairclough and Wodak. In his case study, Ngeh tests Fairclough's (2001) stepwise methodological approach to discourse analysis.[20]

In a joint publication, Fairclough and Wodak (1997, p. 258) define *discourse* as language use in speech and writing and as a form of social practice; a definition that explains the strong focus on different kinds of text analysis in their research. They also stress a dialectical dimension; namely, that discourses or discursive events are socially constitutive, as well as shaped by situations, institutions and social structures. Furthermore, they claim that discourse is affected by, and affects, how objects of knowledge are constructed and how power, social identities and relationships are formed. Even though other variations of the discourse concept have been presented by both scholars over the years, the core themes of the one described above are frequently referred to and remain largely intact (cf. Wodak 2008, p. 3).[21] I am thinking here of the understanding of language use in terms of social practice/action, including nonverbal communication and visual images, and a distinction between the discursive and the non-discursive.

Fairclough's (1992, p. 73; 1995b, p. 59) model for how to analyse communicative events is a good illustration of the latter theme (see Figure 1). In short, the model distinguishes between three levels: the specific *text*, the institutional *discursive practice*, and the surrounding wider 'non-discursive' context, which he labels *sociocultural practice*.[22] The text is placed at the centre and the discursive practice, which includes text production as well as consumption, mediates between the textual, the social and cultural respectively (Fairclough 1995b, pp. 57–62). The purpose of the analysis is, then, to scrutinise 'how texts work within sociocultural practice' (Fairclough 1995a, p. 7).[23]

In his thesis *The Materiality of Media Discourse*, Peter Berglez (2006) analyses the relationship between the capitalist hegemonic order and the mass media in terms of journalistic modes. By inte-

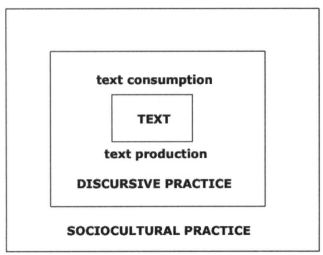

Figure 1. A framework for critical discourse analysis of a communicative event (Fairclough 1995, p. 59).

grating previously separated perspectives from the field of political economy with cultural studies/discourse analysis, Berglez strives to develop a 'cultural materialist oriented CDA'. Such an alternative approach aims to take fully into account both discursive and economic/material aspects when analysing capitalist society and the role of the journalistic institution within it. For democratic reasons, Berglez calls for new journalistic modes to be developed that fully embrace a transnational epistemology and that include the reality of global capitalism in everyday (local) news reporting.

Already in one of his earlier books, *Discourse and Social Change*, Fairclough (1992) expressed his hope of developing an approach to language analysis that would be useful for studies of social and cultural change. This theme runs throughout his writings and has been explored in different contexts; for instance, regarding the commodification of public services in the UK (Fairclough 1992), or more recently in Romania, one of the Central and Eastern European countries in 'transition' (Fairclough 2005a).

Text, genre, intertextuality, interdiscursivity and context are all core concepts within CDA and, like discourse, myriad definitions have been articulated with different emphases (Wodak 2008).[24] In a recent textbook that introduces these different key concepts and methods, Wodak (2008, p. 6) defines *text*, in its most simple form, as 'a specific and unique realization of discourse' and further points out that every text belongs to a *genre*, understood as a conventionalised use of language and associated with a particular type of social activity (Wodak 2008, p. 14). Wodak's (2001a, p. 11) influence from critical theory is visible in another definition, which states that texts are 'often sites of struggle in that they show traces of differing discourses and ideologies contending and struggling for dominance'.

Intertextuality refers 'to the fact that all texts are linked to other texts, both in the past and in the present' (Wodak 2008, p. 3). As Fairclough (2003, p. 218) defines the concept, there is a presence of elements from other texts within all texts. Links can be established in different ways: 'through continued reference to a topic or main actors; through reference to the same events; or by the transfer of main arguments from one text into the next' (Krzyżanowski & Wodak 2008, p. 205).[25] Joakim Isaksson (Chapter 4) combines Fairclough's definition of intertextuality with two other analytical concepts from DT (*articulation* and *aspect change/dawning*) when studying how pupils in need of special support in school have been, and are, constructed in Swedish education policy. In the analysis, the role of the researcher is to identify which other texts, and discourses, the analysed one is built on or borrows from; what I would express as linking a text to possibly relevant contexts (cf. Fairclough 1995b, pp. 61–62). Our roundtable participants spoke in unison about the immense importance of 'contextualisation' in discourse analytical research.

The discourse-historical approach (DHA), a particular form of CDA developed by Ruth Wodak and her Vienna Group, incorporates what she describes as a 'theory of context' (Kendall 2007, p. 3). This entails a triangulatory analytic approach that is interdisciplinary, multi-methodological, and based on a variety of different empirical data (Wodak 2001b, p. 67; 2008, pp. 12–13).[26] As the name DHA indicates, the historical perspective is of special importance (Wodak 2001b; 2006, p. 184).[27] Another key component is the socio-cognitive dimension, that Wodak argues has been unjustly dismissed by previous CDA scholars, but which she maintains plays a pivotal role because it mediates between discourse and society (Wodak 2006, p. 179). One could say that the socio-cognitive level links social structures with the field of action or the individual. 'The discourse-historical approach elaborates and links to the sociocognitive theory of Teun van Dijk ... and views "discourse" as a form of knowledge and memory, whereas text illustrates concrete oral utterances or written documents' (Wodak & Weiss 2003, p. 13; cf. van Dijk 2003). The DHA research programme has been used to analyse a wide range of subjects and a variety of methods have been applied. Politics relating to the European Union constitute one important theme (Wodak 2009; Wodak & Weiss 2005; Triandafyllidou et al. 2009; Krzyżanowski 2005, 2010), and discrimination another; for example, in anti-Semitic, right-wing populist and racist discourses (Riesigil & Wodak 2001b; Krzyżanowski & Wodak 2008).[28]

Discourse theory

DT, or PDT as representatives have been labelling their perspective recently, where the 'P' most often has come to stand for *political,* has, as mentioned earlier, emerged from pioneering work by the political theorists Ernesto Laclau and Chantal Mouffe (Glynos et al. 2009; Torfing 2005, pp. 3, 12). The 'P' could also refer to the post-Marxist, poststructuralist, postmodern, post-analytical or psychoanalytical perspectives that are all associated with this 'well-established political science research programme' (Howarth & Stavarakakis 2000, p. 1). In *Hegemony and Socialist Strategy. Towards a Radical Democratic Politics,* Laclau and Mouffe (1985/2001; 2008) try to tackle the problem of class reductionism and economic determinism in Marxist theory. They use the work of Antonio Gramsci (1973/2007; 1973), and in particular his notion of hegemony, to move away from preset categories that are embedded in the Marxist framing of how to understand politics, identity and social change. They also revise Louis Althusser's (1971/2001; 1976) writings on ideology for the same purpose (Glynos et al. 2009, p. 7). The poststructuralist Jacques Derrida and his deconstructive 'method', alongside Jacques Lacan's psychoanalysis, also provided pivotal input for the authors in their formulation of this post-Marxist position that embraces both an 'anti-essentialist ontology' and an 'anti-foundationalist epistemo-logy' (Torfing 2005, p. 13).

Such a poststructuralist outlook on the world, including how to gain knowledge about it, forms a vital part of what could be called a more general 'DT-grammar'. This grammar serves as the common ground for an otherwise heterogeneous, growing group of research-ers from a variety of disciplines around the globe (Torfing 2005, p. 3).[29] DT scholars share the viewpoint that 'all objects and actions are meaningful, and that their meaning is conferred by histori-cally specific systems of rules', or discursive formations (Howarth & Stavarakakis 2000, p. 2). They also subscribe to the perspective that discourse(s) partially fix the meaning of objects and actions, yet emphasise that they have no transcendental centre or pre-given essence (Torfing 2005, p. 13). Instead, discourse theorists stress that meaning is always 'contextual, relational and contingent' (Howarth 2004, p. 317). This strong emphasis on the radical contingency of meaning is, in my interpretation, a crucial part of the novelty in the DT approach.[30]

While Laclau and Mouffe agree with Foucault about the con-nection between power and discourse, they take issue with any distinction between the discursive and the non-discursive (Laclau & Mouffe 1985, p. 107). Such a division is sometimes implied in Foucault's writings (cf. 1971/1993; 1981). Instead, Laclau and Mouffe (1985, p. 108) point out that 'every object is constituted as an object of discourse', but such an argument 'has *nothing to do* with whether there is a world external to thought'. An earthquake certainly exists, they argue, but its meaning completely depends on the particular, always contingent 'discursive conditions of emergence' (Laclau & Mouffe 1985, p. 108). These ongoing historical construc-tions make any discursive formation vulnerable to change. Yet it is the ever-changing orders, or discourse(s), that constitute an object's identity and significance, as Howarth and Stavrakakis (2000, p. 3) express it. Discourse, according to them, is understood as a social and political construction that establishes a system of relations between objects and practices and that constitutes social reality. According to Laclau (2005, p. 68), discourse is even 'the primary terrain of the constitution of objectivity as such'. It also offers (subject) positions that social agents or individuals can identify with (Howarth & Stavrakakis 2000, p. 3).[31]

These acts of identification, specifically regarding the formation of cutter identities in personal accounts of self-harm, are the focus of Anna Johansson's (Chapter 7) contribution. She applies many of Laclau and Mouffe's concepts, such as 'hegemonic intervention' and 'floating signifier'. Johansson argues that these enable a political analysis of identification acts that are not always regarded as such (see also Johansson 2010). Jenny Gunnarsson Payne (2006) also explores identification processes from a DT perspective in her thesis *Syster-skapets logiker*, and more specifically the meaning of feminist zines among their diverse groups of producers. She identifies 'sisterhood' as an 'empty signifier'. Both the concept of an empty signifier and a floating signifier shed light on the ever- shifting meanings of objects and practices, and have often been used to illustrate the contingent and conflictual construction of otherwise reified or taken-for-granted understandings of certain phenomena (cf. Torfing 1999, p. 301; Winther Jørgensen & Phillips 1999, p. 39). Gunnarsson Payne (2006) takes inspiration from Laclau's (2005) *On Populist Reason*, that focuses on the nature and logics of the formation of collective identities, or articulations of social demands. Gunnarsson Payne (2006, p. 194) shows how the feminist zine community 'springs forth from its antagonistic relation with the patriarchal oppressor', which constitutes the all- important collective 'enemy' in this otherwise potentially fragile alliance of diverse feminist groups. This 'constitutive outside' of a discourse forms its exteriority and limits its content. An enemy represents that which cannot be incorporated within a discursive formation, but the constitutive outside is vital for its very existence, even if it threatens the current stability of the same discourse and blocks the identity of the inside (Torfing 1999, p. 299).

After the publication of *Hegemony and Socialist Strategy*, Laclau continued to 'spell out in an even more coherent fashion the framework of his political post-structuralism' (Critchley & Marchart 2004, p. 5). Part of this work is presented in *New Reflections on the Revolution of Our Time* (1990), where Laclau reformulates some of his basic ideas; for example, regarding the subject and identification processes. The influence of Lacanian psychoanalysis and the notion of a fundamental 'lack' in the subject, as well as in the social or society at large, both become stronger. The more structuralist concept of 'subject position' is, for example, replaced by 'identification'. The intention is to break loose from any sense of identity formation as a structurally pre-determined process. The central DT term 'dislocation', which relates to the disruption or destabilisation of discourses when ' the contingency of discursive structures is made visible', is also linked to the same psychoanalytical influence (Howarth & Stavrakakis 2000, p. 13).[32]

Laclau and Mouffe (1985/2001, p. 1) point out that *Hegemony and Socialist Strategy* was written during a time when Marxism was on the decline. The Left movement faced several challenges. They could identify a great need for the articulation of another, 'new', kind of socialist strategy that moved away from the dominant class perspective to also allow for other, non-predefined, types of political struggles. Their proposal was formulated as a plea for 'radical plural democracy' (1985/2001, pp. 149–194; 2008, pp. 241–260). Laclau and Mouffe have continued to develop this alternative conflict-theoretical perspective ever since, but published their work for the most part separately.

Mouffe (2000; 2005) has written extensively about the meaning of politics, including dominant viewpoints on Western democracy. Mouffe (2000, p. 6) argues that if the neo-liberal hegemony remains unchallenged, the democratic institutions of today are at severe risk. As an alternative to previous understandings of democracy, she puts forward an *agonistic model*. Mouffe argues (2000, p. 11) that her non-essentialist approach – informed by deconstruction and post-structuralism – is absolutely necessary for a 'proper understanding of democracy'. Furthermore, she strongly contests any consensus-oriented ideal in politics. The refusal of confrontation and an overly strong desire for conformism can lead to apathy among citizens and result in a widespread disaffection when it comes to political participation. Pointing to a worst case scenario, Mouffe claims that such an ideal even threatens the very basis of civility (2000, pp. 98–107). The growing success of right-wing politics in contemporary Europe is an example of a development in a direction that very much concerns her (Mouffe 2005, pp. 64–89). Here, we can identify a clear parallel in research interest with CDA scholars; for example, Wodak (Wodak & Riesigl 2001; Krzyżanowski & Wodak 2008).

One of Mouffe's (2000, p. 104–105) main targets of her critique is the Habermasian influenced theory of deliberative democracy, with its idea that power can be dissolved through a rational debate (cf. Dryzeks 2000; Permfors & Roth 2004).[33] Furthermore, Mouffe (2005, pp. 8–34) distinguishes between 'the political' and 'politics'. The political is constitutive of human societies and refers to 'the dimension of antagonism that is inherent in human relations', while politics refers to a diversity of 'practices, discourses and institutions which seeks to establish a certain order and organize human coexistence' (Mouffe 2000, p. 101).

In *Aversive Democracy: Inheritance and Originality in the Democratic Tradition*, the DT scholar Aletta Norval (2007) – like Mouffe and Wodak before her – bases her theories on Ludwig Wittgenstein's later writings.[34] She also roots her work in Derrida's textual analysis. The main aim for Norval (2007, p. x) is to develop a novel and distinct Wittgensteinian approach to what she calls 'democratic politics'. This approach takes into account the far-reaching unease and disappointment with current political institutions and democratic practices, instead of focusing on 'what in the best of all possible worlds we ought to do', which so many before her have tried to do (Norval 2007, p. 4). The process of making claims, and the question of how we become democratic citizens, constitute the main focus. Norval's (2007, p. 12f.) 'post-analytical' arguments are formulated as a critique of both deliberative democracy and post-structuralist accounts of radical democracy.[35] In essence, *Aversive Democracy* can be read as a sincere attempt to get to grips with the relation between tradition and novelty in democratic politics, but as Norval (2007, p. 12) herself phrases it, without treating tradition as mere repetition or novelty as radical breaks.

Sara Carlbaum (Chapter 3) starts her analysis of education policies in upper secondary education with a quote from Mouffe about our understanding of citizenship, and how it reflects ideals of politics and the kind of society we want. Carlbaum argues that education policies are central sites for political struggles regarding citizenship.

Her study shows how the construction of future workers, as pupils are addressed in the analysed report, is also clearly gendered. Joakim Isaksson (Chapter 4) is also inspired by DT and uses education policy reports as the main empirical material in his study of how pupils with school difficulties are framed. He applies two concepts borrowed from Norval (2007); namely, 'aspect change' and 'aspect dawning'.

The 'logics approach' that was developed by Glynos and Howarth (2007) is of significant interest among discourse theorists today and has also inspired this volume's authors. This interest is of no surprise because the authors sketch a whole framework for conducting research. Their aim is to present 'an ontological stance and a grammar of concepts, together with a particular research ethos, which makes it possible to construct and furnish answers to empirical problems' (Glynos & Howarth 2007, p. 7). They also try to deal with previous criticism of DT, such as methodological arbitrariness and historical particularism. Glynos and Howarth (2007, pp. 133–164) propose the use of a threefold typology of logics for conducting critical explanations of how regimes or social practices are transformed, stabilised and maintained. The first, *social logic*, helps to characterise a particular social practice and stands for the 'rules' or non-controversial aspects of a regime – what is regularly taken for granted. The second, *political logic*, relates to the contestation or disruption of regimes and speaks to the transformation of social practices and processes of collective mobilisation. The third and final, *fantasmatic logic*, has an ideological dimension and concerns the reasons why particular regimes 'grip' subjects. These logics enable an understanding of, and serve to explain, continuity as well as regime changes. The psychoanalytical influence in Glynos and Howarth's approach is most visible in this third type of logic and it constitutes the least explored dimension in terms of applied research. That has inspired Angelika Sjöstedt Landén (Chapter 10) to explore how the fantasmatic, in conjunction with a theory of emotions, can help to shed light on narratives about possible futures, and 'the good life' that is associated with a relocation process. The participants in her interview study are new recruits transferees to a public sector agency that has been moved from the capital to a small town in the rural north of Sweden. Anna Sofia Lundgren (Chapter 11) also applies the logic concept when analysing stories of ageing in interviews with older people living in sparsely populated areas of northern Sweden. Lundgren shows that even though the collective identity of 'Norrlanders' is constituted, the stories lack a unifying 'enemy'. No corresponding demands are therefore articulated; something DT otherwise identifies as crucial in order to mobilise social change.

Similarities and differences

Let us focus our attention on the similarities and differences between CDA and DT and summarise the main observations that have been made in this brief review. As has been discussed, even if scholars use the theories in various ways, one can easily identify overlaps between CDA and DT with regard to intellectual 'heritage'. Foucault's perspective on discourse is a paramount resource within both traditions. Gramsci's work on hegemony, and Althusser's views on ideology, are also crucial influences. Conflict theoretical perspectives on society, including eventual changes within it, are also applied in both schools, and are linked to the legacies of critical theory and Marxism. The former, however, seems to have a stronger presence in today's CDA, while the latter has clearer links to DT.

Even if these discourse analytical traditions subscribe to the notion that knowledge, and our understanding of the world, are 'socially constructed' or discursively formed, there is an important difference between the two perspectives regarding the amplitude of such a poststructuralist view. Postmodern thinkers, such as Derrida, seem to have made a stronger mark on DT than CDA. These ontological differences are partly reflected in the concept of discourse itself. While a discourse theorist would claim that 'everything is discursive', a CDA scholar is more likely to distinguish between the discursive and the non-discursive. That is *not* to say, however, that the former ignores the 'real' impact of discourses, or that the latter plays down the far-reaching power of discourse(s), or believes that one can easily step outside them. On the contrary, they share Foucault's (1971) view that discourses are productive forces, and that we, in our diverse roles as subjects/agents, are constantly part of their ongoing (re)production.

This contingency of discourses is, in my interpretation, what makes resistance to inequalities meaningful. In other words, the possibility of change is a necessary condition in the joint effort of both schools to critically engage with contemporary social problems such as racism and other kinds of discrimination. Even though the meaning and possibility of social change are problematised more by some than others, both CDA and DT articulate a will to contribute to social change.[36] It is also evident that many researchers within both traditions place emphasis on the need to be reflexive when undertaking research. The practice of doing so, however, differs widely between individuals.

The importance of analysing every text in its context is yet another commonality for these discourse analytical traditions. Contextualisation was spoken of as a crucial aspect of analysis by all the participants of the roundtable discussion. Further views included the importance of integrating theory and method, and the linkage of micro and macro perspectives, or the understanding of agency and structure to each other. However, *how* this integration is undertaken is something that varies between them. CDA scholars often structure their analysis according to predefined models for this type of multilevel analysis, while DT researchers are likely to resist any such general advice or solution, because they, as Howarth (2005, p. 317) phrases it, believe that any discourse theorist 'ought to reflect upon and theorize the way they conduct research'.[37]

Howarth's argument touches upon another dimension that, in my view, separates the two from each other; namely, the relation to discipline(s). What is somewhat of a trademark of CDA is its interdisciplinary, multidisciplinary or transdisciplinary perspectives that promote eclectic approaches. Wodak even argues that the investigation of complex social phenomena would not be possible with linguistics alone (Kendall 2007, p. 4). The DT perspective lacks any such suggestion, even if a multitude of philosophies and other influences, such as psychoanalysis, are discussed by various researchers and incorporated within this political theory's own 'grammar'. However, CDA scholars tend to borrow theoretical concepts from other disciplines, such as 'politics', 'democracy', 'identity' and so on, and combine them with linguistic analysis. DT researchers are, in turn, much more likely to explore and problematise the very meaning of any used concept or perspective, whether it is part of the 'core' in political philosophy or not. This variation constitutes a significant difference between the perspectives and is, in my view, best understood in relation to their original disciplinary locations. On the one hand, discourses of political philosophy that mainly focus on abstract theoretical discussions influence DT, while, on the other, discourses of linguistics that primarily embrace the empirical analysis of languageuse frame CDA and its viewpoints. They generally, and to even a greater extent then I initially expected, given their 'integrative ethos' and the last few decades' general push for different forms of cross-disciplinary investigations in the humanities and social sciences. The disciplinary discourses form a vital part of the explanation why the dialogue between DT and CDA has been so scarce earlier, at least in my understanding.

I also believe that another crucial reason for this absence is the different understandings of the discourse concept itself, and these differences reflect the ontological views of each tradition. DT's and CDA's respective standpoints were also expressed during the roundtable debate; for example, when a scenario of the ceiling in the room falling down on us and its meaning was discussed. The articulated views regarding how to understand the relationship between the discursive and the non-discursive to a great extent echoed the main disagreement between Laclau and Bhaskar when they met in a similar debate in Essex, England, back in 1998 (Laclau & Bhaskar 1998, 2005). The main aim of the meeting was to compare DT with critical realism, a philosophical perspective that has influenced CDA (Fairclough et al. 2004). Just like the dialogue among the panel participants that took place a decade later in Umeå, Sweden, the conversation between Laclau and Bhaskar mainly revealed areas in which they agreed, such as their fundamental critique of empiricism. However, one pivotal difference between them concerned the ontological understanding of the 'extra-discursive reality', or the non-discursive. First of all, they agreed that it existed. Bhaskar then stated that he 'believes in the possibility and actuality of a world without human beings, and therefore without discourse' (Laclau & Bhaskar 1998, p. 11). Furthermore, he argued that even if all 'extra-discursive realities' are constituted and made intelligible within discursive practices, they can still be captured by so-called transcendental arguments. This viewpoint, he continued, is not to be understood as if causal impact is constituted in discursive practice. Laclau contested this perspective. Instead, he stressed that everything is constituted within discourse and that any kind of practice is embedded in the linguistic world. Furthermore, he defined discourse as 'the level of constitution of any objectivity', which, according to him, also counts for the external world (Laclau & Bhaskar 1998, p. 13).

Methodological issues are also a shared interest for contemporary DT and CDA.[38] CDA scholars have proposed a variety of stepwise approaches for how to conduct discourse analysis in practice, even if they are not meant to be used in a strictly linear fashion. However, any such predefined procedure could easily be understood as 'balkanization and reification of methodology' by discourse theorists, who seem to strongly oppose similar attempts (Howarth 2005, p. 317). Their resistance to such predefined 'solutions' was confirmed in the roundtable conversation, but so was the conclusion that, in the end, when it comes to the actual analysis of text, the differences between the perspectives were not that great. This similarity has also been noted by Torfing (2005, p. 9) in his comparison of different 'generations of discourse theory', and more specifically in the work by Fairclough with Laclau. Torfing's use of metaphor to map the field is problematic in many ways because it places different perspectives in a chronological order, as if they developed from each other. DT is placed at the very front as the latest and more advanced perspective here, thus leaving 'previous' generations, such as CDA, behind. Such a narrative does not communicate that both traditions very much represent contemporary perspectives on discourse analysis. Both alternatives have inspired many Swedish researchers interested in politics, democracy and social change, and which we, in turn, hope to have shown examples of in this volume.

Concluding remarks

Finally, a few concluding remarks concerning the previous discussion on the meeting points and standpoints in CDA and DT. Firstly, as suggested in the roundtable discussion, and as the next step, it would be interesting to look systematically, and in more depth, at how some of the core concepts such as 'power' or 'democracy' are applied in each tradition, and then to compare them. This would enable a more thorough understanding of the differences that are otherwise easily overlooked due to a similar vocabulary, etc.

Secondly, I would suggest that the identified differences in theoretical perspectives between CDA and DT – often related to divergent ontological standpoints – lead to missed opportunities for dialogue and critique, especially when it comes to specific research areas that they share. The spread of right-wing politics and racism in contemporary societies is one example. Citizenship and the problems of democracy in the European Union is another.

Thirdly, one lesson that can be learned from this comparative exercise concerns the influence of disciplines on our thinking. Despite transdisciplinary ambitions and sincere criticism directed towards established traditions, the original disciplinary location of each perspective still seems to frame many of the views within it, including the analytical practices. The degree to which this disciplinary frame was maintained was unexpected, in my view of things. Therefore, the impact of discipline partly explains why CDA and DT have developed separately, despite what appears at first to be common ground.

In my view, this comparative analysis has only just begun. As was concluded in our roundtable discussion, a corresponding dialogue between leading representatives of CDA and DT would be very useful in terms of increasing our understanding of similarities and differences. There is still much more to discover about different meanings of politics in each theory, about how formations of identities are understood and, perhaps most importantly, regarding if and how discourse analytical research can deepen our understanding of – an contribute to – possibilities for social change.

Overall structure of the book

One of the main ambitions with *Tracking Discourses* is to fill a gap in the existing body of English literature that reflects the widespread interest for CDA and DT in Scandinavia, and Swedish academia in particular. The majority of the authors concentrate their energies on the empirical use of discourse theoretical concepts when analysing different forms of texts: policy documents, news items, corporate reports or interview excerpts. This focus on application also represents one of the commonalities between contemporary scholars of both CDA and DT. We are therefore far from alone in our methodological interest in the practical use of the rich conceptual framework that CDA and DT provide us with. This subject has engaged many researchers in the last decade. This activity has been partly generated as a response to the criticism of the field's non-transparent application of theoretical and conceptual understandings (Bergström & Boréus 2000, p. 352; Torfing 2005, p. 2; Howarth 2005, p. 316; Howarth 2000, p. 14), or in some cases even more forceful accusations from quantitative researchers that 'anything goes' in discourse analysis (Antaki et al. 2003, p. 16; Howarth 2007, p. 22).[39]

The first two chapters of this book, including this introduction about meeting points and standpoints in CDA and DT, mainly focus on theoretical and conceptual issues. Payne and Gunnarsson Payne work on the significance and understanding of emancipation. An initial comparison between the two studied traditions' respective understanding of 'critique' is followed by a more in-depth exploration of the Laclauian approach.

The rest of the volume is dedicated to different case studies that explore the meaning of discourse(s) and influential institutions within a Swedish context and contemporary Western societies in general. We have grouped the contributions subject-wise, and the first three of these chapters (Carlbaum, Isaksson and Ngeh) have in common that they study discourses of education. As it happens, all of them also offer perspectives on the importance of educational policies and practices for the possibility of social change regarding inequalities and discrimination. The subsequent trio (Sylwan, Johansson and Faye Hendrick) are dedicated to exploring the meaning of traditional and online (mass)media discourses in relation to identity. Here the reader will meet additional perspectives on discourse analysis, such as a Foucaultian interpretation by Sylwan, and Faye Hendrick's analysis of pseudonymous blogging practices that is inspired by MDA and nexus analysis (Norris & Jones 2005; Scollon 2001). The subsequent case study is Lischinsky's linguistic-rooted analysis of corporate discourses, in which he applies the identity concept at the organisational level; a relatively unusual focus within CDA, but, as he argues, pivotal for researchers who wish to contribute to social change. The last two chapters (Sjöstedt Landén and Lundgren) both bring to the fore the meaning of (geographical) places and their importance for individuals' self-understandings – whether as newcomers to a region, or part of an ageing population living in the rural north of Sweden. The reader will also see how these two ethnologists apply parts of the 'logics approach' developed by Glynos and Howarth (2007) in their respective fieldwork.

Notes

1 I am grateful to Maritha Jacobsson and Jenny Gunnarsson Payne, who have provided valuable comments on earlier drafts of this chapter. Martin Shaw has also helped out a great deal to improve the English language. I also want to thank the group of participants in the LIP (Language-Ideology-Power) group, led by Professor Ruth Wodak at Lancaster University, UK, who commented on a presentation of this text during my stay as a visiting scholar in 2009. The frequent multidisciplinary encounters at Lancaster provided important input to the whole project, and especially regarding perspectives on CDA and its many varieties.

2 The 'linguistic turn' expression is associated with shifts in both philosophy and political theory and often refers to a book with the same title that was edited by the American philosopher Richard Rorty (1967/1992). For many scholars within the humanities and social sciences, the linguistic turn is closely linked to the notion of reality as 'socially constructed' (cf. Berger & Luckmann 1991/1966; Burr 2003).

3 The main theories or intellectual influences that Chouliaraki and Fairclough are in dialogue with are Marxism (including Gramsci's and Althusser's writings), critical theory (Habermas' work in particular), Bourdieu, Bhaskar and Bernstein, and poststructuralists and postmodernists (Foucault, Lyotard, Baudrillard, Derrida, Laclau, Mouffe, Jameson and Rorty), plus Systemic Functional Linguistic representatives, like Halliday and Hasan (cf. O'Regan 2001).

4 And vice versa; namely, to introduce linguistic students and scholars to *social* analysis (Fairclough 2003). Increased 'Critical Language Awareness' that deals with issues of language and power is another of his pedagogic goals (Fairclough 1995a, pp. 215–252).

5 However, they acknowledge their contribution regarding retroductive reasoning and any rigid separation between the context of discovery and the context of justification (Glynos & Howarth 2007, pp. 18–48). A critical realist ontology has come to be associated with certain CDA scholars, and Fairclough (2005a) in particular. In Fairclough et al. (2004), he discusses the relationship between critical realism and CDA with fellow Lancaster scholars Bob Jessop and Andrew Sayer, and begins on a critical note by stating that the critical realists have tended to take semiosis (intersubjective production of meaning) for granted to a large extent. However, Fairclough (2005b, p. 915) warns against making overly strong 'commitments to postmodernism and extreme versions of social constructivism'. Instead, he promotes a more moderate social constructivist position. He considers this position to be of more value in understanding organisations, and, in particular, changes within them.

6 The representatives who took part in this relatively unusual panel discussion were DT scholars Aletta Norval, Jason Glynos and CDA researchers Michał Krzyżanowski and Peter Berglez. The roundtable discussion was held at Umeå University, Sweden, and lasted for about three and a half hours. It was recorded in full and transcribed thereafter. Before this event the participants in the panel had the opportunity to listen to each other's lectures and different views of discourse analysis. The group of Ph.D. students also took part in the discussion and had prepared questions for the panellists in advance.

7 As a Ph.D. student in Media and Communication Studies towards the end of the 1990s, and the beginning of 2000, I noted that discourse analysis was not only seen as a novelty, but was so popular that it partly constituted a norm about how to conduct research. Very few, if any, corresponding perspectives influenced my fellow doctoral students and myself to the same degree. Winther Jørgensen and Phillips (1999, p. 9) use the fashion metaphor to describe the same phenomenon. As it was so widely used, it even became something that I tried to avoid in my own work for quite some time. Key concepts, such as 'discourse', came to mean very different things to different researchers. However, this dissonance was neither articulated nor acknowledged, and I found this problematic (Fairclough 1995b, p. 18; Mills 1997, p. 8).

8 Social *practices* and mediated *actions* are the main units of analysis in MDA, and not discourse *per se* (Norris & Jones 2005, p. 4). In other words, discourse *in action* is the main interest, and not discourse *as action*. Scollon (2001, p. 140) also argues that even if MDA shares the goals of CDA, such as its concern with social problems, it also tries to 'reformulate the object of study from a focus on the discourses of social issues to a focus on the social actions through which social actors produce histories and habitus of their daily lives'.

9 Of course, there are exceptions to this main observation, like a meeting between Laclau and Bhaskar (1998, 2005).

10 Whatever the case may be, I see it as a great opportunity to undertake this type of work because it gives me a chance to revise and reformulate my own discourse analytical understanding. The need to be self-reflexive as a researcher, and above all to problematise one's own position in relation to the discourse or actual issue being studied, is very much part of what scholars across the whole field place emphasis on in their writings (Winther Jørgensen & Phillips 1999, pp. 148–154; Börjesson 2003, p. 25; Chouliaraki & Fairclough 1999, p. 66).

11 As the popularity of discourse analysis has increased, so has the amount of literature that is devoted to introducing beginners to it (cf. Howarth 2000, 2007; Wetherell et al. 2001a, 2001b; Börjesson 2003; Bergström & Boréus 2005; and Neumann 2003). One of the first, and still a very useful book, is Winther Jørgensen and Phillips' (1999) *Diskursanalyse som teori och metod*, that compares DT, CDA and Discourse Psychology. An English edition was published in 2002.

12 Weiss and Wodak (2003, p. 12) confirm this observation when they state that 'CDA has never been and has never attempted to be or to provide one single or specific theory, and one specific methodology is not characteristic of research in CDA'. Understandably, they also emphasise that any criticism of CDA should always be specific and directed towards the research concerns.

13 The two main types of texts that I collected and analysed in detail throughout the whole time period were mass media outlets (local newspapers and television news broadcasts), and interviews with politicians, civil servants, experts, authorities, journalists, engaged citizens, and industry as well as NGO representatives.

14 The definition that Mill (1997, p. 7) regards as the most used by theorists understands discourse as 'a regulated practice which accounts for a number of statements'.

15 Foucault's contributions relating to the early archaeological and the later genealogical period are described in Howarth (2000, pp. 48–84 or 2007, pp. 59–98) and in Fairclough (1992, pp. 37–61). Regarding genealogy, see also Beronius (1994, 1999).

16 Jürgen Habermas is often mentioned as the successor of the Frankfurt School, and his work, for example on communicative action, has influenced both Chouliaraki and Fairclough (1999, pp. 83–89) and Wodak (Fairclough & Wodak 1997, p. 261).

17 The material consequences and costs of taking a political stand as a researcher against anti-Semitism, racism and right-wing populist rhetoric are described in an interview with Ruth Wodak (Kendall 2007, p. 4).

18 The tradition of discursive psychology (DP) is described by Winther Jørgensen and Phillips (1999, pp. 105–142). See also Wetherell et al. (2001a,2001b). DP has much in common with CDA. Both perspectives have devoted a considerable amount of attention to the empirical analysis of interactions and conversations between individuals and groups, and often interpreted them as both expressions and constructions of identities.

19 In other publications Wodak emphasises other aspects, as in, for example, Riesigl and Wodak (2001), where they delineate three dimensions of the concept (text-immanent critique, socio-diagnostic critique and prospective critique). Different meanings of a critical perspective have also been taken up for discussion in different CDA forums, for example in relation to the increased use of the perspective in non-Western cultures (Chilton & Wodak 2005, pp. x–xvi). See also Maingueneau (2006).

20 This framework is divided into five main steps: (1) focus upon a social problem that has a semiotic aspect; (2) identify obstacles that stand in the way of the problem being tackled; (3) consider whether the social order 'needs' the problem; (4) identify possible ways past the obstacles; and finally (5) reflect critically on the analysis (Fairclough 2001). Note that the researcher moves back and forth between these steps during the analysis; the research process by no means refers to a simple, straightforward procedure (cf. Wodak 2001b).

21 In more recent publications, Fairclough (2005a) prefers to use the term *semiosis* instead, defined as 'intersubjective production of meaning' (Fairclough et al. 2004, p. 23), to avoid confusion and to clarify certain aspects of the discourse concept.

22 In my reading of Fairclough, I am not entirely sure whether he argues that sociocultural practice is entirely non-discursive. However, he points out explicitly that it includes economic, cultural and political aspects (Fairclough 1995b, p. 62).

23 This particular framework, presented in full in *Media Discourse* (Fairclough 1995a), has been adopted by many media and communication scholars because it focuses specifically on media language and the power of mediated communication (cf. Richardson 2007; Olausson 2005; Phillips 2000). DT perspectives, however, have been picked up later and to a lesser degree than CDA, and one reason for this is because of DT's 'rather abstract nature' and strong 'realm of Political Studies' (Carpentier & De Cleen 2007, p. 265; see also Carpentier & Spinoy (2008).

24 Power, hegemony and ideology are three other key concepts in CDA that are part of the critical perspective on discourses.

25 For a longer discussion about intertextuality and CDA, see Fairclough (1992, pp. 101–136). Foucault's understanding of the role of the commentator in discourse(s), referring to the one who only repeats what has already been stated beforehand by others, generates intertextuality and interdiscursivity (Foucault 1970/1993; Sjölander 2004, pp. 165–167).

26 The contextual analysis in DHA takes account of four levels (which are similar to the ones mentioned in Fairclough's model, see Figure): (1) the immediate, language or text-internal co-text; (2) the intertextual and inter-discursive relationship between utterances, texts, genres and discourses; (3) the extralinguistic social/sociological variables and institutional frames of a specific context of situation (middle-range theories); (4) the broader socio-political and historical contexts, in which the discursive practices are

embedded and related to (macro theories) (Wodak 2001, p. 13; Wodak 2008, p. 67).

27 For an introduction to DHA and the analytical procedures, see Wodak (2001b).

28 Several of these projects have been undertaken in collaboration with Michał Krzyżanowski (2005, 2010). In a number of projects, Krzyżanowski has studied discourses of EU politics, and political identities in Europe and the EU. He has worked within the discourse-historical framework and applied its multi-methodological approach; for example, used focus groups, interviews and ethnographic fieldwork, alongside more traditional linguistic methods for text analysis, like focusing on topoi, arguments, etc. (Krzyżanowski 2008; Oberhuber & Krzyżanowski 2008). *Topos* (plural: *topoi*) is taken from argumentation theory and refers to generally used or accepted arguments, so-called commonplaces (Krzyżanowski & Wodak 2008, p. 208). Topoi connect the argument with the conclusion, the claim (Wodak & Reisigl 2001, pp. 74–75). How topoi are identified by the researcher was one of the questions raised during the roundtable discussion, and since they play a central role in DHA it was also suggested that it would be interesting to look into how they relate to DT concepts such as, for example, *floating* or *empty signifier*.

29 One question raised during the roundtable debate and directed towards the DT researchers was how their strong analytical emphasis on dissent, antagonism and plurality related to this notion of a 'strong intellectual grammar', in the form of set categories, etc. The respondents acknowledged that there is a certain kind of grammar to the programme, but stated that there are still huge differences within it, largely because researchers are informed by different philosophies.

30 The importance of social antagonisms in any sense-making process is another, and these antagonisms 'occur because social agents are *unable* to attain fully their identity' (Howarth & Stavrakakis 2000, p. 10).

31 'Articulation' is also a pivotal concept in DT and crucial for the understanding of discourse(s). Laclau and Mouffe (1985, p. 105) write that 'we will call *articulation* any practice establishing a relation among elements such that their identity is modified as a result of the articulatory practice'. According to their definition, articulation establishes relationships and changes identities, and it is the 'structured totality resulting from the articulatory practice' that they subsequently call *discourse* (Ibid.). Hence, the concept refers to more than just labelling or 'words' (Howarth 2007, p. 117). Articulation is a practice that does something.

32 The possibility of emancipation(s), and more specifically the relation between the universal and the particular in any such movement, continues to be of central importance in Laclau's writings and was a major theme in his book with the same name, *Emancipation(s)* (1996).

33 Mouffe (2005, pp. 35–63) is also highly critical of Giddens' (1996) and Beck's (1992) work on 'reflexive modernity' in late modern societies.

34 For example, Wittgenstein's (1953/2001) understanding of language games presented in *Philosophical Investigations*.

35 Norval (2007, p. 12f.) claims that the deliberative theory fails to understand the actual institution and process of democratic subjectivity, while the theory of radical democracy makes use of simplistic dichotomies and has a tendency to place too much emphasis on the political as disruption and dislocation.

36 DT scholars tend to use the concept of 'hegemonic intervention' when discussing similar issues, and CDA researchers generally describe their perspective as a 'bottom-up' approach. Laclau (1996), Wodak (2001, p. 10) and Fairclough (2001, p. 127) all write about 'emancipation', but in different ways.

37 Inspired by Foucault, among others, Howarth (2005) has developed what he calls a 'method of articulation'; this in order to be able to apply DT more easily, but at the same time avoid any mechanical methodological procedure that he identifies in other research approaches, for example within CDA (Howarth 2005, pp. 317–318). Anna Sofia Lundgren (Chapter 11) has been working with this 'method of articulatory practice'.

38 Representatives from both try to develop better ways to apply theoretical views on empirical texts and vice versa, and the proposals from CDA and DT scholars contain similar features. The former, for example, undertake 'problem-oriented' research and often deal with social problems, while the latter prefer to call their approach to social and political analysis 'problem-driven', and their focus is on pressing practical issues of the present. Another example of similarities is the 'abductive approach' that Wodak (2001, p. 70n) promotes in DHA, where the researcher constantly moves back and forth between theory and empirical data; this versus 'retroductive reasoning' in Glynos and Howarth's (2007, pp. 18–48) logics approach. Retroduction is their response to the shortcomings of induction and deduction respectively.

39 Howarth & Torfing (2005); Neumann (2003); Börjesson (2003); Börjesson & Palmblad (2007); Bergström & Boréus (2005); Wodak & Krzyżanowski (2008); Winther Jørgensen & Phillips (1999); Wetherell et al. (2001b) and Wodak & Meyer (2001) are all examples that in different ways try to tackle the 'methodological deficit' within the field and to better articulate how to apply theories to empirical objects of investigation.

References

Althusser, L., 1976. *Filosofi från proletär klasståndpunkt*. Lund: Cavefors.

Althusser, L., 1971/2001. *Ideology and Ideological State Apparatus (Notes Towards an Investigation)*. New York: Monthly Review Press.

Alvesson, M. & Kärreman, D., 2000. Taking the Linguistic Turn in Organizational Research: Challenges, Responses, Consequences. *Journal of Applied Behavioral Science*, 36 (136), pp. 136–158.

Archer, M., Bhaskar, R., Collier, A., Lawson, T. & Norrie, A., 1998. *Critical Realism: Essential Readings*. London: Routledge.

Beck, U., 1992. *Risk Society: Towards a New Modernity*. London: Sage.

Berger, P. & Luckmann, T., 1991/1966. *The Social Construction of Reality: A Treatise in the Sociology of Knowledge.* London: Penguin Books.

Berglez, P., 2006. The Materiality of Media Discourse. *On Capitalism and Journalistic Modes of Writing.* Örebro Studies in Media and Communication No. 4, Örebro: Örebro University.

Bergström, G. & Boréus, K., 2005. Diskursanalys. In: Bergström, G. & Boréus, K., *Textens mening och makt: metodbok i samhällsvetenskaplig text- och diskursanalys.* Lund: Studentlitteratur, pp. 305–362.

Beronius, M., 1994. *Bidrag till de sociala undersökningarnas historia – eller till den vetenskapliggjorda moralens genealogi.* Stockholm/Stehag: Symposion.

Beronius, M., 1999. *Genealogi och sociologi. Nietzsche, Foucault och den sociala analysen.* Stockholm/Stehag: Symposion.

Billig, M., 2003. Critical Discourse Analysis and the Rhetoric of Critique. In: Wodak, R. & Meyer, M. (eds), 2001. *Methods of Critical Discourse Analysis.* London: Sage, pp. 35–46.

Börjesson, M., 2003. *Diskurser och konstruktioner. En sorts metodbok.* Lund: Studentlitteratur.

Börjesson, M. & Palmblad, E. (eds), 2007. *Diskursanalys i praktiken.* Malmö: Liber.

Burr, V., 2003. *Social Constructionism.* London: Routledge.

Carpentier, N. & De Cleen, P., 2007. Bringing discourse theory into Media Studies. The applicability of Discourse Theory Analysis (DTA) for the Study of media practices and discourses. *Journal of Language and Politics,* 6(2), pp. 265–293.

Carpentier, N. & Spinoy, E., 2008. *Discourse Theory and Cultural Analysis: Media, Arts and Literature.* Cresskill: Hampton Press.

Chilton, P. & Wodak, R., 2005, Preface. In: Wodak, R. & Chilton, P. (eds), *New Agenda in (Critical) Discourse Analysis.* Amsterdam: Benjamins, pp. x–xvii.

Chouliaraki, L., 2004. *Media Discourse in the Public Sphere.* In: Howarth, D. & Torfing, J. (eds), *Discourse Theory in European Politics: Identity, Policy, and Governance.* London: Palgrave Macmillan, pp. 275–297.

Chouliaraki, L. & Fairclough, N., 1999. *Discourse in Late Modernity: Rethinking Critical Discourse Analysis.* Edinburgh: Edinburgh University Press.

Critchley, S. & Marchart, O., 2004. Introduction. In: Critchley, S. & Marchart, O. Eds. *Laclau: A Critical Reader.* London: Routledge, pp. 1–15.

Dryzeks, J., 2000. *Deliberative Democracy and Beyond: Liberals, Critics, Constestations.* Oxford: Oxford University Press.

Egan Sjölander, A., 2009. Rare and Fruitful – the Concrete use of Foucault's Discourse Theory in Media and Communication Research. Paper presented at the ESRC Networks for Methodological Innovation's Conference in Discourse Analysis held at University of Essex, UK April, 2009.

Fairclough, N., 1992. Discourse and Social Change. Cambridge: Polity Press.

Fairclough, N., 1995a. Critical *Discourse Analysis. The Critical Study of Language.* Boston: Addison Wesley.

Fairclough, N., 1995b. *Media Discourse.* London: Edward Arnold.

Fairclough, N., 2001. Critical Discourse Analysis as a Method in Social Scientific

Research. In: Wodak, R. & Meyer, M. (eds), 2001. *Methods of Critical Discourse Analysis*. London: Sage, pp. 121–138.

Fairclough, N., 2005a. Critical Discourse Analysis. *Marges Linguistiques*, 9, pp. 76–94.

Fairclough, N., 2005b. Peripheral Vision: Discourse Analysis in Organizational Studies: The Case for Critical Realism. *Organization Studies*, 26 (6), pp. 915–939.

Fairclough, N., 2003. *Analysing Discourse: Textual Analysis for Social Research*. London: Routledge.

Fairclough, N. & Wodak, R., 1997. Critical Discourse Analysis. In: van Dijk, T. (ed) 1997. *Discourse as Social Interaction*. Los Angeles: Sage, pp. 258–284.

Fairclough, N., Jessop, R. & Sayer, A., 2004. Critical Realism and Semiosis. In: Joseph, J., & Roberts, J. (eds), *Realism, Discourse and Deconstruction*. London: Routledge, pp. 23–42.

Foucault, M., 1970/1993. *Diskursens ordning*. (The Discourse on Language) Stockholm: Symposion.

Foucault, M., 1981. The Order of Discourse. In: Young, R. (ed), *Untying the Text: A Post-Structralist Reader*. London: Routledge & Kegan Paul, pp. 48–78.

Foucault, M., 1969/1993. Vad är en författare? In: Entzenberg, C. & Hansson, C. (eds), *Modern litteraturteori. Från rysk formalism till dekonstruktion*. Lund: Studentlitteratur, pp. 329–347.

Glynos, J., 2001. The Grip of Ideology: A Lacanian Approach to The Theory of Ideology. *Journal of Political Ideologies*. 6(2), pp. 191–214.

Glynos, J. & Howarth, D., 2007. *Logics of Critical Explanation in Social and Political Theory*. London: Routledge.

Glynos, J., Howarth, D., Norval, A. & Speed, E., 2009. *Discourse Analysis: Varieties and Methods*. ESRC National Centre for Research Methods Review Paper. ESRC National Centre for Research Methods. NCRM/014. August 2009.

Giddens, A., 1996. *Modernitetens följder*. Lund: Studentlitteratur.

Gramsci, A., 1973. *Selections from the Prison Notebooks*. London: Lawrence & Wishard Limited.

Gramsci, A., 1973/2007. *Brev från fängelset*. Stockholm: Ruin förlag.

Gunnarsson Payne, J., 2006. *Systerskapets logiker. En etnologisk studie av feministiska fanziner*. (The Logics of Sisterhood. An Ethnological Study of Feminist Fanzines.) Etnologiska skrifter 38. Umeå: Institutionen för kultur och medier, Umeå universitet.

Howart, D., 2000. *Discourse*. Buckingham: Open University Press.

Howart, D., 2007. *Diskurs*. Liber: Malmö.

Howarth, D., 2005. Applying Discourse Theory: The Method of Articulation. In: Howarth, D. & Torfing, J. (eds), *Discourse Theory in European Politics: Identity, Policy and Governance*. Basingstoke: Palgrave Macmillan, pp. 316–349.

Howarth, D. & Torfing, J., 2005. *Discourse Theory in European Politics: Identity, Policy and Governance*. Basingstoke: Palgrave Macmillan.

Howarth, D. & Stavrakakis, Y., 2000. Introducing discourse theory and political analysis. In: Howarth, D., Norval, A. & Stavrakakis, Y. (eds), *Discourse Theory and Political Analysis. Identities, Hegemonies and Social Change*. Manchester: Manchester University Press, pp. 1–23.

Johansson, A., 2010. *Självskada. En etnologisk studie av mening och identitet i berättelser om skärande.* Umeå: Bokförlaget h:ström – Text & Kultur.

Kendall, G., 2007. What is Critical Discourse Analysis? Ruth Wodak in Conversation With Gavin Kendall. *Forum Qualitative Sozialforschung / Forum: Qualitative Social Research,* 8(2), Art. 29.

Krzyżanowski, M., 2005. 'European identity wanted!' On discursive and communicative dimensions in the European Convention. In: Wodak, R. & Chilton, P. (eds), *New Agenda in (Critical) Discourse Analysis. Theory, Methodology and Interdisciplinarity.* Amsterdam: Benjamins.

Krzyżanowski, M., 2008. Analysing Focus Group Discussions. In: Wodak, R. & Krzyżanowski, M. (eds), *Qualitative Discourse Analysis in Social Sciences.* Basingstoke: Palgrave Macmillan, pp. 162–181.

Krzyżanowski, M., 2010. *The Discursive Construction of European Identities: A Multilevel Approach to Discourse and Identity in the Transforming European Union.* Frankfurt am Main: Peter Lang.

Krzyżanowski, M. & Wodak, R., 2010. *The Politics of Exclusion: Debating Migration in Austria.* New Brunswick, NJ: Transaction Publishers.

Laclau, E., 1990. *New Reflections on the Revolution of Our Time.* London: Verso.

Laclau, E., 1996. *Emancipation(s).* London: Verso.

Laclau, E., 2005. *On Populist Reason.* London: Verso.

Laclau, E. & Bhaskar, R., 1998. Discourse Theory vs. Critical Realism. *Alethia,* 1(2), pp. 9–14.

Laclau, E. & Bhaskar, R., 2005. Diskursteori kontra kritisk realism. *Fronesis,* No. 19/20, pp. 178–192.

Laclau, E. & Mouffe, C., 1985/2001. *Hegemony and Socialist Strategy: Towards a Radical Democratic Politics.* London: Verso.

Laclau, E. & Mouffe, C., 2008. *Hegemonin och den socialistiska strategin.* Göteborg: Vertigo förlag.

Maingueneau, D., 2006. Is Discourse Analysis Critical? *Critical Discourse Studies,* 3(2), pp. 229–235.

Mills, S., 1997. *Discourse.* London: Routledge.

Mouffe, C., 2005. *On the Political.* London: Routledge.

Mouffe, C., 2000. *The Democratic Paradox.* London: Verso.

Norris, S. & Jones, R. (eds), 2005. *Discourse in Action: Introduction to Mediated Discourse Analysis.* London: Routledge.

Norris, S. & Jones, R., 2005. Discourse as Action/Discourse in Action. In: Norris, S. & Jones, R. (eds), *Discourse in Action: Introduction to Mediated Discourse Analysis.* London: Routledge.

Norval, A., 1999. *The Things We Do With Words: Contemporary Approaches to the Analysis of Ideology.* Essex Papers in Politics and Government. No. 12. Essex: Department of Government, University of Essex.

Neumann, I.B., 2003. *Mening, makt och materialitet. En introduktion till diskursanalys.* Lund: Studentlitteratur.

Oberhuber, F. & Krzyżanowski, M., 2008. Discourse Analysis and Ethnography. In: Wodak, R. & Krzyżanowski, M. (eds), *Qualitative Discourse Analysis in Social Sciences.* Basingstoke: Palgrave Macmillan, pp. 182–203.

Olausson. U., 2005. *Medborgarskap och globalisering: Den diskursiva konstruktionen av politisk identitet.* Örebro Studies in Media and Communication No. 3, Örebro: Örebro University.

O'Regan, J., 2001. Review of *Discourse in Late Modernity: Rethinking Critical Discourse Analysis* by Lilie Chouliaraki & Norman Fairclough. *Language and Intercultural Communication*, 1(2), pp. 151–161.

Phillips, L., 2000. Risk, Reflexivity and Democracy: Mediating Expert Knowledge in the News. *Nordicom Review*, 21 (2), pp. 115–135.

Premfors, R. & Roth, K., (eds), 2004. *Deliberativ demokrati.* Lund: Studentlitteratur.

Reisigl, M. & Wodak, R., 2001. *Discourse and Discrimination.* London: Routledge.

Richardson, J. E., 2007. *Analysing Newspapers. An Approach from Critical Discourse Analysis.* Basingstoke: Palgrave Macmillan.

Rorty, R. (ed.), 1967/1992. *The Linguistic Turn: Essays in Philosophical Method: With Two Retrospective Essays.* Chicago: University of Chicago Press.

Schegloff, E. A., 1997. Whose Text? Whose Context? *Disourse & Society*, 8, pp., 165–187.

Scollon, R., 2001. Action and Text: Towards an Integrated Understanding of the Place of Text in Social (inter)action, Mediated Discourse Analysis and the Problem of Social Action. In: Wodak, R. & Meyer, M. (eds), *Methods of Critical Discourse Analysis.* London: Sage, pp. 139–185.

Sjölander, A., 2004. *Kärnproblem. Opinionsbildning i kärnavfallsdiskursen i Malå.* (Core Issues. Opinion Formation in the Nuclear Waste Discourse in Malå.) Medier och kommunikation, No. 7, Umeå: Institutionen för kultur och medier, Umeå universitet.

Torfing, J., 1999. *New Theories of Discourse: Laclau, Mouffe and Žižek.* Oxford: Blackwell.

Triandafyllidou, A., Wodak, R. & Krzyżanowski, M. (eds), 2009. *Europe in Crisis: The 'European Public Sphere' and National Media in the Post-War Period.* Basingstoke: Palgrave.

Weiss, G. & Wodak, R. (eds), 2003. Introduction: Theory, Interdisciplinarity and Critical Discourse Analysis. In: Weiss, G. & Wodak, R., *Critical Discourse Analysis: Theory and Interdisciplinarity in Critical Discourse Analysis.* London: Palgrave, pp. 1–32.

Weiss, G. & Wodak, R. (eds), 2003. *Critical Discourse Analysis: Theory and Interdisciplinarity in Critical Discourse Analysis.* London: Palgrave.

Wetherell, M., Taylor, S. & Yates, S. (eds), 2001a. *Discourse Theory and Practice: A Reader.* London: Sage.

Wetherell, M., Taylor, S. & Yates, S. (eds), 2001b. *Discourse as Data: A Guide for Analysis.* London: Sage.

Winther Jørgensen, M. & Phillips, L., 1999. *Diskursanalyse som teori och metod.* Fredriksberg: Roskilde Universitetsförlag/Samfundslitteratur.

Wittgenstein, L., 1953/2001. *Philosophical Investigations.* Oxford: Blackwell Publishing.

Wodak, R., 2001a. What CDA is about – a Summary of its History, Important Concepts and its Developments. In: Wodak, R. & Meyer, M., (eds), *Methods of Critical Discourse Analysis*, London: Palgrave MacMillan, pp. 1–13.

Wodak, R., 2001b. The Discourse-Historical Approach. In: Wodak, R. & Meyer, M. (eds), *Methods of Critical Discourse Analysis*, London: Palgrave MacMillan, pp. 63–94.

Wodak, R., 2006. Mediation between Discourse and Society: Assessing Cognitive Approaches. *Discourse Studies*, 8(1), pp. 179–190.

Wodak, R., 2008. Introduction: Discourse Studies – Important Concepts and Terms. In: Wodak, R. & Krzyżanowski, M. (eds), *Qualitative Discourse Analysis in Social Sciences*. Basingstoke: Palgrave Macmillan, pp. 1–29.

Wodak, R., 2009. *The Discourse of Politics in Action: Politics as Usual*. Basingstoke: Palgrave Macmillan.

Wodak, R. & Chilton, P. (eds), 2005. *New Agenda in (Critical) Discourse Analysis. Theory, Methodology and Interdisciplinarity*. Amsterdam: Benjamins.

Wodak, R. & Krzyżanowski, M. (eds), 2008. *Qualitative Discourse Analysis in Social Sciences*. Basingstoke: Palgrave Macmillan.

Wodak, R. & Meyer, M. (eds), 2001. *Methods of Critical Discourse Analysis*. London: Sage.

Wodak, R. & Reisigl, M., 2001. *Discourse and Discrimination. Rhetorics of Racism and Antisemitism*. London: Routledge.

Wodak, R. & Weiss, G., 2005. Analyzing European Union Discourses: Theories and Applications. In: Wodak, R. & Chilton, P. (eds), *New Agenda in (Critical) Discourse Analysis. Theory, Methodology and Interdisciplinarity*. Amsterdam: Benjamins, pp. 121–135.

CHAPTER 2

Critique Disarmed, Ideas Unharmed

A Laclauian Approach to Emancipatory Ideas

David Payne & Jenny Gunnarsson Payne

Can social and political theory do without an idea of critique? And if not, what is the purpose, the function, of critique? What is the Idea or the hope that a critically invested theory bears within itself when it engages in an unmasking, an exposé, or a denaturalisation of 'concrete' social practices that harbour exclusions, that exercise force over a particular subset of a society's population, venting untold violence against a group or collectivity? There need not be one principle that functions as the unifying instance of *all* critique. However, this would raise its own questions about the competing claims that any putative theoretical discourse makes on the world and raises against other theories. Minimally speaking, even if we place to one side the plural ends to which critique can be put, to separate critique from scepticism requires that an interrogation of society preserves an Idea (whatever this idea may be) irreducible – or 'undeconstructible' – to the actual state of affairs it is questioning.[1]

Critical syntaxes

In the theoretical discourses both discussed and applied in this volume there is a commitment to critique. 'critical discourse analysis' wears its fidelity on its sleeve, so to speak. The very way it wishes to be addressed is as a discourse analytic approach with a critical sensibility. Here the adjectival mark (*critical* discourse analysis) indexes that its mode of analysing discourse is identifiable in relation to other variants of discourse analysis on account of its critical orientation. This goes also for – for want of a better descriptive – 'discourse theory', which, in its many formulations, articulates an idea of critique as a central component in its theoretical armature, thus taking its place beside the dual imperatives of explanation and contextual interpretation. The work of David Howarth and Jason Glynos can be taken as exemplary in this regard:

> Our central aim … is to construct an explanatory logic, together with the grammar of concepts and assumptions that serve as its conditions of possibility, and to articulate a typology of basic logics – social, political and fantasmatic – which can serve to characterize, explain and *criticize* social phenomena (Glynos & Howarth 2007, p. 8, emphasis added).

In both approaches, 'critical discourse analysis' (CDA) and 'discourse theory' (DT), the question of critique, and its place within political and social theory, seems already decided. If this is indeed the case, then it might not be too much of a stretch to say that the 'critical' value of these perspectives functions more as a supposition, and, as such, can, by its exponents, be too readily taken for granted.[2] However, it must not be forgotten how the struggle for the acceptance of critique as a legitimate theoretical task has been long and hard-fought. Albrecht Wellmer, himself a proponent of a critically informed theory – this time operating within the horizon of the Frankfurt School – has stressed the precarity of the critical thinker's position in relation to both the sciences and politics. Constituting something of a hinterland, a non-place – strictly speaking, *neither* a science *nor* a politics – critique is at risk of being a poor substitute for the vicissitudes of political practice, and inadequately scientific to furnish any putative critical theory with a rigorously developed system of deductions and propositions that would enable it either to predict or to explain social and political phenomena (Wellmer 2002, pp. 32–41). There is the risk that critique amounts to little more than being the unhappy conscience of its times!

Doubtless, this redoubled problematic, according to which critique lacks both scientificity and political efficacy, is one to which both CDA and DT have not only been alive, but is an obstacle they have actively sought to surmount in their respective traditions. Each has, in their own way, sought a more rigorously developed articulation between critique and theory. The critical moment of the research process is neither foisted at the end – simply as the ad hoc expression of the political preferentiality of the particular researcher – nor is its critical direction welded to a set of fixed theoretical concepts and axioms. The meaning of critique derives always from the imperatives of an immanent critical engagement, on account of which the act of critique must show a sensitivity to the contextual specificity of the case which constitutes the object of criticism.

The semantics of critique: the idea of emancipation

While one would not wish to deny the importance that, as a theoretical resource, critique has in the social and human sciences, doubt might nonetheless be cast over the operation it performs on the Ideas with which theoretical critique gains its vitality (cf. Ricoeur 2002, p. 135). We have in mind the theoretical practice of 'emancipatory critique'. Note that here, the critical method undergoes predicative qualification; critique is placed in the service of an Idea of emancipation. Consequently, we read in the literature on Critical Discourse Analysis how, with specific reference to Jürgen Habermas, critical discourse analysts understand any would-be critical social science as investing in an 'emancipatory knowledge interest' (Chouliaraki & Fairclough 2007, p. 29; Habermas 1998, pp. 313–317), that

> in the name of *emancipation* critical discourse analytical approaches take the side of oppressed social groups ... with the overall goal of harnessing the results of critical discourse analysis to the struggle for radical social change (Winther Jørgensen & Phillips 2002, p. 64).

Critical social science does not proceed in a disinterested manner; any theoretical activity that operates under its name is involved in the world, comporting itself in such a way that it does not seek to take the world as it finds it, which is to say to conduct its affairs descriptively and interpretatively. Rather, it comports itself towards the world critically in order to contribute to its immanent transformation. In this sense, even if not in all senses, the critical discourse analyst remains responsive to a certain injunction of Marx; namely, to put theoretical activity in the service of positively changing the world.[3] This would be to sharpen the normative edge of its own theoretical discourse, inasmuch that this is what a critical social science *ought* to do. However, CDA would, at the same time, wish to focus its attention on a certain ontological condition of social research: that social research *is* always-already 'involved' in the very social practices about which it theorises, and that, epistemologically, the object about which knowledge is to be accrued, and the knower assigned to accrue such knowledge, co-appear on the same epistemic plane. It is therefore unavoidable that social research, in the categories and concepts it deploys to describe and understand the world, already transforms the appearance of that world; and concomitantly, that specific worldly practices, serving as the backdrop against which the researcher plays out his or her own part, predispose him or her to relate to the world in a particular way. The point, then, is to carry out research in a manner that is sensitive to this reciprocal relation, and in a way that impresses on the researcher the inextricable linkage between the orders of description and prescription, as well as the critical judgements that are inseparable from any empirical enquiry.[4]

The connection that is forged between the critical sciences and a practical emancipatory interest seeks further support from the critical realism of Roy Bhaskar, for whom 'the possibility of an explanatory critique constitutes the kernel of the emancipatory potential of the human sciences' (Bhaskar 1989, p. 102). From the suppositions upon which Bhaskar grounds his particular variant of a critical social science (many of which are shared by CDA), the emancipatory possibility of the social sciences reveals itself in a twofold sense. The possibility rests on both the demand to explain social processes and practices as well as to offer a critique of whatever discloses itself as harmful and unjust. If a social science is to make good on its nominal 'scientificity', then 'explanation' is a requisite characteristic. Critique, regarded as an attempt to put into question a state of affairs, must be grounded on some secure footing, providing for it both the necessary and sufficient reasons why a particular critique waged at a certain social practice has about it an irresistible force that goes beyond the particular whims and desires of the critic. In Kantian vernacular, we might choose to summarise this position by way of the following maxim: while critique without explanation is blind, explanation without critique is empty.

More specifically, however, what does it mean to be committed to a form of explanatory critique that would keep within it the burning desire for emancipation? For Bhaskar's meta-theory – along with the applied theories that take some variant of critical realism as their theoretical ground (notably here, CDA) – the task of theory is not, contra positivism, to remain at the level of appearance; that is, along the surface of what is immediately visible and directly perceptible. For the critical intervention to have potency, it must penetrate beneath the changing and transitive, and instead provide an account of the very conditions under which these phenomena appear as such. The task is to isolate a set of intransitive processes that operate within a given social system, and that are formative in constructing and shaping phenomenal appearances themselves. The aim is thus to solicit knowledge about those underlying processes and embedded structures, which, while not perceptible, are none-theless objects about which knowledge can be positively obtained – structures and processes that work behind the backs of subjects, both foreclosing and enabling certain possibilities, and that, moreo-ver, researchers themselves risk reproducing in their own unreflexive scientific practices.[5] The significance of explanatory critique in rela-tion to the Idea of emancipation comes to have, here, a particular perspicuity. Explanatory critique becomes a method by which social agents who engage in practices that function in the production and reproduction of certain obdurate relations – and which generate effects of subordination and oppression – might come to recognise their own unconscious duplicity in, perhaps, another's oppression, but, almost certainly, in their own subordination.

Even if in a very different manner, DT gives its assent, albeit qualified, to the claim that a 'well-founded explanatory theory has intrinsic implications for critique and thus for human emancipation'

(Glynos & Howarth 2007, p. 10). Though it picks up the thread of 'explanatory critique' and its relation to emancipatory ends, by both pulling and twisting this relation in inventive and important ways which will make such a task compatible with its own social ontology (Glynos & Howarth 2007, p. 11). In their formulation of the discourse theoretical approach, they seek to

> steer a course between an unapologetic positivism, which denies any role for critique and values in scientific investigation (other than those intrinsic to science itself), and a partisan approach that is prepared to compromise the virtues of scientific study – objectivity, impartiality, systematicity, consistency, and so on – in the name of an explicit set of political commitments and values (Glynos & Howarth 2007, p. 191).

The first thing that needs to be said, therefore, is that the critical task seemingly finds its feet in the contribution it makes to emancipatory transformation; which is to say, in the social sciences and the humanities, the Idea of emancipation gives orientation to critique. Here, from the very outset, this causal direction needs to be emphasised; a causal relation about which, in principle, Bhaskar is more than aware, when he writes how it is to the benefit of any scientific enlightenment that it be dependent upon *a* politics (Bhaskar 1989, p. 176).[6]

That various strands of critical social and political theory (whether or not discourse is taken as its datum) coalesce around some Idea of emancipation (the content of which can be left underdetermined for the present time) is *because* a critical sensibility towards the world has emerged out of specific historical conjunctures. It is the concrete and historically situated 'emancipatory' struggles that have widened the horizon of both what is politically possible and what is theoretically visible. From out of actual emancipatory struggles theoretical continents have emerged. Such is the case with the workers' movement for Marxism, the women's movement for feminism, the anti-colonial struggles for postcolonialism. It is the emancipatory hope, which is carried by concrete political movements, that sets the critical sciences on their way.

And yet so often has it been the case that the causal direction between critique and emancipatory Ideas comes to be read in the reverse direction, so that the furtherance of emancipation, the flame of emancipatory promise, is kept alive not by political forces, but by the travails of the critic alone. The figure of the critic, in the wake of defeats and setbacks, reversals and blind alleys, can all too easily be led by a sense of vexation, by an exasperation about the very forces that pushed him into a state of theoretical activity and political commitment, where, as Herbert Marcuse was to retort, the last vestiges of 'hope' seem to spring from hopelessness alone (Marcuse 1968, p. 257).[7]

A fine line exists between expectation and disquiet, between hope and hopelessness. This is admittedly a risk that is harboured by any critical discourse which operates within the fields of social and political enquiry, and should not be regarded as a problem specific to either CDA or DT. All the same, the question to be pursued in this chapter can be put as follows: if the circulation of emancipatory Ideas is one important way of accounting for theory's critical sensibility in the social sciences, is the only way to affirm such Ideas through critique? Might there be another approach in which, at the level of theory, commitment to emancipation can be shown? Ultimately, we shall go looking in the writings of Ernesto Laclau for another possibility, which keeps in operation emancipatory Ideas without passing through theoretical critique as the means by which to gain access to such Ideas. It sees its aim not in directly contributing to emancipatory ends – not therefore as an *emancipatory* theory working in synergy with concrete political struggles – but as, in part, a *theory of* emancipatory Ideas; a theoretical discourse that focuses its attention on the political logics that make possible the appearing of any emancipatory struggle – seeking to explain the emergence and genesis of historically situated emancipatory discourses. If it has something to transmit to political discourses, it is not as a partner that seeks to bring about a particular set of determinate objectives for a certain oppressed collective or group, or indeed, as the bestower of some prescient insight, which, through some metaphysical contrivance, would provide that particular struggle with the foundations and justifications so that it is looked upon as the aperture through which to view the universal liberation of humanity as such. Rather, it is to convey something of the primacy of political processes that would accord to situated collectivities absolute centrality and to return to politics a certain importance that has otherwise been neglected and underestimated, all in order that human beings can recognise themselves as 'the true creators' of the world (Laclau 1996, p. 16).

Laclau and the tempering of the 'arms of critique'

It is possible to unfold a logic interior to Ernesto Laclau's discourse theoretic approach that presents something of a rethinking of how, from a theoretical point of view, thought can seize emancipatory Ideas in a way that does not take up the mantle of the critic, and whose critical intervention is said to gain its legitimacy by working 'in the name' of emancipation. Laclau admonishes both the naïvete and the abstruse sanctimony of such a position. There is always a risk, when the stakes are high and the passions reach a fervent pitch, that, in political matters, the political theorist might exchange the 'obstinate rigour' of analysis for 'the terrorism of words', and to settle instead for the opportunism of polemical brinkmanship – caught up, as it is, in the gestures of 'complacent sleights of hand that seek only to safeguard an obsolete orthodoxy' (Laclau 1990, p. 97). Such is the line that Laclau both consistently and unflinchingly tacks in the course of his theoretical work; they are thoughts he holds up for public reception, on more than one occasion, a general warning against the blind assaults made on otherwise unknown territories. We find such warning signs in an early text, entitled 'Post-Marxism Without Apologies', that sees Laclau (along with his erstwhile collaborator Chantal Mouffe) having to fend off the criticisms offered by Norman Geras, displeased as he is with how what is said in their work is not directly transposable into his own theoretical idiom. In a later text, *On Populist Reason,* while the context is somewhat altered, the same motif is encountered. This time citing Freud, we are told how the problem is always that of jumping headstrong into a polemical exchange, and ceding ground too early on what is most substantive for what is the most politically expedient: 'One can never tell where that road may lead one; one gives way first in words, and little by little in substance too' (Laclau 2005, p. 249).

The problem today, Laclau diagnoses, 'is when condemnation replaces explanation' (2005, p. 249) or equally when heavy praise is a substitute for the rigours of theoretical construction; when precisely the long and laborious theoretical task of thinking the political is sacrificed, for what is most expedient and capricious. Laclau names such acts a 'faintheartedness' in the face of what is truly needed; namely, a rigorous analytic of the political (Laclau 2005, p. 250). The dual temptation is both an *ethicism* and a *politicism*: two conditions that can easily come over the would-be critic, to the detriment of theoretical vitality. Such is the case when one's theoretical mission is couched in terms of a critique that works 'in the name' of emancipation. The trouble is that as a theoretical gesture emancipatory critique harbours a fundamental ambiguity:

Either, as a theoretical intervention that works under the name of 'emancipation', the contribution that a critique makes to the Idea is identical with how the Idea operates within a localised context. Therefore, a critique that works 'in the name of' emancipation is a critique that takes its specific form from the precise way in which the name comes to be articulated in that particular context with a set of determinate demands. In this way, both the critique and the Idea of 'emancipation', in the name of which theoretical critique gains its efficacy, is particular; it is part of the political process that it is intervening in. The effects of the theoretical contribution are limited by the case. Its intervention is *politicist* and its theoretical valence is compromised because of it.

Or, as a theoretical intervention, working 'in the name of' emancipation, the Idea of emancipation it operates under is general and abstract, and the concrete case with which it critically engages is subsumed by this global understanding that transcends it. From a theoretical point of view, one not only sacrifices the specificity of the case, but one also circulates within a rarefied atmosphere of generality where 'emancipation' operates as an empty slogan. The possibility is not politicist in this case but *ethicist* or *moralist*, but once more its theoretical value is all the same compromised. This latter alternative brings to mind what Louis Althusser once derided as a growing consensus between intellectuals expunging Ideas of all their material value: 'an International of Decent feelings' who would speak of socialism 'without speaking of class struggle', who would rally around 'the flag of a United Europe' with a 'moral sermonising', which, in all cases, conjures away all notions of 'social antagonism' (Althusser 1997, pp. 21–30).

How can a theoretical understanding of emancipation avoid these two alternatives? How might a thinking of emancipatory Ideas be countenanced that preserves their material and concrete force—so that one remains vigilant to the multiple ways in which such Ideas appear in the world—but at the same time, as an Idea, allows one to think a certain consistency in its appearing across a range of cases? What is it that allows one to name an instance of politics as 'emancipatory'? How might one mobilise this adjectival marker, thus allowing a theorist to see unity through a dispersal of cases? Rather than suffering a bout of faintheartedness, of falling foul of either a *politicism* or *ethicism*, Ernesto Laclau's task is nothing short of a scrupulous investigation of the conditions that make any emancipatory political discourse possible, therefore allowing him, precisely in the name of emancipation, to retain unity among a dispersion of cases without this unifying instance operating as but an empty abstraction.

Certainly, the 'faintheartedness' of the critic need not show itself as either a *politicism* or an *ethicism*. Neither of these terms would account for the attempts made on behalf of 'critique' to furnish it with the security of a positive ground; an explanatory principle that would ensure the authority of its own critical statements. A third possibility can be added to the first two presented. 'Faintheartedness' can show itself as a *theoreticism*, and such a tendency is in need of further elaboration. Via a problematisation of the practice of ideologycritique, Laclau further adds to the disquiet about theory following the path of criticism in pursuit of emancipatory Ideas – bedevilled as this path is by detours and cul-de-sacs, circulars and u-turns – and proposes why one might instead find advantage in pursuing an alternative route towards the affirmation of Ideas of emancipation.

'Emancipatory critique' as 'ideology critique'

The thrust of Laclau's suspicion regarding emancipatory critique can be summed up by the assumed homonymy said to exist between 'emancipatory critique' and the 'critique of ideology'. Putative emancipatory theories have operated within the tripartition of 'ideology', 'critique' and 'emancipation' – according to Laclau, 'expressed in its purest terms by classical Marxism and prolonged today by Habermas' regulative idea of undistorted communication' (Laclau 1997, p. 218). Functioning as mutually exclusive terms, ideological mystification operates as the other of emancipation; emancipation comes to function as the release from the machinations of both ideology and relations of power.

Two simplifying assumptions are operative here and Laclau seeks to dispel both: firstly, the opposition drawn between ideological opacity and emancipatory transparency, and, secondly, the further assumption that the critical theorist occupies a privileged position as the overseer of this transitional move. Accordingly, theoretical critique acts as the relay between the points that would take a specified group from a state of collective misrecognition to the realisation and fulfilment of emancipatory ends. Against these two suppositions, Laclau advances two theses of his own. First, that the distinction between ideological mystification and rational transparency is untenable, and, second, that understood in terms of the contrast between opacity and transparency, emancipation becomes the victim of a game within which the critic will hold it captive. Emancipation contains within it its own dialectical reversal; namely, a critical discourse that appoints itself as bringing about emancipatory effects by way of a process of demasking, unveiling, exposing, etc. In sum, the strategy of providing knowledge to those who know not what they do can easily be its own form of command, and thereby perpetuate relations of inequality and political subordination. First, such a thinking must know where to draw the line between ideological subordination and emancipatory enlightenment so that the point of positivity is fixed, and then specify the conditions under which thought can seize, beneath the layers of ideological subterfuge, the point of rational knowledge. This is easier said than done.

The history of ideology as a concept has undergone a set of revisions in which the reductive assumptions of that very category have slowly been dispensed with. 'False consciousness', 'alienation', the antipodes of 'ideology' and 'science', the distinction between the 'essential' and the merely 'apparent' have been shorn of their explanatory value – too simplistic to offer a complex account of social and political phenomena. The analytical complexification of ideology has correlatively placed in question the possibility of critique (cf. Laclau 1997). Or to be more precise, the gradual deconstruction of the markers that the critique of ideology as emancipatory critique took as its guide has cranked up the demands for an effective critique to such a pitch that it barely remains audible. Laclau both acknowledges and assents to this conceptual tendency. Alluding to the work of Louis Althusser and Michel Foucault, Laclau sees a twofold process in operation whereby an ideological creeping is met with a concomitant retreat of the space that would circumscribe any neutral space for the raising of epistemic claims, right up to the point at which the distinction between what is said to be ideology and what is extra-ideological is indiscernible (Laclau 1997, p. 228).

The problem, then, for ideology critique – and a notion of emancipatory critique that it has often been paired up with – hangs on the following questions: what if there is no 'outside' of ideology? What if an appeal to an objective set of relations is foreclosed in advance? What if the very attempt to seize the truth is an act that is already discursively mediated; that, in Kantian vernacular, the 'thing-in-itself' is debarred from ever being known? (cf. Kant 1929).

To put this within a scheme of reference that is closer to Laclau's, let us say that we encounter a physical object. How might that object be described? Are descriptions about that object exhaustive of its physical properties, or, alternatively, can we speak of a semantic latitude regarding the way in which an object 'appears' and is 'phrased' in the world? It is doubtless the case that both positions can be accommodated and that an interior fold serves as the dividing line between the interiority and exteriority of ideology; that is, between the ideological and extra-ideological. On this basis it is certainly possible to make a distinction that would separate the essential and invariant features of a given thing from what is accidentally and contingently ascribed to it. To give an example: an object is unearthed; it is identified by the local geologist as a diamond. It has both a particular atomic classification and an elemental structure that is identifiable from the periodic table. However, at the very point of it being exhumed, the diamond is not reducible to its mere physical presence. It circulates within a system of relations in which its meaning will undergo a set of descriptive variations and deictic permutations. Let us say, for example, that the diamond will be an invaluable source of local pride for the mayor of a township, the discovery of which would keep him in the mayoral office for another term. The venture capitalist will not see so much of the symbolic pride bestowed upon the local community, but the opportunity to mine, and increase profit margins; for the environmentalist the mining for diamonds will mean the further destruction of the local environment. The unemployed miner will see the diamond as the possibility of future employment. The local union representative will caution against any over-enthusiasm for employment possibilities, which will doubtlessly pay little and pit the local workers against one another in the competition for a limited number of job opportunities, etc. In this example, the thing encountered does not reveal itself univocally. For the one object, an innumerable set of descriptive statements and normative claims can be made. Are any of these statements derivable from the mere presence of the diamond? No. There is nothing in the diamond itself that would predispose it to any particular statement. In light of this, Laclau will say that the mere thing-hood of the thing (its brute physical existence) is the point of departure for social analysis, and not the salvation of that analysis (Laclau 1990, p. 105). Rather, it is the indexing of possible ways in which a thing, an object, an event, a happening, comes to be signified that a political theory realises its full explanatory capacity.

Nonetheless, theory has often played the game of finding the right lexical ordering of possible statements about a particular object, an event, a set of processes – to place thereby the statements in order of veracity: from descriptives that are most felicitous to statements that are most erroneous. This would be the point of entry for a critical interjection, and for the emancipatory credentials of theoretical critique to reveal themselves. The task would be to sift through a set of discourses, and ascertain the truth content of each in order finally to better identify a set of claims that misrecognise the situation of which they are a part. The problem is how to find the best way to sort through the possible descriptions about a given set of relations? A measure will need to be put forward that can evaluate all the possible statements. Such a measure must submit to three criteria:

1. It must have a consistency that ensures its successful functioning outside the set of statements it is presiding over. It must have a theoretical significance that traverses the otherwise localised situation with which it is analytically engaged.

2. A measure that serves to bring accord to a multiple set of statements must submit itself to the order of a description, to the dictates of the sentence; it must be intelligible, and for it to be intelligible it must operate as any other discourse would.

3. It cannot be just another statement related paratactically with other possible statements; to be so means that it must be a part of the descriptions to be ordered and not that which permits the ordering of possible statements. It must therefore operate as that which grounds the intelligibility of all other sentences. Such a statement must be both a part of, as well as being an exception to, the order of discourses it places under the analytical microscope. Its point of reference is the same phenomenon, but it must account for that object in a way that transcends the understandings that particular subjects give to themselves. The double requirement is, however, untenable.

Consistently throughout Laclau's work there is, first, the circumscription of this theoretical problem and, second, the extrication of his own thought from this dilemma. His starting point is, he writes, 'the negation of any such metalinguistic level' (Laclau 1997, p. 299). A metalanguage would set itself up as a neutral field by which to account for all possible discursive permutations. On the contrary, for Laclau, ineradicable in any discourse is a set of rhetorico-discursive devices; the corollary being that 'there is no extra-discursive ground from which a critique of ideology could proceed' (Laclau 1997, p. 299).

If Laclau takes as axiomatic that there is no extra-discursive or extra-ideological principle that may function as the court of appeal to arbitrate over discourses, he does so not in order to assert either the inefficacy or impossibility of critique. Rather, the intent is to query the understanding of emancipation that such a mode of theoretical critique supposes – which is, an investment in an idea of transparency, in the recovery or reclamation of a rational or a material principle, functioning behind the backs of otherwise unsuspecting subjects, and about which their enlightenment constitutes the emancipatory task. An attentiveness to the implications deriving from the lack of a resort to an extra-ideological substratum will have profound consequenses in the way emancipatory Ideas are seizable theoretically. Laclau's problematisation of the classical form in which a commitment to emancipation shows itself (i.e., emancipatory critique) is his way of clearing the ground for thinking the political processes that – in their plurality, novelty and heterogeneity – give rise to emancipatory Ideas. If one is to understand something of the genetic logic by which emancipatory struggles appear in the world then one must take seriously, in a rigorously analytical way, the logic of the political.

Beyond critique: the elements of a theory of emancipatory ideas

How does Laclau go about thinking this logic that undercuts the usual manner in which theory relates to emancipatory Ideas?

Firstly, Laclau's contribution to a renewed understanding of emancipatory Ideas is not a secret hidden deep within the author's work needing to be carefully exhumed from beneath an array of other concerns. Arguably, the question of emancipation has been an explicit point of thematic commentary and re-thematisation in his corpus of work to date: from his very first Althusserian inflected studies on populism, which comprise his first book, *Politics and Ideology in Marxist Theory*, through his collaborative writings with Chantal Mouffe in *Hegemony and Socialist Strategy*, up to his most recent systematic inquiry into the logics of populism, which avowedly positions itself against a general 'denigration of the masses' in much of political and social theory (Laclau 2005), the possibility of a rethinking of political sequences that have, in the past, and that may, in the future, speak for the 'universal' – for the 'collective emancipation' of all – has been a constituent feature of his more general reflections on 'the political'. And, even if his 1996 volume, *Emancipation(s)*, begins with an essay, suggestively entitled 'Beyond Emancipation' – an essay that closes with the rather bold claim that 'today we are at the end of emancipation and at the beginning of freedom' (Laclau 1996, p. 18) – the general impetus of Laclau's thinking is not to join others in the denunciation of the desire for emancipation or related Ideas, but of seeking to provide a theoretical grammar more consequent in thinking the actual emergence and endurance of such Ideas within the vicissitudes of political struggle. Indeed, notwithstanding the prior indications that might be interpreted, on casual inspection, as portents for a rejection of this Idea, within the short confines of that essay, between the Scylla and Charybdis of the title and the closing refrain that would seemingly ward off any possible retreading of the Ideas of emancipation, there is, amongst its procedural deconstruction, nonetheless the claim that they should not be abandoned (Laclau 1996, p. 2).

What, then, to make of this mixed message, which, on the one hand, clearly extols a movement 'beyond' the task of emancipation and yet, on the other, re-lands in the very space that Laclau otherwise claims to leave behind? Clearly, the distance shown towards the Ideas is a particular understanding of the emancipatory hope, and not the Idea of emancipation as such. In an essay on Jacques Derrida's *Spectres of Marx*, collected as part of the same volume as 'Beyond Emancipation', Laclau implores us not to make the mistake of conflating a certain theoretical discourse with the destiny of all emancipatory discourses (Laclau 1996, p. 82). His warning, on this occasion, was aimed at an important recuperation of Marx (made, for one, by Derrida), which sought to combat the vitriol of a re-amped liberalism – that, after the seismic geo-political changes precipitated by the collapse of communism in Eastern Europe, needed no second invitation to dismiss and denounce Marxism (Fukuyama 1993; Gray 2004; Furet 1999). The risk, though, in the important activity of keeping in check the self-congratulatory excesses of liberalism, was constructing something of an isonomy between the recuperation of Marxism and emancipation as an 'Ideal', as if it were the case that the latter necessitated the former. However, as Laclau was to note on that occasion, even if one must remain respectful towards the spectres of Marx and Marxism, in rethinking the Idea of emancipation, '[m]any more ghosts than those of Marx are actually visiting and revisiting us' (Laclau 1996, p. 82). True, Marxism as a critical theoretical discourse could not do without the retention of the Idea of emancipation, but the Idea need not require the service of Marxism. Here we find a disarticulation of Marxism and emancipation, but in order to phrase anew emancipatory Ideas, to broaden their sphere of influence.

What form does this rephrasing take? We must consider the function of *Hegemony and Socialist Strategy* from 1985, which, as we know, was an attempt, first and foremost, to think beyond the impasses of a theoretical paradigm that had begun to flag under the weight of political disappointments and missed opportunities; whose myopia had become clearly diagnosable in its incapacity to come to a proper and serious understanding of the irruption of political struggles that were not so easily domesticated within the confines of class politics (Laclau & Mouffe 2001, pp. 2–4). It was a lesson in the art of both reconfiguring and rearticulating the coordinates by which both to think, analytically, and engage actively in politics with greater acuity and efficacy. Laclau and Mouffe were to do so still within the broad tradition of Marxism,[8] but wresting the left away from, as they expressed it, any last 'redoubts' of dogmatism and essentialism (Laclau & Mouffe 2001, p. 75); seeking to embrace thereby a more pragmatic and contextually nuanced understanding of social and political phenomena, one that would be more attuned to the 'infinite intertextuality of emancipatory discourses in which the plurality of the social takes shape' (Laclau & Mouffe 2001, p. 5).

Some fifteen years after its original publication, the authors would take the opportunity to add some retrospective comments on the status of their work. But if, in the original publication, the text was ultimately overdetermined by a set of normative and practico-political concerns, they would on this occasion seek to place the emphasis elsewhere; this time considering the ontological contribution they saw themselves making in both an *analytical* deepening and broadening of the logics of politics: 'Any substantial change in the ontic content of a field of research', they wrote, 'leads to a new ontological paradigm' (Laclau & Mouffe 2001, p. x). *Hegemony and Socialist Strategy* would be part of this paradigmatic shift, according to which their approach, 'grounded in privileging the moment of political articulation, and the central category of political analysis ... [of] hegemony' (Laclau & Mouffe 2001, p. x), opens itself towards a more transcendental line of enquiry, and therefore comes to unearth a set of primordial questions, namely, 'how does a relation between entitites have to be, for a hegemonic relation to become possible?' (Laclau & Mouffe 2001, p. x). It is from here that the category of discourse reveals itself as the prima principii for thinking, in its most rigorous way, the possibility of politics, and by extension the terrain on which politics itself is staged; that is, the continual struggle for hegemony.

For Ideas of emancipation to be properly and meticulously thought through, they must pass through the political conduit of hegemony, which now becomes the most consequent category in thinking about the implications subtending the ontological axiom that the social field is structured discursively (Laclau & Mouffe 2001, p. 112).

Laclau reaches the same conclusion in a contribution to his debate with Judith Butler and Slavoj Žižek. However, the implications he wishes to draw from this conclusion broach, more directly, the question of the Idea of emancipation. A thinking of the specificity of an emancipatory politics will benefit from taking the hegemonic turn (Laclau 2000, p. 47). From these two statements, we can render Laclau's reasoning syllogistically, threading together the logic of hegemony, the category of the political and emancipatory Ideas. This can be put in the following way:

P1. The logic of hegemony provides the resources for thinking the political.
P2. Emancipatory Ideas must be thought in terms of their political operation.
C. The category of hegemony is the way in which to understand the formation of emancipatory Ideas.

We have, then, the major premise that binds together the concept of the political with the category of hegemony; a minor premise which serves to institute a break with the dominant way in which emancipatory Ideas have been mobilised at the level of theory – inattentive as they have been to the immanent political logics constitutive in the formation of such Ideas. Finally, we have the general inference that articulates an understanding of emancipatory Ideas with the general logic of hegemony. The category of hegemony, which is itself a receptacle for thinking a wider set of political processes, reopens the theoretical task of engaging with Ideas of emancipation. It is via this three-stage logical deduction that an understanding of Laclau's rephrasing of the category of emancipation can be secured.

However, if an understanding of the way in which Laclau seeks to re-treat emancipatory Ideas can be rendered syllogistically, obviously there is, from within the confines of this syllogism, much that needs unpacking and demonstrating. What Laclau means by the 'political', by 'hegemony', and how these two terms come to transfigure the way in which Ideas of emancipation are to be thought in their political appearing, requires a more extensive commentary.

From within the theoretical development of Marxism, Laclau fastens onto the category of 'hegemony', because, interior to that history, the category is what might be termed an 'immanent exception' to that *dispositif*. Theoretically, it emerged from within the bounds of a Marxism continually intent on refining and complexifying its understanding of societal relations in response to all manner of anomalous events and unforeseen circumstances. Yet, at the same time, some of the implications were exceptions to the very theoretical field in which the category first took root and, if properly worked through, would question some of the founding axiomatic commitments of historical materialism (whether this be the claim that 'class struggle is the motor of history', or the topographical model of society upon which the analytical distinction between the economic *infrastructure* and the juridical and political *superstructure* was predicated).

The categorial emergence of hegemony (a theoretical advance attributed to Antonio Gramsci) is something akin to a 'watershed' moment interior to the history of Marxism, as Laclau and Mouffe were to make plain through their genealogical account in the second and third chapters of *Hegemony and Socialist Strategy* (Laclau & Mouffe 2001, pp. 65–71). Through the very supplementation of the category of hegemony, there was an acknowledgement that an account of the conditions of emergence for an emancipatory subjectivity could no longer be traced back to any underlying structural cause. It could no longer be rendered in terms of a systematic reflex, in the way that, according to Marx and Engels (from *The Communist Manifesto*), the bourgeoisie are said to be responsible for creating their own grave-diggers (Marx & Engels 1985, p. 87). Only through the analysis of contingent and pragmatic discursive practices might one come to a fuller understanding of the possibility of an emancipatory struggle and the specific articulation of demands and tasks that irrupt from within a given situation: 'More than any other theoretician of his time, Gramsci broadened the terrain of *political* recomposition and hegemony, while offering a theorisation of the hegemonic link which clearly went beyond the Leninist category of class alliance' (Laclau 2001, p. 66). Why was this the case? Clearly, Gramsci occupied a place both in space and time that forced him to grapple with the vicissitudes and the indeterminacy of social relations, for which no ruse of History or systemic design could have legislated (cf. Gramsci 1998). Specifically, this meant, in the case of Italy during the third and fourth decades of the twentieth century, a society that was still in the infancy of capitalist development, ravaged by geo-political divisions and gripped by fascism – which became the emergent political solution to the twin problem of political fragmentation and economic underdevelopment. The constellation of historical events, of tendencies and counter-tendencies, were such that ortho-dox Marxism, as an explanatory theory, was inadequately attentive to contextual differences, lacking thereby the rigour of detail that was necessary to save any analysis it sought to provide from empty generalities and superficiality; an analytical impoverishment that would, by implication, leave such a theory ill-equipped to meet the specific demands that were set by a given situation.[9] Gramsci was, analytically, more experimental in his attempt to understand his own contemporaneity, riven as it was with acute contradictions, and, practico-politically, was more pragmatic in seeking a workable political strategy for the left. He readily acknowledged that a progressive and emancipatory political project would have to be composed from an array of social groups and classes (the peasants, the working class, the intelligentsia). Imperative was the formation of a collective will – itself an active political task. What the situation demanded was the construction of a collective will that harnessed an effective political ideology, which, in expressing 'neither … a cold utopia nor … a learned theorising', would necessitate rather the 'creation of a concrete phantasy, [acting] on a dispersed and shattered people to arouse and organise its collective will' (Gramsci 1998, p. 126). Whence the emphasis placed upon hegemony as the practical act of constructing a unified emancipatory will from a fragmented set of elements (which, for Gramsci, still meant the working class as the *archein* of this movement, even if it was necessary that other progressive sectors of that society were to follow it, and perhaps, more importantly still, even if it was necessary that the proletariat be at the centre of a constellation of demands and interests which, in assimilating them, transcended its own immanent concerns).[10] With Gramsci, and with the categories that he was in part responsible for introducing, one can discern a shift in the analytical balance of power from knowledge of the formation of modes of production, analyses of economic relations and the emergence of social classes, to an analysis of the genesis of political struggles and the possibility of their endurance. The category of hegemony, then, emphasises the importance of the political constructability of a collective identity.[11] For Laclau, what this points towards is an opening up of some primitive political operations that were otherwise neglected or displaced in social theory (whether Marxist or non-Marxist) up to that point.

We must show a little focus here, thus ensuring that, rather than the general articulation between hegemony and the political be broached (with the full force of concepts and logics this unleashes), we confine our comments to how, according to Laclau, the logic of hegemony comes to transfigure the way in which emancipatory Ideas might be seized theoretically.

It is important that one comes to terms with the precise status of the category of hegemony in Laclau's work, one which is at variance with how both the noun ('hegemony') and its adjectival form ('hegemonic discourse') are deployed in some other theoretical fields. A case in point (very much relevant to this volume) is Critical Discourse Analysis. Lilie Chouliaraki and Norman Fairclough deploy the category of hegemony, but see it only as 'helpful in analysing relations of power as domination' (Chouliarki & Fairclough 2005, p. 24). In this sense, the hegemonic relation takes on a distinctly pejorative guise. Emancipation would be attained through the elimination of relations of domination and hegemonic relations as such. Hegemonic discourses would relate to emancipatory discourses as alpha relates to omega. In this way, it is of a piece with how the category of ideology has often been harnessed in social and political theory, namely, as something to be identified and critiqued. The emancipatory contribution made by theory to society would be its attempt to eliminate such instances. This double restriction placed on hegemony, and analogously the category of ideology, puts a particular normative weight on theoretical engagements with political phenomena. While the restrictive sense in which both hegemony and ideology are employed doubtlessly sharpens the efficacy of critique, something ends up being sacrificed: something of the nuance and subtlety – which is to say nothing of the complexity – of political existence and the logics constitutive of political struggles.

For Laclau and DT more generally, the category of hegemony (and the same applies to ideology too) is not a restrictive concept that applies only to questionable institutions, relations and political regimes, in which their immediate contestation is called for. The hegemonic relation suffuses the social as such, and in this way is inextricably bound up with the very possibility of politics (whether as part of a strategy to maintain the status quo or as part of an emancipatory struggle to overthrow an unjust system). Domination, therefore, does not necessarily take the form of a hegemonic relation – if by domination one is to deploy this appellation normatively; that is, as a system of relations that ought to be questioned and replaced with a more 'democratic' and 'open' system.[12]

As Laclau writes in response to a question posed by Judith Butler about the extent of the utility of the category of 'hegemony': '"hegemony" is more than a useful category, it defines the very terrain in which a political relation is actually constituted.' (Laclau 2000, p.

44). For Laclau, hegemonic power does not have as its counterpoint emancipatory resistances. Hegemony is the terrain on which political subjects play out their struggles; the hegemonisation of the social field is the telos for all would-be contesting political imaginaries. This applies to all *modes* of politics (whether liberal, emancipatory, bureaucratic, totalitarian, etc.), even if, ontically, there are fundamental differences between such modalities. And it is precisely here that a fundamental faultline can be drawn between DT and CDA, upon which the relation between critique and emancipation undergoes a certain modulation in the respective traditions.

Concluding reflections

It is the merit of Laclau that he fastens onto an immanent understanding of how emancipatory Ideas come to be articulated politically, *hic et nunc*, in the very throws of specific struggles. He writes: 'the demands of a lesbian group, a neighbours association or a black self-defence group are all situated on the same ontological level … [i]n this way the absence of a global emancipation of humanity allows the constant expansion and diversification of concrete emancipatory demands' (Laclau 1990, p. 216). The problem with putative emancipatory theories is that they have never managed to provide a successful account of emancipation that would transcend the historical possibilities of emancipation to which they believed they were contributing. Either they function as a theory that takes as its understanding of emancipation the particular demands tied to a certain political sequence (emancipation from patriarchal tutelage, in the case of feminism emancipation from the wage relation, in Marxism emancipation from heteronormativity, in queer theory), or what it has thought was a theory of emancipation meant merely to elevate a particular emancipatory struggle as the ontological elect for the ultimate and universal instantiation of liberation. Laclau raises the analytical bar considerably higher, which involves a coming to terms with a set of questions pertaining to the political as such.

This searching into the political is, precisely, a move not for the 'fainthearted'; such a task, once assented to, must inquire into the conditions that make politics possible – to offer a theory of the political that transforms significantly the topographical setting for theoretical inquiry, and places particular restrictions on what can rationally be demanded of critique. There is, then, an attentiveness to the limits of the figure of the critical thinker; a line of thought that, prima facie, would align Laclau with the most unyielding of sceptics. However, it is a merit of Laclau's thought that he does not shirk from the task of plumbing the depths of a most volatile storm. There is, on his part, a sentience towards a twofold crisis – a crisis of critical rationality (which we have spoken of) and the crisis regarding the equivocity of the values and Ideas in which modern man has invested so deeply. But, as has been intimated already, emancipatory Ideas are not to be relinquished. The tone is set by the title under which the diagnosis of the present is granted space for articulation: *New Reflections on the Revolution of Our Time* is an attempt to recast emancipatory Ideas in a new theoretical idiom that would not play on the contrast between light and dark that has otherwise befallen the present. Against nostalgia for a more certain past, which might lead the theorist, faced with the vicissitudes of the present, to either court nihilistic despair or to become trenchantly dogmatic, thus cleaving to old methods and certainties, the point of intervention for Laclau would be to do 'exactly the opposite':

> Far from perceiving in the 'crisis of reason' a nihilism which leads to the abandonment of any emancipatory project, we see the former as opening unprecedented opportunities for the formulation of liberation projects hitherto restrained by the rationalist 'dictatorship' of the Enlightenment (Laclau 1991, p. 3).

The Idea of emancipation need not be vanquished; it might be better served by being freed from the baggage of a critical theory. Extricated from the clutches of the classical ways by which theory has sought to seize the Idea, the issue is given a new orientation:

> To what extent does placing in question the rationalism character-ising the project of modernity not mean undermining the founda-tions of the emancipatory project linked to it? … It is a question

of historically constituting the subject to be emancipated – indeed, emancipation and constitution are part of the same process. But in that case why prefer one future over another? Why choose between different types of society? There can be no reply if the question is asking for a kind of Cartesian certainty that pre-exists any belief. But if the agent who must choose is someone who already has certain beliefs and values, then criteria for choice – with all the intrinsic ambiguities that a choice involves – can be formulated. Such an acceptance of the facticity of certain strata of our beliefs is nothing but the acceptance of our contingency and historicity. We could even go so far as to say that it is the acceptance of our 'humanity' as an entity to be constructed; while in the case of rationalism, we have been given 'humanity' and are merely left with the secondary task of realising it historically (Laclau 1991, p. 83).

An interior distinction is drawn about how one is to comport one-self in the theoretical task of thinking Ideas of emancipation. The path forks between the high road of philosophical rationalism and the low road – what we might wish to call more subterranean – of political reason. Such a distinction is drawn between the givenness of Ideas and their constructability, between their eternity and their historicity, between their transcendent and imperious authority and their immanent and auto-legislative capacity. What separates these two approaches is two different understandings of both politics, and the relation that politics has to Ideas. Are Ideas donated to politics so that politics must realise them in practice, or does their force only ever derive from their localised and immanent construction? For Laclau, who wants no less than a theory of the political, there can be little room for equivocation. The problem with the former position is that Ideas are transcendentally deduced; their power lies prior to their historical conditions of possibility. Even if the first move is to assent to the derivative nature of emancipation, that any seizure of the Idea – and the specifiable meaning attributable to that Idea – must be drawn from the resources of a given situation, there is a further move that accompanies the former and which undermines the founding principle of immanence.

Emancipation as an Idea has an inescapably derivative status. It becomes an operative term precisely in the presence of conditions of social injustice – experienced by particular collectivities, and verifiable through meticulous analysis via a description of the structural and historical conditions of emergence of a given situation of oppression. It is *because* of the empirical fact that oppression exists in one form or another that the demand for emancipation appears. Its derivative status can be registered by way of the syntactic form under which the demand for emancipation is phrased. One speaks of 'emancipation from'. The preposition is such that emancipation does not so much contain within it the futural of the towards-which. It operates by way of its reference to an extant set of conditions from which it seeks to break free. It could be said of emancipation that its sense and meaning are derived entirely from the specificity of a struggle and the particular situation out of which that struggle emerges. One speaks therefore of 'emancipation *from*' as one would talk of a deliverance *out of* a certain set of relations; it is the determinate set of relations from which one wishes to escape that has centrality. 'Servitude', Louis Althusser writes:

> is a form of captivity *from which* one can escape because it is a real prison, with real walls and bars ... every day the proletarian experiences the concrete reality of the content of his condition; every day he repeats his efforts to get the better of it, and this daily experience furnishes him the double proof that he is not wrestling with the shadows, but confronts a real object in his struggle, and that this object, inasmuch as it exists and resists, can be overcome. (Althusser 1997, p. 26).

Such, then, is the case with the proletarian who hopes to be emancipated *from* the shackles of wage labour and the insidious relations of capital, etc., or the slave, who hopes to be emancipated *from* his/her condition as an object that is entirely at the disposal of its master's volition, or women who hope to be emancipated *from* the yoke of patriarchal authority, etc. In each case the conditions at stake have both a historical and structural specificity that is not easily assuaged.

In drawing our attention back to the derivative status of emancipation, Laclau does not wish to reduce emancipation to the relations of power, from which a particular collectivity seeks to break free. If

74

this were the case, emancipation would be no more than a structural effect, not a political construction. Consisting of more than the break of a particular cohort from a state of minority, emancipatory Ideas are the political articulations of novelties, of unexpected and contingent happenings that, while taking their cue from historical and structural conditions, are themselves never reducible to them.

What ultimately Laclau wishes to affirm in politics (which is his way of affirming emancipatory Ideas) is how 'human beings see themselves as the builders and agents of change of their own world, and thus come to realise that they are not tied by the objective necessity of history or any institutions or way of life' (Laclau 1990, p. 216). In doing so, it is arguably the case that in his disarming of critique, he leaves the Idea of emancipation unharmed.

Notes

1 The reader of this text should note a typographical decision taken here by the writers. For the most part, the 'Idea' appears capitalised, and not as 'idea', expressed in lower-case. This ostensibly rather strange decision, one that flies in the face of convention, has been taken for strictly philosophical reasons. Philosophically, it is important to differentiate between 'ideas' we might have of, say, a table, a chair (that is, of any 'object' in the world) and a species of Ideas, for which there exists no direct correspondence with an object of experience. Here, the inspiration is Kant, who in his *Critique of Pure Reason* beseeches his readership that 'those who have the interests of philosophy at heart … must be careful to preserve the expression "idea" in its original meaning, that it may not become one of those expressions which are commonly used to indicate any and every species of representation, in a happy-go-lucky confusion …' (Kant 1929, A319=B376). It is in the particular manner that Kant intended the deployment of the term 'Idea' – i.e. where our object is only in our brain, and therefore cannot be empirically given and known in accord with laws of experience (Kant 1929, A484=B512) – that the term is hereafter used.

2 This is a particular concern of Michael Billig, who in his pointedly entitled essay 'Critical Discourse Analysis and the Rhetoric of Critique' cautions against self-complacency, which can all too easily result in 'new forms of … linguistic orthodoxy.' Instead, he implores his peers 'to draw back from treating "Critical Discourse Analysis" as if it were a recognisable product and to unpick the rhetoric that has led from "critical approaches" to the abbreviated and capitalised "CDA".' (Billig 2003, p. 44).

3 Marx's Eleventh Thesis on Feuerbach: 'Philosophers have hitherto interpreted the world, the point is to change it' (Marx 1977, p. 145).

4 This point is immaculately presented by Glynos & Howarth, who explain how far the binding between the significance they ascribe to the political dimension of practices 'already implies a normative point of view, which regards certain norms or social logics as *worthy* of public contestation' (Glynos & Howarth 2007, pp. 191–193).

5 For critical realism this distinction between the transitive and the intransitive must be kept sacrosanct. Otherwise, at least according to Bhaskar, 'the possibility of rationally defensible conceptual criticism and change, most fully in the development of the concept of ideology' is impugned (Bhaskar 1998, p. 23).

6 Politics is described by Bhaskar as 'any practice oriented to the transformation of the conditions of human action; more concretely, as practices oriented to or conducted in the context of struggles and conflicts over the development, nature and distribution of the facilities and circumstances of human action; more starkly, as practices oriented to the transformation of the structured sets of social relations within which particular social structures operate and particular social activities occur' (Bhaskar 1989, p. 176).

7 Thus Marcuse writes: 'The critical theory of society possesses no concepts which could bridge the gap between the present and its future; holding no promise and showing no success, it remains negative. Thus it wants to remain loyal to those who, without hope, have given and give their life to the Great Refusal.' (Marcuse 1968, p. 257). It is a final meditation that finds a certain solace in Walter Benjamin's refrain that 'Nur um der Hoffnungslosen willen ist uns die Hoffnung gegeben' (Walter Benjamin, cit. Marcuse, 1968, p. 257).

8 *Hegemony and Socialist Strategy* developed out of a spirited agonistic relation with Marxism. Famously, in the introduction, both Laclau and Mouffe speak of their general itinerary as being post-Marxist. But, rather than the prefix 'post', designating a strict departure and discontinuity with both Marxist theory and practice, a more refined and complex relation is articulated (Laclau & Mouffe 2001, p. 4).

9 In Laclau's own words: 'Gramsci was writing at a time when it was already clear that mature capitalism was not advancing in the direction of an increasing homogenisation of the social structure but, on the contrary, towards an ever greater social and institutional complexity ... In this new historical situation it was clear that any "universal class" was going to be the effect of a laborious political construction, not of the automatic and necessary movements of any infrastructure' (Laclau 2000, p. 52).

10 Gramsci made an important distinction to clarify two tendencies in thinking the role of the workers' movement. The corporate interests of the working class, which meant any act of politics that resulted in the promotion of a set of immanent and restrictive interests of the working class, e.g., trade union politics, such as the demand for better working conditions, improvements in wages, etc., and a universal interest, where the working class would transcend its own immediate interests and put forward a set of demands that addressed the 'all' of a political community composed from a plurality of collective identities (Gramsci 1998, pp. 181–182).

11 We should recall what Gramsci found so appealing about the thought of Niccolo Machiavelli. Gramsci attributed to Machiavelli the modern invention of 'politics as an autonomus science'; a species of activity not subsumable by any other branch of science (Gramsci 1998, p. 136).

12 Indeed, were one to think instead the category of domination descriptively, then, in a sense, all struggles have as a constitutive aim the *suturing* of the social – emancipatory political sequences serve as no exception here. Historically, politics of emancipation have spoken in the name of the 'all'; mobilising around a set of articulated demands waged against a given social order. Emancipatory political discourses not only, therefore, contest the existing organisation of the social, but offer an alternative envisioning of the social as such. One social order replaces another social order, and not, as some have claimed, that universal emancipation would be the end of the function of order-ing *tout court*. For some extensive reflections on this issue by Ernesto Laclau, see: 'Why do Empty Signifiers Matter to Politics', an essay in the volume entitled *Emancipation(s)* (Laclau 1996).

References

Althusser, L., 1997. *The Spectre of Hegel: Early Writings*. London: Verso.

Althusser, L., 2001. *Lenin and Philosophy and Other Essays*. New York: MRP.

Bhaskar, R., 1986. *Scientific Realism and Human Emancipation*. London: Verso.

Bhaskar, R., 1989. *Reclaiming Reality: A Critical Introduction to Contemporary Philosophy*. London: Verso.

Bhaskar, R., 1998. *The Possibility of Naturalism: A Philosophical Critique of the Contemporary Human Sciences*. London: Routledge.

Billig, M., 2003. Critical Discourse Analysis and the Rhetoric of Critique. In: G. Weiss & R. Wodak (eds), *Critical Discourse Analysis: Theory and Interdisciplinarity*. London: Palgrave Macmillan, pp. 35–46.

Chouliaraki, L. & Fairclough, N., 1999. *Discourse in Late Modernity: Rethinking Critical Discourse Analysis*. Edinburgh: Edinburgh University Press.

Derrida, J., 1994. *Specters of Marx: The State of the Debt, the Work of Mourning and the New International*. London: Routledge.

Foucault, M., 1980. *Power/Knowledge: Selected Interviews and Other Writings 1972–1977*. London: Longman.

Fukuyama, F., 1993. *The End of History and the Last Man*. London: Harper Press.

Furet, F., 1999. *The Passing of an Illusion*. Chicago: Chicago University Press.

Glynos, J. & Howarth D., 2007. *Logics of Critical Explanation in Social and Political Theory*. London: Routledge.

Gramsci, A., 1998. *Selections from the Prison Notebooks*. London: Lawrence & Wishart.

Gray, J., 2004. *Heresies: Against Progress and Other Illusions*. London: Granta Books.

Habermas, J., 1998. *Knowledge and Human Interests*. London: Polity Press.

Jørgensen, M. Winther & Phillips L., 2002. *Discourse Analysis as Theory and Method*. London: Sage Press.

Kant, I., 1929. *The Critique of Pure Reason*. London: Palgrave.

Laclau, E., 1977. *Politics and Ideology in Marxist Theory*. London: NLB.

Laclau, E., 1991. *New Reflections on the Revolution of Our Time*. London: Verso.

Laclau, E., 1996. *Emancipation(s)*. London: Verso.

Laclau, E., 1997. The Death and Resurrection of the Theory of Ideology. *Journal of Political Ideologies*, 3(1), pp. 201–220.

Laclau, E., 2005. *On Populist Reason*. London: Verso.

Laclau, E., Butler, J. & Žižek, S., 2000. *Contingency, Hegemony and Universality* London: Verso.

Laclau, E. & Mouffe, C., 1985/2001. *Hegemony and Socialist Strategy*. London: Verso.

MacKenzie, I., 2004. *The Idea of Pure Critique*. London: Continuum.

Marcuse, H., 1968. *One-Dimensional Man: Studies in the Ideology of Advanced Industrial Society*. London: Routledge.

Marx, K., 1978. The Eleven Thesis on Feuerbach. In: R. Tucker (ed.), *The Marx-Engels Reader*. London: Norton Press.

Marx, K. & Engels, F., 1985. *The Communist Manifesto*. London: Penguin Press.

Ranciere, J., 2009. *The Emancipated Spectator*. London: Verso.

Ricoeur, P. 2002. Ethics and Culture: Habermas and Gadamer in Dialogue. In: D. Rasmussen & J. Swindal (eds), *Jürgen Habermas: Sage Masters of Modern Social Thought*; vol. 1. London: Sage Press, pp. 129–44.

Wellmer, A., 2002. Empirico-Analytical and Critical Social Science. In: D. Rasmussen & J. Swindal (eds), *Jürgen Habermas: Sage Masters of Modern Social Thought*; vol. 1. London: Sage Press, pp. 32–41.

CHAPTER 3

Reforming Education

Gendered Constructions of Future Workers

Sara Carlbaum

As political theorist Chantal Mouffe states, the 'way we define citizenship is intimately linked to the kind of society and political community we want' (Mouffe, 1992, p. 225). Therefore, in my view it is important to recognise that citizenship is not a natural entity, but a constructed and contested concept. As the notion of citizenship most commonly refers to the membership of a community, these constructions constantly involve mechanisms of exclusion and inclusion; that is, of who belongs and who does not (Lister et al. 2007; Siim & Squires 2008). A person's occupation plays an important part of identification in the construction of citizenship, because it involves a sense of community, belonging and loyalty. In Western societies citizenship is often understood not only as rights but also in terms of obligations. That a person works is viewed as necessary in order to contribute to the community's or the nation's welfare (Lister 2003; Siim & Squires 2008). The definition of citizenship is constituted in different contexts, one of which is education. This makes it essential to deconstruct notions of citizenship in education policy. The meaning of education is contextually formed and fills different functions in different places at different historical times. Therefore, what are conceived of as the most important values and skills of education are continuously being contested and renegotiated. New educational reforms always raise questions about what aspects of the current system should be preserved, what should be changed and whose interests should apply (Assarson 2007; Linde 2006). The feminist political scientist Carol Bacchi (1999, pp. 1–4) states that what should be studied is precisely how certain policy problems are materialised through policy discourses. Therefore, policies related to education can be seen as a prime site of political struggles over the meaning of citizenship. Guidelines are set up in these policies that form certain discourses, which involve consequences for how we perceive ourselves and our relationships with others (Bacchi & Beasley 2002, p. 331). Aspects of power are involved in the interpretation and construction of problems with education. Various subject positions are constructed that are not open for everyone to occupy (Bacchi 1999; Foucault 2002). The subject positions of workers[1] and citizens are always gendered, racialised, sexualised and class-oriented, etc. (Crenshaw 1995). However, in this chapter I will particularly focus on how the subject positions of workers are gendered.[2] By gendered I mean that the categories of women and men are constituted as significant distinctions in education policies, and that these distinctions construct relations of subordination and domination that leave different opportunities for women and men respectively.

Upper secondary education in Sweden has not changed substantially since the mid-1990s, but it is now facing a new reform. The Upper Secondary School Commission has submitted the report *Path to the Future*[3] (SOU 2008:27) and the government has followed the majority of the report's suggestions. A bill was subsequently presented to parliament in May 2009. The forthcoming reform has received some scholarly attention (cf. Bergström & Wahlström 2008) and this research has focused on the strong emphasis in the reform on work, labour market needs and the consequences of these reforms on social divisions such as class and ethnicity. However, as of yet, no study has drawn attention to how this reform constructs future workers and particularly how these constructions are gendered. As the reform appears to constitute a change in education policy, it is important to describe and analyse these gendered constructions and problematisations through a discourse theoretical perspective (cf. Lundahl et al. 2008).

Aim and outline

The aim of this chapter is to analyse and discuss the ways in which upper secondary education (USE) in Sweden is understood in the Upper Secondary School Commission's report, *Path to the Future*. How have the purpose, aims and perceived problems of upper secondary education been represented in the report? The problems of USE, and the justifications made for the forthcoming reform, are analysed with regard to how future workers are constructed and how these constructions are gendered. This chapter attempts to deconstruct subject positions in the contemporary discourse of education policy.[4]

I shall begin by presenting the theoretical perspectives and analytical strategies that I will use in order to deconstruct the proposed reform and the gendered construction of future workers that it implies. A description of the Swedish education system, particularly upper secondary education, is also presented. This is followed by an analysis of the representations of the problems and aims of upper secondary education and how these articulations in the reform are linked together in a hegemonic process.[5] The next section analyses how these articulations construct specific subject positions of gendered workers. Finally, some concluding remarks are presented.

A discourse theoretical approach

The discourse theoretical approach is based on a post-structuralist perspective in which all objects and practices are conceived as meaningful, and hence inevitably discursive (Laclau & Mouffe 2001, p. 113). Meaning is always contingent and always constructed in a specific context in relation to other meanings or objects, and, therefore, discourse encompasses more than just 'speech and writing'. We cannot understand a practice or an object without understanding it *as* something that stands in relation to other practices or objects (Laclau & Mouffe 1987, p. 2; Smith 1998). This perspective also corresponds to my own ontological view, and thus by education policy discourse I refer to temporary systems of meaning of the purpose of USE. These education policy discourses structure power relations in their articulation of certain subject positions of gendered future workers. Consequently, these discourses limit and open up possibilities for different people in terms of social practices of inclusion and exclusion (Torfing 2005, pp. 8–9; Winther Jørgensen & Phillips 2000).

Discourse, in this sense, is viewed in terms of 'systems of meaning', while the terms of reference and the report *Path to the Future* are viewed as containing acts of articulation that link together and order a meaningful structure of education practices. These articulations are sometimes constructed in new ways that may shift certain discourses (Laclau & Mouffe 2001, p. 113). Laclau and Mouffe (2001, p. 105) define articulation as 'any practice establishing a relation among elements such that their identity is modified as a result of the articulatory practice'. These articulatory acts of temporarily fixing the meaning of education can be viewed as a hegemonic process in the sense that they determine a set of problems and solutions of USE within a particular system of meaning that becomes dominant. The organisation of consent – by making the goals of education appear to be natural, true, real, valid and unconditional – constitute what is involved in a hegemonic process. I refer here to 'hegemonisation' as a struggle to constitute a certain education policy as stable and fixed, which indicates that it is more dominant and sedimented (Laclau 1990, pp. 27–31; Laclau & Mouffe 2001, p. 136).

Methodological discussions

Political struggles over meaning and practices are constantly articulated in policies, because these specific documents formulate the problem at hand, and thereafter propose solutions to it. This is why I see it as essential to study policymaking using a problematisation strategy. This term refers to how discursive practices construct problems that are contingent and political, rather than naturally given or 'necessary'. Policies are not mirrors of reality, but create meaning which imbues a specific question or a particular phenomenon with value (Bacchi 1999, pp. 1–4; Howarth 2007, p. 152). Problematisation has been used by a number of critical theorists as a strategy for problem-driven research (Bacchi 1999; Foucault et al. 1997; Glynos

& Howarth 2007). According to Foucault (2002, p. 14), problematisation is a method of analysis which combines his archaeological and genealogical approaches. The archaeological approach refers to the formation of a problem in the present, whereas the genealogical approach analyses its contingent formation in history. The analysis should focus on how problems are thought about and what follows from these problematisations. Justifications of different forms of solutions depend on the construction of perceived problems (Foucault 2002, p. 14; Foucault et al. 1997, pp. 115–119; Howarth 2007, p. 151). Therefore, the strategy of problematisation directs attention to how problems of USE are represented, and what solutions they justify. It also focuses on which signifiers are made central, and what subjects are made responsible as well as the objects for adjustment. In order to answer how education policy discourses are formed, logics of equivalence and difference are used as an analytical tool. The hegemonic process of linking together and uniting the representations of problems and essential signifiers in logics of equivalence fix the purpose of upper secondary education in a specific way; a way that appears natural, real and valid (Laclau 1996, pp. 38–43; Laclau & Mouffe 2001, pp. 154–155).

These representations of problems that are linked together in logics of equivalence also construct subject positions. Subject positions refer to 'differential' positions within discourses that construct social agents (Howarth 2007, p. 125). The social agent cannot be viewed as a homogeneous entity; instead, its identity is made up of intersecting subject positions that are constituted in various discourses. Therefore, education policies construct certain gendered subject positions such as pupil, worker and citizen.[6] The categories of woman and man are political and historical constructs, and gender is thus viewed as a system of organising people into different sexes; that is, of subject positions as men and women (Mouffe 2005, p. 77). These subject positions are more or less fixed representations of gender that postulate what it means to be female/male. Gender is discursively constituted and the 'female' is defined in relation to the 'male'; a process that ascribes certain qualities, characteristics, practices and subjects as either feminine or masculine. This discursive construction organises a heterosexual matrix in which gender is intimately linked to heterosexuality, policing and constructing womanhood and manhood as the only available positions – positions that are essentially different from each other (Butler 1999, pp. 42–43). The organisation of the feminine in relation to the masculine normalises different anatomical bodies to appear as two 'natural' sexes and not as political and historical constructs (Laclau & Mouffe 2001, pp. 117–118). This notion of women and men as discursive categories of subject positions argues against an essentialist notion of the subject as rational, homogeneous and transparent to itself (Mouffe 2005, p. 77). There is no prior extra-discursive sex from which gender is retrieved. Sex is not something that is before or outside gender; it is only through discourse that we make sense of the meaning of constructions of sexual difference (Butler 1999, pp. xxii–xxiv; Mouffe 2005, p. 77). Even though gendered subject positions like worker and citizen are discursive categories, it is not possible to totally step outside this organisation of the world and be anything we want to be. Whereas gender is constituted through repeated performative acts (Butler 1999, p. 173), we always interpret the world, act and identify ourselves through the mediating effects of political discourses about gender (Laclau 1990, pp. 44–60; Smith 1998, p. 99). The constructed subject positions of education policy discourses define how ideal gendered future workers should be and how they should act.

The Swedish education system

The Swedish education system is in the beginning stages of a major reform that encompasses everything from compulsory comprehensive school to higher education. The reforms involve changes regarding grading assessment, structures, as well as curricula (Prop. 2009/10:1). There is a three-year upper secondary education that is optional and free of charge. This education is aimed at pupils between the ages of 16 and 20 and falls between the compulsory school and higher education. The vast majority of the young people in the country attend USE today (Skolverket 2009) and it is even seen as a minimum requirement in order to successfully make the transition from school to work (Lundahl et al. 2008).

At the beginning of the 1970s, USE, vocational education and 'academic' or study-oriented education were integrated in the sense that they were governed by the same curriculum and legislation (Richardson 2004). This integration was further developed during the reform in the mid-1990s, which meant that all the study programmes changed so that they were three years in length. Each study programme included common core (academic) subjects that constituted a third of the total amount of study time. These changes gave all the pupils on each programme a basic eligibility for higher education (Skolverket 2009). The social democratic government's mid-1990s USE reform introduced a goal-related grading assessment and a programme-oriented education system. Today, upper secondary education consists of 17 national programmes which are comprised of 35 national specialisations, specially designed local programmes and so-called individual programmes (Dir. 2007:8, p. 2). These changes in the mid-1990s also involved a decentralisation of responsibilities. Instead of the state, municipalities were now made responsible for the implementation and organisation of the nationally adopted objectives and goals for USE, which still had the ambition of achieving national equivalence. The reform highlighted the pupils' need of so-called lifelong learning and individual development aims preparing them for active participation in a knowledge economy that follows a 'Bildung' tradition (Prop. 1990/91:85).

A further reform had been planned by the social democratic government and was to be implemented in 2007. However, in the wake of the 2006 elections, and the consequent shift in power to the four-party, right-wing coalition, 'The Alliance', the reform was stopped because the changes were found to be insufficient to meet the requirements of a reformed USE (Prop. 2006/07:1). Instead, an expert was commissioned to carry out the Upper Secondary School Commission report, with the task of proposing a new structure for Swedish USE.[7] The report was submitted in March 2008.[8] It was common that earlier official reports that focused on education reform were carried out by a parliamentary commission or with the involvement of a commission of several experts. One trend has developed in the Swedish political system, and that is the move from large

commissions that take a relatively long time to arrive at a conclusion to an increasing number of single expert commissions, where
clearer objectives have been stated in advance by the government.
The terms of reference that state this USE commission's task are specific in a number of ways, such as the differentiation of vocational,
academic and apprenticeship training. The report closely follows
these government intentions. The official report contains suggestions and basic data for the reform of upper secondary education,
and the government has drawn on the contents of this report in the
bill that was presented to parliament in May 2009. Therefore, the
report has had a great influence on the reform that was presented
to parliament. The new and reformed USE, in line with the suggestions from the report presented in the bill, was implemented in
the autumn of 2011 (Prop. 2008/09:199).[9] As the bill was being
prepared by the government while this chapter was being written,
the Upper Secondary School Commission report *Path to the Future*
and the terms of reference for this report constitute the main material analysed in the following sections.[10]

Employability and production of workers

The report *Path to the Future* represents the present state of USE
as unable to make pupils employable, and therefore the goal of
educating to meet the needs of the labour market is not fulfilled.
This positions the current educational system's inability to provide
a supply of people with the necessary national and regional skills as
a problem. It is hoped that the reform 'will contribute to a positive
development for youth employability and that the present high age
of entering the labour market will thus be lowered' (SOU 2008:27,
p. 179). The report also states that 'a pupil with a vocational diploma
should be employable' (SOU 2008:27, p. 379). This implies a view
that the main purpose of USE is to provide the labour market with
employable citizens. Furthermore, USE should be seen as a strategic part of the national and regional infrastructure and economic
growth (SOU 2008:27, p. 59).

In order for education to satisfy the needs of the national and
regional labour markets, a closer cooperation between schools and

receivers is proposed, where stakeholders such as employers and universities will have a significantly stronger influence over the content and goals of the different programmes. 'In my [the expert commissioner's] assessment, the receivers should be able to strengthen upper secondary education's role in different ways by providing for the supply of skills at national level' (SOU 2008:27, p. 532).[11] This cooperation is necessary, as 'the skill supply perspective means that municipalities and regions need to find out what the whole of the education supply should look like so that it can accommodate working life requirements' (SOU 2008:27, p. 602). The cooperation between receivers and schools is suggested at national and local levels, and will provide the receivers with influence over the goals, contents and the workplace learning of the different programmes and national tests and diploma requirements (SOU 2008:27, pp. 59–60, 180, 321, 329).

> I therefore propose that the task of upper secondary schools to satisfy the skills supply needs of working life and the higher education sector be further clarified in the Swedish Education Act. I also propose a clear role for receivers, i.e. working life and the higher education sector, when it comes to formulating educational objectives. It is also valuable if they participate in ensuring the quality of the education (SOU 2008:27, p. 59, original excerpt from English summary).

There is no mention of the general problem that education has in being able to satisfy the supply of skills needed. This issue is viewed in terms of an easy fix if the receivers are involved and command influence over education:

> With a national council, with representation from receivers, it would be possible to capture developmental needs and to satisfy the future needs of future industries, which have no established patterns of interaction at present. In doing so, it would be possible to continuously renew upper secondary schools and ensure that the urgent development needs are met (SOU 2008:27, p. 329).

However, how are the different problems with upper secondary education represented and how are they linked together by logics of equivalence that make employability the main purpose of education?

Too academic

One of the representations of the problem with USE is that the current education is *too academic*. 'Upper secondary education has become increasingly homogeneous. The differences between the various programmes have been reduced and the number of theoretical courses has increased' (Dir. 2007:8, p. 3).

> The current upper secondary education is too uniform. What this means is that vocational education is too theoretical and that many pupils find it difficult to pursue their education. It also means that the preparatory education for further studies is not adequately preparing the pupils for successful higher education (SOU 2008:27, p. 371).

It is also argued that too much time is spent on so-called core subjects that are common for all programmes. The terms of reference state that:

> All pupils in the national and the specially designed programmes are forced to study for basic eligibility to university, regardless of the goals, talents and interests held by the individual pupils. Core subjects are largely driven by a traditionally academic perspective... Many vocational programmes with programme specific subjects have become too theoretical with too little time for vocational subjects (Dir. 2007:8, p. 3).

According to the report, the increase of core subjects like mathematics and English has come at the expense of programme specific subjects, and has resulted in vocational skills that are too basic. This overt theorisation of vocational programmes has caused problems with high drop-out rates and a lack of efficiency.[12] The report, which makes reference to empirical studies, also argues that pupils have difficulties seeing the benefits of these too abstract and theoretical subjects (SOU 2008:27, pp. 237, 379–380). Therefore, the aim of basic eligibility for higher education does not make pupils employable, but leads to a late entry into the labour market because of long education and dropouts. If you are unable to find gainful employment, the risk of social exclusion increases and limits your ability to participate in society. [13]

This representation of problems leads to a proposed solution: to differentiate between vocational and academic education, whereby pupils who attend vocational programmes are not forced to study for basic eligibility for higher education (SOU 2008:27, p. 394). This solution is similar to the system that was in operation before the mid-1990s reform. The differentiation involves an increase in more practically oriented subjects; that is, the so-called programme specific subjects, more workplace learning within vocational programmes and the possibility to choose the vocationally oriented programmes, such as apprenticeship training (SOU 2008:27, pp. 379–380). The suggested apprenticeship training is viewed as a way to alleviate the problem of high youth unemployment[14] and as an alternative for pupils who have problems finishing upper secondary education. In the report, some references are made to research that sees apprenticeship training as a positive alternative for those pupils who are struggling or are tired of school (SOU 2008:27, pp. 250, 475). The unmotivated pupils are mainly boys. The report quotes an educational researcher, Margreth Hill, who states that a relatively large proportion of teenage boys feel that school is not made for them.

> Much of what the school offers them, they cannot see that they need … They don't see any advantages with the education unless they are to become engineers, which they don't have in mind. So 'loser' does not stand for 'we who have failed in school' but instead for 'we who do not have a school that suits us'. To get out and earn money is what lures. Moving away from home and living independently as well (SOU 2008:27, p. 250).

The image represented is that the problem for young men is that today's education system is unsuitable for them because it is too theoretical and academic, and this causes them to drop out of school. In contrast, the problem for young women is that they are not perceived as having any well-functioning vocational education at all, which makes them choose the more study-oriented Social Science Programme instead (SOU 2008:27, p. 315). Therefore, in relation to women's employability, the vocational programmes are too academic in a different way, because they do not provide workplace contacts, such as networks. By not receiving a good practical vocational training that prepares them for employment straight after school, the women are forced to turn to higher education in much greater numbers than men (SOU 2008:27, pp. 611–612).

> The option to choose attractive vocational programmes that lead to good working relations and employability are present for men but much less so for women. This is probably also one reason why there is an increasing proportion of women who continue to higher education (SOU 2008:27, pp. 315–316).

There is an inconsistency here. The underlying argument is that young men seem to have stable vocationally oriented programmes with traditional work paths to follow, and these paths make them employable after they have graduated. The previous statements concerning the over-academic nature of vocationally oriented programmes making young men unemployable seem to contradict this. Furthermore, there is a strong tradition of apprenticeships associated with the male dominated programmes, but these traditions do not exist to the same degree in female dominated programmes, such as the Child and Recreation Programme and the Health Care Programme. It is argued that young women's employability benefits from mandatory workplace training. Neither has there been a tradition of providing opportunities for constructing apprenticeship training in these programmes. In the report it is argued that the suggested closer cooperation between employers and schools is essential for this workplace and apprenticeship training to be successful, especially for girls (SOU 2008:27, pp. 85, 612).

> It is also important that apprenticeship training can gain a foothold and develop in industries and occupations where a weak or no ap-

prenticeship tradition is present. I refer here to occupations such as childcare, health and trade and administration. From a gender perspective, I believe it is important to open up and develop opportunities for apprenticeship training even in traditionally female dominated areas (SOU 2008:27, p. 472).

There is a distinct focus in the report on making women employable through specialised training. This will benefit women because more female dominated occupations will require a specific type of education and trained personnel, which will improve the status of female dominated work (SOU 2008:27, p. 466). The claims that education is too academic, and the proposal that vocational and academic education should be differentiated, lead us to the articulation of upper secondary education as generally 'too vague'.

Too vague

The representation of education as being *too vague* is articulated to justify the idea of clarity in education programmes to make pupils employable. The argument is presented in terms of the lack of clarity concerning whether a programme is vocationally oriented or prepares the pupils for further studies. It is argued that some programmes seem to be aiming for both of the aims simultaneously, but succeeding in neither (SOU 2008:27, pp. 234–235). The report states that 'It should be clear what an education includes, where it leads and that it should deliver what it promises' (SOU 2008:27, p. 186). The contents, goals and possible occupations are vague and unclear, which leaves receivers confused.

> Employers often think that it is unclear what the results of a vocational programme are and they have difficulty, on the basis of programme descriptions and governing documents, to understand what pupils are expected to know and be able to do (SOU 2008:27, pp. 279–280).

Neither the receivers nor the pupils seem to know what a certain study path entails or what it is training pupils for, and the result is that pupils become unemployable. It is also argued that this vagueness contributes to social segregation.

> Today's information for young people on working life; where an
> education leads, and on working conditions, is undeveloped. Many
> young people have no knowledge of the labour market or which
> occupations are possible after university studies. It paves the way
> for the young to make traditional choices and may thus reinforce
> social segregation (SOU 2008:27, p. 177).

The more female dominated programmes such as the Child and Recreation Programme, the Health Care Programme, the Business and Administration Programme and the Handicraft Programme are the main programmes that are described as ambiguous. It is unclear whether they lead to vocational or academic training, and they are considered to function badly because they prepare pupils for both (SOU 2008:27, p. 235). The Healthcare Programme is vague as it does not 'lead to a career that starts directly after upper secondary education' (SOU 2008:27, p. 465). The Child and Recreation Programme is also considered vague because more than one in five pupils choose further studies at college or university as a result of the programme's inability to educate for any particular occupations directly after education (SOU 2008:27, p. 446). Furthermore, the name of the programme is considered particularly problematic.

> Another problem is that the current Child and Recreation Pro-
> gramme has a name that suggests that the programme is exclusively
> directed at work with children, when it is really about working with
> people of all ages. Moreover, there is a current imbalance in the
> programme's gender distribution [about 73 per cent of the pupils
> are women] (SOU 2008:27, p. 446).

Therefore, a suggested move to improve women's employability is that an emphasis should be placed on health and leadership and that the programme focuses on the care of people of all ages. This leads to a proposed change in the name of the programme to the Leadership and Preventive Healthcare Programme. Claims are made that such a change will make it possible to attract more males, because the focus would then be on leadership and sports, rather than children. 'My assessment [the expert commissioner's] is that the new programme, with a clear social orientation and a new emphasis on sports, health and wellbeing, will attract both boys and girls' (SOU 2008:27, p. 447). The feminine nature of the programme, with its focus on traditional female qualities such as childcare, and the female overrepresentation are clearly identified as problems.

What needs to be made clear in order to increase the chances of a person's employability is where a study path leads, and especially to what type of employment it leads. The suggestion is to make a clear distinction between vocational training and academic training that prepares pupils for higher education. Pupils should either be made employable directly after they have completed their education or they should be well prepared for further studies (Dir. 2007:8, pp. 6–7). Another argument is that it is unclear what level, skills and competences each pupil has after USE, because the pupils do not receive a specific diploma (SOU 2008:27, pp. 393, 534). The vagueness of the programmes in this particular representation is understood in relation to contemporary USE being too fragmented.

Too fragmented

Education is also represented as *too fragmented* because there are so many choices available for pupils and schools. These choices include study programmes, programme-specific subjects and individual subjects that make it possible for pupils to make the so-called wrong choices; ones that do not lead to employment (SOU 2008:27, p. 581).

> However, I believe that this flexibility and the scope of pupil choice has gone too far. The system has become difficult to grasp and it is very cost-inefficient. … There is also a risk that pupils are enticed to choose study paths and courses that do not lead to employability or a good preparation for further studies (SOU 2008:27, p. 266).

It is also asserted that there is too much freedom and flexibility of choice for schools to provide particular local courses and local specialisations and profiles. This is viewed as a problem because these courses and specialisations are not considered to be relevant for the study path chosen by the pupil or for labour market needs (SOU 2008:27, p. 179). These choices are especially problematic for young women; their education choices are represented as the wrong choices to a much greater extent. 'One such example is hairdressing. As the supply is tailored after the pupils' requests, it is not certain that the supply is consistent with the labour market's demand for workers' (SOU 2008:27, p. 266, see also p. 430). Another education path that is chosen by young women and articulated as problematic for their employability consists of specialisations like the care of horses or small animals within the Natural Resource Use Programme. These specialisations do not respond to labour market requirements, unlike forestry; a more male dominated branch that supposedly leads to employability (SOU 2008:27, pp. 403–404).

Although there are solutions that have been suggested for making education more diversified, in order to combat the claim that the programmes are too uniform, they mainly refer to the small differences in general subjects and workplace training between vocational programmes and preparatory programmes for higher education. Instead, what is prominent within the articulation of education being too fragmented is the emphasis on much more national control and the wish to reduce local variation. The pupils' influence over educational pathways is also said to have gone too far, and is perceived as being of no benefit to the pupils or the needs of the market.

> The Commission has seen examples where the competitive aspect is more important when an attractive local branch is created in a municipality than whether the local variant really responds to a regional or local need. This can create problems, particularly because such a local focus on a vocational programme has no roots in the local labour market and can lead, at worst, to the pupil not being employable (SOU 2008:27, pp. 272–273).

One suggestion is that restrictions should be put in place so that schools cannot provide local and regional specialisation and local course alternatives. The control of education should be placed in the hands of the state, but mostly in the hands of the receivers because their influence is perceived as the best solution to meet market needs (SOU 2008:27, pp. 304–305, 362). By positioning employers as the solution to the current fragmentation, a paradox is made apparent in the report because these receivers will influence both national and local programmes. Therefore, local variation should not be reduced.

The market-oriented discourse of personal choice that has been developed within education policy (cf. Bunar 2004, 2008; Lund 2008) has given too much control to producers, according to the report. In other words, the educational institutions themselves have too much control. Neo-liberalism's emphasis on personal choice has in some way failed (cf. Olssen et al. 2004). Too much control has been placed in the hands of schools as producers of education, and they follow the demands of pupils' interests and wishes. The analysed report proposes a shift in the market-oriented discourse of choice, but still follows a market-oriented supply and demand chain. This market-oriented discourse of skill supply is said to limit the control of the producer as schools now are meant to follow a different demand: the demand of receivers instead of the pupils. The pupils are pretty much absent subjects in this reform and are no longer the consumers of services in the education sector. They are simply the workers who are produced for consumers such as employers and higher education representatives. The control of the producer who follows the demands of the pupils is criticised in the report for fragmenting education, focusing too much on pupils' choices and not responding to the needs of the labour market. Pupils are mainly viewed as making the wrong choices, and making themselves unemployable. These representations of pupils making the wrong choices are linked to the last problem, namely the inefficiency of the current education system.

Too inefficient

Another articulated problem is that education is *too inefficient*. The effectiveness of today's upper secondary education is not at a sufficiently high level and there are particular problems within vocationally oriented programmes' (SOU 2008:27, p. 177, see also pp. 309–310).

> Almost all pupils continue from compulsory school to upper secondary school, but far from all complete their education. It must be seen as a serious failure that one in four boys and one in five girls do not receive their school-leaving certificate within four years, despite the fact that it is a three-year education. Of the pupils in year 1 October 15, 2004, 13 per cent had changed their chosen path a year later and just over seven per cent in year 1 had dropped out. In particular, the proportion of pupils who did not receive their school-leaving certificate is particularly high in vocational programmes. ... Overall, this contributes to a later entry into the labour market (Dir. 2007:8, p. 2).

This inefficiency is not only perceived as a problem for individuals but also for society: the costs can be high when these individuals become dependent on the social welfare system. In this sense, they do not contribute to growth in society. They are not only constructed as *at* risk but also as *the* risk.

> Dropping out from upper secondary education represents a high risk that the pupil will not complete his/her upper secondary education. Young adults who do not have a completed upper secondary education are over-represented in the group of welfare dependent, long-term unemployed. These people may have a difficult situation on the labour market and can generate high costs in terms of welfare provision and unemployment, etc (SOU 2008:27, p. 310).

Although the terms of reference state that upper secondary education is voluntary (Dir. 2007:8, p. 1), it is described in the report as being, in principle, mandatory in order to minimise the risk of social exclusion, and to encourage a sense of belonging and being an active citizen (SOU 2008:27, pp. 226, 379).

A completed vocational training is crucial for the entry of young people into the labour market; it helps to compensate for differences in social background and to reduce social risks such as economic inactivity and long-term welfare dependency. Another conclusion is that clear, profiled vocational education that responds to industry's requirements is a prerequisite for accelerating the transition from school to work (SOU 2008:27, p. 379).

In order to increase efficiency in USE (the number of pupils who finish their education), a more stringent admission requirement that differentiates between vocational training and academic training is suggested (SOU 2008:27, pp. 548–549). By providing clearer information on the prerequisites for the desired education, the expert believes that the pupils who are admitted will have a better chance of successfully completing their education. Clearer information will prevent those with poor knowledge from failure and stop them from attending more study-preparatory programmes, which they are likely to fail (SOU 2008:27, p. 556).

These representations of inefficiency also have gender dimensions. In practice, USE is described as providing one type of education for young men, and another for young women. This segregation is foremost perceived as an outcome of the gender segregated labour market in Sweden (SOU 2008:27, pp. 314–316, 382, 611–612). However, dropout rates and problems with employability are viewed as much more common when pupils make untraditional choices; that is, when they break gender boundaries.

In Sweden there is strong gender segregation in employment and my [the expert commissioner's] analysis is that this cannot be changed within upper secondary education unless representatives of working life contribute. There is also evidence that men and women who make untraditional choices in upper secondary education and dare to break the gender pattern have a higher dropout rate and meet more resistance after upper secondary education (SOU 2008:27, pp. 314–316, see also p. 382).

By claiming that gender segregation is the responsibility of the labour market, the influence of the receivers over education is once again put forward as the solution to making education more efficient and gender balanced. The gender balance in the programmes receives some attention through basic headcounts. However, the low percentage of women who attend male dominated areas (see discussion about the Child and Recreation Programme above) is not given the same attention as the opposite scenario and not formulated as a problem.

Employability as the empty signifier

The representation of upper secondary education as too academic, too vague, too fragmented and too inefficient, linked together through logics of equivalence, constructs an education policy discourse of skill supply. These represent particular problems, but they are also articulated and linked together to form the universal problem of employability. Employability is the key concept and presented as the main aim of education. Therefore, employability can be understood as the empty signifier that represents the whole chain of problem representations (cf. Laclau 1996, pp. 38–43). The representations of problems and solutions are not mutually exclusive, but are internally split and not entirely separable from each other. They all lead to the same universal argument of employability. This linking process is crucial for the hegemonic process to be successful in partially fixing the meaning of upper secondary education and making that meaning dominant; in this case in terms of employability (Laclau 2005, pp. 131–133; Laclau & Mouffe 2001, pp. 154–155). By articulating the aim of USE in terms of its ability to educate pupils for labour market needs, that is, of making pupils employable, the receivers are represented as solutions to the problem. This emphasis on the receivers' influence on education involves a shift of power in who determines the goals and needs that education is supposed to fill in society at large, and for the individual citizen. Receivers are now positioned as the primary actors in defining skills, contents and goals, instead of politicians, school leaders, teachers and the pupils themselves. The report assigns power to the receivers not only through their direct and active participation in the councils, but also by making employability the hegemonic purpose of education, which teachers, school leaders, pupils and politicians must try to fulfil. This hegemonisation also involves the gendered constructions of future workers.

Gendered constructions of future workers

The emphasis on employability, study path differentiation, finishing on time and study path destinations segregates the two categories women and men. This hegemonisation constructs the gendered subject positions of future workers. Wider divisions are constructed between those pupils who are being made employable and those who are designated for higher education. This process is in stark contrast to the mid-1990s reform that emphasised integration. According to Lundahl (2008, p. 29), the 'proposed reform constitutes a major break with the previously dominant integration trend, as its aim is a clear division of students into three separate streams [vocational, academic and apprenticeship]'. Lundahl (2008, p. 29) considers the reform to be 'aimed at restoration rather than formulating solutions for an unknown future' because it reflects the consistent policy of the political right. The proposed 'path to the future' is a step backwards to an education system similar to the one before the 1970s' integration. This restoration of education policy is also formulated in the policy document of teacher education with regard to pupils with difficulties in school and in need of special support (cf. Isaksson, this volume).

The constructions of subject positions define who is viewed as an asset and resource for the national and regional labour markets. This involves the construction of certain types of ideal and undesirable behaviour. According to the current reform, a person who is 16 years of age is expected to know what they want to do after upper secondary education and what he or she want out of life in general. A young person is not only supposed to choose a study path according to these lifetime goals, but also according to his or her capacities and talents. As long as a young person selects a clear study path that leads to a specific occupation, he or she is thought to do 'the right thing'. The pupil is expected to stick to his or her choices and finish on time. Anything else is a failure. Furthermore, the pupil seems to be expected to make traditionally gendered choices of education because these choices seem to improve the pupil's chances of finishing within the set time frame and the chances of becoming employable in a highly gender segregated labour market. This behaviour will produce employable citizens who are assets to regional and national labour markets. According to the report, the pupils who follow this path will contribute to society in terms of being active and employable workers who do not delay their entry into the labour market.

Simultaneously, and in stark contrast to the above-mentioned pupils who do 'the right thing', there are those subjects who are positioned as a burden to society. They are the ones who do not know their lifetime goals, capacities and interests. They change study paths, drop out and do not choose their education according to the labour market needs. This delays their entry into the labour market or can even make them unemployable. They do not contribute to society and are at risk of social exclusion. These subject positions that I have called 'ideal future workers' are also gendered, because it is mainly girls within vocational programmes who make the so-called 'wrong' choices and therefore become unemployable. They fail to choose the right study paths which force them to continue into higher education (SOU 2008:27, p. 241). Women's employability is problematised to a greater extent than men's because the latter tend to make the 'right' choices. With regard to the employability of men, the problem is not said to lie so much in men making the 'wrong' choices, but rather that education fails *them*. In contrast, young women always seem to make the wrong choices. Young women in vocationally oriented programmes are portrayed as a burden to society because they continue into higher education. They are not supposed to be there. The prolongation of young women's education means that they are unproductive over a longer period of time and therefore embody a cost to society. This seems to be reproducing a heteronormative male worker. Schools are also considered to have become too feminised because women achieve better results than men in terms of test scores, grades and higher education (cf. Bacchi 1999; Epstein 1998; Francis 2006; Francis & Skelton 2005). In this context, the gender dichotomy that had previously been constructed around an understanding that theory and academic training were constructed as 'masculine', and practice and workplace training as 'feminine', seems to have been rearticulated. In the report, theory and academic knowledge are degraded and practice and workplace training or apprenticeship training are viewed as the answer for those boys who do not benefit from this rearticulated 'feminised' theoretical education.

It is of interest that gender is problematised in the report; attention is drawn to upper secondary education's failure to provide good workplace training in the more female dominated work sectors. However, the proposed new and improved vocational programmes for these female dominated sectors are also subject to different requirements than the more male dominated ones. As most of the female dominated sectors concern service professions, it is suggested that programmes such as the Trade and Administrative Service Programme, the Hotel and Tourism Programme, the Leadership and Preventive Healthcare Programme and the Health and Social Care Programme, should include more language courses (SOU 2008:27, p. 342). By reducing the range of general compulsory subjects in many of the male dominated programmes, while simultaneously including more subjects that are necessary to enter higher education in the female dominated ones, the effect will probably be a reproduction or even a strengthening of the gender division between the programmes. Thus in practice this will almost certainly mean that those who study the more female dominated programmes will find it easier to attain basic eligibility for higher education. In other words, these programmes will be more general and theoretical than many of the male dominated programmes. By differentiating men from women and placing them into separate sectors, language, communication skills and services will most likely be reproduced as feminine, thus maintaining differences in their traditional places and in line with the heterosexual matrix and the gendered heteronormative labour market in Sweden (Butler, 1999).

Although articulations of employability and the education of workers for labour market needs dominate the report, there are also traces of the need for education to foster citizens for active participation in society (cf. SOU 2008:27, p. 340; Hjort Liedman & Liedman 2008, p. 17). The mission to educate for active participation in society is placed mainly in compulsory education in the report, but the common core subjects and workplace learning in USE are also accorded a role in this respect (SOU 2008:27, pp. 339–340, 539–540). As there is a suggestion that common subjects should be reduced, more emphasis is placed on workplace learning, which provides certain skills that are essential for active citizenship, as well as for employment.

> Workplace learning also provides good opportunities for pupils to practise and to acquire the more general skills that, together with professional skills in a narrower, technical sense, are becoming increasingly important. Social and communication skills, problem solving ability, service mindedness and entrepreneurship are generalised competences that are important (SOU 2008:27, p. 385).

However, the articulation of active participation is marginalised by the simultaneous emphasis on educating people for labour market needs. Educating for active participation takes on a somewhat different or new meaning, as it is claimed that educating for employability and work are necessary in order to prepare people for active participation in society.

> Preparation for a profession or higher education also means being prepared for life in society. Professions and higher education are aspects of social life. ... The skills that are essential to be employable in the profession that you have been trained for, or to complete higher education, are also important for active participation in society (SOU 2008:27, p. 540).

The role of educating people for active participation in society is included and linked together in the logics of equivalence, and constructs education as essentially a matter of national and regional skill supply. In this way, educating for 'active participation' could be viewed as a floating signifier, a signifier that is present within different and competing logics of equivalence (Laclau 2005, pp. 131–133). Therefore, the floating signifier of active participation has different meanings attached to it depending on which logics of equivalence it is united with. Here the meaning of an active citizen or active participation in society is foremost about being active in terms of paid employment. This fixation of meaning is what Lister (2003, p. 19; 2007, pp. 52–53) claims to be a shift towards a citizenship of obligation rather than rights. According to Lister, this can be seen as part of a neo-liberal rhetoric, which is gaining more ground in countries like the US, the UK, Australia and Europe, where the emphasis on active citizenship is constructed in terms of being active in paid work. Less focus is put on rights and personal choice and more on obligations. The prime obligation for citizens is to engage in paid work, and avoiding state dependency. This is a contributory factor in class constructions, because the individual is held responsible for making him- or herself employable (cf. Garsten & Jacobsson 2004).

Different kinds of skills that are necessary for being an active citizen, such as problem solving, critical thinking, entrepreneurship and communication skills, as well as the eight EU key competences for lifelong learning, are only fleetingly mentioned in the report.[15] This discussion is largely missing from the texts, and the aspects of flexibility and lifelong learning which are prominent in the notion of a knowledge economy (cf. Nicoll 2006) and present in the mid-1990s reform are now almost absent. Surprisingly, the concept of a knowledge economy is not mentioned at all. It seems as though the future worker is constructed geographically and occupation-wise immobile, inflexible (cf. Isopahkala-Bouret et al. 2008). This construction of workers is contradictory to the conception that is prominent in the notion of the knowledge economy, as well as to the Bologna Process regarding higher education, which both promote universal standards to improve labour flows over national borders (cf. Fairclough & Wodak 2008; Olssen et al. 2004). In contrast to what Olson (2008) describes as a shift from education fostering a 'nation builder' to a 'market nomad' in the 1990s, this new reform seems to suggest a return to the concept of nation builder. However, this nation builder is fostered for the needs of the labour market and follows what Båth (2006) refers to as a 'Qualification Discourse', which was the main theme of education just before and after 2000 and placed emphasis on specific skills and abilities instead of citizenship.

As the reform proposes an education where receivers have greater control over the goals, objectives and the content of USE, these receivers will also have much more control when determining and defining the skills which future workers are supposed to possess in order to become employable. Therefore, pupils are constructed to fit into certain subject positions which are determined neither by themselves nor by the educational system, but mainly by the presumptive employers. It is no longer professional teachers and school leaders who will have control over USE. Nor are the pupils any longer viewed as the active actors in terms of choosing education from a variety of schools, programmes and branches. In this new reform the actors and the problem solvers are the employers, who effectively fill the role of shaping and defining skills and objectives for upper secondary education.

Concluding discussion

To recapitulate my argument, the main goal and purpose of USE is represented in the new reform and formulated as education's ability to provide the supply of national and regional skills in order to make pupils employable. By increasing the receivers' control over education, schools are represented as merely producers of workers, and this constructs a market oriented discourse of education for the supply of skills. This discourse is combined with certain representations of problems and justifications of particular solutions that seem to be required in order to make pupils employable. The empty signifier of employability is what unites the different representations of education as being too academic, too vague, too fragmented and too inefficient. This signifier also unites the suggested solutions of increased clarity, more national control, differentiation of educational programmes and more receiver influence. The receivers are in turn represented as the problem solvers and the ones with the knowledge and control of what skills future workers are supposed to have. The role of the local school and its professionals is simultaneously played down.

Certain personal traits concerning discipline and control over desired behaviour and constructions of belonging accompany this new education policy. Those pupils who know their long-term life goals and are able to choose a study path that leads to employment without dropping out or changing their minds, and thereby finishing within the stipulated time, are represented as an asset and a resource to society. They are desirable, contributing and productive workers. Those who are uncertain and change their study path, or drop out and thereby either prolong their time in education or perhaps become unemployable, are represented as either burdens or risks to society. They are not seen as contributing to society, but as being more likely to depend on the state. This type of behaviour is represented as something that will exclude one from society as well as creating a feeling of not belonging.

The empty signifier of employability and the representations of problems that are linked together in logics of equivalence also construct gendered future workers. The academic nature of today's USE is represented as making young men unemployable. The theoretical feminised nature of vocational programmes means that young men drop out of education, and are, therefore, not contributing to society. Instead, they are excluded from society and dependent on social welfare. However, this group of men is not as much of a burden or risk to society as the young women who are described as those who finish their education in larger numbers, but constantly make the wrong choices of education. As they are 'forced' to continue into higher education, they are not employable. In practice, when young women continue their education, they depend on the state instead of being productive directly after USE. The differentiation of who is regarded as employable also has consequences for the production and reproduction of social class. Gender and class are linked through the emphasis on choosing the right path and not prolonging your time in education. Gender does not appear to be a problem or even discussed in the study-oriented programmes that have a higher proportion of pupils from middle class backgrounds. However, the young working class women who frequently choose vocational programmes such as the Child and Recreation Programme are constructed as a problem when they go against the idea of direct productivity by continuing into higher education. One can even get the impression that the report suggests they are not supposed to be there. The middle-class women who do the same, however, are not positioned as a problem, either from a gender or a class perspective. We need to recognise, as I try to do in my own analysis, that these constructions of so-called good productive workers do affect people's lives. They represent embodied categories, and these concrete bodies are 'differentially situated in terms of gender, class, ethnicity, sexuality, ability, state in the life cycle, etc' (Yuval-Davis 2008, p. 160).

As the quote in the beginning of the chapter from Mouffe (1992, p. 225) emphasised, the construction of citizenship and its links to the organisation of the political community positions the analysed education reform in a wider context. The arguments that are said to create a 'path to the future' can be viewed as part of a struggle to fix the meaning of citizenship in terms of obligation instead of rights. The active citizen is the employed one. This policy development of social responsibility in relation to the rhetoric on 'dependency culture' is prominent in many Western nations (Lister et al. 2007, pp. 54–55). Sweden does not seem to constitute an exception to this. The current political administration has placed much emphasis on work and employability as the solution to social exclusion. In order to emphasise this new work obligation, policies such as higher costs for unemployment insurance, tax cuts for those currently in paid work, lower unemployment benefits, and harder restrictions and time limits for payments of social insurance have been implemented. The termination of the former social democratic government's upper secondary education reform can, in this perspective, be viewed as part of a wider struggle over the meaning of citizenship and democracy that is also present within other policy domains. The current government's education policy constructs citizens as active workers who make a smooth transition from school to work, and who do not depend on social welfare and unemployment benefits. This hegemonisation process of the active citizen is also gendered and, as my analysis has shown, the ideal is very much a male productive worker.

Notes

1 By 'worker' I refer to the Swedish term *arbetare*, which in this context has the main meaning of being active in paid work.

2 This chapter is part of an ongoing Ph.D. project financed by Umeå University that deconstructs upper secondary education policy from the 1970s until today. The aim is to analyse the intersectional construction of future workers (*arbetare*) as constituted as part of citizenship discourses. While this chapter focuses on the aspect of gender, my forthcoming thesis will have a more intersectional approach because I recognise that gender is not the only relevant social category. I would like to thank Chris Hudson and Linda Rönnberg at the Department of Political Science, Umeå University, for their valuable comments on this chapter.

3 The Swedish original is entitled *Framtidsvägen – en reformerad gymnasieskola*.

4 By deconstruction I refer to making visible the constructions of subject positions and their constant ordering of exclusions and inclusions that are necessary for an 'imaginary fixed identity' (Derrida 1998).

5 By hegemonic process I refer to constructions of discourses through logics of equivalence and difference, constructing dominating discourses and organising consent (Laclau & Mouffe 2001).

6 I argue that the concept of subject position is more relevant for my study as it refers to different positions constructing social agents within discourses, rather than what Laclau refers to as political subjectivity, which instead refers to the way social agents act in identifications in times of dislocation (Howarth 2007, p. 125; Laclau 1990, pp. 39–41).

7 Anita Ferm was the expert who was commissioned to carry out the report. She has a Master of Science degree in Engineering and has worked as an upper secondary teacher for 15 years. Between 1991 and 2003 she was in charge of USE and adult secondary education (*Komvux*) in the city of Stockholm. During eight of those years she was Director of Education. Ferm has also worked as a departmental secretary at the Ministry of Education and Research and at the Swedish National Agency for Education, in charge of issues concerning USE.

8 In the Swedish political system the government often chooses to appoint a committee of inquiry to thoroughly examine important topics before a draft proposal is formulated by the government. The committees are supposed to look into the issues and the problems to be solved, which are stated in the terms of reference. The results from the committee are then published in the Swedish Government Official Report Series (SOU). Stakeholders, such as central government agencies, special interest groups and local government authorities that are affected by the issue at stake then have the opportunity to respond to the suggestions made by the commission in what is called a referral process. This provides feedback in terms of levels of support for the recommendations made, before the bill is drawn up and presented to parliament. For the official report *Path to the Future*, the referral process showed a high level of support for the recommendations made.

9 The bill presented to parliament corresponds to the overall suggestions in the official report; however, some differences brought forward in this chapter are noticeable. The proposed change in name of the Child and Recreation Programme to the Leadership Programme will, for example, not be implemented, due to the argument that the concept of leadership is linked to a more professional status than is applicable to upper secondary education. Another example is the concept of entrepreneurship, which is central to the presented bill but almost absent in the official report.

10 The terms of reference and the report *Path to the Future* are written in Swedish, but there is an English summary in the report. The quotes are therefore translated by me, except when mentioned that they are original excerpts.

11 In the report the Swedish term used is *avnämare*, referring to employers, both within the private sector and public sector, and higher education. The term *avnämare* is very central in the report and the English summary translates this into the English term 'receivers'. I have therefore chosen to use the same term. This concept was not as prominent in the mid-1990s reform. It has, however, been a more common term during the 1990s and refers to clients and consumers of public services.

12 Of those pupils who started upper secondary education in 2004, one in four boys and one in five girls did not receive their school-leaving certificate within four years after starting, and approximately seven per cent of the pupils had dropped out in the first year.

13 The term used in Swedish is *utanförskap*. In a wider Swedish context, especially in regard to immigration, work and multiculturalism, the concept could be viewed as being re-articulated, and the essential meaning of social exclusion (*utanförskap*) is constructed in terms of unemployment. Social exclusion tends to refer to both work and active participation in society as a whole; of being integrated in society. However, by being unemployed one is not an actively participating citizen in Swedish society.

14 In comparison to other countries, youth unemployment in Sweden has been relatively high since the mid-1990s' economic crisis and has ranged between 12 an 20 per cent.

15 The eight EU key competences for lifelong learning are: communication in the mother tongue, communication in foreign languages, mathematical competence and basic competences in science and technology, digital competence, learning to learn, social and civic competences, a sense of initiative and entrepreneurship, and cultural awareness and expression. Competences are here defined as knowledge, skills and attitudes. For a discussion of the eight EU key competences and their impact on upper secondary education in Sweden, see (Liedman 2008).

References

Literature

Assarson, I., 2007. *Talet om en skola för alla: pedagogers meningskonstruktion i ett politiskt uppdrag.* (Diss.) Malmö: Malmö högskola.

Bacchi, C. L., 1999. *Women, Policy and Politics: The Construction of Policy Problems.* London: Sage.

Bacchi, C. L. & Beasley, C., 2002. Citizen Bodies: Is Embodied Citizenship a Contradiction in Terms? *Critical Social Policy*, 22(2), pp. 324–352.

Båth, S., 2006. *Kvalifikation och medborgarfostran: En analys av reformtexter avseende gymnasieskolans samhällsuppdrag.* (Diss.) Gothenburg: Göteborgs universitet.

Bergström, Y. & Wahlström, N., 2008. TEMA: En reformerad gymnasieskola – med vilka ambitioner? *Utbildning och Demokrati. Tidskrift för didaktik och utbildningspolitik*, 17(1), pp. 5–16.

Bunar, N., 2004. *Komplement eller konkurrent: fristående skolor i ett integrationsperspektiv.* Norrköping: Integrationsverket.

Bunar, N., 2008. The Free Schools 'Riddle': Between Traditional Social Democratic, Neo-liberal and Multicultural tenets. *Scandinavian Journal of Educational Research*, 52(4), pp. 423–438.

Butler, J., 1999. *Gender Trouble: Feminism and the Subversion of Identity.* New York: Routledge.

Crenshaw, K., 1995. Mapping the Margins: Intersectionality, Identity Politics and Violence Against Women of Color. In: K. Crenshaw (ed.), *Critical Race Theory. The Key Writings that Formed the Movement.* New York: New Press, pp. 357–384.

Derrida, J., 1998. *Of Grammatology.* Baltimore: Johns Hopkins University Press.

Epstein, D. (ed.), 1998. *Failing Boys? Issues in Gender and Achievement.* Buckingham: Open University Press.

Fairclough, N. & Wodak, R., 2008. The Bologna Process and the Knowledge-based Economy: A Critical Discourse Analysis Approach. In: R. Jessop et al. (eds), *Higher Education and the Knowledge Based Economy in Europe.* Rotterdam: Sense Publishers, pp. 109–125.

Foucault, M., 2002. *Sexualitetens historia. Bd 2, Njutningarnas bruk.* (*The History of Sexuality*, vol. 2) Göteborg: Daidalos.

Foucault, M., Rabinow, P. & Hurley, R., 1997. *Essential Works of Foucault, 1954–1984. Vol. 1, Ethics: Subjectivity and Truth.* New York: New Press.

Francis, B., 2006. Heroes or Zeroes? The Discursive Positioning of 'Underachieving Boys' in English Neo-liberal Education Policy. *Journal of Education Policy*, 21(2), pp. 187–200.

Francis, B. & Skelton, C., 2005. *Reassessing Gender and Achievement: Questioning Contemporary Key Debates.* London: Routledge.

Garsten, C. & Jacobsson, K. (eds), 2004. *Learning to be Employable. New Agendas on Work, Responsibility, and Learning in a Globalizing World.* Basingstoke: Palgrave.

Glynos, J. & Howarth, D., 2007. *Logics of Critical Explanation in Social and Political Theory.* London: Routledge.

Hjort Liedman, M. & Liedman, S-E., 2008. The Lifelong Apprentice. *Utbildning och Demokrati. Tidskrift för didaktik och utbildningspolitik*, 17(1), pp. 17–28.

Howarth, D., 2007. *Diskurs*. Malmö: Liber.

Isopahkala-Bouret, U., Lappalainen, S. & Lahelma, E., 2008. *Educating 'Proper Workers: Vision and Division in Curriculum Texts*. 36th Nordic Conference on Educational Research. Copenhagen, Denmark, 6–8 March 2008.

Laclau, E., 1990. *New Reflections on the Revolution of Our Time*. London: Verso.

Laclau, E., 1996. *Emancipation(s)*. New York: Verso.

Laclau, E., 2005. *On Populist Reason*. London & New York: Verso.

Laclau, E. & Mouffe, C., 1987. Post-Marxism Without Apologies. *New Left Review*, 166 (November–December), pp. 79–106.

Laclau, E. & Mouffe, C., 2001. *Hegemony and Socialist Strategy: Towards a Radical Democratic Politics*. 2nd edn. London: Verso.

Liedman, S.-E., 2008. *Nycklar till ett framgångsrikt liv? Om EU:s nyckelkompetenser*. Stockholm: Skolverket.

Linde, G., 2006. *Det ska ni veta! En introduktion till läroplansteori*. Lund: Studentlitteratur.

Lister, R., 2003. *Citizenship: Feminist Perspectives*. Basingstoke: Palgrave Macmillan.

Lister, R., et al., 2007. *Gendering Citizenship in Western Europe: New Challenges for Citizenship Research in a Cross-National Context*. Bristol: Policy.

Lund, S., 2008. Choice Paths in the Swedish Upper Secondary Education: A Critical Discourse Analysis of Recent Reforms. *Journal of Education Policy*, 23 (6), pp. 633–648.

Lundahl, L., 2008. Separate Paths to the Future: Perspectives on the Swedish Upper Secondary Reform of the Early 2000s. *Utbildning och Demokrati. Tidskrift för didaktik och utbildningspolitik*, 17 (1), pp. 29–51.

Lundahl, L., Erixon Arreman, I., Lundström, U. & Rönnberg, L., 2008. *From Expansion and Integration to Marketisation and Restoration: Policies of Swedish Upper Secondary Education 1968–2008*. In: European Conference on Educational Research. Gothenburg, Sweden, 10–12 August 2008.

Mouffe, C., 1992. Democratic Citizenship and the Political Community. In: C. Mouffe (ed.), *Dimensions of Radical Democracy: Pluralism, Citizenship, Community*. London: Verso, pp. 225–239.

Mouffe, C., 2005. *The Return of the Political*. London & New York: Verso.

Nicoll, K., 2006. *Flexibility and Lifelong Learning: Policy, Discourse, Politics*. London: Routledge.

Olson, M., 2008. *Från nationsbyggare till marknadsnomad: om medborgarskap i svensk utbildningspolitik under 1990-talet*. (Diss.) Linköping: Linköpings universitet.

Olssen, M., Codd, J. & O'Neill, A.-M., 2004. *Education Policy: Globalization, Citizenship and Democracy*. London: Sage.

Richardson, G., 2004. *Svensk utbildningshistoria: skola och samhälle förr och nu*. Lund: Studentlitteratur.

Siim, B. & Squires, J., 2008. Contesting Citizenship: Comparative Analyses. In: B, Siim, and J. Squires (eds), *Contesting Citizenship*. London: Routledge, pp. 403–416.

Smith, A. M., 1998. *Laclau and Mouffe: The Radical Democratic Imaginary*. London: Routledge.

Torfing, J., 2005. Discourse Theory: Achievements, Arguments and Challenges. In: Howarth, D. & Torfing, J. (eds), *Discourse Theory in European Politics: Identity, Policy and Governance*. New York: Palgrave Macmillan, pp. 1–32.

Winther Jørgensen, M. & Phillips, L., 2000. *Diskursanalys som teori och metod*. Lund: Studentlitteratur.

Yuval-Davis, N., 2008. Intersectionality, Citizenship and Contemporary Politics of Belonging. In: B. Siim & J. Squires (eds), *Contesting Citizenship*. London: Routledge, pp. 159–172.

Official documents

Prop. 1990/91:85. *Växa med kunskaper: om gymnasieskolan och vuxenutbildningen*. Stockholm: Utbildningsdepartementet.

Prop. 2006/07:1. *Budgetpropositionen för 2007*. Stockholm: Finansdepartementet.

Dir. 2007:8. *En reformerad gymnasieskola*. Stockholm: Utbildningsdepartementet.

SOU 2008:27. Gymnasieutredningen, 2008. *Framtidsvägen – en reformerad gymnasieskola: betänkande*. Stockholm: Fritze.

Prop. 2008/09:199. *Högre krav och kvalitet i den nya gymnasieskolan*. Stockholm: Utbildningsdepartementet.

Prop. 2009/10:1. *Budgetpropositionen för 2010*. Stockholm: Finansdepartementet.

Online sources

Skolverket, 2009. *Gymnasieskolan*. Available: http://www.skolverket.se/sb/d/2398. [Accessed 28 January 2009].

CHAPTER 4

Re-Evaluating the Meaning of School Difficulties

Joakim Isaksson

Do certain pupils *have* special support needs regardless of the environment or *are* some pupils *in need of* special support in their regular school environment? This question is one of the central questions in the Swedish educational discourse about pupils' school difficulties and seems to divide the main stakeholders into two divergent groups. These contrasting perspectives on pupils' difficulties in school have also to some extent characterised the public and scientific debate regarding these issues in Swedish education policy since the late 1970s. From a discourse analytical perspective I would also argue that these viewpoints carry with them consequences for how pupils' difficulties are interpreted in school, including how the support measures take on a segregated or inclusive character. If pupils are considered to *have* special support needs, it signifies that the pupils should be 'corrected' or 'normalised' in relation to fixed knowledge goals and the norms and values of the school. On the other hand, if pupils are seen as *being in need* of special support, it would imply that difficulties at school are interpreted as a result of the interplay between the individual and the environment. As a consequence, the focus is directed towards the removal of barriers in the teaching environment and to the adjustment of teaching to the pupils' varying needs. In practice, if school difficulties are seen as the result of individual shortcomings, they often tend to be a matter for experts, transferred to somewhere outside of the regular classroom. However, if school difficulties are seen as the result of an interplay between the individual and the environment, the support measures are placed in a larger context and it becomes the responsibility of all the school staff to create conditions for inclusive education (cf. Emanuelsson, Persson & Rosenqist 2001; Persson 2001).

Two commonly used concepts found in educational policy documents during the 1960s were 'pupils with special needs' and 'pupils with difficulties'.[1] These concepts indicated that pupils' school difficulties could be related to individual shortcomings and/or individual pathology. The general idea was that school difficulties were due to individual deficits– specific traits that a child was said to 'have'. Despite a shift in this terminology during the 1970s – from the word 'special' to the word 'particular'[2] – frequently used formulations in educational policy documents still indicated that pupils' needs were mainly the results of individual deficits. However, a larger shift in perspective occurred during the 1980s. The shift made it explicit that it was the support rather than the pupil that should be focused on, and that the pupil could *be in* some sort of difficulty. Furthermore, such difficulties could be related either to individual deficits or to barriers that were extrinsic to the pupil; for example, in the very teaching environment in which the child was immersed. Consequently, the concept of 'pupils with special support needs'[3] became more common during the 1980s. The focus on potential barriers in the teaching environment and their effect on pupils' school difficulties were to be given greater priority during the 1990s, when the former concept of 'pupils *with* special support needs' was largely replaced with the concept 'pupils *in need* of special support'.[4] After having appeared for the first time in the national curriculum in 1994, the concept 'pupils in need of special support' has been used since 2001 in all official Swedish policy documents, such as the National Education Act (SFS 1985:1100) and The Compulsory School Ordinance (SFS 1994:1194).[5]

The changes in the use of terminology is illustrative of historical discourses concerning pupils' school difficulties, and shows how a hegemonic intervention[6] has taken hold in Swedish education policy during the past three decades, aimed towards an environmental and relational understanding of the causes of such difficulties. However, despite this hegemonic intervention questions concerning these pupils' recommended support measures have been regularly raised, and the answers to these questions have been rearticulated in various educational debates. Such debates are indicative of political struggles over meaning in education policy. My intention in this chapter is to investigate the ways in which these issues are articulated within a recent proposal for a new teacher education programme in Sweden (SOU 2008:109).[7] The reason that this particular report was chosen is that it stands in sharp contrast to earlier education policies related to pupils in need of special support and special education practices. Therefore, I will argue in this chapter that the proposal might contribute to a 'dislocation'[8] of the former dominant meaning of pupils' school difficulties in education policies that may give rise to 'the need for new identifications, the use of new words, and new ways of depicting practices' (Norval 2007, p. 127).

Aim and outline

The overall aim of this chapter is to analyse and discuss how the meaning of pupils in need of special support is articulated in the 2008 proposal *Sustainable teacher education* (SOU 2008:109). A central question is *how* pupils in need of special support are described in the report; that is, how is the problem of pupils' school difficulties constructed and what are the recommended measures that are provided in the report to 'solve' the problem? Furthermore, which types of problems are seen as essential elements of a child's personality and which types of problems are regarded as 'special needs'? Another intention is to focus on how the proposal justifies specific measures for pupils in need of special support, especially if the recommendations and guidelines contradict or call existing school practices into question.

I will now present the theoretical approach and the analytical strategies that I will use to discern the construction of pupils' school difficulties and the recommended support measures that the report suggests. In order to contextualise the report, a presentation of earlier education policies and education reforms in Sweden will be provided so that specific traits of various periods of education policy during the last decades can be pointed out. This presentation will be followed by a closer presentation of the 2008 proposal

Sustainable teacher education, and include the background, aims and purpose of the proposal. The presentation will then be followed by an analysis of the report's contents. Finally, the analysis section will be followed by a concluding discussion about a potential hegemonic intervention (Laclau 1996) and what I have chosen to call an *aspect change* (Norval 2007) regarding school difficulties and special education that the proposal exemplifies. This will be followed by some concluding remarks on the potential consequences of these discursive changes in the Swedish education policy.

A discourse analytical approach to education policy

A theoretical framework that mainly draws upon a poststructuralist discourse theoretical perspective will be used in the analysis of the empirical material (cf. Laclau & Mouffe 2001; Howarth 2007). Such a perspective implies that all objects and practices are discursive; that they are provided with meaning by discursive structures. An object and/or practice is/are not able to constitute themselves as objects or practices 'outside any discursive condition of emergence' (Laclau & Mouffe 2001, p. 108). Consequently, this perspective rejects the distinction between discursive and non-discursive practices that is central to other perspectives within the field of discourse analysis, such as critical discourse analysis (CDA) (cf. Fairclough 1992).

The concept of discourse is described as a fixed *meaning* within a particular domain by Laclau and Mouffe (2001, p. 105). More specifically, a discourse includes several fixed signifiers called moments. These moments are given meaning by means of articulatory processes that fix their differential positions to each other. Consequently, meaning is always relational; it is always created through specific relations between the moments within a discourse, and such relations are constructed by means of articulatory practices. Accordingly, the meaning of 'school difficulties' is discursively constituted, and not given as a 'natural fact'. What we take for granted as bare facts are the results of complex historical and social constructions (Laclau & Mouffe 1990, p. 102).

Articulation and *articulatory practices* are central theoretical concepts within discourse theory (DT) and refer to constructions of meaning. Laclau & Mouffe (2001, p. 105) define articulation as 'any practice establishing a relation among elements such that their identity is modified as a result of the articulatory practice'. The concept of element is used by Laclau and Mouffe (2001, p. 110) to describe signs that are more open and have not been given a definite meaning; that is, they have not been discursively articulated as moments.[9] Such articulatory practices of fixing or stabilising the meaning of school difficulties, which are carried out by linking them to various elements that may not previously have come into play in policy documents, might be viewed as a hegemonic intervention concerning the way that such difficulties should be understood and what kinds of solutions (special support measures) should be provided. Articulation is a key theoretical concept in the DT perspective and explains changes in relations between different elements (Winther Jørgensen & Phillips 1999, p. 133).

The concept of articulation is also frequently used in CDA, and is often related to the concepts *interdiscursivity* and *intertextuality* (cf. Fairclough 1992, pp. 84–85). Interdiscursivity refers to articulations within and between orders of discourses, while intertextuality refers to how a text draws upon other texts; that is, how a text includes elements from other texts (Winther Jørgensen & Phillips 1999, p. 77). In education policy, such intertextual relationships might be identified by focusing on what a new policy document incorporates from earlier policies (and also which parts of earlier policy texts that are not referred to). The function of intertextuality is described by Fairclough as follows '[it] sees texts historically as transforming the past – existing conventions and prior texts – into the present' (1992, p. 85). A similarity between Laclau & Mouffe's concept of articulation and Fairclough's concept of intertextuality is that they both emphasise that discursive practice builds on earlier patterns, but at the same time questions them (Winther Jørgensen & Phillips 1999, p. 133).[10]

The main reason why I intend to use both articulation and intertextuality in the analysis is that the latter provides more concrete guidelines for what to focus on in the documents compared to articulation. Intertextuality means looking at how a text 'responds to, reaccentuates, and reworks past texts, and in so doing helps

to make history and contributes to wider processes of change'
(Fairclough 1992, p. 102). These two concepts will be used as a
theoretical 'box of tools' to analyse how the meaning of pupils in
need of special support are constituted through articulatory practices in the report.

This strategy for analysing the chosen policy document is inspired
by what Glynos and Howarth (2007) describe as a problem-driven
approach (cf. Carlbaum's chapter in this book). Education policies,
as well as policies in general, are characterised by a struggle over
meaning, and I would argue that this approach provides a fruitful
strategy to problematise how objects and practices are formulated
and constructed in policy making. In comparison with method-
driven or theory-driven approaches to research, the object of study
in a problem-driven approach is regarded as constructed, rather than
as an outcome of chosen techniques of data-gathering or theory
(Glynos & Howarth 2007, p. 167). Furthermore, the problem-
driven approach is closely linked to the concepts of articulation and
articulatory practices that have been described above (cf. Howarth
2005, pp. 326–329).

Contextualising the 2008 proposal
A sustainable teacher education

As I mentioned in the introductory section, the official terminology
for pupils who are considered to have school difficulties has changed
in education policy since the 1960s and onwards. These shifts illustrate various intentions to stabilise the meaning of pupils' school
difficulties at a national policy level. However, the development
towards a hegemonic understanding of pupils' school difficulties
has not been a straightforward process because Sweden has undergone an educational policy shift during the last 20 years; a period
that has also been characterised by educational policy conflicts (cf.
Englund & Quennerstedt 2008). In this section I will present a
brief review of various periods of education policy and describe the
specific traits of each period of importance for pupils in need of
special support and the work procedures of schools. Lundahl (2005)
identifies three distinct time periods in Swedish education policy

during the last couple of decades, and I will use these periods as a way of structuring the presentation.

The first time period (late 1970s–1990) was characterised by increased local autonomy, which meant that much educational decision making was transferred from the national to the municipal level. During this period, the 'inner work' of schools was criticised and focused on in education policy. An investigation of 'the school's inner work' led to a rearticulation of the meaning of school difficulties by stating that the prevailing term 'pupils with difficulties in school' could be largely replaced by 'a school with teaching difficulties' (SOU 1974:53, p. 217 ff.). Furthermore, in line with the ideological goals of integration/inclusion,[11] a growing emphasis on further training in special education knowledge for *all* teachers was advocated in future teacher education (SOU 1978:86). With an ambition to bring special education closer to 'regular' education, new organisational work practices were introduced and the role of special teachers was changed slightly at the end of this period (cf. DsU 1986:13; Prop. 1988/1989:4).[12] A common theme in policy documents during this period was the emphasis placed on a relational perspective on pupils' school difficulties.

During the second time period (1991–1998) the decentralisation process accelerated at a rapid pace under the government in office (1991–1994), which consisted of a minority coalition of conservative and liberal parties. A new national curriculum that was adapted to the new steering principles of management by objectives was introduced, as well as a new grading system for the comprehensive school.[13] This new system of governing by objectives, however, led to a focus displacement in which *results* seemed to take centre stage instead of *objectives* (cf. Wahlström 2002). This meant that those who failed to reach the objectives and passing grades were considered to be pupils in need of special support;[14] that is, candidates for special education practices. This system meant that individual shortcomings and needs were in focus at the expense of the impact of the social environment, and the meaning of special education measures came to mean the prevention of pupils failing to reach the recquired knowledge targets. Another key feature of this period was deregulation and a market orientation of the school. The practical result of this was increased competition between schools and a strengthening of parents' and pupils' possibilities to choose schools. Due to an economic crisis that accompanied this period, a new system of resource distribution through unspecified block grants was also introduced; this led to competition for resources between schools in the same municipality.

During the third period (late 1990s – early 2000s) the social democratic government had ambitions to dampen the former government's escalating focus on objectives and results in schools. Two bills that placed emphasis on the impact of environmental factors on pupils' school difficulties were presented that had relevance for pupils in need of special support (Prop. 1999/2000:135; Prop. 2001/02:14). Even though neuropsychiatric disorders or symptoms, such as ADHD and DAMP,[15] were given more attention in these documents, it was still emphasised that teachers should possess sufficient special education knowledge in order to organise their work in relation to these pupils' needs (Prop. 1999/2000:135, pp. 58–59). Special education was also included in the broader concept of pupil health activities in school, together with school health services and pastoral care. Consequently, the function of pupil health activities broadened the schools' work with pupils in need of special support and introduced professionals with competence in care, medicine, psychology and the field of social work (Prop. 2001/02:14, p. 31). Furthermore, it was emphasised that special educational needs should be seen as a result of a combination of several factors and not as individual shortcomings. The period was also characterised by a degree of return to state governance in terms of economic governance, while at the same time measures were taken to accelerate the process of decentralisation.

As mentioned above, Swedish educational policy since the late 1980s might be characterised by an increased stress on individual agency, knowledge acquisition and results in school. However, perspectives on pupils' difficulties in policy texts have differed. The introduction of the new curriculum in the mid-1990s focused on individual failures, while an overall perspective was the focus in documents from the late 1990s to the early 2000s. These later bills also stressed the importance of regular teachers being more involved in the work with pupils in need of special support, and their ability to support these pupils within the regular classroom. The different foci can also be partly related to the two agendas of the governments which were in power during the periods: social democrat, or conservative and liberal. Even though there seems to be a general ambition to develop the schools' overall work with pupils in need of special support during all the stated periods (in later years described as the pupil health activities), the descriptions of which actors should be responsible for this work varies in policy documents over time (cf. Isaksson & Lindqvist 2009).

Other factors have, however, also influenced the development described above. For example, the new system of resource distribution that was implemented during the 1990s encouraged schools to identify more pupils in need of special support, since that could generate additional economic resources for the school (Johannesson, Lindblad & Simola 2002). The use of medical diagnoses also increased significantly during the 1990s and has, more or less, come to function as a method of securing and maintaining the flow of resources to special support measures. As a result, pupils are constructed as 'diagnosable subjects', which, in turn, signifies what Jóhannesson (2006, p. 113) calls a 'defective-approach'. This development has also been described in terms of a 'medicalisation'[16] of social and personal problems and has also had an impact on the understanding of pupils' difficulties.

From the early 2000s, the use of national, as well as international, comparisons of knowledge acquisition has also become more common and been used as arguments in the educational policy debate. International comparisons are often used as evidence to show that Sweden is lagging behind other countries[17] (cf. Emanuelsson 2006). This has placed further pressure on schools to show good results in knowledge acquisition and has also led to competition between schools.[18] Clearly, this causes ambivalence in the implementation process because of the demands for competition and selection on the one hand, and inclusive education on the other (cf. Barton & Slee 1999).

The fact that national tests have been increasingly used as indicators of pupils' knowledge acquisition may well bring into question whether state governance has actually decreased due to the decentralisation process or just become differently focused (cf. Lundahl 2005). For example, the formulation of objectives and the control of results are still firmly in the hands of the state, and the control of how the schools work has also been sharpened by inspections and quality audits[19] (Lundahl 2005, p. 11). However, educational policy goals and national guidelines are vague and do not specify the form and content of schools' internal work (Isaksson 2009, pp. 26–28). Therefore, official policy documents such as official reports (SOU) and governmental bills are vital to study as 'texts' because acts of articulation in these documents shape the practical work in schools, including how pupils' school difficulties should be understood and what form of support measures are to be provided.

Constituting aspect change in teacher education

Norval (2007) uses the Wittgensteinian concepts of *aspect change* and *aspect dawning* as a fruitful way of understanding changes in political grammars. Aspect change is defined as 'a shift in perspective that establishes different relations between objects or words' (Norval 2007, p. 114). This definition is similar to Laclau and Mouffe's (2001, p. 105) definition of articulatory practices, and aspect change might be seen as a result of concrete articulations of the relationship between elements. More specifically:

> Things are no longer the same; our way of looking at things has changed. But, as I have argued, this is not a break that denies all that has gone before. To the contrary, it is dependent upon what has gone before, but that before is also rearranged – resignified – in important respects. *It is precisely this emphasis on rearrangements that allows one to think through a conception of political change that steers a path between radical rupture and continuity* (Norval 2007, p. 117, my emphasis).

Furthermore, the concept of aspect dawning is related to a distinctive account of change. It is related to a dislocation and disorientation of the social that gives rise to new ways of depicting and understanding various practices. Politically, such an aspect change occurs when sedimented practices or perspectives are questioned, and when traditional ways of doing or looking at things become disrupted; for example, by linking together elements that did not belong together before (Norval 2007, p. 114). According to Norval, a change of aspect within politics often carries with it a great deal of re-evaluation of a previous perspective (Norval 2007, p. 114). As the proposal that I have chosen to analyse in this chapter contains such a re-evaluation of the perspective on pupils' school difficulties, I will apply Norval's concepts in the analysis.

In 2007, the government, which consisted of a right-wing, four-party coalition, appointed a special investigator whose task was to write a proposal for a new teacher education.[20] The special investigator appointed was the former Chancellor of the Swedish Universities, Professor Sigbrit Franke.[21] One important reason for appointing such an investigation and tabling such a proposal for a new teacher education was the fact that nearly 25 per cent of all schoolchildren failed to attain the set knowledge goals in every subject in school (SOU 2008:109, p. 458). Another reason was that the current Swedish teacher education had received major criticism in evaluations and inspections that were carried out by the Swedish National Agency for Higher Education (HSV).

One of the political directives included a review of the school situation for pupils with various kinds of learning and concentration difficulties and the support offered to them.[22] This directive further relates to teachers' general knowledge about the pupils' various difficulties, and the possibilities to accomplish the overall mission of the school in society:

> In order to be able to realise the mission of the school, teachers need more than just subject knowledge. The education for the majority of the educational tracks also needs to include knowledge about children's speech and mathematical development. Accordingly, the situation for children and pupils with various forms of learning and concentration difficulties will be the subject to special attention by the investigator. *All the educational tracks of the teacher education shall provide the teacher with special education knowledge* (SOU 2008:109, p. 467, my emphasis).[23]

The call for an increase in the amount of special education knowledge that teachers should have resembles the content of earlier post-1970 teacher education reforms. However, in terms of intertextuality, such knowledge is re-accentuated (Fairclough 1992) from past texts because it is proclaimed in the report that it should be used in order to *identify* pupils 'with difficulties', rather than to *support* them in the ordinary classroom. The reintroduced special teachers are described as having the main responsibility for providing support for these pupils. Therefore, compared to earlier reforms, the investigator does not place the same emphasis on the whole school's responsibility for these pupils. Instead of emphasising the vision of inclusion and making all school staff involved in such work, the intention is rather to strengthen and cultivate teachers' professional role and mission in schools. This means that pupils who are in need of special support are to a greater extent placed within the purview of special education and something that demands expert competence. The realism of inclusive education is also questioned by the investigator:

> 'A school for all' is a matter of course in a democratic knowledge society. However, this does not necessarily mean that all the pupils must be taught at the same time by the same teacher. An individually adjusted education worth its name also takes into consideration that some pupils have special needs that cannot be provided for in the regular class (big group). *The so-called inclusive perspective is an ideological vision that, when it faces reality, leads to pupils in need of special support running the risk of not receiving this support* (SOU 2008:109, p. 188, my emphasis).

The argument against the all-inclusive vision is that it is considered to be a task that is unrealistic to realise at school. Therefore, it is stated by the investigator that 'it is the special teachers that, on behalf of their expert competence, have the key role of supporting the knowledge development of these pupils' (SOU 2008:109, p. 188). In order to emphasise the professional role of teachers, it is further stated that they 'cannot have competencies to work with the whole range of special needs that might be apparent in a class' (SOU

2008:109, p. 188). Hence, some pupils' needs are constructed as being too complicated to deal with by regular teachers. Such articulations can, in turn, be seen as part of an aspect dawning (Norval 2007). Some pupils' needs are characterised as too demanding for regular teachers, and in comparison with earlier policy documents this is a new way of seeing certain 'special needs' and a different way of defining those actors in school who should be responsible for the support of these pupils.

Sustainability in the educational sector is also a central concern in the report, since several school reforms have taken place in the past decades. In the report, the term sustainability implies (among other things) that the teacher education should not 'be subjected to radical makeovers every ten years', and that future teachers should be given 'a solid knowledge base and effective tools that enable them to exercise the profession in a professional and secure manner' (SOU 2008:109, p. 31). Furthermore, the investigator is quite straightforward regarding the claims of the report and its ideological position:

> This investigation claims that the structure of the teacher education *should be sustainable in the long term and therefore not characterised by temporary prevailing winds in the societal and educational debate.* ... The ideological position that this investigation takes is rather to claim that there are central and universal areas that today's as well as tomorrow's teachers should be oriented towards. (SOU 2008:109, p. 224, my emphasis).

The fact that the report strives and even argues for sustainability in teacher education in relation to its contents implies the proposals are to be cemented in the teacher education of the future, not subject to change as the result of further educational debate. 'Those perspectives, knowledge and skills that this investigation identifies and proclaims are assumed to be sustainable in the long term' (SOU 2008:109, p. 56). Here, the investigator attempts to 'fix' the meaning of pupils' school difficulties and the recommended support measures proposed, intending them as long term solutions in future teacher education.[24] But how are pupils in need of special support constructed in the report? Which perspective on pupils' school difficulties should prevail in teacher education and what are the recommended support measures to 'solve' the problem?

The individual perspective revisited

A striking feature of the report is its rather straightforward perspective on pupils that are deemed to have difficulties in school for various reasons. In earlier policy documents about pupils in need of special support and special education, such questions had often been discussed in much more general and vague terms, with the traditional agent-centred perspective on pupils' difficulties in school problematised (cf. Prop. 1999/2000:135). However, such difficulties are explicitly linked to individual deficits in the 2008 proposal. Now, as in policy documents from the 1960s and early 1970s, the pupils are seen as *having* difficulties:

> Obviously, some children do fall short in school. In spite of extensive school reforms, the problem that some pupils *fail* has not been solved. They develop slower than others and *have* more difficulties learning how to read, write and count. Some *have* difficulties sitting still, concentrating fully and keeping up with school work. Others show aggression towards their friends, bully them and are disruptive, defiant and noisy (SOU 2008:109, p. 207, my emphasis).

The description that certain pupils fail to achieve the stipulated goals of knowledge is an example of the increasing focus that has been placed on grades during the last few years in Sweden.[25] Therefore, it is apparent that the report articulates the meaning of pupils' difficulties by linking them to individual deficits and results, rather than to environmental factors such as the work methods, teaching methods and organisation of the school. Regarding the hitherto dominating relational/social system perspective on pupils' school difficulties in education policy, the author acknowledges that such a perspective has been 'thought-provoking' by focusing more on the school as a system and the pedagogical environment, rather than the individual. However, this perspective is also described as problematic in the report because it has led to very few successful practical results:

> Pupils with difficulties must attain qualified help here and now and cannot wait for reforms that might take decades to realise. Therefore, there is still a significant space for an *individual perspective* (SOU 2008:109, p. 208, original emphasis).

The author argues for the need to re-evaluate the traditional perspective on pupils' school difficulties because it is believed to provide more concrete results in school. Consequently, the meaning of school difficulties is defined in terms of *effectiveness*. This re-evaluation of the traditional perspective can be seen as an aspect dawning (Norval 2007, p. 113). It is argued that pupils' school difficulties should be considered of in a different way so that their school results can be improved.

Another striking feature of the investigation is the one-sided reference to research within developmental psychology and neuropsychiatry presented in relation to the causes of difficulties in reading, writing and maths, as well as concentration difficulties. Such articulatory acts that link school difficulties to elements of a medical/health discourse, however, become problematic in relation to the scientific debates on the topic of medicalisation, which have taken place between neuropsychiatric scholars and social scientists on the subject of diagnoses such as DAMP (cf. Kärvfe 2000); attention deficit/hyperactivity disorder (ADHD) (Brante 2006); and to some extent also reading and writing difficulties (dyslexia) (Solvang 1998), and maths difficulties (dyscalculia) (cf. Sjöberg 2006). These debates have been related to the increasing use of medical diagnoses in schools, as well as the validity and usage of such diagnoses. Such diagnoses may be attractive because biological explanations are used instead of explanations that place the responsibility on social actors like teachers or parents (Solvang 1998). If school difficulties are strongly linked to elements of a medical/health discourse through articulatory acts, less attention is paid to inadequate pedagogy and the organisational shortcomings of the school.

This medicalisation debate is mentioned in the report, but only in a few sentences in relation to ADHD, in this paragraph:

> During the last few years there has been an intense debate regarding the concept of ADHD. From a sociological point of view, the neurobiological base has been questioned and child psychiatrists have been accused of a medicalisation of social problems. The child's problem, it is stated, has to be understood on a societal and cultural level, and it is especially on this level that the measures must be provided (SOU 2008:109, p. 215).

The critique of the use of ADHD as a diagnosis is an important feature of the report because it is articulated as if such critical remarks came from a rather modest group of sociologists. This is quite a simplification of the substantial scientific and public debates in Sweden regarding the concept of ADHD and DAMP, but also dyslexia and dyscalculia, since the late 1990s (cf. Solvang 1998; Kärfve 2000; Sjöberg 2006). The author's stance on this subject is, however, quite straightforward:

> Within the school one might hardly sweep serious behavioural problems of children under the carpet and wait for the societal changes that could eliminate these problems. One has to find ways to help the children and in that case make use of all the scientifically grounded knowledge that has been developed in different fields, but at the same time be careful with the apparent risk of over-diagnosing (SOU 2008:109, p. 215).

An underlying inconsistency is present in the above citation. On the one hand, the scientific knowledge presented in the report is more or less limited to research within developmental psychology, brain research, and similar disciplines that are rooted in a psychological/medical research tradition (SOU 2008:109, p. 203). On the other hand, the recommendations imply that knowledge from different fields should be used in order to support the pupils' development. This contradiction becomes even more apparent when the risk of over-diagnosing children is mentioned, because this has been one of the main arguments in the critique levelled at the individual perspective. This is also something the author seems to be aware of. As will be evident in the next section, such an individual/medical perspective on pupils' difficulties has significant effects on the recommended support measures to be used in schools.

Recommended support measures
– differentiated or inclusive solutions?

As has been indicated above, the investigation's recommended support measures imply that the character of special support for this group of pupils is undergoing a change of meaning. It also questions the inclusive school vision. It is stated in the report that most classrooms cannot offer the social and physical environment that is required to provide pupils with precise instructions and positive feedback. Furthermore, a one-to-one teacher/pupil ratio is considered to enable the possibility of creating the necessary time for work assignments to be completed. Compared to the suggestions in earlier policy documents, which were oriented more to the vision of inclusion, these newer suggestions constitute a shift from earlier policies that recommended support first and foremost within the regular education and the ordinary classroom. A further interesting feature of the text is that it stated that several studies have shown that a one-to-one teacher/pupil ratio might be effective, although no references are made to such studies, or for that matter studies that have shown some negative effects of differentiated work forms.[26] In terms of intertextuality, what has been described above might be seen as both a response to past texts, as well as an example of what is incorporated and not from previous policies with the aim of creating changes.

The author stated that the newly reintroduced teacher training for special teachers[27] would fit well with a so-called individual perspective (SOU 2008:109, p. 208). The right-wing government's reintroduction of special teachers was considered to be essential in correcting a 'mistake' made by the social democratic government during the 1990s:

It brings me great satisfaction to report that the government is
rectifying a major mistake that was committed seventeen years ago
when the Special Teacher Education Programme was abandoned
(Utbildningsdepartementet 2009, my translation).

Contrary to the special educationalists, the special teachers should
work more closely with those pupils who need special support. The
task of special educationalists is instead described as solving individual
problems in specific school situations and teaching environments.
Instead of social and organisational factors, the report's articulated
meaning of special education is constructed in terms of focusing on
individual pupils' shortcomings. Consequently, the support measures
that are prioritised involve special skills training that are there to
avoid 'failures' of pupils not matching the expected school results.
In comparison with the earlier meaning that was ascribed to special
education – that is, a specific area of knowledge in schools and as
a complement to basic teacher competence – the report constructs
special teachers as 'the experts' that should work directly with those
pupils in need of special support. This particular view of education
policy was criticised as early as during the 1970s. However, the
author argues that because the regular teachers are the first to face
the various special educational needs, they should also be able to use
basic special educational knowledge so that they can identify various learning difficulties and 'call for the expert help that the special
teachers can provide' (SOU 2008:109, p. 208). Therefore, by linking
pupils' school difficulties with elements such as 'individual deficits'
and 'failures', it is easy to envisage that pupils who are in need of
special support would be handed over to special teachers outside
the ordinary classroom. The author is also positive to the suggestion made by teaching unions that teachers should have the right
to demand that specific support measures be provided for pupils in
need of special support. This forms a further argument supporting
the idea that pupils in need of special support are constituted as a
group demanding expert competence beyond the scope of teachers'
basic knowledge (SOU 2008:109, p. 208).

Sustainability as a hegemonic intervention

The decentralisation processes that accelerated during the 1990s signalled a change in the educational sector, as well as in other social arenas in society. Furthermore, a dislocation took place within the discourse of education policy; that is, it became unstable (cf. Shül-lerqvist 1995) and hence open for articulatory practices. Concrete study results in schools took centre stage and knowledge acquisi-tion related to educational goals was highlighted. Consequently, an increased focus was placed on individual agency and the pupils themselves were, by and large, constructed as responsible for their own academic success. The discourse of education policy in relation to the meaning of pupils' difficulties might, however, be described as a struggle between a *disability discourse*, which involves a contextual understanding of how difficulties arise, and a *curriculum discourse*, where difficulties are articulated in relation to objectives and results in school (Isaksson & Lindqvist 2009).

The examination of how pupils' school difficulties are constructed by articulatory acts does not solely involve looking at concrete articulations within the text, but also that which is absent from the texts, i.e. 'the silences in the official maps of policy making' (Lind-blad & Popkewitz 2002, p. 23). In this respect, it is relevant that the investigation neglects and silences special education research, as well as other research within disability studies; that is, research that highlights the negative effects of the individual perspective and dif-ferentiated solutions for pupils. I would argue that these questions were given adequate scope within earlier policy documents (cf. Prop. 1999/2000:135). In a similar way, the report effectively silences the critique of the 'medicalisation process' of pupils' difficulties in school, and this silencing includes research that has problematised the increasing use of medical labelling in school and the pathologi-cal perspective on pupils' difficulties. Consequently, the reading, writing and concentration difficulties of pupils are constructed as medical and psychological problems, whereas social factors are given less attention as the possible causes of such difficulties.

Even though there is an intertextual relationship in the analysed texts in terms of the emphasis on special education knowledge within the general teacher education, the meaning of such knowledge for teachers is rearticulated as a means of identifying rather than supporting pupils, and this implies a changed meaning of special education knowledge within schools. I would argue that this articulation constitutes a new way of depicting special educational practices in schools, as well as a re-evaluation of the hitherto dominant relational perspective of pupils' school difficulties in education policy in Sweden. By representing pupils' school difficulties almost exclusively in relation to medical and psychological research, the meanings of such difficulties are constituted as individual failures. These failures involve various forms of neurological disorders that are associated with deficits of the individual child, rather than a result of the interplay between the individual and the environment. In this respect, I would argue that the report contributes to a new dislocation in the discourse of education policy. The explicit claims that focus on the need to re-evaluate the individual perspective in schools, which was largely abandoned in education policies during the 1970s, can further be understood in terms of what Norval (2007, p. 114) describes as an aspect dawning; a new way of understanding the causes of pupils' school difficulties and the role of special education in schools. However, such an aspect dawning is dependent on the fact that one *sees* things differently; that the way of looking at these things has actually changed (Norval 2007, p. 117). In the report, a disparate set of elements are linked together in the name of sustainability, which is an example of articulatory acts that fix the meaning of pupils difficulties and support measures. These, in turn, can be seen as an intention to construct a universal political project (cf. Howarth 2005, p. 323).

The call for an individual perspective, as well as the report's strong reliance on research within a psycho-medical paradigm, can also be interpreted as a hegemonic intervention (Laclau 1996, p. 89), or what Howarth (2005, p. 323) describes as an operation of the hegemonic logic, serving to fix the meaning of pupils' school difficulties in future education policy. The articulated need for an individual perspective that provides quick practical results for schools might construct 'political alliances and coalitions between differently positioned social actors' (Howarth 2005, p. 323). This, in turn, might contribute to an aspect change in education policy discourse. However, the success of such an intervention depends on how such a fixation of meaning is supported by other social actors. This is, however, a question that remains to be answered.

Concluding discussion

In this chapter I have argued that the proposal for a sustainable teacher education can be seen as contributing to a dislocation within Swedish education policy, and that this gives rise to what Norval (2007) calls an aspect dawning regarding the meaning of pupils' school difficulties and special educational practices. Pupils' school difficulties are mainly articulated as individual failures in the report and understood in terms of various forms of neurological disorders. This articulation implies that pupils' difficulties in schools are the result of individual shortcomings and not the teaching environment. Furthermore, a change in the meaning of special educational practices is also evident, and this change places the focus on differentiated solutions for these pupils and a 'handing over' of them to a 'special track' within schools, where special teachers have the main responsibility for these pupils.

As Carlbaum (in this book) points out, there is a trend in the Swedish political system of moving away from the previous vague terms of reference and larger (parliamentary) commissions to single-expert-led commissions with clear objectives stated by the government. I would argue that these new types of reports also signify a new genre of policy texts (cf. Fairclough 1992, p. 126). This genre includes an argumentative rhetorical mode, largely missing in former reports. The possibility of constructing the 'problem' of pupils in need of special support and recommended support measures in new ways is thus given more leeway compared to earlier investigations, where more political parties were represented and divergent viewpoints included.

The claims in the report are largely made in the name of sustainability, and arguments have been made that the content of teacher education, as well as education policy, should be sustainable in the long term. However, the fact that the prevailing perspective on pupils' school difficulties is questioned is an apparent contradiction because this perspective has been proclaimed in educational reforms since the 1970s. Therefore, it seems relevant to ask the question whether it is sustainable to abandon a perspective that has been important in shaping teacher education, the development of special educationalists' roles in schools, and the practical work guided by a vision of inclusion. It is indeed tempting to raise the question – who gains from this sustainability?

The fact that the bill (Prop. 2009/10:89) which draws upon this investigation, does not discuss these issues makes it difficult to estimate the impact of the investigator's proposals. However, as the investigator's call for an individual perspective is neither commented on nor rejected, this could well imply that it is seen as valid. There is also a good chance that it will influence the direction of practical work in schools because the proposal shows how such matters are articulated and given meaning on a policy level. One reason for this is that even though the social system and the more relationally oriented perspective on pupils' school difficulties has been important in shaping the direction of education policy since the 1970s, the individual perspective has been deeply rooted in the practical work of schools for a long time (cf. Persson 2001). The recommendations that are presented in the report might therefore function as further arguments for teachers to stick to this tradition, instead of focusing on the potential barriers in the teaching environments that might obstruct certain pupils' learning processes, like poor organisation and inadequate pedagogy. The clear-cut role of teachers presented in the report suggests that their role is solely to identify pupils with school difficulties and then call for the expert knowledge that the special teacher can provide. As the proclaimed individual perspective suggests that differentiated support measures will be applied – that is, special support outside the ordinary classroom – it might also be questioned whether the intentions are to increase all pupils' knowledge acquisition, or whether these measures mean that teachers can be rid of disruptive elements within the ordinary class that could bring down the average results.

Finally, it seems reasonable to sum up the discussion by returning to the question of the use of terminology that was presented in the introductory part of this chapter. As the articulated meaning of pupils' school difficulties is constructed as the result of individual shortcomings, and not the result of an interplay between the individual and the school environment, this forms an apparent discrepancy between the language used in policy documents and the former meaning that was ascribed to the concept of 'pupils in need of special support'. If pupils are portrayed in policy texts as 'having difficulties', rather than 'being in difficulties', then perhaps it is time to wonder whether to make this visible by also changing the terminology. Consequently, instead of using the concept 'pupils in need of special support', which indicates that school difficulties are bound to the social context, it might perhaps be more correct to use the old term 'pupils with special support needs', in order to bring clarity regarding which perspective should prevail in contemporary Swedish education policy, as well as in the teacher education of the future.

Notes

1 The concepts that I refer to are the Swedish concepts *elever med speciella behov* and *elever med svårigheter*.

2 I am here referring to the Swedish terms 'speciella' and 'särskilda'.

3 The Swedish term is 'elever *med* behov av särskilt stöd'.

4 The Swedish term is 'elever *i* behov av särskilt stöd'. Compared to the earlier terms that indicated that school difficulties were related to individual deficits, this term indicates that school difficulties are bound to the social context and arise in the meeting between the individual and the environment. That is, instead of *having* the needs, the pupil is – depending on the situation and context – *in need* of special support. Therefore the terminology has undergone a displacement of focus, and the focus is more on pupils' various development possibilities in relation to their needs (cf. Ekström 2004, for a further discussion on the use of terminology in Swedish policy documents).

5 Although the term *'pupils with special educational needs'* is well established internationally and used in most international scientific journals, I will use the term *'pupils in need of special support'* in this text. The main reason for this is that I find the first term rather paradoxical since it relates the needs mainly to the individual, while the latter one captures the relational/contextual meaning of such needs to a higher degree and hence is more in line with the meaning ascribed to the Swedish term *'elever i behov av särskilt stöd'*.

6 Laclau (1969, p. 89) describes a hegemonic intervention as a 'contingent intervention taking place in an undecidable terrain'; that is, an articulation

that by force restores an unambiguous fixation of elements to moments (Winther Jørgensen & Phillips 1999, p. 55). Even though these changes in terminology were not characterised by antagonistic forces, I would argue that they can be seen as a hegemonic intervention in terms of 'fixing' the meaning within education policy of how the origins of school difficulties should be interpreted.

7 This chapter builds on empirical material that was part of my Ph.D. project *Spänningen mellan normalitet och avvikelse: om skolans insatser för elever i behov av särskilt stöd* (The tension between normality and deviance: on schools' support for pupils with special educational needs) (Isaksson 2009), financed by the Swedish Research Council (Vetenskapsrådet). The aim of the thesis was to analyse the tension between normality and deviance that is manifested in the compulsory schools' work procedures for pupils with special educational needs. My thesis consisted of four different studies, and one of them focused specifically on how pupils with special educational needs and special education have been articulated in national policy documents during recent decades (Isaksson & Lindqvist 2009). In part, this chapter draws upon the results of that study, but also narrows down the analysis to one specific policy document which is studied in more detail here.

8 With 'dislocation' I refer to a process by which the contingency of discursive structures becomes visible (Laclau 1990, pp. 39–41); that is, when the relationship between moments in a discourse become 'blurred', making possible the articulation of elements that may not previously have come into play (Norval 2007, p. 83).

9 Due to the impossibility of 'absolute fixity' of a discourse, the transition from elements to moments is never entirely complete, which makes articulatory practices possible (Laclau & Mouffe 2001, pp. 110–11).

10 However, although proponents of the CDA perspective find the concept of articulation useful, this does not imply that they agree with the overall theoretical framework of Laclau and Mouffe. It seems that the dividing point between the two perspectives on discourse analysis, as well as the usage of articulation, lies within their understanding of the social; that is, whether the social constitutes or is constituted by discourse. On this topic, Chouliaraki and Fairclough (as well as other CDA proponents) state that Laclau and Mouffe overrate the openness, the radical contingency, of the social (1999, p. 25).

11 The concept of integration was largely replaced by the concept of inclusion during the 1990s in the public, as well as the scientific, pedagogical debate in Sweden (cf. Tideman et al. 2004). Related to education, the concept of inclusion often refers to a vision that all pupils should participate in the ordinary classroom. The application of the concept, which is often described as inclusive education, suggests that all teaching should be provided within the ordinary classroom and that social fellowship is prioritised. The concept might be seen as having radical implications, since it implies that schools should be organised in relation to the fact that individuals have different needs. Therefore, instead of the traditional special education practices which, to a great extent, located

the pupils' difficulties within the child and implied individual compensating support, the concept of inclusion implies that 'differences between pupils should be seen as natural and something that the school system both value and adapt to' (Nilholm 2006).

12 The Special Teacher Education Programme was abandoned in 1990 and replaced by the Special Educationalist Programme. Compared to special teachers working directly with pupils in need of special support, the special educationalists' role in school was to function as supervisors to teachers and their role was also more closely related to the overall organisational work in school.

13 The bill was entitled *En ny läroplan för grundskolan och ett nytt betygssystem för grundskolan, sameskolan, specialskolan och den obligatoriska särskolan*, Prop. 1992/1993:220).

14 What is also striking is that the author of the bill used the old term 'pupils with special support needs' (*elever med behov av särskilt stöd*), while the author of the curriculum proposal used the term 'pupils in need of special support' (*elever i behov av särskilt stöd*). Such an articulation reveals an ambiguous attitude towards different perspectives on what causes the difficulties; that is, whether individual shortcomings (expressed in the former) or shortcomings of the environment (expressed in the latter) are the most important factors.

15 The term ADHD stands for attention deficits/hyperactivity disorder, while DAMP stands for deficits in attention, motor control and perception. The latter diagnosis has mainly been used in Sweden and the main difference between the two diagnoses is that DAMP includes motor control, i.e. motor functioning of the body.

16 With 'medicalisation' I refer to a process by which an increasing amount of (social and personal) problems are interpreted in medical terms and that an increasing trust is placed in the medical professions (cf. Illich 1995; Zola 1975; Conrad & Schneider 1992). To put it simply, such processes indicate that medical expertise is given the power to define what is normal (healthy) and who is deviant (sick), something similar to what Johansson discusses in terms of the 'psychiatrisation' of cutter identities in her chapter in this book.

17 The vision of the right-wing, four-party coalition government has been depicted by the powerful slogan of creating the 'best school in Europe'.

18 For example, competition between schools within the same municipality regarding resources, and it has also become much more common that the results of national tests are made public in newspapers, which further increases the competition between schools.

19 Since 1 October 2008, educational inspections and quality audits are carried out by the Schools Inspectorate (*Statens skolinspektion*). The Schools Inspectorate, which was established as a new state authority in 2008, took over this responsibility of making educational inspections from The National Agency of Education (*Skolverket*).

20 As Carlbaum points out in this book, special commissions (read: single experts) have become more common in the Swedish political system, in contrast to

larger commissions with broad political representativeness that were the case before (cf. Lärarutbildningsutredningen, 1999). Another striking feature of educational reforms during later years is that there has been a decrease in educational research's influence on educational policies (cf. Persson 2009).

21 Even though the appointed special investigator of the commission had an expert group at hand, I will refer to the 'author' or 'investigator' as one person.

22 I only present these directives since they relate to questions regarding pupils' school difficulties and the support available to these pupils. Since these questions mainly relate to special education, the main part of the text excerpts that follow are taken from the chapter in the report that specifically discusses special education (pp. 207–215).

23 The proposal *Sustainable teacher education* is written in Swedish, although including an English summary. The quotes are therefore translated by me.

24 The following bill, *Bäst i klassen – en ny lärarutbildning*, was presented to parliament in the beginning of February 2010. In the bill, questions of perspectives on pupils' school difficulties and recommended support measures are surprisingly absent and therefore neither commented on nor rejected by the government. Despite this silence, the investigator's proposals are still important and might have influence since they identify a problem area and point out the direction for practical work in schools. The investigation's potential impact will be further discussed in the concluding section of this chapter.

25 The grading system in Sweden was changed in the 1990s from a relative system to an absolute system, i.e. pupils' study results would be assessed in relation to stipulated objectives and acquired knowledge targets. During the first decade of this century, issues regarding grades have continued to be debated within Swedish educationpolicy circles, especially in relation to international comparative examinations of pupils' knowledge.

26 A great number of studies since the 1970s have pointed out negative, stigmatising effects of such support measures for pupils (cf. Westling Allodi 2002; Groth 2007; Karlsson 2007; Ljusberg 2009, for more recent Swedish studies). Furthermore, a review of research presented not long after the report by the National Board of Education (Skolverket 2009) found that such support seemed to have no significant effect on pupils in terms of increasing their knowledge acquisition.

27 In 2008 the government decided to reinstate the Special Teacher Education Programme alongside the Special Educationalist one.

References

Literature

Barton, L. & Slee, R., 1999. Competition, Selection and Inclusive Education: Some Observations. *International Journal of Inclusive Education*, 3(1), pp. 3–12.

Brante, T., 2006. Den nya psykiatrin: exemplet ADHD. In: G. Hallerstedt (ed.), *Diagnosens makt. Om kunskap, pengar och lidande*. Göteborg: Daidalos.

Chouliaraki, L. & Fairclough, N., 1999. *Discourse in Late Modernity: Rethinking Critical Discourse Analysis.* Edinburgh: Edinburgh University Press.

Conrad, P. & Schneider, J.W., 1992. *Deviance and Medicalization: From Badness to Sickness.* Philadelphia: Temple University Press.

Ekström, P., 2004. *Makten att definiera. En studie av hur beslutsfattare formulerar villkoren för specialpedagogisk verksamhet.* (Diss.) Gothenburg: Göteborgs universitet.

Emanuelsson, I., 2006. Betyget godkänd i en obligatorisk skola för alla. In: E. Forsberg & E. Wallin (eds), *Skolans kontrollregim – ett kontraproduktivt system för styrning?* Stockholm: HLS Förlag.

Emanuelsson, I., Persson, B. & Rosenqvist, J., 2001. *Forskning inom det specialpedagogiska området: en kunskapsöversikt.* Stockholm: Skolverket.

Englund, T. & Quennerstedt, A., 2008. Linking Curriculum Theory and Linguistics: The Performative use of 'Equivalence' as an Educational Policy Concept. *Journal of Curriculum Studies,* 40(6), pp. 713–724.

Fairclough, N., 1992. *Discourse and Social Change.* Cambridge: Polity Press.

Glynos, J. & Howarth, D., 2007. *Logics of Critical Explanation in Social and Political Theory.* London: Routledge.

Groth, D., 2007. *Uppfattningar om specialpedagogiska insatser: aspekter ur elevers och speciallärares perspektiv.* (Diss.) Luleå: Luleå tekniska högskola.

Howarth, D., 2005. Applying Discourse Theory: The Method of Articulation. In: D. Howarth. & J. Torfing (eds), *Discourse Theory in European Politics: Identity, Policy and Governance.* New York: Palgrave Macmillan.

Howarth, D., 2007. *Diskurs.* Malmö: Liber.

Illich, I., 1995. *Limits to Medicine. Medical Nemesis: The Expropriation of Health.* London: Marion Boyars Publishers.

Isaksson, J., 2009. *Spänningen mellan normalitet och avvikelse: om skolans insatser för elever i behov av särskilt stöd.* (Diss.) Umeå: Umeå universitet.

Isaksson, J. & Lindqvist, R., 2009. Articulatory Practices on the Meaning of Special Education in Swedish Policy Documents. In: J. Isaksson, *Spänningen mellan normalitet och avvikelse: om skolans insatser för elever i behov av särskilt stöd.* (Diss.) Umeå: Umeå universitet.

Johannesson, I., Lindblad, S. & Simola, H., 2002. An Inevitable Progress? Educational Restructuring in Finland, Iceland and Sweden at the Turn of the Millennium. *Scandinavian Journal of Educational Research,* 46(3), pp. 325–339.

Jóhannesson, I.A., 2006. 'Strong, Independent, Able to Learn More …': Inclusion and the Construction of School Students in Iceland as Diagnosable Subjects. *Discourse: Studies in the Cultural Politics of Education,* 27(1), pp. 103–119.

Karlsson, Y., 2007. *Att inte vilja vara problem: social organisering och utvärdering av elever i en särskild undervisningsgrupp.* (Diss.) Linköping: Linköpings universitet.

Kärfve, E., 2000. *Hjärnspöken. Damp och hotet mot folkhälsan.* Stockholm/Stehag: Brutus Östlings Bokförlag Symposion.

Laclau, E., 1996. *Emancipation(s).* London: Verso.

Laclau, E. & Mouffe, C., 1990. Post-Marxism without Apologies. In: E. Laclau (ed.), *New Reflections on the Revolution of our Time.* London: Verso, pp. 97–132.

Laclau, E. & Mouffe, C., 2001. *Hegemony and Socialist Strategy: Towards a Radical Democratic Politics.* London: Verso.

Lindblad, S., Lundahl, L. & Zackari, G., 2002. Sweden: Increased Inequalities – Increased Stress on Individual Agency. In: S. Lindblad & T. S. Popkewitz (eds), *Education Governance and Social Integration and Exclusion: Studies in the Powers of Reason and the Reasons of Power.* Uppsala: Uppsala University, pp. 299–329.

Lindblad, S. & Popkewitz, T.S., 2002. Introduction to the Problematics. In: S. Lindblad. & T. S. Popkewitz (eds), *Education Governance and Social Integration and Exclusion: Studies in the Powers of Reason and the Reasons of Power.* Uppsala: Uppsala University, pp. 9–29.

Ljusberg, A.-L. 2009. *Pupils in Remedial Classes.* (Diss.) Stockholm: Stockholm University.

Lundahl, L., 2005. A Matter of Self-governance and Control: The Reconstruction of Swedish Education Policy: 1980–2003. *European Education,* 37(1), pp. 10–25.

Nilholm, C., 2006. Special Education, Inclusion and Democracy. *European Journal of Special Needs Education,* 21(4), pp. 431–445.

Norval, A., 2007. *Aversive Democracy. Inheritance and Originality in the Democratic Tradition.* Cambridge: Cambridge University Press.

Persson, B., 2001. *Elevers olikheter och specialpedagogisk kunskap.* Stockholm: Liber.

Persson, B., 2009. Den pedagogiska forskningen måste ta plats i utbildningsdebatten. *Tvärsnitt: Humanistisk och samhällsvetenskaplig forskning,* 3, pp. 21–22.

Shüllerqvist, U., 1995. Förskjutningen av svensk skolpolitisk debatt under det senaste decenniet. In: T. Englund (ed.), *Utbildningspolitiskt systemskifte?* Stockholm: HLS, pp. 44–106.

Sjöberg, G., 2006. *Om det inte är dyskalkyli – vad är det då? En multimetodstudie av eleven i matematikproblem ur ett longitudinellt perspektiv.* (Diss.) Umeå: Umeå universitet.

Skolverket, 2009. *What Influences Educational Achievement in Swedish Schools? A Systematic Review and Summary Analysis.* Stockholm: Skolverket.

Solvang, P., 1998. Velferdsstatens problemlogik i lys av en debatt om dysleksi. *Sociologisk forskning,* 2, pp. 5–24.

Tideman, M., Rosenqvist, J., Lansheim, B., Ranagården, L. & Jacobsson, K., 2004. *Den stora utmaningen. Om att se olikhet som resurs i skolan.* Halmstad: Högskolan i Halmstad.

Wahlström, N., 2002. *Om det förändrade ansvaret för skolan. Vägen till mål- och resultatstyrning och några av dess konsekvenser.* (Diss.) Örebro: Örebro universitet.

Westling Allodi, M., 2002 *Support and Resistance. Ambivalence in Special Education.* (Diss.) Stockholm: The Teacher Education Office in Stockholm.

Winther Jørgensen, M. & Phillips, L., 2000. *Diskursanalys som teori och metod.* Lund: Studentlitteratur.

Zola, I.K., 1975. Medicine as an Institution of Social Control. In: C. Cox & A. Mead (eds), *A Sociology of Medical Practice.* London: Collier-Macmillan.

Official documents

SOU 1974:53. *Skolans arbetsmiljö. Betänkande angivet av Utredningen om skolans inre arbete – SIA.* Stockholm: Utbildningsdepartementet.

SOU 1978:86. Lärarutbildningsutredningen, 1978. *Lärare för skola i utveckling: betänkande.* Stockholm: Utbildningsdepartementet.

DsU 1986:13. *Specialpedagogik i skola och lärarutbildning.* Stockholm: Utbildningsdepartementet.

Prop. 1988/89:4. *Om skolans utveckling och styrning,* 1989. Stockholm: Utbildningsdepartementet.

Prop. 1992/93:220. *En ny läroplan för grundskolan och ett nytt betygssystem för grundskolan, sameskolan, specialskolan och den obligatoriska särskolan.* Stockholm: Utbildningsdepartementet.

SOU 1999:63. Lärarutbildningsutredningen, 1999. *Att lära och leda – en lärarutbildning för samverkan och utveckling: slutbetänkande.* Stockholm: Utbildningsdepartementet.

Prop. 1999/2000:135. *En förnyad lärarutbildning.* Stockholm: Utbildningsdepartementet.

Prop. 2001/02:14. *Hälsa, lärande och trygghet.* Stockholm: Utbildningsdepartementet.

SOU 2008:109. *En hållbar lärarutbildning: Betänkande av Utredningen om en ny lärarutbildning (HUT 07).* Stockholm: Utbildningsdepartementet.

Prop. 2009/10:89. *Bäst i klassen – en ny lärarutbildning.* Stockholm: Utbildningsdepartementet.

Online sources

Utbildningsdepartementet, 2009. *Speciallärarutbildningen återinförs.* (Press release.) Available at: http://www.regeringen.se/sb/d/9076/a/81477. (Accessed 14 February 2010.)

CHAPTER 5

Cameroonian Students in Higher Swedish Education

Jonathan Ngeh

Migrants in many countries are known to face problems of discrimination or exclusion (Abiri 2000; Delanty et al. 2008). There are several studies carried out in Sweden that have highlighted this problem, and indicated that migrants are excluded from different spheres of life (Bråmå 2006; Räthzel 2006; Bunar 2007; Behtoui 2009). The meaning of exclusion in this chapter follows Ruth Wodak (2008, p. 60), who defines it as the '*deprivation of access* through means of explicit or symbolic power implemented by the social elites'. Wodak continues by stating:

> I assume that 'inclusion/exclusion' of groups, people, nation-states, migrant groups, changes due to different criteria of how insiders and outsiders are defined in each instance. In this way, various typologies, or group memberships, are constructed, which sometimes include a certain group, and sometimes do not, depending on socio-political and situational contexts and interactions (Wodak 2008, p. 55).

What Wodak highlights is that the inclusion/exclusion of people is not fixed, but changes under different circumstances and in relation to different people (cf. Neergaard 2009). This chapter is part of my Ph.D. project that uses theories of conflict and social exclusion to analyse the discrimination of migrants from Cameroon and Somalia in Sweden.[1] The chapter pays particular attention to Cameroonian students who attend Swedish universities. The aim is to apply the theoretical perspective of critical discourse analysis (CDA) to show how structural/institutional factors in Sweden discriminate against these students. A further aim is to show how the students resist (or submit to) such constraints. The analysis is based on interviews and periods of participant observations that were carried out in Malmö during the first six months of 2008. In total, eight interviews have been selected and the sample consists of four women and four men between the ages of twenty-four and thirty-four.[2] The students come from different social backgrounds and local areas in Cameroon and therefore have different local identities and experiences (see Nyamnjoh & Rowlands 1998; Pelican 2008). These differences certainly have an influence on how they respond to the challenges they face in Sweden, and studies about Cameroonian migrants in South Africa and in the UK have shown this (Pineteh 2008; Mercer et al. 2008, 2009). An analysis of the internal differences between Cameroonian migrants and how such differences affect their transition in Sweden is beyond the scope of this chapter, which instead is primarily concerned with their shared experiences of subordination as Cameroonians and Africans studying in Sweden.

Background of the study

According to official statistics, the majority of migrants in Sweden are from Europe and Asia (Statistiska centralbyrån [Statistics Sweden] 2007, pp. 18–19). In the city of Malmö, where this study was conducted, 61 per cent of migrants came from Europe, 30 per cent from Asia, 4 per cent from Africa and the rest from other continents (Pålsson 2007). Official statistics in Sweden also show that a significant number of Africans started migrating to Sweden in the 1980s and the majority of them came from Ethiopia and Somalia (Statistiska centralbyrån 2007, pp. 18–19). In general, most of the people who migrate to Sweden from this continent come from economically and/or politically unstable countries. As a consequence of this fact, and the dominant Swedish discourse that represents immigration from the Global South (economically poor and less industrialised countries) as refugees on the move, migrants from this area are commonly perceived as refugees (cf. Westin 2006, p. 2; Norman 2004).[3] This is problematic because the label refugee is negatively charged. One expression of this negative labelling is that the immigration of refugees has been listed as a threat to national security since the 1980s (Abiri 2000, p. 190), and in ordinary conversations some people in Sweden associate refugees with anti-social behaviour like crime (Norman 2004). By focusing on students, this chapter tries to avoid the customary representation of migrants from Africa as refugees and therefore a problematic category.

The perspective of CDA

According to Fairclough (2006, p. 12), discourse is used to refer to the semiotic elements of social life as opposed to its non-semiotic components. Semiosis, as used by Fairclough, is an irreducible part of material social processes, and includes all forms of meaning making such as visual images and body languages, as well as written and spoken language (Fairclough 2001, p. 122). He also uses the term discourse to refer to particular ways of representing certain aspects of the world (Fairclough 2006, p. 12). Central to Fairclough's notion of discourse is the primacy of social life, understood in terms of processes which are composed of two distinctive parts: a meaning making component (semiosis) and a material component (Chouliaraki & Fairclough 1999, p. 51). These different components constitute what are described in CDA as the discursive and non-discursive elements of social life.

When, for example, people from a small Swedish town protested against a settlement of refugees, one of the complaints they made was that 'refugees dirty the area and steal our belongings' (Norman 2004, p. 212). Let us assume that some of the protesters became worried that refugees would do these things, and therefore reacted by refusing to rent out apartments to them. The first act, that is, the statement that refugees are dirty and thieves, is linguistic and hence an example of semiosis. As a result of its semiotic character, it constitutes what was described above as a discourse (Chouliaraki & Fairclough 1999, p. 51; Fairclough 2001, p. 122). The second act, which consists of the refusal to rent apartments to refugees, could be seen as the 'speech act' of 'refusing'. This is in itself discursive, but of course the actual physical 'shutting out' of some people from some places (such as houses) would be material. The effects of these acts, such as potential homelessness, would also be material in Fairclough's sense of the word. The non-linguistic or material aspects of the second acts are non-discursive. Even though CDA does differentiate between the discursive and non-discursive, it also insists that both elements are linked in a dialectic relationship that constitutes parts of the same social reality (Fairclough 2006, pp. 30–31). In the discussed example, the discursive and non-discursive acts are part of the same social reality; that is, direct discrimination against refugees.

Another important concept in Fairclough's theoretical framework is the 'order of discourse', which is best explained by using what he calls 'social practice'. Social practice(s) is/are defined as 'habitual, ritual or institutionalised ways of *going on*, which are associated with particular institutions (such as the law or education) and, at a more concrete level, particular organisations (such as a school or a business)' (Fairclough 2006, p. 30). Fairclough explains that any institution or organisation is characterised by a specific network of social practices. Such networks of social practices or social practices in general have a semiotic component, which he describes as an 'order of discourse'. 'We can characterise the order of discourse of an organisation such as a school as the semiotic or discourse moment of the school (of the network of social practices that constitutes it), which is dialectically related to other moments' (Fairclough 2006, p. 31). Furthermore, he explains that an order of discourse is a combination of three sorts of entities: discourses, 'genres' and 'styles'. Genre refers to different ways of acting and producing social life in the semiotic mode, like for example in everyday conversations or formal meetings, whereas styles are ways of being and identities associated with the semiotic aspects that are connected to a certain position, like for example a doctor or an opera singer (Fairclough 2001, pp. 123–124; 2006, p. 31). According to Fairclough's analysis, a particular order of discourse contains different discourses, different genres and different styles, which may be complementary to each other, or alternative and even conflicting. In situations where there are different or competing discourses, Fairclough notes that one of the discourses is dominant: 'different discourses, genres and styles are articulated together in particular relations – for instance, where there are (conflicting) alternatives, there will be a tendency for one to be the dominant one, the officially recognised and approved one' (Fairclough 2006, p.31). van Dijk (1997, p. 165) comes to the same conclusion when arguing that the discourse of minority groups and anti-racist proponents, which forms a contrastive perspective in relation to racist discourse, is often marginalised, problematised or ridiculed. In my study, the concept of an order of discourse is used to analyse specific institutions/organisations that work with the issue of immigration (migrants) and those that influence public opinion on this topic. In each specific case, different discourses, genres and styles can be identified, and it can be shown how they complement a general discourse that constructs migrants as a problem or how they provide alternative or contrasting possibilities.

Other key concepts in Fairclough's (1992) analysis are 'ideology' and 'hegemony'. He considers these concepts to be central in the (re-) production of structural inequalities and transformations of society. Ideology, as used by Fairclough, is 'significations/constructions of reality (the physical world, social relations, social identities) which are built into various dimensions of the forms/meanings of discursive practices' (Fairclough 1992, p. 87). He explains that ideologies that are embedded in discursive practices are at their most effective when they become naturalised and appear as 'common sense'. The earlier example concerning refugees who are perceived as 'dirty and thieves' is a way of suggesting that refugees (migrants) are responsible for these kinds of anti-social behaviour, which are disruptive to cohesion in society. When negative representations of migrants are deeply embedded in institutions, as shall be seen later, they become common sense notions and in many cases justify the subordination of migrants. In this respect they can be seen as ideological.

Fairclough's concept of hegemony is influenced by the works of Gramsci (1971) and Laclau and Mouffe (1985; Laclau 1996). Laclau and Mouffe have developed Gramsci's idea of hegemony using the concept of chain of equivalence. A chain of equivalence is the link that exists between a variety of concrete or partial struggles and mobilisations, which are related because of their shared opposition to a common 'enemy' (Laclau 1996, pp. 40–41). Using the concept of a chain of equivalence, Laclau and Mouffe theorise the political process of hegemony as the articulation of differences within a discursive system. Moreover hegemony is formed through acts of 'social antagonism' that exclude what is beyond their limit. Drawing from Gramsci and Laclau and Mouffe, Fairclough (1992, p. 92; 1995, p. 76) explains that hegemony is about constructing alliances, and integrating rather than simply dominating subordinated classes, through concessions, physical force or through ideological means, in order to win consent. He highlights two major ways in which hegemony and discourse are related. First, he argues that hegemonic practices and struggles for hegemony are to a significant degree discursive practices. The concept of hegemony entails the development of practices that naturalise particular relations and ideologies, and these practices are largely discursive. Second, he argues that discourse is itself a sphere of cultural hegemony and the hegemony of a 'group' over society or a section of it (Fairclough 1995, pp. 94–95). In my analysis, the representation of migration/migrants from the Global South as problems for the dominant Swedish society clearly portrays it/them as different and threatening. This negative characterisation often carries with it the consequence of either directly or indirectly legitimising the exclusion of migrants from society (van Dijk 1997, pp. 68–69). Consequently, the discourse that constructs migration/migrants from the Global South as in societal problem, and the tendency for people in the dominant society to accept this as a fact and to use it as a basis for excluding these migrants means that we can see this discourse as hegemonic.

Methodologically, Fairclough (2001) proposes an analytical framework for CDA consisting of five key steps that the researcher should follow. (See Table 1 below for a summary.) The computer software programme MAXQDA was used to organise and analyse the data. The interviews were first coded in an open way; the codes were partly inspired by the research questions and review of the literature. These codes were later refined by looking for redundant codes and by grouping similar codes into larger themes (Strauss & Corbin 1990). This process helped to develop the major themes and sub-themes and to form a perspective on each of them.

Table 1. Analytic framework for CDA (based on Fairclough 2001)[4]

Step	Explanation
1. Focus on a social problem that has a semiotic aspect.	In this study the problem of analysis is the exclusion, through various discursive practices, of Cameroonian students in Sweden.
2. Identify obstacles to the social problem being tackled.	This step deals with diagnosing the problem under study. The aim of this step is to reveal how differences between social collectives are hierarchical. To carry out this task in my study, we need to focus on how structural and institutional conditions in society exclude migrants. In other words, we need to show that dominant structures and institutions embrace discursive practices that exclude migrants.
3. Consider whether the social order in a sense 'needs' the problem.	This step entails posing questions related to ideology. For example, to what extent are the semiotic aspects of the social problem under study helpful in sustaining the present social order, with its patterns of power and domination? In my study, anti-immigration rhetoric and perceived homogeneity of Swedish society provide legitimacy for institutionalised practices that exclude migrants. Fairclough explains that it is important to show this connection in order to convince people that change is needed.
4. Identify possible ways past the obstacle.	Aside from the elements holding the semiosis together, we must also analyse the variations, gaps and contradictions within the orders of discourse that we study. This can, according to Fairclough, be a way of discerning previously unrealised potentials for change. An example could be to show that there are other voices or ways of representing social reality.
5. Reflect critically on the analysis.	Finally, we must reflect on how the results of our CDA can contribute to emancipatory change.

Analysing the experiences of Cameroonian students in Sweden

The section below examines the difficulties that some Cameroonian students face when they encounter Swedish institutions. The analysis here focuses on excerpts, which highlight some of the recurring themes in the interviews. However, the size of the sample and qualitative nature of the study means that the results cannot be generalised as is customary in quantitative research.

Migrant encounters with dominant institutions

The interview below describes an encounter between a man from Cameroon and two customs officers. The interview was conducted at the home of the interviewee on a weekend afternoon.

> *Tala*[5]: Another incident was with customs officers when I was travelling by train from Copenhagen to Malmö. Some customs officers came with police dogs, you know how when they see a black[6] guy they like to bring the dog to him, even when it walks away they try to force it on you. The customs officers were patrolling the train and one of them came with a dog and the dog passed me, but he stopped and pulled the dog towards me. I asked why he was forcing the dog on me and he started yelling and wanted to start a fight. I reported the matter to my school the next day, but they said the man apologised, and that I should let it go.
>
> *Interviewer*: Why did you report this to the school authorities?
>
> *Tala*: I felt that only the school could back me up, they [customs officers] collaborate with the police and I felt that the police would support the customs officers if I reported what happed to them, it would have been like complaining to their colleagues.

The above interview highlights Tala's perception of injustice and his reaction to it. The statement 'you know how when they see a black guy they like to bring the dog to him' suggests that it is common knowledge among black men living in Malmö that customs officials in the area always subject black people to that kind of treatment. As the interviewer was a black man and fellow Cameroonian, Tala could have expected him to recognise this particular narrative as an aspect of common knowledge. The statement suggests that Tala considers his background as a black person to be the reason why the customs officer wanted the dog to search him. In this regard, the statement represents Tala, and black people in general, as victims of a system that is 'out to get them'. In this sense, Tala's representation of what happened can be seen as minority discourse and also constitutes a genre of its own that has developed in opposition to the majority discourse. It is different from the dominant discourse that mainly represents migrants as a problem. Tala's negative representation of the police and the criminal justice system as biased and less than impartial can be contrasted with his much more 'positive' representation of the university, to which he turned for help after his encounter with the customs official. His perception of discrimination in this particular example links a specific institution (and not the entire Swedish state) to the problem.

It is possible that the customs officer wanted to perform a thorough search of Tala because he had reason to be suspicious of him. Tala, however, seems certain that his appearance was the cause of the officer's action. The question is: Why would he think so? A recent report about the criminal justice system in Sweden by Martens et al. (2008) indicates that people with visible immigrant origin and other minorities are more likely to be subjected to 'random' stops and searches by law enforcement officers. The report shows that there are highly prejudiced informal codes and attitudes among professionals of the criminal justice system in Sweden. These informal codes and attitudes, as indicated in the report, are often based on generalised preconceptions about individuals with a non-Swedish background. In addition, the report shows that the prejudiced attitudes and behaviour are often legitimised by routine work practices, institutional/organisational argots and directives. Examples given in the report include racial profiling and directives that identify minority ethnic groups as more prone to criminality. This report and other studies strongly suggest that the criminal justice system in Sweden treats migrants unfairly (Martens et al. 2008; see also Bunar 2007). In addition to the criminal justice system, other influential dominant institutions like the press and welfare institutions show similar prejudice against migrants/minorities. In a study about how the media represent robberies by youths in Sweden, Lindgren (2009, p. 70) argues that 'youth robberies' are represented in the media as crimes that are perpetrated by migrants against Swedes. Similarly, in political debates, as shown by Norman (2004, p. 214), criminality is represented as an integral part of migrant culture. These representations by the media, political elites and state institutions directly influence ordinary people's views of migrants (cf. van Dijk 2007).

In conclusion, the idea that migrants are prone to criminality seems to be deeply embedded in major institutions in Sweden, including those charged with the maintenance of law and order. As a result, the action of the customs officer who brought the dog to Tala can be seen as a common practice that is influenced by a certain ideology. It is ideological because the treatment of migrants as suspect by officials of the criminal justice system is influenced by a deep-seated belief that migrants are prone to criminality. This can also be seen as hegemonic because it successfully constructs migrants as the 'enemy' that threaten cohesion and stability, positioning them as outsiders who do not belong (cf. Laclau & Mouffe 1985).

In the next example, we examine an encounter between two men from Cameroon and officials at the tax office. The interview was conducted at the university after the day's classes and a follow-up interview took place in a café a few days later. In both cases we used a quiet and 'private' place for the interviews.

> *Njoya*: A guy from Cameroon had a one-year student visa to study in Sweden, and the law in Sweden allows people with a one-year visa to get a 'personnummer' [personal identity number, or the Swedish national identification number]. I took him to the tax office where the 'personnummer' is issued and the man we met was reluctant to serve us, he took the passport from the guy and asked where he got it. I was like wow! Because on every passport there is the nationality of the bearer and you could see that the visa on the passport was issued in Sweden. After some time he [the tax office official] said, you cannot get the 'personnummer' because you have

already stayed for some time. I am very sorry, bye. I just laughed because I am a bit used to the system. It was a very funny attitude and I told the guy who was with me that in order to avoid any confrontation we should leave and try to talk to a different person the next day. We returned to the tax office the next day and met a different man. He looked at the passport, made a copy and a week and half later the 'personnummer' was sent to us. This is how people in different offices treat you and it is up to you to handle the problem in your own way.

The purpose of many governments, use of identification numbers and documents is to keep track of their citizens and residents in areas such as work, taxation and welfare benefits. In welfare research, relations between the state and its people are often defined in terms of rights and obligations, and the encounter between the state and its people often takes place through bureaucratic agencies (Hasenfeld et al. 1987). The bureaucracies, according to Hasenfeld et al. (1987, p. 397), are mandated to determine eligibility, levels of entitlements, and the actual benefits people can receive from government. With respect to this particular case, the Swedish personal identification number is very necessary. It is required for personal services at different institutions like health care, banks, insurance companies, house rental companies and so on. In relation to migrants, it can provide them with many of the rights and obligations that Swedish citizens have. It is, however, important to note that bureaucratic institutions and organisations, like the tax office, are structured to reflect and reaffirm the broad cultural, normative and symbolic justification for the welfare state (Hasenfeld et al. 1987, p.398). What this means from a CDA perspective is that bureaucratic institutions and organisations function in ways that sustain and reproduce power relations that we also find elsewhere in society.

> [C]onsequential power relationships, and gross inequalities of income, can be seen to be sustained by networks of reasonable people all doing perfectly normal and routine things, sustained by a symbolic discourse which legitimates some actions and denigrates or prohibits others (Dennis & Martin 2005, pp. 208–209).

In the encounter between Njoya/his friend and the tax office official, it can be argued that eligible people's routine processes of obtaining and renewing ID cards at the tax office enforce and reproduce power relations and inequalities in society. These processes create a distinction between those who have a Swedish 'personnummer' and those who do not, thus facilitating exclusionary practices which take place in habitualised everyday encounters between migrants and bureaucrats in Swedish institutions. This notion of power resonates strongly with the view that power is omnipresent. 'Power is everywhere; not because it embraces everything, but because it comes from everywhere' (Foucault 1990, p. 93). Ordinary people's daily interactions within established institutions produce structures of domination. In this particular case, Njoya and his friend succeeded in acquiring the necessary document at a later date, but it is also important to note that the tax office strictly regulates the issuing of the 'personnummer' to migrants. This function of the tax office makes it look like an agent of border control within the nation-state, and the action of the tax officer who refused to issue Njoya's friend with a 'personnummer' can be seen as an attempt to enforce the 'internal border' control.

The next section examines the discursive practices that discriminate against migrants as they come into contact with 'ordinary' Swedes and classmates at the university.

Migrant interaction with 'native' Swedes

In the interview below, Dugah describes some of the challenges that he has had to face as a student at the university. The interview was conducted in his home. In a follow-up question about his experiences of Sweden – where, among other things, he talked about the difficulties that he had faced since arriving in the country – I asked him about his experiences of the university in Sweden.

> *Dugah*: First, the way of teaching and doing things are different and it is difficult at the beginning. Here, they [students] work in groups most of the time, whereas back home it is not like that. The first major difficulty, which I had, was that in class [study] groups had

already been formed; friends got together to form a group and I found myself trying to work alone. And the social sciences require that you work in groups. It is not like mathematics, for example, where you can work alone. In the social sciences it is very important that you exchange ideas with other people.

Interviewer: Did you succeed in getting into a group later on?

Dugah: You try to find a group that is accessible; what you do is look for a group with people who are open and welcoming. You can figure this out from the way that they behave towards you.

Interviewer: Could you explain the kind of behaviour that can make you know if people are open to you?

Dugah: First, everything begins with the way we sit and interact in class. The teacher sometimes asks us to discuss with the people around us in groups for about ten minutes during lectures, and when you talk to the people in your group you pay attention to the way they respond to you. Even after class you might try to interact with them, and the way that they respond helps you to make a judgement about them.

Dugah highlights two main problems that affect him. The first is that he did not have a study group at the beginning, adding it was difficult for him to work alone. His understanding of the problem was that 'friends' had already formed groups, implying that he did not have any 'friend' in the class. The second problem, which is closely related to the first, is that he did not conceive of his peers as readily accessible for interaction within and outside classroom situations. Both problems highlight the importance of social ties and the disadvantages involved in not having them. Studies about social ties show that they are not formed randomly, but often between people who find each other resourceful in one way or another (Bourdieu 1997; Putnam 2000, p. 20). This is perhaps why social ties are possible between some people and not between others. Studies in Australia and Norway show that there is a degree of social distance between students from abroad and those from the host country (Sam 2001; Rosenthal et al. 2007). A study by Rosenthal et al. (2007, p. 76) provides further evidence that students from abroad easily form social ties with people whose cultural background is similar to their own. The above interview with Dugah simply tells us that he worked alone in class even though the task required work in study groups, and he did this because there was nobody to form a study group with. It also appears as if he could not join any of the established study groups because he felt that the members were not quite open to him. Later on in the interview, he elaborated further on the reasons why he was the only person in class without a study group.

> *Dugah*: They [students] came from different countries, but often you can find two or three students from the same country. Even if they come from different parts of the country it is easy for them to stick together since they speak the same language.
> *Interviewer*: The students on the course that you are talking about came from which national backgrounds?
> *Dugah*: I was the only African, the rest came from Germany, France, Sweden, Finland, the Czech Republic, Russia; no, not Russia, but Poland. These were the countries where most of the students came from.

It seems that if there were other students from Cameroon or any other African country, Dugah might have formed a group with them. The fact that he found it difficult to join a study group, or informal social network with the European students, highlights the importance of the argument that social distance exists between students with different cultural backgrounds (Rosenthal et al. 2007, p. 76; Bhopal 2008, p. 189). Social ties, whether weak or strong, can in this respect be said to be of 'structural' significance because they are based on the 'social' traits of the people involved. A proponent of this view is Michael Eve (2002), who argues that it is not only cultural similarities or so-called categorical characteristics that structure the formation of friendship, but also a strong configurational logic.

> Who becomes a friend seems to be determined not solely by individual attraction but above all by the potential for enriching and maintaining another relationship which is already important. A neighbour may become a friend when the respective children play

together happily, or when there is some basis for distinguishing oneself from others in the neighbourhood, thus constructing an identity as 'more enlightened', 'more respectable', etc. So some friendships may not be a question of reinforcing certain important relationships, but also of distancing oneself from others (whether one's husband or one's neighbour), marking the social boundary of one's separate identity (Eve 2002, p. 401).

From the above argument, a conclusion can be drawn that friendship both reinforces and produces exclusive identities that have the potential to perpetuate existing structures of inequality in society. This can be the case, for example, when the network of friends in a particular setting is composed of people with a middle class background or members of another dominant group in society. Given that supporting each other is one of the things friends do (Eve 2002, p. 401), we can say that it is more beneficial to have social ties with people who are well-connected and 'successful' in society than it is with those who are not. Excluding the latter from the social networks of the former also has the effect of excluding them from resources in society, because the more successful or privileged people in society control pivotal resources (Bourdieu 1997; Behtoui 2009). What can be said about this is that if social ties among students at the university reinforces and reproduce the notion of a homogenous Swedish or even European identity, they also serve to buttress existing structural relations that exclude people with non-European backgrounds in Sweden.

The next interview with Njoya involves a similar problem, as he explains that it is easier to socialise with students from abroad than with Swedish students.

Njoya: With due respect to Swedish lecturers and to all Swedes, it is my observation that Swedes are a bit reluctant to share their emotions with people they do not know.[7] They like to keep to themselves. This is something which is not just peculiar to those you meet on the street but also with those you meet in school. They do not open up, so no matter what you are going through it is difficult to know how they feel about you [laughing]. That is how it is and I have learned to accommodate it. I even find this attitude with my schoolmates, I mean my Swedish schoolmates. It was very hard to talk to them, very hard to share my experiences with them, but it was easy to talk to people from outside Sweden and to understand each other, especially when it comes to challenges that we face.

Njoya points out that there is some social distance between him and 'native' Swedes. From his point of view, the cause of the problem is that Swedes do not like to interact with people they do not know. Njoya's laughter in the interview appears to be an expression of disapproval of 'native' Swedes; later on, he states that 'it was easy to talk to people from outside Sweden'. This can be taken to imply that everybody from outside Sweden is easy to talk to and socially accessible, whereas 'native' Swedes are not.[8] This is a stereotypical view of 'native' Swedes and is clearly denigrating. Still, the focus of my analysis is not to discredit this stereotype, but rather to reflect on the reasons *why* 'native' Swedes are viewed in this way and the possible implications.

In CDA, stereotypes are depicted as negative characterisations, and they are often attributed to the *stigmatisation* of a social collective (Krzyżanowski & Wodak 2009, p. 15; cf. Goffman 1963, pp. 13–14). In this field, stereotypes are portrayed as (re-) producing an exclusive identity and as associating a particular social collective with characteristics that are often undesirable. However, the precise material consequences of the stereotype depends on power relations (Link & Phelan 2001).

> [S]tigmatisation is entirely contingent on access to social, economic, and political power that allows the identification of differentness, the construction of stereotypes, the separation of labelled persons into distinct categories, and the full execution of disapproval, rejection, exclusion, and discrimination (Link & Phelan 2001, p. 367).

From this notion of stereotypes it can be stated that migrants and minorities produce their own stereotypes of the dominant group, but such stereotypes generally do not have the same impact as the ones about migrants produced by the dominant group. However, stereotypes about 'natives' by migrants challenge the popular perception of the former as the ideal and perfect identity. They do so by representing 'natives' as an undesirable category and implicitly suggesting that the migrant identity is the better one.

Njoya explained in the quote that it was very difficult for him to interact with 'natives' and that he learned to accommodate the problem. Remember that earlier on, Njoya and his friend encountered a problem with a tax office official and dealt with it by walking away. If walking away is how he deals with his problems, it is possible that his way of dealing with the problem of 'natives' not interacting with him was by avoiding them. This suggests that he formed social ties with mostly other migrants. If 'natives' and migrants avoid interacting with each other, the outcome will be the (re-)production of exclusive social networks and identities. Such outcomes clearly suggest that the actions of 'natives' and migrants can contribute to the problems. However, the formation of exclusive social networks and identities by 'natives' and migrants cannot be viewed in the same way because of the power relations between the two groups. While exclusive 'native' social networks and identities (re-)produce the exclusion of migrants, exclusive migrant social networks and identities need to be seen as a form of resistance or empowerment:

> The idea of being marginalised and different was emphasised by many of the women. It was one of the reasons why women felt they wanted to belong to a group that consisted of women with whom they could identify. It was also about being accepted by women who would not marginalise or discriminate against them based on where they came from, their religion, their dress (Bhopal 2008, p. 189).

The concept of hegemony can be used to explain the impact of social distance between students from Cameroon and 'native' Swedes. It can be argued that the social distance between them (re-)produces homogenising identities on each side. This perpetuates structural relations of power that in turn exclude the students from Cameroon or indeed any other migrant group. The formation of homogenising identities also needs to be understood as a social process that attempts to minimise internal differences within each group.

Some of the most common and severe forms of discrimination against migrants in Sweden can be found in the area of employment and the acquisition of accommodation (Bråmå 2006; Neergaard 2009). The next and final section examines the experience of Cameroonians in the housing and labour markets.

Immigrant access to material resources

The limited access to good and affordable accommodation constitutes a major problem in the city of Malmö (Andersson 2003). Migrants generally face severe housing problems such as overcrowding and living in disreputable residential areas (ibid.). The majority of the people in this study live in student housing, but the stories of how they acquired their accommodation reveal some major difficulties which they face. The interview below is with a woman, Ebango, who gave up after having failed several times to rent a flat. In the first three academic terms she stayed in different sublets, often in overcrowded flats, before a Cameroonian neighbour finally helped her to get her own flat.

> *Interviewer*: How did you get your flat?
>
> *Ebango*: There was a Cameroonian living close to me and when I was asked to move out he sympathised with me. He was going to Brussels and did not plan to come back to Sweden. He went to the housing company and explained that I was his girlfriend, that he was going to Brussels and when he came back he would want us to move to a different flat in the building. He said he would be happy if I could move in straight away because he had already signed out of his flat. The man we met said I should choose any flat on the fifth floor where all the flats were newly constructed and vacant. I chose the flat which I have now.
>
> *Interviewer*: Do you think without his intervention it would have been difficult to get the flat?
>
> *Ebango*: Yes, because so many people tried to get housing in the building and did not succeed. I do not know why they gave John

[the man who helped her] preference, because what he said was simply that I did not have a place to live so it would be nice if they could give me an flat. The man at the housing company asked if he should use John's name on the contract and John said no, he should use my name. By then I did not have a 'personnummer' and the man said they do not give housing to people who do not have a 'personnummer'. John asked if it was the 'personnummer' or money that pays the rents and convinced the man to give me the flat.

There does not seem to be any specific cause that made it difficult for Ebango to get housing. However, there are different factors that could account for this problem. First, the general housing shortages in Malmö certainly contributed to the problem. Second, the rental policies of the major housing providers in the city also appear to place limitations on students from abroad. For example, among the major housing companies that provide student housing in Malmö, only MKB Fastighets AB has translated some of the information on its website into English. The rest only communicate in Swedish. This is, of course, a problem that mostly affects students from abroad, because many of the study programmes and courses for foreign students are in English and knowledge of the Swedish language is not a prerequisite for admission. With the exception of exchange students who are able to get housing through the university, most so-called free-movers who do not understand Swedish have to go through a great deal of trouble to obtain information about housing. In *Language and Symbolic Power* by Bourdieu and Thompson (1991, p. 37), it is explained that language is not simply an object of contemplation; rather, it is an instrument of action and power. This argument echoes the view in CDA that language, as well as other forms of semiosis, is intertwined with structures (economic, political and cultural) of subordination (Fairclough 2006, pp. 30–31). Language in this case excludes those who do not understand Swedish from the housing market. It is important to note that in many other Swedish university towns the providers of student housing supply all the important information about their accommodation on their websites in both Swedish and English. Finally, it also appears that individual officials in housing companies can influence whether a potential tenant gets a flat or not. It can be discerned from the interview that other people had tried to get accommodation in the same building where Ebango had managed to acquire hers, but they failed. However, it is not known why they were unsuccessful or if they met the same official who gave Ebango the accommodation. The fact that the official rented out the flat to Ebango without a *personnummer* suggests that individual officials in housing companies (and other organisations) can perpetuate or inhibit structural/institutional discrimination against migrants.

The next interview is about the labour market. It shows how some Cameroonian students use social ties to tackle some of the challenges of the labour market.

> *Abega*: You can see that the majority of the people working got their jobs through third parties who introduced them to the right contacts. I think that is how many people get jobs [in Malmö]. If you take my case, for example, it took me one week to get a newspaper job [distributing newspapers in the morning] and there were people who had struggled for more than a year to get a job at the same place. What helped me is that an African man who works there recommended me to the boss. The African man got a job at the place through his wife [a 'native' Swede]. After getting the job he has recommended many other people. I was the sixth or seventh person [all from Cameroon and Nigeria] who got a job through his recommendation.

The first of two major points made is the importance of social ties for gaining employment and how difficult it can be for job seekers to find work if they do not have the right contacts. This is clearly what Abega implies when he explains that he was able to secure a job one week after the recommendation, whereas others had tried to find work during the previous year with no success. It is remarkable that the man from Africa gained employment at the company through his 'native' Swedish wife. This suggests not only that social ties are generally important, but also that it is important to know people who are actually in a position to help you.

The second point is that the interview with Abega shows how one

African employee is influential in the employment of a further seven Africans in the same company. In the interview with him I realised that it is the same type of job that all of them are doing. The general labour market statistics there show that migrants from Africa have one of the lowest employment rates in Malmö (Broomé et al. 2007, p. 21). This is also the case in the rest of the country (Integrations-verket 2006, p. 47). The study by Broomé et al. shows that Swedes, and especially men, occupy the top managerial positions, followed by people who are born in the other Nordic countries and the EU. The statistics also illustrate that people from Latin America, Asia and Africa are less likely to occupy top managerial positions (Broomé et al. 2007, p. 21). The findings suggest that there is a segmentation of the Swedish labour market and that there seem to be distinctive ethnic niches consisting of migrants from countries in the Global South at the bottom of the labour pyramid. The people involved in the previously described scenario and Abega's situation indicate the presence of subordinated inclusion (Neergaard 2009), because they are not completely excluded from the labour market. They are, however, employed in unskilled and low-paid jobs.

Conclusion

This chapter has shown Cameroonian students in this study to be included and excluded in Swedish society in different spheres of life. They are included as legal residents, with many rights and benefits. For example, they have access to education, healthcare and other resources/services on more or less the same terms as Swedish citizens. However, they are subject to discrimination by specific institutions like the criminal justice system, which perceives them as an interior threat to public security. Structural and institutional conditions, such as the labour and housing markets do – as we have seen – make it difficult for them to secure good employment and housing.

Fairclough (2001) outlined a methodological guide for carrying out CDA, which entails moving through a number of steps. I have systematically employed this method in my analysis. The first step requires that we focus on a problem which has a semiotic aspect. The analysis has shown that a widespread negative representation of migrants promotes discrimination against them. In the second step, Fairclough states that attention should be paid to the obstacles that stand in the way of the problem that is being tackled. The social problem in this study is the exclusion of Cameroonians who study in Sweden and how they experience it. As legal residents and students in Sweden, they have many rights, and discrimination against minorities in general is unconstitutional in Sweden and thus illegal. This means that it is difficult to convince people that structural/institutional conditions in Sweden exclude migrants. By applying the analytical framework of CDA, it has been shown that the exclusion of Cameroonian students in Sweden has very little to do with legalised discrimination. The problem has more to do with structural and power relations generally taken for granted. Here, the concept of power helps to show that everyday practices like the formation of closed network ties can have the effect of excluding minorities if they are not accepted in the social networks of members of the dominant society. This appears to be one of the problems facing the Cameroonian migrants in this study because they are also members of a racialised group within Swedish society (Pred 2004; Schmauch 2006). They belong to a minority; namely, people with an African background who are highly overrepresented among the unemployed, have limited access to quality accommodation and occupy lower positions in the labour market (Bråmå 2006; Neergaard 2009; Ngeh 2009). In the third step, Fairclough suggests that we should find out whether the problem that is being studied helps to sustain the social order. In this particular case, discursive practices within various institutionalised settings such as the criminal justice system exclude migrants in the sense that they discursively construct them as threatening 'outsiders'. Furthermore, the false image of migrants as threatening outsiders appears to be widely accepted and used to legitimise their exclusion. In this case it is clear that the exclusion of migrants helps to maintain the existing social order, with its patterns of unequal power relations and domination of minorities. The fourth step requires that the gaps and contradictions are shown within the order of discourse. The studied discursive practices exclude migrants in some respects and include them in others. This indicates that there are different discourses at work at any given time. In the last step,

Fairclough recommends that researchers should reflect on how their analyses can contribute to emancipatory change. By drawing attention to how power and structural/institutional practices exclude minorities, this study hopes to create awareness about these issues which are often ignored because the production of discourse is carried out in a way that conceals both its power and danger (Foucault 1981, p. 52).

Notes

1 The project is funded by the Department of Sociology, University of Umeå, Sweden.
2 All respondents were enrolled in undergraduate or Master's degree programmes at the time of the interviews. They attended the universities in Malmö and Lund but only the material of the informants who lived in Malmö is used in the analysis. All interviews were recorded and are kept by the author.
3 The Aliens Act (1989: 529 'Utlänningslagen' in Swedish) defines a refugee as someone 'who is outside the country of which he is a national, owing to well-founded fear of being persecuted for reasons of race, nationality, membership of a particular social group, or religious or political opinion and who is unable or, owing to such fear, is unwilling to avail himself of the protection of that country' (Lithman 1987, p. 16). I adopt this definition of refugee in my analysis.
4 My analysis also draws on Lindgren's (2009, p. 68) interpretation and application of the analytical framework proposed by Fairclough.
5 In order to protect the informants' identities, all names used in the interviews are pseudonyms.
6 In the interview, Tala uses the term 'black' to refer to a person from sub-Saharan Africa or a person of visible sub-Saharan descent. I use it in the same sense throughout the text.
7 The term Swede, as used by Njoya, refers to 'native' Swedes.
8 In the interview, Njoya explained that he had good social contacts with foreign students and lecturers from other European countries and the USA.

References

Abiri, E., 2000. *The Securitisation of Migration: Towards an Understanding of Migration Policy Changes in the 1990s, the Case of Sweden.* Gothenburg: Department of Peace and Development Research, University of Gothenburg.

Andersson, B., 2003. *Fyra stadsdelar – fyra vägar mot integration. Storstadssatsningen i Malmö: utvärdering av demokratiarbete och skolprojekt.* Malmö: Malmö stad.

Behtoui, A., 2009. Social Capital and Stigmatised Immigrants. In: A. Neergaard (ed.), *European Perspectives on Exclusion and Subordination: The Political Economy of Migration.* Maastricht: Shaker Publishing, pp. 223–237.

Bhopal, K., 2008. Shared Communities and Shared Understandings: The Experiences of Asian Women in a British University. *International Studies in Sociology of Education*, 18(3–4), pp. 185–197.

Bourdieu, P. 1997. The Forms of Capital. In: A.H. Halsey et al. (eds), *Education: Culture, Economy, and Society*. Oxford, New York: Oxford University Press.

Bourdieu, P. & Thompson, J. B., 1991. *Language and Symbolic Power*. Cambridge: Harvard University Press.

Brämå, Å., 2006. *Studies in the Dynamics of Residential Segregation*. Uppsala: Department of Social and Economic Geography, Uppsala University.

Broomé, P. et al., 2007. Quantitative Indicators of Diversity: Content or Packaging? *Current Themes in IMER Research*. Malmö: IMER, Malmö University College.

Bunar, N., 2007. Hate Crimes against Immigrants in Sweden and Community Responses. *American Behavioral Scientis*, 51(2), pp. 166–181.

Chouliaraki, L. & Fairclough, N., 1999. *Discourse in Late Modernity: Rethinking Critical Discourse Analysis*. Edinburgh: Edinburgh University Press.

Delanty, G. et al. (eds), 2008. *Identity, Belonging and Migration*. Liverpool: Liverpool University Press.

Dennis, A. & Martin, P., 2005. Symbolic Interactionism and the Concept of Power. *British Journal of Sociology*, 56(2), pp. 191–213.

Eve, M., 2002. Is Friendship a Sociological Topic? *Archives Europeennes de Sociologie*, 43(3), pp. 386–409.

Fairclough, N., 1992. *Discourse and Social Change*. Cambridge: Polity.

Fairclough, N., 1995. *Critical Discourse Analysis: The Critical Study of Language*. London: Longman.

Fairclough, N., 2001. Critical Discourse Analysis as a Method in Social Scientific Research. In: Wodak, R. & Meyer, M. (eds), *Methods of Critical Discourse Analysis*. London: Sage Publications Ltd.

Fairclough, N., 2006. *Language and Globalization*. London: Routledge.

Foucault, M., 1981. The Order of Discourse. In: R. Young (ed.), *Untying the Text*. London: Routledge & Kegan Paul Ltd, pp. 48–78.

Foucault, M., 1990. *The History of Sexuality. Vol. 1, An Introduction*. New York: Random House, Inc.

Goffman, E., 1963. *Stigma: Notes on the Management of Spoiled Identity*. Englewood Cliffs, N.J.: Prentice-Hall.

Gramsci, A., 1971. *Selections from the Prison Notebooks of Antonio Gramsci*. New York: International Publisher.

Hasenfeld, Y. et al., 1987. The Welfare-State, Citizenship, and Bureaucratic Encounters. *Annual Review of Sociology*, 13, pp. 387–415.

Integrationsverket, 2006. *Pocket Facts: Statistics on Integration*. Norrköping: Integrationsverket.

Krzyżanowski, M. & Wodak, R., 2009. *The Politics of Exclusion: Debating Migration in Austria*. New Brunswick, London: Transaction.

Laclau, E., 1996. *Emancipation(s)*. London: Verso.

Laclau, E. & Mouffe, C., 1985. *Hegemony and Socialist Strategy: Towards a Radical Democratic Politics*. London: Verso.

Lindgren, S., 2009. Representing Otherness in Youth Crime Discourse: Youth

Robberies and Racism in the Swedish Press 1998–2002. *Critical Discourse Studies*, 6(1), pp. 65–77.

Link, B. & Phelan, J., 2001. Conceptualizing stigma. *Annual Review of Sociology*, 27, pp. 363–385.

Lithman Lundberg, E., 1987. *Immigration and Immigrant Policy in Sweden*. Stockholm: Swedish Institute.

Martens, P. et al., 2008. *Discrimination in the Criminal Justice Process in Sweden*, Brottsförebyggande rådet (BRÅ) report No. 2008:4. Stockholm: Brottsförebyggande rådet.

Mercer, C. et al., 2008. *Development and the African Diaspora: Place and the Politics of Home*. London & New York: Zed Books.

Mercer, C. et al., 2009. Unsettling Connections: Transnational Networks, Development and African Home Associations. *Global Networks – A Journal of Transnational Affairs*, 9(2), pp. 141–161.

Neergaard, A., 2009. Racialisation in the Labour Market: In Search of a Theoretical Understanding. In: A. Neergaard (ed.), *European Perspectives on Exclusion and Subordination: The Political Economy of Migration*. Maastricht: Shaker Publishing, pp. 201–221.

Ngeh, J., 2009. Challenges and Aspirations of Somali Youth Immigrants in Sweden. In: G. Katsas (ed.), *Sociology in a Changing World: Challenges and Perspectives*. Athens: ATINER, pp. 191–202.

Norman, K., 2004. Equality and Exclusion: 'Racism' in a Swedish Town. *Ethnos*, 69(2), pp. 204–228.

Nyamnjoh, F.B. & Rowlands, M., 1998. Elite Associations and the Politics of Belonging in Cameroon. *Africa*, 68(3), pp. 320–337.

Pelican, M., 2008. Mbororo Claims to Regional Citizenship and Minority Status in North-West Cameroon. *Africa*, 78(4), pp. 540–560.

Pineteh, E., 2008. Cultural Associations, Clothing and Food as Markers of Cultural Identity in Testimonies of Cameroonian Forced Migrants in Johannesburg. *African and Black Diaspora: An International Journal*, 1(1), pp. 87–99.

Pred, A., 2004. *The Past is not Dead: Facts, Fictions, and Enduring Racial Stereotypes*, Minneapolis: University of Minnesota Press.

Putnam, R.D., 2000. *Bowling Alone: The Collapse and Revival of American Community*. New York: Simon & Schuster.

Räthzel, N., 2006. From Individual Heroism to Political Resistance: Young People Challenging Everyday Racism on the Labour Market. *Journal of Education and Work*, 19(3), pp. 219–235.

Rosenthal, D. et al., 2007. Social Connectedness among International Students at an Australian University. *Social Indicators Research*, 84(1), pp. 71–82.

Sam, D., 2001. Satisfaction with Life among International Students: An Exploratory Study. *Social Indicators Research*, 53(3), pp. 315–337.

Schmauch, U., 2006. *Den osynliga vardagsrasismens realitet*. (Diss.) Umeå: Sociologiska institutionen, Umeå universitet.

Strauss, A. & Corbin, J., 1990. *Basics of Qualitative Research: Grounded Theory Procedures and Techniques*. Newbury Park, Calif.: Sage.

Statistiska centralbyrån, 2007. *Tabeller över Sveriges befolkning 2006, Sveriges officiella statistik.* Örebro: Statistiska centralbyrån.
van Dijk, T.A., 1997. Discourse, Ethnicity, Culture and Racism. In: T.A. van Dijk (ed.), *Discourse as Social Interaction. Discourse Studies: A Multidisciplinary Introduction.* London, Thousand Oaks, New Delhi: Sage. 2, pp. 144–180.
van Dijk, T.A., 2007. Discourse and the Denial of Racism. In: T.A. van Dijk (ed.), *Discourse Studies.* Los Angeles, London, New Delhi, Singapore: Sage. 5, pp. 208–237.
Westin, C., 2006. Sweden: Restrictive Immigration Policy and Multiculturalism. Stockholm: Centre for Research in International Migration and Ethnic Relations, Stockholm University.
Wodak, R., 2008. 'Us' and 'Them': Inclusion and Exclusion – Discrimination via Discourse. In: G. Delanty et al. (eds), *Identity, Belonging and Migration.* Liverpool: Liverpool University Press, pp. 241–260.

CHAPTER 6

The Construction of Paternity Leave in Swedish Television

Mathias Sylwan

The question of why men choose not to stay at home with their children has caused a great deal of political and scholarly debate in Sweden, a country that is internationally renowned for its progressive welfare policies. The reasons behind the debate have been interpreted and explained in many different ways. During the 1960s, an intense debate on gender took place in Sweden. Radical debaters argued that gender roles were the result of upbringing rather than innate individual characteristics (Hill 2003, p. 51). The result of the debate was a call for male liberation: If roles were not congenital, they could be changed. Men could then have the opportunity to develop 'their whole person' and free themselves from old-fashioned and imprisoning gender roles (Hill 2003, p. 51). In 1974 the Swedish parliament voted for the implemetation of an insurance for parents. The reform can be described as an important juncture for family politics in the country (Klinth 2002, p. 30). This insurance includes the idea that both parents are entitled to economic compensation for loss of income during the time that they are at home taking care of their children. However, the aim is not solely to strengthen the family economy, but includes creating conditions for parents to combine paid work or studies with parenthood so that children have access to both parents (SOU 2005:73, p. 77). In other words, the insurance has the child's best interests at heart and contributes to a greater degree of gender equality. The latter coincides with the political ambition to transform gender relations in the family. The goal with a flexible and generous insurance for parents is to encourage fathers to use their parental leave to a greater extent, and to increase the ability of mothers to participate in the labour market on equal terms (Klinth 2002, p. 220). In this chapter the subject is how fathers' parental leave is mediated in the Swedish television news.[1]

From the debate in the 1960s, and the consequent debates over the last thirty years, a new perception of fatherhood has emerged. Society's expectations and demands on fathers' participation in the care of children are greater than ever before. Traditionally, the figure of the good father was synonymous with the breadwinner who worked for his wages outside of the home (Brandth & Kvande 1998, p. 299). The men of today are generally more inclined to be family-oriented and to adopt the role of the everyday dad (Bekkengen 2003). However, this does not necessarily mean that the care of and responsibility for the children is shared or that the relationship between the parents is equal. Nowadays men are torn between traditional paternity and greater involvement in family life (Plantin 2003, p. 159). Bekkengen (2003, pp. 188–191) describes this as a 'child-oriented masculinity', and explains that being oriented towards children is not the same thing as being oriented towards the woman and/or the household. The men of today should form good relations with their children for their own sake. Even if the relationship between fathers and children has changed on a discursive level in the public sphere, the relationship between the parents has remained relatively unaffected (Bekkengen 2003, p. 189).

The mass media has an important function in today's society in relation to people's knowledge about politics (Mårtensson 2003, p. 14), and the question of how parental leave should be divided is no exception. The contents of television programmes play a central role in this context, with news channels being perceived by people as a particularly reliable source of information (Dahlgren 1988, p. 54; Ekström 1999, p. 179). However, the news media are not just information providers, but also supply material for making sense of society and serve to make certain ideas significant. In these ways, television plays an important role because it contributes to reproducing and establishing conceptions of social identities and positions, as well as of knowledge of both societal concerns and individual responsibility.

Aim and material

The aim of this chapter is to examine constructions of fatherhood in Swedish television news from a perspective that is grounded in Michel Foucault's discourse theory.[2] The main source of inspiration is *The Order of Discourse* (Foucault 1993), in which Foucault describes discourse as both objects of knowledge and the exercise of power, and further suggests that they can be studied.[3] I have chosen to focus on what Foucault (Foucault 1993, pp. 7–14) calls *systems of exclusion*. The concept refers to various procedures that combine and contribute to the exclusion of certain objects of knowledge (phenomena, individuals, groups, ideas, perspectives) from a discourse, and the inclusion of others.

The analysed material consists of televised news reports on paternity leave between 1981 and 2005. These reports are from the two popular Swedish public service programmes *Aktuellt* and *Rapport*. The material is taken from the database of the Swedish National Archive of Recorded Sound and Moving Images (SLBA, Statens ljud och bild arkiv). The keyword 'paternity leave' (*pappaledighet* in Swedish) was used in the database search. A total of 66 hits were identified from the period 1 January 1974 to 1 January 2006: 26 from *Aktuellt* and 40 from *Rapport*. A selection of nine articles was chosen for closer analysis because they included interviews with fathers who were on paternity leave and fathers who were not.[4]

The next section in this chapter describes journalism as a discursive practice. In the subsequent section the theoretical perspectives and analytical tools are presented, and the empirical analysis follows. In the last section the results of the analysis are discussed in the light of a Foucauldian perspective. I argue that the news reporting on paternity leave can be understood in terms of Foucault's 'systems of exclusion'; that is, a dividing and at the same time normalising practice. The examples included in this last section should be regarded as an argument for this perspective.

Journalism as a discursive practice

A frequently used concept in Foucault's terminology is *discursive practice* (Foucault 1993; Foucault 2002). The concept can be understood as having a double meaning. Firstly, 'discourse' encompasses everything that is written and spoken about a subject; that is, a practised language by which something is described (Beronius 1987, p. 65). Secondly, the concept is described as a 'practice'; a term that Foucault often relates to institutions such as schools, hospitals and prisons. However, practices are not just places, but represent 'the whole practice [all human acts] which produce a particular type of statement (Foucault 1993, p. 57).[5] Therefore there is no clear boundary between 'discourse' and 'practice'; a relationship that the concept 'discursive practice' is intended to capture. Furthermore, the production of discourses is not random. On the contrary, rules, interests and values uphold them. Discourses maintain, organise and monitor the boundaries through internal discursive self-control and external systems of exclusion (Foucault 1993, pp. 7–32; Foucault 2002, p. 145).

Journalism can be regarded as such a discursive practice. It is an institutionalised activity in which knowledge is constructed on the basis of rules and conventions that specify what good journalism is, how it should be conducted, by whom, and how reality should be described.[6] What counts as good journalism is also the ability to choose what is considered to have news value. The production of news can briefly and simply be described in three steps.[7] The first step is that an event is selected, and the second that the event is made interesting and understandable for an audience. In this step, the event is processed into a news story in accordance with different dramaturgical and narrative devices. In other words, events and phenomena are adapted to the journalistic form, and not vice versa as Berglez argues (2000, p. 205). The third step is that the news story is distributed to an audience.

The interview is one of the most basic forms of news narrative (Ekström 2006, p. 112). A crucial characteristic of an interview is that it consists of certain pre-established roles, and the participants are expected to act according to these roles. The journalist is the one who asks the questions, and the responding interviewee provides the answers. The interviewee, in turn, has to be considered important in relation to the news subject that is covered. This choice is often based on an evaluation of whose knowledge is considered to have the most weight and legitimacy. These interviewees are often given a greater degree of freedom to express themselves than others (Dahlgren 1988, p. 59). Generally, this freedom is only given to individuals from the elite of society and to people with special roles, like politicians and experts of various kinds. When 'ordinary people' are interviewed, they are normally not treated in the same way as people from more privileged groups. Journalists often interview the 'man on the street' first to ask about their opinions, and then let an expert explain what the hard facts of the matter are considered to be.

News interviews are in other words arenas where power is exercised (Ekström 2006, p. 75). The questions of the journalist are usually formulated in such a way that the person being interviewed must respond in some way. An interviewee may for example be given the freedom to comment on or judge something, or the degree of freedom may be more limited because the person is forced to explain a specific point or defend a particular point of view. In other words, a journalistic interview can be said to involve an assessment of the interviewee. What is said during an interview can also be considered to be part of a discourse. Into a special order of utterances that organises the meaning of what is said, as in this case when ideas and opinions regarding paternity leave are expressed in relation to a broader discourse on parenting.

Power and practices

One of Foucault's major contributions was to challenge traditional conceptions of power (Watson 2000, p. 67). Rather than seeing power as a 'punishing' force from above, he proposes that power should be thought of as relational; that is, always a matter of the relationship between, for example, people. However, the relationship between individuals, groups and various structural phenomena can also be referred to as relationships of power (Hörnqvist 1996, p. 29). Power should also be understood as a desire to elevate a certain understanding of reality; that is, what is considered to be common sense. Consequently, power contributes to determining how the world, or parts of it, should be understood, while at the same time pointing out certain acts as possible and relevant within a particular discourse. Power, in Foucault's terms, is a productive force and constitutive of 'reality' (Foucault 1993, p. 227). Therefore, knowledge and truth are produced within power relations. Thoughts and actions are formed and framed by the basic assumptions about reality that exist within a particular discourse. This means that what is perceived as taken for granted or 'natural' could always be different. Hence, the task of the discourse analyst is not so much to investigate who wants power, or why, but rather to describe *how* power is *exercised* (Foucault 1991, p. 59; Foucault 1982, p. 219). In other words, the focus is on practices, not motives.[8] In this particular case the focus is on journalistic practices.

Systems of exclusion

Practices can be investigated by studying institutionally anchored statements and the images of reality they produce. These statements and images are part of what Foucault (1993) calls 'the three great systems of exclusion' that control the production of discourse. These procedures are the *prohibited words*, the *division of madness from reason* and the *will to truth*. The prohibited words govern discourse by regulating what it is possible to speak of, who may speak, when, and in which situations speaking is possible. A speaker must have certain qualifications, a certain role, or speak from a certain position in order to be able to speak with authority (Foucault 1993, p. 7). The basic line of thought is that certain statements are given greater importance than others in any given discourse. A speaker's education, position, way of speaking and other institutional characteristics may influence individuals to listen to certain people and not to others. Experts and representatives of various institutions, such as academics, politicians and journalists, are examples of people who are listened to (Watson 2000, p. 70). They occupy discursive key positions through their power to define a debate, or how a problem should be understood and resolved. Those whose voices will not be attributed equal importance in a discourse are people who are subjected to 'prohibition', and those whose various practices position them as problematic or in some way deviant. Following Foucault, these absent people can be described as 'the other'. They are also frequently the object of discourse because they are described as a problem by the experts (Järvinen 1996, p. 55). The sick, maladjusted and criminals are representatives of subjected groups in Foucault's own texts, but what he describes does not only apply to these groups. They are more general examples of how various discursive practices exclude certain individuals, groups and perspectives and include others.

The second principle, the division of madness from reason, refers to practices that cause rejection or separation. This is a separating mechanism between binary opposites in which one of the 'poles' is counteracted or rejected. In *Discipline and Punish* (1993), Foucault describes how various practices in prisons, schools, the army and the factory have helped to separate and categorise individuals. Monitoring and classification create particular individuals and groups, such as the criminal, the obedient student and the worker. Foucault refers to these processes as forms of discipline. Through various systems of control, classification and punishment, undesirable, erroneous and deviant behaviour is rejected, while behaviour that is considered desirable is rewarded. The combination of different disciplinary practices affects the human psyche and causes people to be reflexive. By being ever-present in people's minds, the disciplinary practices produce a desire to act in line with approved behaviour. In the long run, disciplinary practices contribute to a process of self-transformation in which the individual is actively involved (Foucault 1982, p. 208). The purpose of these discursive processes is to 'normalise' (Foucault 1993, p. 214).

Since journalistic work is largely based on classification, journalism can be regarded as a form of classificatory practice (Ekström 2002). By regularly addressing and representing people in simple terms such as woman/man, mother/father, on parental leave/not on parental leave, journalistic work supplies and reproduces social categories that people can identify with (or reject). Furthermore, the practice of news production often defines anomalies. For example, the comparison of parents' behaviour with an imaginary standard that defines good parenting is a means of evaluating the parents' behaviour.

The third principle is the will to truth. This is about the distinction between truth and falsehood. In the news, this principle is put to work through an argumentative, factual, neutral and supposedly objective narrative style, where different states of affairs are 'proved true' by experts, images and other statements such as statistics. As will be shown, all three principles of exclusion are at work in the news items about parental leave.

Discursive inclusion and exclusion

As previously mentioned, the Swedish parental insurance policy was implemented in 1974. For the first time in history, Swedish men were given the same opportunity as women to stay at home with their children. The 'new man' became a concept and a desirable ideal in the 1970s (Hill 2003, p. 50). Gender equality was a keyword, and men were now expected to participate fully in the family and do their share of the household tasks. At the beginning of the 1980s, the phenomenon of the 'everyday dad' began to gain ground in the media, and in due course this representation of 'modern masculinity' became common as a role model (Plantin 2003, p. 152). Simultaneously, warnings could be heard on the radio and in the press: Men should not be *too* involved in caring for children. In 1983, the 'mother role' that was adopted by men was widely debated in what in colloquial terms became known as 'the velour-father debate' (*velourpappadebatten* in Swedish).[9] A number of psychologists argued that the father's involvement in child-raising could threaten or disrupt the relationship between the mother and the child. The male 'mother role' was also said to pose the risk of creating difficulties in the child's development of his or her gender identity (Hill 2003, p. 53).

Two news features from the period show how the aforementioned trends were reflected in the media. The first example is taken from *Aktuellt* (SVT1, 8 September 1981), which is one of Sweden's most popular news programmes. The news presenter referred to a study in his introduction which found that men on paternity leave 'do not take on the role of a mother when on paternity leave, and that positive things happen with the fathers' attitudes to the whole family when they are at home'. The presenter continued by telling the viewers that 'it is unusual for men from the trade unions to be on paternity leave, and the motives for not staying at home may sound like this…'. The scene then changes to a shopfloor where three men in blue overalls are in the process of being interviewed. A reporter asks them if they might be willing to stay at home with their children. One of the interviewees states that he might be willing to do it for two months. After this reply the reporter addresses the other two men:

> *Reporter*: Would you mind staying home for four months, for example?
> *Second male interviewee*: Nah. I don't think so.
> *Reporter*: Why?
> *Second male interviewee*: No, I can't be bothered with that.
> *Reporter*: But is it okay to ask your wife to do it?
> *Second male interviewee*: No, but she is, she is the one who wants to – so to speak.

The news anchor's introduction foregrounded a particular view of the interviews before the interviewees spoke. The viewers have already learned that families benefit when fathers are on paternity leave. The underlying assumption in the journalist's initial question is that fathers could choose to act differently and this is also what the journalist suggests; namely, that the interviewee has had the opportunity to be on paternity leave but has chosen to work instead. The reporter is implicitly reproaching him for his lack of responsibility and perhaps even morals. The responsibility for the child seems to rest solely on the wife, which means that she is believed to be responsible for all the daily routines like feeding, changing nappies, cleaning and washing. The man is not asked to answer any follow-up questions concerning the reasons behind his answer, or the degree of consensus between himself and his wife regarding childcare and other tasks. Instead, the reporter turns to the third man in the group. The moralising journalistic tone now turns into what can be interpreted as ridicule:

> *Reporter*: How is it, do you feel inadequate when it comes to small children?

Third male interviewee: Nah, not, not so much. It would be changing
nappies, then [laughter from colleagues], then I feel a bit inadequate
… for certain reasons.

Reporter: Why?

Interviewee: Well, it is a bit disgusting really [more laughter from
colleagues].

After this statement from the interviewee, the scene changes. The
viewer now meets a new man, who stands in what appears to be his
home environment changing the nappies of a child. The contrast
between this image and the concluding remark about how disgusting
it is to change nappies makes the scene function as a remark on the
previous statement. The man on the shopfloor *can* change nappies,
but prefers not to because he simply does not like it. The laughter
from his colleagues is also a distinct indication that they also think
in a similar way. In comparison, the person who changes nappies is
treated differently by the reporter:

Reporter: When did you decide to stay at home with your daughter, Sara?

Fourth male interviewee: Actually, I decided that as soon as I, uh,
knew that I could. As I have several children but not had the opportunity to be with them the first years, this was obvious to me.

Reporter: Is it a positive experience?

Fourth male interviewee: Yes, definitely, definitely.

Reporter: Did you have any idea that it was so much work with
small children?

Fourth male interviewee: Yes, I guess I had, because, as I said, I have
a lot of children. And this is a job even when one does not have to
change nappies. Eh, but then one has to take care of them and so
on, and have dinner ready, to ask how it has been in school. So,
there is a lot to do at home and taking care of a baby if you have
several children.

Criricism of the men on the shopfloor is here replaced by kindness
and respect, and the journalist's questions are more open and focused
on an exchange of knowledge on the subject:

Reporter: Has being at home in any way changed your role as a man?
Interviewee: You'd probably not change that because of paternity leave. It's more about generational change. Perhaps my children will benefit from that change and the job I have done bringing them up. They will take that to their hearts and think of it as obvious. I hope that both girls and boys will do their share of work in the household.
Reporter: But this little girl whose nappies you are changing, you must have a rather special relationship with her because you have been with her since she was born?
Interviewee: Uh, yes, it is obviously a different relationship ... But I also think that I am rather mature and capable of taking care of a child. Since I am almost forty, I have quietened down, and I think this is kind of fun.

Compared with the men who were interviewed previously in the news report, this father is given a greater degree of freedom to speak. He is given the opportunity to comment on the reporter's questions, to share his thoughts and reflect on his situation in his own terms. He is also given the opportunity to comment on the public debates of that time because the interview focuses on the role of the man and the mother. According to this particular man, caring for his children is a matter of a developed sense of responsibility. He uses his own words to state that he has such a sense of responsibility, and this sense of responsibility is confirmed visually through his own actions.

At the end of the news report an expert psychologist and researcher is interviewed. The psychologist confirms what the news anchor initially told the viewers; namely, that 'positive things happen with the fathers' attitudes to the whole family when they are at home'. The consequence of this statement is that the expert verifies and legitimises paternity leave, while simultaneously emphasising the failure of the men on the shopfloor. In both of these scenes the image of two different kinds of fathers can be discerned: those blue-collar workers who work, and those who attend to their children. The working man, who is traditionally seen as the breadwinner, is contrasted against a 'new and modern man'. The latter of the two takes paternity leave and is depicted in terms of a conscious and verbal actor. Therefore, this man fits into the societal goal of changing the imbalance of equality in gender relations.

Parental leave as a norm and no 'luxury'

The second example, which was shown in the 1980s, is taken from another important television news programme *Rapport* (SVT2, 7 February 1982). This news story does not focus so much on the male role, but more on why men do not choose to stay at home with their children. In the news report the viewer meets a male laboratory assistant who is on paternity leave. This man is also interviewed in the comfort of his own home. His daily life seems to revolve around childcare activities such as changing nappies, reading stories and playing. A reporter says that he has previously been on paternity leave for eight months because he considers it to be important to develop a close relationship with his son. He now has a new child and plans to stay at home for a further five months. The viewer also learns that he is 'atypical', and that most men are reluctant to stay at home with their children 'because they often face attitudes, and that paternity leave is a luxury in the harsh economic situation we find ourselves in'. The man confirms and comments on the journalist's claim:

> *Interviewee*: An entire career is perhaps forty-five years, and the vacation for that time is fifty months. And during that time one is perhaps on sick leave for ten months. Then there are like four or six months that one spends at home with children, it is a very small part of the total, it makes no difference to production.

Treating paternity leave as a 'luxury' can be understood as a reply to the industry sector's rhetoric. In the late 1970s and early 1980s there was an economic crisis in Sweden. During the 1980s a number of Swedish business leaders attacked paternity leave on the grounds that it was to be regarded as an extravagance in difficult economic times (Klinth 2002, pp. 277–79). Men's responsibility should be primarily focused on the economy of the nation because it was through paid work, and not paternity leave, that fathers could actively contribute to the recovery from the financial crisis. The male interviewee on paternity leave disagrees with this perspective. In his view the Swedish economy will not break down for the sole reason that men choose to stay at home with their children. Paternity leave is not a burden on society. Therefore, he dismisses the arguments that the industry representatives put forward and claims that there are no economic reasons for not taking paternity leave. Men who choose to work against their own wishes can be understood to have listened to the views of their employers and colleagues too much. The reporter does not ask any more questions, which can be interpreted as an acceptance of the opinions that are voiced by the man on paternity leave.

Statistics as 'truths'

Throughout the 1980s, the reason that men did not utilise the parental insurance was put down to 'faulty attitudes' (Klinth 2002, p. 309). The politicians' main task was to help men combat these attitudes, and help them resist the pressure that was exerted on them by employers and workmates. One step that was taken in order to change men's attitudes was to enlighten them (Klinth 2002, p. 307). Through public information campaigns, men would become convinced that it was acceptable to stay at home with their children.

One such example is taken from *Rapport* (SVT 2, 12 August 1989). The news report begins with the news anchor presenting a problem:

> Too few fathers stay at home and take care of their children. And this happens even if the parents' insurance has been improved. Only one in five fathers take paternity leave and usually only for six weeks. And in order to change this, the government has decided to launch a campaign to make fathers reconsider.

The image of the news presenter is then replaced by another scene in which a man and woman are seen in a park. The man is interviewed while a woman with a pram sits beside him. At the bottom of the screen a caption can be seen which states that the man is a bank clerk.

Reporter: Have you been on paternity leave?
Interviewee: No, I have not.
Reporter: Why not?
Interviewee: No, I think, partly I have an important job, I think. I have not thought about it, my wife is managing it very well.

Another man is then interviewed in the same surroundings:

Reporter: Have you ever thought of taking paternity leave?
Interviewee: No, not now. Because I have such an unusual job, so I cannot be on paternity leave, I think.
Reporter: What do you work with?
Interviewee: With horse racing.

The next scene shows a drawn image of a smiling man carrying a child, with the figure '6%' written to the right of him. An animated woman carrying a child can also be seen to the left of the man and next to a vertical bar. The bar is filled in to the level that corresponds to 6 per cent: the amount of parental leave that is taken out by men. A further drawn image of some 20 men is then displayed, and to the right of this image is the text '22% only 1.5 months'. A reporter says:

Yes, there are still many men who do not use the opportunity to be on paternity leave. Statistics show that fathers only use six per cent of their parental leave [the total number of months at that time was 15]. The men who are at home, that is, twenty two per cent, are on parental leave for one and a half months on average.

The news feature ends with an interview of a female researcher who answers questions concerning the degree to which parental insurance is used. According to a study she has conducted, men believe that it is their work that prevents them from staying at home. The reasons given for why these men do not take parental leave focus on the feeling that they are indispensible at their place of work, that they do not want to place their colleagues in a difficult situation, and attitudes at work in general.

Reporter: But doesn't the pressure on the men increase if they are told to stay home more?

Expert: I would rather see it as an opportunity for them, because I think most of them want to be closer to their children. If you have a newborn child, and you have the opportunity to be on paternity leave, it would be very rewarding; I think many would like it. But they feel pressure from work and find it difficult to take that conflict.

The news report ends with the researcher's words, and the men in the park are left to represent all the men who fail to take the opportunity of staying at home on paternity leave. Just like the men on the shopfloor, these men have also left the immediate care of their children to the children's mothers, i.e. their wives. Another common denominator is that both sets of men were asked simple questions by the journalists, and these questions were not so open-ended. Therefore, there seems to be little difference between how the white-collar and blue-collar workers were treated by the reporters during the interviews.

Not just a fun dad

The reasons why men did not take out their paternity leave gradually changed during the 1980s and 1990s. The image of the soft and 'gender-crossing' dad was replaced with the image of the 'real man' (Nordberg 2003, p. 80). The 'real man' did not suffer from a damaged emotional life and was not in need of liberation. Gender equality also changed at this time: women and men were seen as opposites and the emphasis was on differences between the sexes (Nordberg 2003, p. 83; Klinth 2002, p. 340).

The next report that I will analyse is from 1994 and taken from *Aktuellt* (SVT1, 23 September 1994). Even if the reasons for the men not taking out their paternity leave differ from the previous examples, they are still treated with the same degree of freedom in the interviews. The news anchor begins by stating that the 'fathers of Örebro County are second best in the country at using parental insurance and staying at home with their children'. A scene is then shown of a man sitting on the floor and playing with what is presumably to be his own child. The same man is then shown changing the child's nappy. A reporter asks him if it is fun to be on paternity leave, and the man replies in the affirmative.

The reporter is then heard saying that the man 'does something unusual. The son is eighteen months old and Mats [the father] is on paternity leave ... for six months'. The scene then shifts once more to an interview situation in which the man is seen sitting on a sofa. On the upper part of the screen a caption states that he is on paternity leave.

> *Interviewee*: I can be there when he is growing up and ... get a deeper relationship with him. Before, when I worked I could just be the fun dad who came home at five in the evening, and he would go to bed at seven, one could just play and have fun and so on.

A new scene follows in which a father and his son are outdoors playing with a ball. A reporter says: 'More than seven out of ten fathers do not use their paternity leave at all. And those who do, do not take as many days as they are entitled to.' The statistics in this example focus on those who do not take paternity leave. However, the news report does not follow the same script or pattern as the previous example; the father on paternity leave is given an opportunity to explain in his own words what his reasons are for staying at home.

Ten years later, this way of treating men on parental leave remained unchanged. The next news report is from *Aktuellt* (SVT2, 7 March 2004). The news presenter begins the story by saying that 'just over fifteen per cent of all parental leave can be attributed to fathers, and this number has even decreased slightly. More fathers are going on paternity leave, but they stay at home for less time with their children, and there remain great differences around the country.' The next scene shows a man placing his child into a pram. A reporter says that some fathers certainly do leave their work and use their paternity leave, and the man in the picture is an obvious example father. The viewers then see a close-up of the man in the process of being interviewed. A caption at the bottom of the screen informs the viewer that the man is on paternity leave.

Interviewee: Now, I will take my responsibility and really take care of these children and get the feeling of being on paternity leave.
Reporter: How is it going being at home with the children?
Interviewee: Very well, but it is not as easy as you might think before the paternity leave. Before, I just thought it was a matter of being at home with the kids, but it is almost a job, actually, I do not get as much done as I had planned to.
Reporter: What do you think is the reason why so few men are at home with their children?
Interviewee: Well, I do not know if it is tradition, or if, I hope it is not the mothers who force them to work. I think they are stupid not going on paternity leave because it feels like it is the best thing I have ever done, to be at home with them.

Although men do not generally use the parental insurance, there are those who actually do so, and the man in the news report proves this point. However, he is not just a man on paternity leave. He is also clearly represented as someone who is different from the majority of men; that is, someone who takes on the responsibility. For him, paternity leave brought a new perspective to his everyday life and his familial relations. He has broken with previous notions of what it means to be at home with children, and it seems as if he has arrived at a new and better insight into what it means to be at home with his children. This insight includes the notion that men who work do not know the 'true happiness' of being a father. The statement also involves an understanding, and an affirmation, of the role that is traditionally attributed to women.

Paternity leave is natural

Since 1975, when the first draft of so-called father months was tabled, information has been the primary means through which men have been encouraged to stay at home with their children. From the 1970s to the 1990s, the main thing had been to depict paternity leave as a chance or an opportunity. In recent years, however, campaigns have described paternity leave as something natural and obvious (Johansson & Klinth 2007, p. 145). On the whole, there has been a broad consensus that information is the best way to make men choose paternity leave. The final example is from *Aktuellt* (SVT1, 10 April 2005). The news anchor begins the feature by introducing a problem:

> Good evening. Yes, for thirty years the Swedish authorities have made a mistake believing that it is the father who determines his paternity leave, when in fact it is the mother. Yes, that is what the government's own commissioner says, and now he is proposing a nationwide advertising campaign for three hundred million crowns to persuade mothers to share their days.

In this news report the viewers meet two fathers. A reporter says that the men have taken their children to a pre-school and that they have stayed at home longer than the average man. They are then seen with other men sitting on the floor, talking to each other and playing with their children. In the next scene the men introduce themselves and tell the reporter how many months they will stay at home. One of them is an engineer who says that he will stay home for five months. The other man is a management consultant and his paternity leave will last for six months. When introducing themselves they look straight into the camera. By this stage, the reporter has stepped aside and relinquished his role as an intermediary between the viewers and the interviewees. This is a breach of the conventions of television interviewing (Ekström 2006, pp. 69–70). To look directly into the camera is normally the exclusive practice of journalists. The close-up creates the feeling that the men are speaking directly to the audience, thereby establishing an (imaginary) relationship with the public. The intimacy that the shot presents is usually something associated with people we are well acquainted with (Jewitt & Oyama 2001, p. 146). The interviewees are also presented as if they either belong to, or should belong to, our group. Furthermore, the viewer is addressed as a special person. A reporter, who is still out of picture, asks one of the men:

> Was it a natural thing for you to choose to be at home with your children?
> *Interviewee*: Yeah, I think so.

Being on paternity leave is explicitly framed as something natural. The interviewee could hardly have answered the question differently. The report ends with an interview with the governmental commissioner. He repeats what the news anchor said in the beginning; that is, that it is the mother who determines how many days the mother and father should stay at home. Even though the mother's attitudes are presented as if they are in need of change, they do not appear in the report. In these short sequences the two men are promoted as representatives of a group who stay at home more than the average man; they are presented as role models. The news report is very normative because it singles out and identifies a certain father role as the ideal. There is also a degree of moralising evident in the report. To be on paternity leave is not only constructed as a natural consequence of being a father, but also something that is clearly desirable. Like the man in the previous news report, the two men can be seen as good examples of fathers. They only do what should be expected of any man.

Visual distinctions

A further question of importance is how the fathers who work or are on paternity leave are visually described. A first observation is that working fathers are not shown as often as fathers on paternity leave. In fact, the only men who are usually interviewed are fathers on paternity leave. Furthermore, the interviews tend to take place in their own homes or on a walk where they can be seen to be engaged in the care of children. Working men are, however, not totally excluded in the reports. They are always present, but presented as the antithesis of men on paternity leave. In the first example above (*Aktuellt*, SVT1, 8 September 1981), a man stands by a stove, cooking. The reporter says that about ten per cent of fathers who live in homes in which both parents are in gainful employment take out paternity leave in the first six months after the child's birth. On average, fathers stay at home for forty days. The next scene shows a father preparing a feeding bottle, and then shifts to show a close-up of an infant. In front of the child's face, there is a caption with the words 'Every 10th dad (with a working wife) stays at home for 40 days'.

Another example from *Aktuellt* (SVT1, 21 July 2002) presents the viewer with the image of a man feeding his children in the kitchen. A reporter then informs the viewer that, despite the existence of a unique 'father month', statistics show that fathers use fewer and fewer days of their paternity leave. 'In 1994 fathers took paternity leave for an average of 39.6 days, but today the figure is about 27.1.' The reporter continues by telling the viewers that 'Fathers with higher education spend more time at home, especially if the mother is well-educated also. Olle is a typical example: both he and his wife are engineers, and right now he is at home with their daughters.' The audience is also shown a picture of adults and children holding hands, and above the picture there is a message: 'Number of days for paternity leave 1994, 39.6, 2001, 27.1.' Another example of this type of news presentation is taken from the programme *Rapport* (SVT1, 11 July 2002). The news feature, which was broadcast ten days before the previous one, begins with the news anchor referring to a report about gender equality from *Statistics Sweden*. According to this report, 'quite a few men choose paternity leave ... The sad reality is that women still dominate the children's world and that men earn seven to eight per cent more than women.' Another image then fills the screen: a baby is shown lying on its stomach with a woman caressing its stomach. After a few scenes from a day nursery, a picture of a child appears. The following words are written above the picture: 'Who takes care of the children?' On the left-hand side of the screen, the words 'paternity leave 14%' can be seen. The reporter then says, 'Dad comes home, and stays at least for a couple of months. It would probably be a dream message for both children and the social democrats, now that the election is coming up. Still, it is women who strongly dominate the world of the children.' In these examples, the viewer is shown the percentage of men who are on paternity leave, but not how many who are working. It is left to the viewer to deduce the percentage of fathers not on paternity leave. The statistics stand in sharp contrast to the images of caring men who have close relationships with their children. Therefore, the mothers are the ones who are considered to be the cause of the problem.

The responsible, equal father and his opposite

How can the theoretical perspective and the findings of the analysis be articulated? The construction of paternity leave in the discussed news features is based on a number of divisions. The creation of divisions is also a central discursive procedure of exclusion. The functions of inclusion and exclusion are expressed in the captions by the organisation, hierarchisation and evaluation of the behaviour of fathers. The main division in this journalistic discursive practice is between fathers who are on parental leave and those who work; a clear creation of an either/or division. Either a man is on paternity leave or he is not. The first alternative is hierarchically superior. By discursively separating fathers from each other, two well-defined groups are constructed. The distinctions between them are based on morally value-laden concepts such as responsible/irresponsible, conscious/unconscious, and equal/unequal (cf. table below). By using these dichotomies or binary pairs in the news reports, the behaviour and performance of men on paternity leave are rated as good, while men who are not on paternity leave are considered to be bad fathers and husbands. There are certain meanings that are produced and legitimised with this either/or logic. Men on paternity leave are described as responsible, sensitive and equally-oriented, whereas working dads are seen as a problem. The problem with fathers who do not stay at home is related to their relationship with other people and society as a whole. According to the presented arguments in the news programmes, these fathers' behaviour endangers both the children's socialisation and the societal project of increased gender equality. The table below shows the conceptual division between men on parental leave and those who are not:

Fathers on paternity leave	Working fathers
Few/minority	Many/majority
Unusual/atypical	Usual/typical
Mature/responsible/conscientious	Immature/irresponsible/unconscientious
Exercise their rights	Fail to exercise their rights
Equal husband/partner	Unequal husband/partner
Natural/obvious behaviour	Unnatural/strange behaviour
Relationship with child important	Relationship with workplace important

More than a playing 'fun dad'	Only a 'fun dad'
Informed/educated/enlightened (white-collar)	Uninformed/not educated or enlightened (blue-collar)
Happy at home	Bored at home
Subject (speaks for himself)	Object (answering questions)

Such discursive divisions are not only constructed in speech about men on parental leave. The division is also visually displayed. Men on parental leave are, for example, allowed to meet the gaze of the viewer. The camera also enables the viewer to see the homes of these fathers, and to watch them doing things that many people recognise and can identify with. One of these dads is shown changing nappies, feeding his daughter and working in the kitchen (*Aktuellt*, SVT1, 8 September 1981). Another news report shows a man doing everyday things like reading stories, playing and nappy-changing (*Rapport*, SVT2, 27 February 1982). Yet another father is in the kitchen feeding his children (*Aktuellt*, SVT1, 21 July 2002). In the scene that follows we see him on a beach playing and swimming with his children. In a later shot, the same father answers the reporter's questions while carrying a child. In yet another news feature, a man is shown preparing to go for a walk with the pram, and busying himself with the child (*Aktuellt*, SVT2, 7 March 2004).

These pictures of men on parental leave have very little in common with the abstract world of statistics, mainly used to show the majority of fathers that are (still) working. In contrast, the news reports about fathers on parental leave show a concrete, everyday reality. The viewer sees men who are involved in daily activities and caregiving. They cook, play, read stories, change nappies and take walks with the pram. The man on parental leave is not only involved in childcare, but also very involved and active in household work. Besides being a responsible father, he appears to care about gender equality as well.

Exclusions in the paternity leave discourse

These linguistic and visual practices do not just create divisions, but also construct the two groups of fathers and the idea of what good fatherhood is. The father on paternity leave is projected as sensitive and caring, and not afraid of taking care of his children. On the contrary, such feelings are natural to him and something he does not hesitate to express in deeds and words. He is always present, active and involved. This type of father takes responsibility for his relationships with others and future generations – and ultimately for society as a whole. On the other hand, the image of the absent and working dad is relatively closely associated with the idea of (father) betrayal. This man is not only absent from the daily lives of his children, but also from the ongoing societal project that promotes gender equality. His role in the news reports is simply to play the opposite of the 'good' father.

The discourse of paternity leave that creates the father ideal is constructed through a contrast to 'the other'; that is, the majority of rejected and excluded men. This emphasis on 'the other' excludes these men from the news coverage, while being on paternity leave is constructed as the norm. A normal father is obviously at home with his children. Men who work are simultaneously construed as abnormal and unequal and do not live up to the new societal norm. The presentation of fathers as either on paternity leave or not indicates that the journalistic discursive practice reproduces simplified social categories that men can, in turn, either identify themselves with or reject. Similarly, when the news media compare behaviour to a standard and then rate it, they provide definitions of what a normal father should be. A man who is not on paternity leave will constantly be reminded of his 'mistake', and that he is working instead of being at home with his children. In other words, he has not lived up to the social norm. In this sense the news features that I have discussed function as practices that normalise, discipline and divide.

Finally, the examples show that the men are depicted through simplified images. A father is either on paternity leave or he is not. This simple division and categorisation is a journalistic construction that fits the production of news. However, this division excludes individual variations and ignore differences related to class, ethnicity and so on. For example, many men do shift work, and in many cases this means that they are off work a number of days a week; days when they can be at home with their children. They can also perform in front of a camera and answer questions – if they are asked to do so. However, it is quite rare for the journalists to give these men the chance to develop their own thoughts. This can be understood as the operation of the prohibited word that Foucault writes about; it governs the content of a discourse by dictating who may speak and about what. A father who is not on paternity leave does not seem to have the right qualifications to speak. Therefore, the news features can be seen as examples of how journalistic practices exclude and reject certain individuals, groups and perspectives through the use of the prohibited word, while simultaneously including others. I would argue that a man who works for a wage instead of being on paternity leave does not necessarily consider a good relationship and contact with his children to be unimportant.

However, the news features can be said to promote such an image when they exclude a wide range of variations. Even the image of paternity leave is very simplified. When men on paternity leave are present in the news, the focus is on fathers who seem to cope very well with the responsibility of caring for their children. A good and earnest fatherhood is (visually) reduced to being at home with the child during the first year of his or her life. There are, however, good reasons to believe that the general view of fathers and parenting is that it is deeper and broader than just staying at home for a few months when the child is an infant. Even though these categories are journalistic constructs, it may be erroneous to think about them *only* as constructed. They certainly rest on and feed societal ideals and beliefs. Journalism can be interpreted as a truth-producing practice (Sjölander 2004, p. 162). It is grounded in a will to truth; that is, to report 'how it really is'. Ideals and beliefs about parental leave are therefore expressed as indisputable and fathers are separated into two distinctive groups. Furthermore, the men who take paternity leave are seen as good fathers. The news reports on paternity leave are part of an ongoing construction of fatherhood. Even if the discourse is influential, it does not necessarily force fathers to think and act in this particular way, but it certainly expresses something about the kind of paternal behaviour that is desirable.

Notes

1 This article is part of an ongoing dissertation project financed by The Centre for Gender Studies at Umeå University and the University of Gävle, with the preliminary title: 'The Mediated Family: Discourses on Family and Parenthood in the Swedish Television News 1974–2006'. The aim is to analyse mediated discourses on family and parenthood from the 1970s until today. I would like to thank Eva Åsén Ekstrand at the Department of Media, Communication and Film, University of Gävle, for her valuable comments on this chapter.

2 The concept of discourse I use is meant to describe statements (voice, caption, picture) which in various ways give meaning to the phenomenon *paternity leave*. In this study, each individual news caption is regarded as a statement that both expresses and reproduces the discourse of which it is a part.

3 This approach is not an obvious starting point in media and communication studies (Sjölander 2004, p. 51; 2006, p. 2), but critical discourse analysis has become more or less accepted as the standard way of studying journalism and its contents (Garret & Bell 1998, p. 6). However, the Sjölander (2006) study of news reporting on nuclear waste management in Sweden during the 1990s is an example of how Foucault's conceptual world can be used in media and communication research. My study has a great deal in common with Sjölander's approach, as I share the same ontological and methodological views.

4 All citations from the news programmes are translated from Swedish to English by the author, and are slightly modified to be more readable.

5 The definition is found in the translator's notes, and the words are thus Mats Rosengren's, not Foucault's.

6 Journalism is based on both written and unwritten rules. The written rules in this context that have status in law are, for example, The Press Act and The Radio and Television Act. The codes of conduct for the press, radio and television are examples of written professional recommendations (Hadenius & Weibull 1999, pp. 23–38).

7 The news media are sometimes described as news or text factories where news is 'manufactured', hence the term 'news production'. See, for example, Nerman (1973) or Hultén (1993).

8 Despite his great influence, or precisely because of it, Foucault's ideas have not been irrefutable. Above all, critics have argued that his influence has led to everything being seen as expressions of power (cf. Fraser 2003, p. 48 and Bergström & Boréus 2000, p. 256). As a consequence, his critics argue that the concept of power will lose its analytical potential. At the same time the breadth of the concept can be seen as its strength. By considering power as an analytical category, and not something that is pre-determined, the question of what constitutes a power relationship or how it is constructed remains open, and is something that can be studied in specific cases (Hörnqvist 1996, p. 29).

9 The description was mainly used during the 1970s, but seldom today. It is a disparaging term, in my understanding. In its literal sense, the phrase means a

dad who is dressed in velour. The non-literal meaning refers to a sensitive man who nurtures his children and engages himself with the household; that is, he is contrasted to what can be traditionally understood as masculinity.

References

Literature

Bekkengen, L., 2003. Föräldralediga män och barnorienterad maskulinitet. In: T. Johansson & J. Kuosmanen (eds), *Manlighetens många ansikten – fäder, feminister, frisörer och andra män.* Malmö: Liber, pp. 181–202.

Bell, A. & Garrett, P., 1988. Introduction. In: A. Bell & P. Garret (eds), *Approaches to Media Discourse.* Oxford: Blackwell Publishers, pp. 1–20.

Berglez, P., 2000. Kritisk diskursanalys. In: M. Ekström & L. Larsson (eds), *Metoder i kommunikationsvetenskap.* Lund: Studentlitteratur, pp. 194–218.

Bergström, G. & Boréus, K., 2000. *Textens mening och makt. Metodbok i samhällsvetenskaplig textanalys.* Lund: Studentlitteratur.

Beronius, M., 1987. Vetandets spel-inledning till Foucaults kulturkritik. In: U. Bergryd (ed.), *Den sociologiska fantasin – teorier om samhället.* Stockholm: Rabén & Sjögren, pp. 55–74.

Brandth, B. & Kvande, E., 1998. Masculinity and Childcare: The Reconstruction of Fathering. *The Sociological Review* 46(2), pp. 292–313.

Dahlgren, P., 1988. Berättande och betydelser i TV-nyheter. In: U. Carlsson (ed.), *Forskning om journalistik.* NORDICOM-NYTT/SVERIGE, 4–88, pp. 53–63.

Ekström, M., 2002. Epistemologies of TV journalism: A theoretical framework. *Journalism* [Internet], vol. 3, no. 3, pp. 259–282. Available at: http://jou.sagepub.com/cgi/content/abstract/3/3/259 [Accessed 15 June 2009].

Ekström, M., 2006. *Politiken i mediesamhället.* Malmö: Liber.

Foucault, M., 1969/2002. *Vetandets arkeologi. (The Archaeology of Knowledge.)* Lund: Arkiv förlag.

Foucault, M., 1971/1993. *Diskursens ordning.* (The Discourse on Language) Stockholm: Symposion.

Foucault, M., 1974/1993. *Övervakning och straff. (Discipline & Punish)* Lund: Arkiv förlag.

Foucault, M., 1982. The Subject and Power. In: H. Dreyfus & P. Rabinow (eds), *Michel Foucault. Beyond Structuralism and Hermeneutics.* Chicago: University of Chicago Press, pp. 208–226.

Foucault, M., 1991. Politics and the Study of Discourse. In: G. Burchell, C. Gordon & P. Miller (eds), *The Foucault Effect: Studies in Governmentality.* Chicago: University of Chicago Press, pp. 53–72.

Fraser, N., 2003. *Den radikala fantasin: mellan omfördelning och erkännande.* Göteborg: Daidalos.

Hadenius, S. & Weibull, L., 1999. *Massmedier. Press, radio and TV i förvandling.* Stockholm: Bonnier.

Hill, H., 2003. Befria mannen. Försök till en ny genusordning. In: T. Johansson & J. Kuosmanen (eds), *Manlighetens många ansikten – fäder, feminister, frisörer och andra män*. Malmö: Liber, pp. 46–61.

Hörnqvist, M., 1996. *Foucaults maktanalys*. Stockholm: Carlsson.

Hultén, L.K., 1993. *Journalistikens villkor*. Stockholm: Natur & Kultur.

Jewitt, C. & Oyama, R., 2001. Visual Meaning: A Social Semiotic Approach. In: T. van Leeuwen & C. Jewitt (eds), *Handbook of Visual Analysis*. London, Thousand Oaks, New Delhi: Sage, pp. 134–156.

Johansson, T. & Klinth, R., 2007. De nya fäderna. Om pappaledighet, jämställdhet och nya maskulina positioner. *Tidskrift för genusvetenskap*, 1–2(8), pp. 143–166.

Järvinen, M., 1996. Makt eller vanmakt? *Kvinnovetenskaplig tidskrift* 1(17), pp. 47–62.

Klinth, R., 2002. *Göra pappa med barn*. (Diss.) Umeå: Boréa bokförlag.

Mårtensson, B., 2003. *Den televiserade ekonomin. Nyheter om statsbudgeten 1980–1995*. (Diss.) Stockholm: Stockholms universitet.

Nerman, B., 1973. *Massmedieretorik*. Stockholm: AWE/Geber.

Nordberg, M., 2003. Jämställdhetens spjutspets. In: T. Johansson & J. Kuosmanen (eds), *Manlighetens många ansikten – fäder, feminister, frisörer och andra män*. Malmö: Liber, pp. 76–102.

Plantin, L., 2003. Mäns föräldraskap. In: T. Johansson & J. Kuosmanen (eds), *Manlighetens många ansikten-fäder – feminister, frisörer och andra män*. Malmö: Liber, pp. 150–163.

Sjölander, A., 2004: *Kärnproblem. Opinionsbildning i kärnavfallsdiskursen i Malå*. (Diss.) Umeå: Umeå Studies in Media and Communication no. 7.

Egan Sjölander, A., 2006: *Rare and Fruitful – The Concrete Use of Foucault in Media Research*. Paper presented at the CRESC-conference: Media Change and Social Theory, Oxford, UK, September 2006.

Watson, S., 2000. Foucault and the Study of Social Policy. In: G. Lewis (ed.), *Rethinking Social Policy*. London: Sage, pp. 66–77.

Official documents

SOU 1999:126. *Politikens medialisering*. Demokratiutredningens forskarvolym III. Stockholm: Justitiedepartementet.

Television programmes

Aktuellt, 1981. SVT1, 8 September 1981, 21.00.
Rapport, 1982. SVT2, 7 February 1982, 19.30.
Rapport, 1989. SVT2, 12 August 1989, 19.30.
Aktuellt, 1993. SVT1, 1 January 1993, 18.00.
Aktuellt, 1994. SVT1, 23 September 1994, 18.00.
Rapport, 2002. SVT1, 11 July 2002, 19.30.
Aktuellt, 2002. SVT1, 21 July 2002, 18.00.
Aktuellt, 2004. SVT2, 7 March 2004, 18.00.
Aktuellt, 2005. SVT1, 10 April 2005, 19.30.

CHAPTER 7

Constituting 'Real' Cutters

A Discourse Theoretical Analysis of
Self-Harm and Identity

Anna Johansson

The Swedish public debate on young women's health has drawn considerable attention to issues of self-harm over the last decade. Concerns have been raised about the proliferation of self-injurious practices since the 1990s, and cutting in particular has been represented as a major problem amongst young women today. This phenomenon is explained in the media and official documents by reference to characteristics that are popularly associated with girls, including being vulnerable, impressionable, inclined to direct their despair at themselves and being prone to mental ill-health (e.g., *Vad vet vi om flickor som skär sig?* 2004). However, little research has inquired into how cutters[1] themselves make sense of their identities (for a few examples, see Hodgson 2004; Adler & Adler 2008).

Therefore, the aim of this chapter is to analyse the formation of cutter identities and acts of identification found in personal accounts of self-harm. The chapter draws on a poststructuralist discourse theoretical approach, or, more specifically, on the ontological and epistemological developments of Ernesto Laclau and Chantal Mouffe (1985; Laclau 1996), and David Howarth (2005). Empirically, the analysis builds on textual material: virtual discussions about cutting that were obtained from three Swedish Internet communities in 2006 and 2007, as well as semi-structured online and IRL[2] interviews with 13 community users (or ex-users) who were recruited by e-mail.[3]

In relation to the textual material, cutting is both considered as a way of managing and expressing emotion, and associated with a range of psychopathological characteristics: cutting is seen as a *devi-*

ant way of managing emotions. This constitution of cutting as an object of psychiatry is sometimes contested through the framing of cutting as a fad or a property of certain youth cultures. Whilst the former conceptualisation attributes cutter identity with authenticity and credibility, the latter constitutes the cutter as illegitimate and inauthentic. The web forums are primarily formed around the notion of psychopathological cutting and authentic cutters. Ideas that associate cutting directly with youth culture are consequently relegated to the margins of the discussion, and writers who seem to identify themselves with such a position are treated with hostility.

In this chapter some of the concepts elaborated by Laclau and Mouffe are deployed as analytical tools in order to account for this conflict between two understandings of cutting and cutters. I aim to show how the struggle for credibility and authenticity is manifested, and how it can be resolved through a hegemonic intervention (Laclau 1996, p. 89). The chapter points to the merits of a discourse theoretical approach for understanding the micro level[4] formation of identities that are not typically considered political.[5]

All the interviewees have personal experiences of self-harm and mental ill-health, even though several identified themselves as healthy at the time of the interview. Whereas some of them had dealt with their cutting in private, the majority had been in contact with therapeutic practitioners – ranging from meetings with school counsellors to in-patient treatment. The analysis of empirical data is a political act that privileges the interpretations of the researcher (cf. Glynos & Howarth 2007, pp. 196–197), and research on critical topics such as self-harm and mental ill-health therefore requires particular attentiveness to ethical issues, which I have discussed at length elsewhere (Johansson 2010).[6] Hopefully, this article will generate new perspectives on self-harm without compromising the self-interpretations of the informants. In order to account for transparency, excerpts from the interviews as well as the web discussions will be drawn on throughout the analysis.[7]

A discourse theoretical outlook

My theoretical approach relies on Ernesto Laclau's and Chantal Mouffe's poststructuralist, post-Marxist discourse theory (henceforward referred to as DT). Here, the concept of 'discourse' includes more than just linguistic aspects of social life. Ontologically, DT postulates an analogy between linguistic and social systems; both are seen as orders of difference where identities are relationally constituted, and both systems can be analysed using the same tools. 'Discourse', accordingly, refers to that which gives meaning to every social configuration by establishing a specific network of relations between different elements (Laclau & Moffe 1990, p. 100; cf. Foucault 1970). The discursive basically refers to the horizon of what can be thought and expressed – it is only through discourses, historically specific sets of meaning, that we can make sense of the world. Distinguishing between discursive-linguistic and other aspects of social practice is therefore impossible, according to Laclau and Mouffe (1985, p. 107), because such a distinction would itself already be discursive.

The two conflicting ways of understanding cutting, as either a sign of mental ill-health or as a property of certain youth cultures, can serve to clarify this point. In fact, the act and effects of cutting are always necessarily discursive. This stance does not deny that an open wound on the arm of a person has a material existence; obviously, such a wound will bleed, heal and leave a scar regardless of how it is referred to. However, the wound will be rendered intelligible by the actual cutter and others through the discourses that are available at the time, and in different ways: as for instance a bodily adornment, a religious stigmata, as damage to dermal cells that needs suturing, an affiliation to a certain youth culture, or as a sign of mental disorder. The wound will be understood and dealt with according to its discursive framing, capturing how discourse is always constitutive of the social (cf. Winther Jørgensen & Phillips 2000, pp. 26–27).

This ontological tenet also underlies my stance on identity. Discourse is what renders us intelligible as human beings – just like other material objects are thinkable through their discursive framings.

Scholars such as Stavrakakis (2005), Glynos and Howarth (2007), and Glynos (2008) have theorised identity from a Laclauan perspective that is informed by Lacanian psychoanalysis. This theorisation of identity presupposes that there exists an inherent instability and lack of completeness in any identity as well as social structure, which means that a subject can never be fully constituted. This fundamental lack of fullness is the driving force behind the continuous acts of identification, whereby subjects come to attach themselves to certain positions in the discursive structure (Laclau 1994, pp. 2–3; Stavrakakis 2005, p. 70; cf. Glynos & Howarth 2007, p. 129). As such, the constitution of cutter identities is seen as processual and constantly in the making through acts of identification.

In this article, I draw on the concepts of 'articulation', 'antagonism', 'floating signifier' and 'hegemonisation' in order to analyse the constitution of cutter identities. These concepts will be clarified in more detail as I put them into practice, but I will briefly present my understanding of them here. My use of the concept 'discourse' refers to a configuration of meaning that constitutes cutting in a specific way. A particular discourse on cutting also constitutes the cutter in certain ways, thus offering an identity for subjects to 'attach' themselves (or others) to. Like any discourse, these configurations of meaning operate by organising a range of disparate elements into a seemingly coherent whole.

The concept of articulation is crucial here, as it designates this linking together of previously separate elements to a new signifying totality – a discourse. This temporary fixation of relations between entities transforms the meaning of each individual entity as well as the totality (Laclau & Mouffe 1985, pp. 93–97). Such a fixation does not arise out of some *a priori* logic or principle, but is an effect of the abundance of meaning that has not been fixed or articulated in a particular discourse. Accordingly, a discourse is an attempt to take control over this abundance by organising meaning around particular privileged signifiers. Hence, a particular discourse on cutting is a way of defining the practice by linking it to other signifiers, such as psychopathology or attention seeking. However, as Laclau and Mouffe have persuasively pointed out, any constitution always involves exclusion and thus the field of discursivity is the possibility of existence for a discourse, at the same time as it always threatens the existence of any stable totality (Laclau & Mouffe 1985, pp. 111–113). According to the same ontological presuppositions, *antagonisms* arise between two discourses or two identities when the existence of one prevents the full constitution of the other (Laclau & Mouffe 1985, pp. 122–127; Laclau 2005, pp. 83–87). The antagonistic sides are constituted through logics of equivalence – the partial cancelling out of differences between particular signifiers, which leads to a simplification of social space (Laclau & Mouffe 1985, pp. 127–130; Laclau 1996, pp. 47–65, 2005, pp. 73–83). I will show how the discursive formation of cutting involves such a polarisation, and how it is manifested as antagonisms between different cutter identities. Furthermore, I will use the concept of *floating signifier* (Laclau 2005, pp. 129–156) to account for the ways in which the frontier between the antagonistic poles is constantly challenged by discursive elements that attach themselves to both sides. Finally, by employing the central concept of hegemonisation I will be able to show how this insecurity concerning cutter identities can be dissolved when one of the antagonistic identities manages to fix the floating element within its own configuration of meaning.

Real or fake: the proliferation of cutter identities

Matilda, a 20-year-old ex-cutter, provides the following account of self-harm in our interview:

> Well, I believe in some way, there has been an increase, amongst youths or sort of in the normal population or so. Because there used to be a lot more, what I can recall, there used to be many more in institutional care only. And people who were very disordered hurt themselves. And now anyone can, someone who doesn't feel well in their teens can harm themselves pretty easily. And I'm sure they're not feeling well, because otherwise you wouldn't have gone so far as to hurt yourself, but it's not like you need to be psychotic to do it, or you don't have to think about suicide in order to do it, but you do it as an expression of your not feeling well, because it has been really normalised.

According to Matilda, the proliferation of cutting amongst young people has been so great that cutting can be regarded as a normalised practice today, and no longer restricted to institutionalised people with severe psychiatric disorders. Although she appears unwilling to point out certain cutters as less 'real' than others, Matilda, continuing her argument, nevertheless refers to what can be described as a generalised belief about cutting as some sort of – potentially illegitimate – attention-seeking behaviour:

> Uhm, and I can imagine there are many who, of course it's frustrating, I mean to parents and stuff, like 'what the fuck are you doing, you can't do that, it's totally sick!' But in our generation it's not that sick anymore. Because it's so common. And since it's so common they don't feel bad or do it because they feel bad and maybe they have, they know people who've been scratching themselves or self-harmed without having a depression or without feeling really really bad, uhm, they regard it as something superficial. Regard it as a, even if it's sort of a cry for help or an expression of, like, 'I don't feel really well right now', then it doesn't have to be much more than that. Maybe it isn't something that you need to have psychiatric care for. And then there might be a lot of people who think, like, 'screw you, you just want attention', kind of, and 'this is your way of getting it'. Uhm, and I mean all people are in need of attention, I mean you *are*,[8] in different ways. Uhm, and so, if you don't get any positive attention but you manage to get negative attention, it's better than no attention in some way.

Matilda's account should be understood against the backdrop of public debates on self-harm and young women's health in recent years. The increasing mental ill-health amongst young people, particularly girls, and the spread of cutting has been discussed at length in Sweden as well as in an international context (see e.g., Madge et al. 2008). Whereas the public debate about cutting has tended to emphasise the *increasing* propensity for mental ill-health amongst young people, Matilda, on the other hand, draws on the rise in cutting in order to *disarticulate* (McRobbie 2008, pp. 24–53) the link between self-harm and disorder. Initially construed as a property of a deviant and exclusive group, she claims that cutting is now a common means of expression in the younger generation.

Another ex-cutter, Emma, refers to a similar rearticulation of cutting when she reflects upon the reception of her lectures about her own self-harm experiences:

> And I think of that guy who was so offensive. He sounded kind of like 'but why?' I mean, and there was someone in a class where I lectured, they're a bit older the people I talk to, but there was this guy who was maybe my age but who worked in nursing. And they were supposed to ask questions at the end and he raised his hand and, like, 'but aren't there quite *a lot* of people doing that?' you know, when I had been talking about cutting myself, and I said like 'well, yes [pause] so what?' Sure it has become more but he made it sound like 'why have you been sitting here talking about that, quite a lot of people do that, don't they?'

From listening to Emma, it is obvious that this young man did not take her as seriously as she had wanted. The significance of Emma's experiences was questioned, as the proliferation of cutting is constituted as making the practice less exceptional and less worthy of attention. I would argue that, again, this can be understood in terms of a rearticulation of cutting and cutter identity. Self-harm practices are no longer necessarily articulated in relation to mental disorders – if that had been the case, the rapid increase would probably be seen as *more* urgent to acknowledge instead of *less* remarkable, as shown above.

In Emma's quotation, the rearticulation of cutting is framed in a way that is reminiscent of what Glynos and Howarth call a dislocatory moment (2007, p. 79). According to Laclau, 'every identity is dislocated insofar as it depends on an outside which both denies that identity and provides its condition of possibility at the same time' (1990, p. 39). However, as Glynos and Howarth (2007, p. 129) have noted, this is experienced as a problem only in times of crisis – when something happens that calls into question the identity of a subject and thus reveals the contingency of being. At such points in time, the subjects are forced to make decisions and identify anew by aligning themselves with certain discourses or political projects (Howarth & Stavrakakis 2000, p. 14; Glynos & Howarth 2007, pp. 110–112). For Emma, as well as the other interviewees, the proliferation of cutters indicates that a disruption of identities is taking place and as such can be grasped in terms of a dislocation. At the same time as the proliferation of cutters tends to normalise the phenomenon, it also appears to signify a crisis in the system of representation of cutting and the cutter (cf. Howarth & Stavrakakis 2000, p. 14), which, in turn, prompts the subjects to adopt alternative acts of identification.

The two interview excerpts above are illustrative of this reorientation towards a new cutter identity – the 'real' cutter identity. In the empirical context, this reorientation should be seen as a general tendency to challenge certain people's claims to the authentic cutter identity, and to relationally position oneself as a 'real' cutter. For example, there are continuous debates in the web material as to who is really depressed, who has the right to be, and who is just pretending. Even though discussions are generally encouraging, emphatic and supportive, ideas about authenticity and credibility seem to regulate the social order in these contexts. In interviews, as seen above, formulations are generally more nuanced than in virtual interactions, but here too, similar arguments are reproduced about cutting and cutters.

The dominant approach in the forums, as well as in the interviews, defines cutting as a sign of mental ill-health and as such it is always constituted against other possible definitions. The hostile position towards such 'others' entails a polarisation of the discursive space. Following a logic of equivalence (Laclau & Mouffe 1985, pp. 127–130; Laclau 1996, pp. 47–65; 2005, pp. 73–83), cutter identities are linked to one of the two poles: either one is an authentic or a 'fake' cutter. Whereas the authentic cutter is construed as 'feeling bad', this is posited against the inauthentic cutter who cuts for what are considered to be more dubious reasons. Here, cutting is often framed not as a sign of pathology but as a cultural expression, be it a mainstream trend or a sub-cultural feature. Theoretically, this can be understood as an antagonistic construal of social space that follows the dislocatory event discussed above. The experience of no longer being taken seriously forces subjects to reorient themselves, and this is accomplished through identification with a psychiatric discourse where cutting is constituted as an expression of some kind of mental disorder. Hence authenticity is linked to psychopathology through a logic of equivalence.

Whilst often absent from the forums, the inauthentic cutter is nevertheless construed as a constant threat to authenticity and credibility, and haunts anyone who claims to be an authentic cutter. In this respect, the inauthentic cutter must be seen as the constitutive outside: that which is present in its absence. As Laclau and Mouffe (1985, pp. 122–127; Laclau 2005, pp. 83–93) have argued, two identities are antagonistic insofar as they negate each other's existence – but this is so because they are always also mutually constitutive. Accordingly, the inauthentic cutter threatens the partial stability and full constitution of the authentic cutter, but is, at the same time, the condition of possibility for its constitution. Without the fake, there would be no authenticity. As a matter of fact, in the context of these web discussions and interviews, authenticity has no positive content of its own. The authentic identity is commonly claimed instead by referring to what one is *not*. In the web forums, the writers commonly constitute their own authentic identities in contrast to, or as negations of, devalued characteristics that are articulated with inauthenticity: One is *not* a poser, one is *not* an 'emo kid', and one is *not* cutting just to attract attention. Here, a community of cutters is defined by what it is *not*, and formed around the notion of a common enemy (cf. Laclau 1996, pp. 38, 40–41).

Even though authenticity and inauthenticity are interdependent entitities, the latter also poses a constant threat to the former. This is shown, for example, in the previously cited interview with Emma. She recounted her experience of not being taken seriously; that is, not being able to fully constitute herself as an authentic cutter because of the existence of another possible cutter identity. Nineteen-year-old Linda, who has been helped by her school counsellor to stop cutting, argues in a similar way. Throughout the interview, she clearly demarcates two cutter categories: those who strive to become 'popular' and those who feel 'genuinely bad'. Simultaneously as she has a tendency to define other cutters as belonging to the former category, she claims the authentic cutter identity for herself. Furthermore, she holds the inauthentic cutters accountable for the way she herself has been treated by the people around her and for her not wanting to tell people about her cutting:

> *Linda:* It's something that, you open up to people who are like you. They don't judge you the same way as someone who, for instance Mum and my usual friends who don't have the same problems. Because you're easily judged. You want to become popular, that's what most people say, if you show off what you've been cutting, and you want to be admired because of that. And there are probably people who do that, too.
>
> *Anna:* But you're saying that such ideas can be found, that you do it in order to become popular?
>
> *Linda:* I think so. In order to be seen, to *be* something.
>
> *Anna:* And you were afraid people around you would think like that about you too, if they knew?
>
> *Linda:* Yes, that I would be seen like that. I don't want that, obviously. I want to be, I don't want to be seen at all. It was just my way of getting rid of the pain.

Linda says she did not want to be seen at all, and thereby she identifies herself in opposition to those cutters who try to make use of self-harm in order to become popular and admired.[9] Here, like in Emma's account, the inauthentic cutters appear to block the constitution of the fully authentic identity.

This blockage is further elucidated through the reworkings of the Lacanian concept of 'enjoyment' (*jouissance*) within a discourse theoretical framework. Enjoyment, in this sense, should not be confused with pleasure but with its opposite: the pain derived from transgressing the culturally affirmed ideals of that which counts as civilised pleasure (see Glynos & Howarth 2007, p. 107). Žižek (1991, in Glynos & Howarth 2007, p. 107) has pointed to the significance of the concept of enjoyment in the analysis of nationalist discourses. The antagonistic constitution of the 'other' is interpreted in terms of conflicting modes of being, where the 'other' is seen as wanting to 'steal our enjoyment' (i.e., interrupting our way of life). As evident from Linda's account, as well as several of the other quotations, the inauthentic cutter is posited as an 'other', who can be analytically understood as someone out to steal the enjoyment of cutting, i.e., the painful enjoyment inherent in the transgressive act of injuring oneself.

To summarise my argumentation so far, the range of identities represented by the signifier 'cutter' seems to have expanded. This expansion can be understood as a dislocatory event that forces some of the cutters to adopt new modes of identification in order to emphasise their status as 'real' cutters. The idea of antagonism is valuable in this context as it sheds light on the complex and seemingly contradictory constitution of cutter identities. Coupled with the notion of enjoyment, it accounts for the ways in which the authentic mode of being a cutter is articulated through the common renunciation of the 'other'. However, this antagonistic relationship is never stable or fully fixed. There are elements that threaten to destabilise the frontier between the authentic cutter identity and its constitutive outside. One such element is the 'attention seeker'.

Attention seekers as floating signifiers

As seen from a DT perspective, the frontier between two antagonistic camps is always vulnerable. Any antagonism might be destabilised in the presence of discursive elements that are not entirely fixed on one side or the other. Such elements can articulate with either one of the antagonistic poles, and their elusiveness renders the frontier unstable. In his theory of social antagonism, Laclau has discussed these elements in terms of floating signifiers (2005, pp. 129–156). As will be shown, floating signifiers are crucial in the constitution of cutter identities. The frontier between authenticity and inauthenticity is constantly destabilised by the presence of 'attention seeking' or, rather, of the identity of the attention seeker. This identity is alternately articulated with authentic and inauthentic cutting.

One way of conceptualising attention seekers is precisely to posit them as people who pretend to feel bad, and thereby as inauthentic cutters. The post below, which was obtained from one of the forums, attests to the idea that some people self-harm even though they feel quite well:

> And then there are lots of people who cut themselves even though they feel well. They cut themselves only to make people feel sorry for them and see them … So what's so good about being seen that people who feel well cut themselves? (Girl, 15)

The author of the post does not explicitly use the term attention, but simply talks of a desire to be seen. Still, I would argue that this formulation acquires its particular meaning in relation to the concepts of attention and attention seeker. Self-harm discourses, online and offline, position the attention seeker as a signifier of central importance, but its meaning does not seem to be given or stable. There are ongoing struggles over the concept, and attempts are made to fix the meaning of 'attention' and 'attention seeker' by attaching the notions to one of the antagonistic camps.[10] As evident from the previous section, attention seeking tends to be articulated as a property of the inauthentic cutter. The latter is constituted with reference to ideas about theatricality, dramatisation and simulation. Linda, for instance, makes a comparison where people writing about their cutting on the Internet are contrasted with those who also post photos of their cuts:

> *Linda:* Those who show their pictures, I guess they're the ones who want to become something through it. They kind of want an as- surance that they are okay, they want to be seen. It's not the same as those who simply write.
> *Anna:* But how do you mean? You don't think they feel bad, or?
> *Linda:* Yes, I believe, yes, they don't feel bad, they just want to be- come popular, so to speak, by cutting themselves, by showing off.
> *Anna:* Is that possible? Can you become popular through cutting?
> *Linda:* Yes, I actually think so. But it's in the wrong way.
> *Anna:* Well, it sounds a bit strange.
> *Linda:* Yeah, but what I've kind of noticed, because there are, well, each and every one has cut themselves today.
> *Anna:* Yes, it's very common today, isn't it?

Linda: Yeah, that's, I think people I've been talking to have tried at least once. And some of them brag about it and those, those who do that, they don't believe that I feel bad. They do it to make a, well, to *be* someone. Become part of the group or, well. They don't do it because they feel bad and want something out of it.

A similar logic is employed by Emma, but she is more nuanced in her description of being provoked by people who display their scars:

Emma: Yes, and most of all people, those who do it, I guess it's quite logical as well considering that there was less before, I mean if it was like that, that they weren't as explicit with it. But now it's like people, and I can be really upset about it, I mean I feel strongly that if you cut yourself you should hide it. And it's not just for me but it's so obvious, why do you want to, it's sort of provocative, I mean I'm provoked when I see people with scars. This girl I met, she cut herself from time to time, I don't know how she's doing now but she could go to parties together with me and kind of have fresh wounds.
Anna: Without kind of covering?
Emma: With scabs and stuff. And I didn't say anything really [laughter]. I have insinuated that *I* didn't show my scars until they were healed, but I didn't really tell it to her that I think her having it is provocative. But it feels kind of like, I don't know why I think it's so hard. But her argument for showing them was sort of 'then it gives me a reason not to make any more'. But she did anyway. I guess she meant that 'if people see which ones I've got, they will see if I make any more'. I'm not really sure how she was thinking.
Anna: It doesn't seem really logical?
Emma: No, or her being ashamed, she thought it was hard to show them, but if she kept on showing them then maybe she wouldn't make any more because that would be even harder. Kind of like that, I think. Uhm, but I think I know that she wants attention. She's one of those who always have the last word and everything, everything must revolve around her, she's one of those very classic types that need attention. And that's sort of how I feel when I see people showing their wounds and stuff. It's not that often you see

wounds but it's mostly on the Internet you see pictures and stuff and that, I can be *mad* about that. Because it's so, so triggering, don't they think about *others* that actually are sick?

Attention seeking is discredited in this quotation as well. From Emma's story it is clear that a person who displays her scars and wounds is not respected in the same way as someone who tries to hide them. The attention seeker seems to be closely linked to the inauthentic cutter identity.

However, even though this might be the most prominent articulation, it is continuously negotiated. One apparent inconsistency in this regard is the frequent framing of authentic cutting as an expressive and communicative act – basically, a cry for help. In the forums, cutting is constituted partly as a way of regulating emotions by letting them out in a controlled manner, thereby providing a cathartic release; and partly as a way of communicating emotions through a physical manifestation. Both conceptualisations build on already sedimented practices regarding emotional management (e.g., Lupton 1998). Cutting is made intelligible mainly through its comparability with other forms of emotional display and expression, such as crying and talking.[11] This would imply that self-harm is always in some sense about attracting attention, and thus any cutter is by definition also an attention seeker. However, due to the manifold meanings of the latter concept, this apparent contradiction can easily be dissolved and attention seekers are instead articulated with the authentic cutter identity. The equivalence of attention seeking and inauthenticity is also explicitly questioned in attempts to fix the meaning of attention seeking firmly within a discourse of psychiatry. Such rearticulations of cutting transform the cutter identity as well, and thus contribute to rendering the distinction between authentic and inauthentic cutters vague and unstable. For instance, a 23-year-old woman writes in one of the forums:

> Sure, there are many 12- to 14-year-olds who have cut themselves to get attention, BUT if they'd been fine they would never have done something terrible like that in order to get that attention. Come on!

The view that is formulated is that anyone who tries to attract attention to themselves must, by definition, feel bad. Attention seeking is itself constituted as a sign of disorder, or at least a sign that a person feels bad. Emma discusses this in a similar way in the interview:

> *Emma:* I mean, it's like, if you hurt yourself there has to be some reason for it. And even if it's because you want attention, which is like *the worst thing* [with exaggerated voice, then laughter]. It sounds terrible, but I did that *myself* in the beginning.
> *Anna:* I guess that's always part of it?
> *Emma:* Yes, exactly, and so, even if it's because of that, it's extremely serious. I mean, it's caused by something that's extremely serious anyway. But it sounds terrible to do it just to get attention, of course.

In both excerpts, the desire for attention is itself constituted as an indication of the presence of serious problems: the reason why people would want to attract attention must be that they feel terribly bad. I would argue that attention seeking is articulated with disorder and psychopathology in such a way that any person who attempts to attract attention through self-harm will necessarily be understood as an authentic cutter.

However, both of the above quotations imply that this is not a self-evident interpretation. The two accounts do seem to be constituted in opposition to the idea of attention seeking as an inherently inauthentic and superficial phenomenon. It is here that the fluctuating nature of the concepts of attention and attention seeker is manifested. As the meaning of attention seeker is partly attached to the inauthentic cutter identity and partly rearticulated as the property of the authentic cutter identity, it is hard to draw a distinct line between the two. In this regard, the practice of 'attention seeking' and the position of the 'attention seeker' should be understood as floating signifiers. Their undecidability and polysemic nature makes attention seeking and attention seekers open to articulation by conflicting discourses (Laclau 2005, pp. 131–132). This floating status of attention seeking is most clearly discernible in the web discussions, as this social space is generally more construed through equivalential logics, and therefore infused with more antagonisms than are the interviews. However, as the previous examples have shown, the interviews also show a certain tendency towards defining attention seeking in different ways. An application of Laclau's theorisation (2005, pp. 131–133) would imply that anyone who claims the authentic cutter identity is calling for an intervention to install order due to the unstable status of the attention seeker. The potentially inauthentic attention seeker must be rearticulated as an authentic cutter.

Psychiatrisation as hegemonic process

From what I have outlined so far, the notion of disorder appears to be crucial for the antagonistic constitution of the two different cutter identities. The frontier between authenticity and inauthenticity appears to be a frontier between those cutters who truly feel bad and those who do not. What I have shown is that attention seekers and the act of attention seeking destabilise this strict frontier. Attention seeking can be attached to a mentally disordered person as well as to a psychologically healthy person. Thus, in order to claim the authentic cutter identity, one would have to establish some kind of closure in the flow of meaning around the concept of attention seeking. Following a DT perspective, alternative interpretations need to be excluded and prevented in order to make the authentic cutter identity emerge as the single possible option.

And this is exactly what happens when a cutter is turned into a psychiatric patient or otherwise positioned vis-à-vis the psy disciplines[12] within a psychiatric discourse. Cutting is then rearticulated, from being a potentially cultural expression into being a defining feature of psychopathology. Hence, the cutter identity is rearticulated along the same lines. To put it simply, any claim to the authentic cutter identity necessitates a legitimate disorder of some sort. In this context, psychopathology articulates credibility and authenticity in an equivalential chain. The extent to which a disorder appears to be present, or the extent to which a subject succeeds in performing disorder, thus becomes a measure of authenticity. The most solid way of accomplishing such a performance is through reference to some sort of psychiatric intervention, whereby the unresolved cutter identity is articulated as an object of the psy disciplines.[13] This process of 'psychiatrisation' (e.g., Foucault 2008) can be understood analytically in terms of a hegemonic intervention (Gunnarsson Payne 2006, pp. 25–26; Laclau 1996, p. 89) that serves to fix the authentic cutter identity and stabilise the frontier in relation to inauthenticity. I will argue here that such hegemonic interventions and the hegemonising property of the psy disciplines are fundamental to any understanding of the constitution of cutter identities, and might also shed light on the transmission and triggers that have been mentioned in relation to self-harm (e.g., Taiminen et al. 1998).

To illustrate the hegemonising effects of psychopathology and thus of the psy disciplines, 18-year-old Helen's account can be used as an example. Although she had a hard time trying to get adequate care, no one ever questioned her authenticity as a cutter:

> And I also think, because I was warded and I, well, not just that I was warded but it was quite a big deal because I didn't go to school and it wasn't like, people often *believed* that I was feeling bad, I was, I don't know. I mean I *wasn't* taken seriously and at the same time I *was* taken seriously. You know, I wasn't dismissed as being sort of an emo teenager anyway, even though I might have been dismissed as 'come on, quit it' sort of 'stop that nonsense'. But maybe that's in a different way.

Listening to her story, Helen seems to have succeeded in performing disorder the 'right' way. According to her, not attending school and getting in-patient treatment for sustained periods contributed to the constitution of herself as an authentic cutter. Analytically, I would argue that these practices are fixed in relatively stable positions as properties of a psychiatric subject, and the articulation between them and the cutter identity is a hegemonic operation which (temporarily) renders impossible other identifications than that of the authentic cutter.

In the above account we are, however, dealing with tangible signs of disorder. Being discharged from school and taken into psychiatric care are factors which make it practically impossible to view the cutter in any other way than as a person in serious distress. By employing these elements as explanations of how she came to be regarded as *not* 'an emo teenager', Helen comes to inhabit the position of the authentic cutter.

The opposite is described in the interview with Emma. Time and again, she bemoans the fact that her scars are not as many or as large as she would have wanted them to be. Stating that she was 'only' sutured once during all those years, she implies that it constitutes a deviation from the cutter norm. She argued that her identity as truly disordered would have been secured had her scars been more conspicuous to other people, and this is equivalent to the desired and normative authenticity.

> It kind of feels like, why didn't I self-harm more when I had the chance, because, to get more out of this. I liked, you know I liked the feeling, this high that you get. ... And to be able to, I, *now* it feels a little *embarrassing* with people seeing my scars and, like people understand what you've done, but it feels so tiny and pointless.

The size and extent of scars is constituted in terms of a verification of psychopathology. As Emma's scars have faded compared to other cutters', her claims to an authentic cutter identity seem somewhat disputable. Several times during our interview I had the feeling that Emma sees herself as some kind of impostor because of the invisibility of her scars. This is constituted as a failure to embody the normative and authentic cutter identity. Likewise, neither Emma nor Matilda have had in-patient treatment, and both of them tend to construe this lack of psychiatrisation as an obstacle to full identification with an authentic cutter identity. Thus, in their accounts, the real cutters are those who have been disordered enough to be in-patients. These examples serve to illustrate how psychopathology – in part defined through the extent of visible signs of self-harm, but primarily constituted through the articulation between a cutter and the psy disciplines – must be present in order to rearticulate a cutter identity from potentially inauthentic to being credible and authentic. Any psychiatric intervention operates as a legitimisation of psychopathology, and psychiatrisation hegemonises the authentic cutter identity so as to exclude all other possible identifications.

I would suggest that the hegemonic force of psychiatrisation is also the driving force behind features such as *contagiousness*, *triggers* and *competitiveness* in the context of cutting. That feeling bad is contagious has been noted by several interviewees, and in other contexts cutting has been portrayed as easily transmitted. As such, it has been known to spread quickly in certain groups, such as those that can be found in schools and treatment centres (see e.g., Taiminen et al. 1998). The web forums studied here are best described as communities that are built on the idea of mutual support and understanding. I have argued elsewhere that 'feeling bad' takes on the status of an empty signifier that mobilises a collective identification in the forums (Johansson 2010). Whilst this is often constituted as one of the benefits of the forums, it also constitutes a potential problem as the mobilisation around 'feeling bad' tends to exclude other possible positions, such as 'feeling well'. One ex-forum user describes it this way in an e-mail interview:

> I think the atmosphere there is very bad. They sit around cheering each other when they self-harm and I think that's just silly and stupid. They often compare with each other. 'I cut myself so much I had to go to the ER and get 4 stitches' then someone else tries to be worse and they build a vicious circle that never ends for those who read and live in this … [The forum] made it worse rather than it made it better.

In another e-mail interview, a girl warns about the potential dangers and contagiousness of mental ill-health:

> I think it's excellent that there are discussion forums on the web where people can talk anonymously, if they for some reason at the moment cannot get the kind of help they might need like a social worker or someone like that, but I don't think it's a long-term solution because (which I realised now after many years of mental ill-health) mental ill-health is contagious. It easily turns into a competition about who feels the worst and who self-harms the most and that's no good at all.

However, triggering is not restricted to the world on the web. Having friends who feel bad and self-harm, or a partner who does, is also constituted as a risk. A 15-year-old girl writes a post in an agitated way about a friend copying her actions:

> I told one of my friends how I felt. I didn't know then that she's the kind of person who tries hard to feel bad. She started scratching her arms a little and then she PROUDLY showed them to me and everyone else!

'She started scratching her arms a little', writes this girl – and stresses that her friend also seemed proud of this and showed off her marks. This forum post articulates a chain of equivalences where attention seeking, superficial cutting, imitation and the endeavours to be disordered are combined so as to constitute this friend as completely lacking credibility. A similar attitude is also insinuated in the following excerpt from an e-mail interview:

> I have 'friends' who have cut, they thought it was so cool when they got to know that I did so they just had to copy me. And that's why they're not my friends anymore.

Discussions about the transmissibility of cutting often refer to the recruitment of new cutters through exposure of the behaviour. The use of concepts such as contagion and contagious effects operates to situate cutting within a medical domain. Presenting oneself as contagious at the same time confirms that one should be taken seriously as a cutter, because contagiousness equals pathology equals authenticity. It can be seen as a way of constituting oneself as a role model, especially when describing one's influences upon friends – self-injurious acts constitute the subject as someone for others to follow (cf. Taiminen et al. 1998). At the same time, however, the idea of being contagious does imply impurity because the subject constitutes a danger to the people around her. In other words, there are both possibilities and risks in being positioned as contagious.

I would argue that contagious effects in terms of transmission to new individuals or groups of people cannot be distinguished from what is usually referred to as triggering effects. Triggering in this context refers to the tendency that knowledge of other people's self-harm prompts even more, often escalating, acts of self-harm in someone who is already familiar with this behaviour. Both of these imitative processes, transmission and triggers, involve an individual being inspired to self-harm by seeing other people doing it. The fundamental logic seems to be the same in both cases: everyone wants to be the best at self-harm.

Pictures are primarily constituted as the greatest triggers,[14] but graphic representations of acts of cutting or very detailed information are sometimes included in this category as well. According to the contents of the interviews, there appear to be many individual variations of what triggering is. Emma and Matilda, for instance, claim that they were triggered simply by hearing about other cutters being warded:

> And it's also about not making comparisons, because that's what makes it triggering, that you actually *can* compare, that you *can* be better or worse at something. And then if you feel bad and feel that you really suck then you have to show that you're worse than someone else perhaps, or that you've been warded for a long time perhaps, because you've been really really ill or something. And when I think about that, or since I started thinking more about it, I've stopped being triggered or attracted to someone being in a treatment facility for instance. And instead try to see it as a strength that I haven't been in a mental institution, and still show that I have felt like shit. And there was nothing that went totally wrong with my treatment, which many people have had, and I don't need to complain that much about BUP[15]. But still I have felt bad and it's totally okay. And I can still feel fine today without having been down at the bottom. And I can still talk about feeling bad, I can still share my experiences. And it still feels, well, it feels kind of important. To show this too. That it isn't that you need to be really, really ill in order to show that you feel bad. Or that you need not compare, because you can't compare your feeling bad. Or feeling well for that matter.

Matilda does criticise the ongoing comparisons, but her account might also be understood as an attempt to contest the hegemonisation of cutting performed by a psychiatric discourse, where only an individual endowed with the legitimisation of psychiatry can be constituted as a complete and authentic cutter. To Emma, on the other hand, stories about in-patients and psychiatric care do still operate as triggers:

> Of course you could think that it's triggering to read about someone being warded and, and this and that. I mean, small things. It *is* for me, I get kind of 'oh, she's on LPT'.[16] [jealous voice, laughs] And it's like Sofia[17] brought up several times, that it was some kind of status, those who were on LPT, that they had a greater worth, they were kind of more important.

Even though Emma sometimes tends to criticise these kinds of valuations and normative orders, where LPT patients are being construed as the most authentic – on top of the hierarchy – there is nothing in her account that explicitly contests this view. Regrets regarding her not being considered disordered enough or not being legitimised through an extensive psychiatric intervention are displayed in the earlier quotations associated with Emma, and these make her identity as an authentic cutter more vulnerable. A similar tendency is shown by Pamela K. Hardin (1999) in her study of processes of identity construction among anorexics. Hardin argues that anorexics make distinctions between authentic and inauthentic patients, a conclusion that shares many characteristics with the distinction observed between the two kinds of cutters in this study. According to Hardin, this distinction reveals the need for a discourse of psychopathology in order to bestow anorexia with legitimacy as a 'real' disease. To be considered anorexic, it is thus necessary to emphasise one's own psychopathology.

Much like eating disorders, contagiousness as well as triggering effects in self-harm imply a willingness to identify as the best (or worst) cutter, the one who is the most disordered, which, in turn, can be seen as a claim to authenticity. From a DT perspective, both contagiousness and triggers can be understood as attempts at resolving cutter antagonism by exceeding others' performances of psychopathology. However, in a wider social context there might be considerable risks of victimisation and disempowerment if the only way of being identified as an *authentic* subject is to embrace the identity of a *disordered* subject.

Conclusion

This chapter is an attempt to apply a discourse theoretical framework to personal accounts of self-harm and cutting on Swedish networking sites as well as in interviews. I have argued that there are two conflicting understandings of cutting and cutters in this empirical material, and using analytical concepts derived primarily from Ernesto Laclau and Chantal Mouffe (1985; Laclau 1996, 2005) I have outlined how these are antagonistically constituted. The chapter has drawn on rich empirical examples of this antagonism, as well as of how it is destabilised by the elusive meanings of attention seeking.

I have argued that the proliferation of cutting might be seen as a dislocation that disrupts the identity of the cutter as pathological and in need of help. In the wake of this dislocatory event, the web forums emerge as arenas for the mobilisation of claims to authenticity and credibility. However, as shown in the study, 'attention seeking' takes on the status of a *floating signifier*, and as such it appears as an object of contestation between the claims in the forums and its threatening constitutive outside, the inauthentic cutter. While 'attention seeking' and 'attention seekers' destabilise the frontier between the two cutter camps, I further demonstrated how authenticity can be hegemonised by rearticulating the cutter as a psychiatric subject.

This implies that any individual with claims to the authentic cutter identity must also succeed in being disordered. It would seem that there is a precariousness involved in taking up such a position within a psychiatric discourse, as it is strongly inscribed in asymmetrical power relations. Whereas the psychiatric discourse renders authenticity to the subject, the authentic cutter's constitution is dependent on its subjection to the knowledge, practices and institutions of the psy disciplines, as discussed by Foucault (e.g., 2008). Not only does the struggle for disorder involve the risk of reinforcing emotional suffering, but also the adoption of a position as a psychiatric subject – to become an object of the psy disciplines – which most likely adds to social stigma and marginalisation. In this case, success in being identified as a real cutter may come at a rather high price.

Notes

1 According to Sternudd (2008, p. 29) in his discussion of international message boards, there are variations regarding the naming of identifications amongst people who self-harm, and the identity 'cutter' is not necessarily adopted by everyone. It should also be noted that the empirical data for this chapter is in Swedish, where there is no term (neither designated nor self-imposed) that is equivalent to the English 'cutter'. Although the more general labels 'självskadare' ('self-harmer') and occasionally 'självskadetjej' ('self-harm girl') occur in the Swedish accounts, this seems more often to be paraphrased as 'person som skadar sig själv' ('person who self-harms'). The lack of a unifying denomination might be illustrative of the floating character of cutting as a signifier. Even though the cutter label is not used in this empirical material, I employ the term here for the purpose of convenience, in order to designate an assemblage of positions that are taken up by the participants in this study.

2 IRL is an abbreviation for 'In Real Life', referring to that which is not on the Internet.

3 This chapter builds on empirical material from my Ph.D. project. The subject of this chapter is also elaborated on and presented in more detail in my thesis (Johansson 2010).

4 My classification of this as a micro level study should be understood in comparison to other empirical studies that draw on discourse theory, which tend to work with official and/or public documents more than personal accounts (cf. Howarth 2005, p. 339; for examples of empirical studies, see Griggs & Howarth 2000; Howarth 2000; Nidia Buenfil Burgos 2000; Stavrakakis 2000, 2005). For a discussion of different types of data and the epistemological status of interviews, see Howarth (2005).

5 The application of discourse theory in works on identity construction is mostly found in analyses of political identities in a rather traditional sense, e.g., studies of new social movements (see Gunnarsson Payne 2006; Howarth & Torfing (eds) 2005; Howarth et al. 2000). Even so, I would argue that a discourse theoretical concept of 'politics' makes it possible to understand all forms of identifications as initially political acts, regardless of whether the identity in question works as a political mobiliser or not (cf. Glynos & Howarth 2007, p. 130; see also Norval 2000).

6 The methodological procedure was reviewed and approved by the Regional

Ethical Vetting Board, Umeå University (dnr 06-091M). In accordance with the decision of the board, the names and web addresses of the Internet communities will not be given here.

7 Empirical examples have been translated from Swedish and the interview extracts are slightly modified in order to enable readability. The names of the interviewees are all fictitious.

8 *Italics* in transcripts indicates interviewee's emphasis.

9 Paradoxically, to completely hide your feelings from view will not result in any validation at all – and so the struggle for authenticity turns out to be a question of balancing between displaying too much and not displaying anything at all. I argue elsewhere that the contents of authenticity in this regard strongly relate to gender normativity and conceptions of girlhood (see Johansson 2010).

10 For instance, in the treatment literature on self-harm, medical staff are often instructed to care for the physical wounds, but pay as little attention as possible to the practice of self-harm in order not to reward this behaviour (e.g., Sterner 2006). Such treatment principles build on behaviourist theories and are primarily aimed at reducing so-called deviant practices by ignoring them. One of the most prominent writers on self-injury from a medical perspective, Armando R. Favazza, refers to cutting as an instance of attention seeking behaviour (1996, p. 254). However, there is also the opposite construal of cutting in the therapeutic literature, when it is conceptualised as a cry for help which needs to be attended to.

11 It should be noted, however, that in the long run cutting is believed to lose its cathartic function and instead tends to be reframed by the cutters as a loss of willpower. This shift is conceptualised by articulating cutting with aspects of a discourse on abuse and dependency, which further transforms the cutter from intentionally and autonomously acting upon his or her body and emotions to being at the mercy of precisely these objects.

12 My use of the concept 'psy disciplines' is influenced by discussions on the 'psy complex' by, for example, Rose (1985), as well as Blackman and Walkerdine (2001). The term implies a Foucauldian understanding of relations between power and knowledge, and it includes more specifically the set of ideas, practices and institutions that are associated with psychology as well as psychiatry. I use the term to refer to institutions and professionals as well as practices (such as psychotherapy and medication) and knowledge (in terms of diagnoses and explanatory models).

13 The analytic use of the term psychiatric intervention is somewhat misleading because in this empirical context it is not of particular importance whether the psy institutions really have been involved in concrete interventions. What is important is rather how these interventions are framed and how patienthood is performed by the writers and interviewees; and further, how a psychiatric discourse – ideas about cutting as psychopathology – seem to hegemonise certain subjects as authentic cutters, whilst others fail to be positioned within a psychiatric discourse and hence fail to attain credibility.

14 However, people publishing photos on the web are often posited as less authentic and credible.

15 BUP is a Swedish abbreviation that refers to Barn- och ungdomspsykiatrin, which are regional centres for youth and child psychiatry and offer publicly funded counselling and treatment. They are principally open to anyone, but, as indicated in Matilda's account, their services (or lack thereof) are often criticised by cutters.

16 LPT is the abbreviation of the Swedish law on compulsory psychiatric care, and being on LPT refers to being forced into care according to this law.

17 Reference to Sofia Åkerman, author of *Zebraflickan* (2004), an autobiographical account of self-harm.

References

Literature

Adler, P.A. & Adler, P., 2008. The Cyber Worlds of Self-Injurers: Deviant Communities, Relationships, and Selves. *Symbolic Interaction,* 31(1), pp. 33–56.

Blackman, L. & Walkerdine, V., 2001. *Mass Hysteria: Critical Psychology and Media Studies.* New York: Palgrave.

Favazza, A.R., 1996. *Bodies under Siege: Self-mutilation and Body Modification in Culture and Psychiatry.* Baltimore: The Johns Hopkins University Press.

Foucault, M., 2008. *Psychiatric Power: Lectures at the Collège de France 1973–1974.* New York: Palgrave Macmillan.

Foucault, M., 1970. The Order of Discourse. In: R. Young (ed.), 1981. *Untying the Text: A Post-Structuralist Reader.* Boston: Routledge, pp. 48–78.

Glynos, J., 2008. Ideological Fantasy at Work. *Journal of Political Ideologies,* 13(3), pp. 275–296.

Glynos, J. & Howarth, D., 2007. *Logics of Critical Explanation in Social and Political Theory.* London: Routledge.

Griggs, S. & Howarth, D., 2000. New Environmental Movements and Direct Action Protest: The Campaign against Manchester Airport's Second Runway. In: D. Howarth, A. Norval & Y. Stavrakakis (eds), 2000. *Discourse Theory and Political Analysis: Identities, Hegemonies and Social Change.* Manchester: Manchester University Press, pp. 52–69.

Gunnarsson Payne, J., 2006. *Systerskapets logiker. En etnologisk studie av feministiska fanzines.* (Diss.) Umeå: Umeå universitet.

Hardin, P.K., 1999. Shape-Shifting Discourses of Anorexia Nervosa: Reconstituting Psychopathology. *Nursing Inquiry* 10(4), pp. 209–217.

Hodgson, S., 2004. Cutting Through the Silence: A Sociological Construction of Self-Injury. *Sociological Inquiry,* 74(2), pp. 162–179.

Howarth, D., 2000. The Difficult Emergence of a Democratic Imaginary: Black Consciousness and Non-Racial Democracy in South Africa. In: D. Howarth, A. Norval & Y. Stavrakakis (eds), *Discourse Theory and Political Analysis: Identi-*

ties, Hegemonies and Social Change. Manchester: Manchester University Press, pp. 168–192.

Howarth, D., 2005. Applying Discourse Theory: The Method of Articulation. In: D. Howarth & J. Torfing (eds), *Discourse Theory in European Politics: Identity, Politics and Governance*. New York: Palgrave Macmillan.

Howarth, D., Norval, A. & Stavrakakis, Y. (eds), 2000. *Discourse Theory and Political Analysis: Identities, Hegemonies and Social Change*. Manchester: Manchester University Press.

Howarth, D. & Torfing, J. (eds), 2004. *Discourse Theory in European Politics: Identity, Politics and Governance*. New York: Palgrave Macmillan.

Johansson, A., 2010. *Självskada. En etnologisk studie av mening och identitet i berättelser om skärande*. (Diss.) Umeå: H:ström.

Laclau, E., 1994. Introduction. In: E. Laclau (ed.), *The Making of Political Identities*. London: Verso, pp. 1–8.

Laclau, E., 1996. *Emancipation(s)*. 2007 edition. London: Verso.

Laclau, E., 2005. *On Populist Reason*. London: Verso.

Laclau, E. & Mouffe, C., 1985. *Hegemony and Socialist Strategy*. London: Verso.

Laclau, E. & Mouffe, C., 1990. Post-Marxism without Apologies. In: E. Laclau (ed.), *New Reflections on the Revolution of our Time*. London: Verso, pp. 97–132.

Lupton, D., 1998. *The Emotional Self: A Socio-Cultural Explanation*. London: Sage.

Madge, N. et al., 2008. Deliberate Self-Harm within an International Community Sample of Young People: Comparative Findings from the Child and Adolescent Self-harm in Europe (CASE) Study. *Journal of Child Psychology and Psychiatry*, 49, pp. 667–677.

McRobbie, A., 2008. *The Aftermath of Feminism: Gender, Culture and Social Change*. London: Sage.

Nidia Buenfil Burgos, R., 2000. The Mexican Revolutionary Mystique. In: D. Howarth, A. Norval & Y. Stavrakakis (eds), *Discourse Theory and Political Analysis: Identities, Hegemonies and Social Change*. Manchester: Manchester University Press, pp. 86–99.

Norval, A.J., 2000. Trajectories of Future Research in Discourse Theory. In: D. Howarth, A. Norval & Y. Stavrakakis (eds), *Discourse Theory and Political Analysis: Identities, Hegemonies and Social Change*. Manchester: Manchester University Press, pp. 219–296.

Rose, N., 1985. *The Psychological Complex: Psychology, Politics and Society in England 1869–1939*. London: Routledge.

Stavrakakis, Y., 2000. On the Emergence of Green Ideology: The Dislocation Factor in Green Politics. In: D. Howarth, A. Norval & Y. Stavrakakis (eds), *Discourse Theory and Political Analysis: Identities, Hegemonies and Social Change*. Manchester: Manchester University Press, pp. 100–118.

Stavrakakis, Y., 2005. Passions of Identification: Discourse, Enjoyment, and European Identity. In D. Howarth & J. Torfing (eds), *Discourse Theory in European Politics: Identity, Politics and Governance*. New York: Palgrave Macmillan.

Sterner, T., 2006. Självskadande beteende. In: K.G. Öst (ed.), *KBT. Kognitiv beteendeterapi inom psykiatrin*. Stockholm: Natur & Kultur.

Sternudd, H.T., 2008. Smärtans gobeläng. Bilder av självskador. *Valör*, 2.

Taiminen, T.J. et al., 1998. Contagion of Deliberate Self-Harm Among Adolescent Inpatients. *Journal of the American Academy of Child and Adolescent Psychiatry*, 37(2), pp. 211–217.

Vad vet vi om flickor som skär sig? 2004. The National Board of Health and Welfare – Socialstyrelsen.

Winther Jørgensen, M. & Phillips, L., 2000. *Diskursanalys som teori och metod*. Lund: Studentlitteratur.

Åkerman, S., 2004. *Zebraflickan*. Västerås: Författarhuset.

CHAPTER 8

A Mediated Discourse Analysis of Pseudonymous Blogging

Stephanie Faye Hendrick

Blogging is a practice by which an author, or authors, can create an online representation of the self, typically through text-based posts set in reverse chronological order. According to Herring et al.'s (2004, p. 11) analysis of the weblog genre, 92 per cent of blog authors provided a name, i.e., a full name, surname or a pseudonym. Additionally, more than half of weblog authors provided explicit demographic information such as age, occupation, and/or geographic location (Herring et al. 2004). Despite the high number of bloggers who include information about their identity on their blog, anonymous blogging is an accepted practice. Blogging 'fictionally' or through a fictional character[1] without revealing that the blog is fictional, however, seems to be quite taboo[2] (Hendrick 2006). This interdiction can be attributed to a conceptualisation of weblogs as containing stylistic elements of both the diary and citizen journalism (Allan 2006; Rosenberg 2009). It is within the cues of these two competing, yet similar, discourse systems that the reader decides whether the author has presented him- or herself truthfully. The predominant response within the blogging community to a weblog that is revealed to have been written by someone other than the openly identified author is often characterised by uproar[3] (Geitgey 2002; Walker Rettberg 2008).

This article will deconstruct the social identity *pseudonymous blogger* through the mapping of identity elements in the presentation posts of two bloggers, and compare these identity elements to a sample of the mass media's presentation of the same two bloggers.[4] I begin this chapter by setting the discourses of diary writing and journalism in historical contexts and relating these contexts to the practice of blogging. I will then argue that the two discourses inform the categories *cultural projections* and *societal currents* in Norris' (2004) *multimodal framework*. I then use Scollon and Scollon's (2004) nexus analysis and Norris' (2004) multimodal framework in order to examine the blogs BitchPhD and Belle de Jour. The aim is to examine the construction of pseudonymous social identities in action and how these constructions dictate, and are dictated by, social practices.

Identity and blogging

The concept of identity can be understood as the story we tell others about who we think we are. It is the 'project of the self' (Giddens 1991, pp. 53–54), and often changes to meet the conversational demands of our perceived audience (Bell 1984). Online diaries and weblogs can provide an insight into how social identity is remediated and translated online and over time (McIlvenny & Raudaskoski 2005). Daniel Chandler (2004) wrote that 'personal homepages may not always be of great importance to those who come across them, but they're profound, creative opportunities for people to reflect on themselves and think about how they want to represent themselves to the world' (Thurlow, Lengel & Tomic 2004). There are often a limited amount of cues to a physical-world counterpart in a blog, and it can be exceedingly difficult to connect physical-world identities with their online representations. Various weblog communities reward transparency and identity play differently. For example, in academic and/or professional blogging communities, your *physical-world identity is reinforced by your reputation*. It is often a simple process to identify whether a professional or academic blogger is who he or she says they are because digital traces of their identity are also located beyond the boundaries of the blog – a university/departmental webpage, appearances at conferences, journal publications, etc. However, in a pseudonymous social identity blog, rather than your social identity serving as a redeeming part of your reputation, *your reputation is your identity*. An example of this can be found in punditry blogs; albeit, these do not have to be, by default, anonymous or pseudonymous. The aspect of reputation as identity does remain equally important, though, as continued success as an expert on his or her blog often results in online and physical-world rewards.[5]

Blogs are more than a representation of their authors, but are simultaneously a monologue and a dialogue. As such, they are both a reflection of the author's thoughts and feelings and a channel through which to report news and commentary. According to Scott Hall (2006, p. 4) in *The Blog Ahead: How Citizen-Generated Media is Radically Tilting the Communications Balance*, a blog is a place 'to inform and to be informed, a *conversation* that is, derived from direct information, and an abundance of *straight talk*'. This duality leads to interesting assumptions in relation to the performance of privacy, accountability, and identity in weblogs. As will be shown in this chapter, elements of diary writing and journalism have been assimilated into a domain of meaning, which I argue has social consequences both online and offline.

The blogging diarist

According to van Dijck's (2004) exploration of the relationship between diaries and blogs, diaries have long been associated with the misconception that they are a private record meant for the author alone. Both the diary and the journal display traits of the private and the public. Diaries are often addressed to an unknown or perceived reader (even if the reader exists only for the author). Moreover, Mallon (2004) posits that the journal was born from the genre of travelogue and associated with the newspaper, which led to ideas of a perceived audience and entries that were made on a daily basis.

> [N]o one ever kept a diary just for himself; pointing out the continuity between the 'journal' and the 'diary', [Mallon] concludes that both are directed towards an audience and 'both [are] rooted in the idea of dailiness, but perhaps because of the journal's links to the newspaper trade and diary's to 'dear', the latter seems more intimate than the former' (Mallon, in van Dijck 2004).

In his article 'Composing the Self', van Dijck (2004) goes on to say that the diary was often perceived as a semi-public record by a community rather than an individual, and used as a way of expressing and remembering, which was shared within, but never outside a community.

> Diaries have thus historically been produced by both individuals and groups, regardless of their degree of intimacy or their potential to appear in print. Since its very inception, the genre has been dialogic rather than monologic, hence obliterating the line between private and public (van Dijck 2004).

The travelogues and diaries that Mallon and van Dijck describe above could describe most blogs today. Blogs are written with a similar duality. They are simultaneously a conversation with oneself *and* with an unknown or perceived audience (Efimova et al. 2005). They are at once intensely public and fiercely private.

The blogging journalist

Both journalism and diary writing have a long-standing tradition of 'getting at the truth'.[6] Previously, diaries were written as part of religious exercises in self-discipline or used as a means to highlight and edify a spiritual journey (Serfaty 2004). These diaries demanded truthful writing in order to fulfil their purpose. Journalism was not the introspective journey for truth, but rather a search for fact through the inclusion of different sources and perspectives that were carefully edited and verified (Prillinger 2004). Weblogs can be seen as a blend of these genres. They are simultaneously a chance for self-reflection and an opportunity to report in a public forum. As 'truthful' reporting is the basis for both of these genres, it therefore becomes clearer why blogging under a veil of secrecy is often met with anger or frustration. It goes directly against an unwritten maxim of weblog writing: 'truthful' disclosure (Blood 2002). Even if you are writing under a pseudonym, truthful disclosure is expected and, in fact, the very reason why a pseudonym may be needed. Blogs are merely a platform from which acts of journalism or acts of self-expression may occur. And while they can be used for journalism, a Pew Internet Research survey conducted in 2006 reported that 65 per cent of the respondents stated that they did not consider their blogs to be a form of journalism (Lenhart & Fox 2006). Rather, blogs can be seen as a subjective medium which filters information through the bloggers' experiences. They are the multiple personality of online writing; a reflection of truth as seen through the lens of the author.

The Kaycee case

There are several cases of blog identity that have been exposed as alternative or as a hoax in the mass media. Possibly the first case, and certainly the first to receive such attention, was a 19-year-old girl who wrote a detailed weblog in which she bravely described living as a teenager with leukaemia. Her name was Kaycee Nicole Swenson. Kaycee quickly garnered a large audience who adored her. They wrote to her both through her weblog and via e-mail. People spoke with her and her family on the telephone, and when she died people grieved. They wanted to know where to send cards or when the funeral was scheduled. When noone in her audience was able to find an obituary to scan in and distribute, or a funeral to attend, this scam – which lasted well over two years – began to unravel. An Internet forum[7] was created to discuss what people actually knew about Kaycee and whether anyone had ever physically seen her. It was soon discovered that Kaycee was actually the fictional creation of a woman named Debbie Swenson and her real-life, perfectly healthy, daughter. In order to make their ruse more convincing, the Swensons used a combination of pictures of a girl at Debbie's daughter's school and the daughter's voice to give life to their blog character.

The Belle de Jour case

Another case that attracted a great deal of interest by the mass media and readers in order to 'correctly identify' the author was that of Belle de Jour, the supposed Internet call-girl who the *Times Online* dubbed, 'a stiletto-heeled sex bomb with the erudition of a college professor' (Woods & Hellen 2004). This weblog had an immense following, which ultimately led to a book deal – one with the stipulation that no one was to know Belle's real identity (Bradberry & Wagner 2004). This stipulation was picked up in the mass media and led to a host of reporters and professors attempting to identify the real 'Belle'. Several people were believed to be the call-girl, including a journalist[8] for *The Register* in San Francisco who replied, 'I'm shocked. To be accused of being a whore is one thing, but to be accused of being a weblogger is actionable' (Vance 2004). Belle's blog, and the media attention surrounding it, will be explored further in this chapter.

Analytical concepts
Mediated discourse analysis

The construction of identity is not always an explicit process. We create the stories of our identity through discursive actions. Furthermore, what may be implicit in one mode of discourse may be made explicit in a different one (Norris 2004). Every action that we effect contributes to the construction of our social identity by accepting, denying, aligning with, or against a discourse. It is through actions that we position artefacts of our identity – foregrounding or backgrounding these artefacts in order to claim socially constructed identities. In order to explore pseudonymous social weblog identities through artefacts or traces left by blogging practices, a model (see Figure 1) based partially on the frameworks of Ron Scollon and Suzie Wong Scollon's *nexus* analysis[9] and Sigrid Norris' *multimodal* analysis has been created. This model traces artefacts of identity that are made explicit through the actions of blogging by identifying cultural projections. One such projection is anonymity=deviance, which can be assigned to the medium as well as various other modes of communication, such as a perceived audience and the affordances of the blog's layout. Scollon and Scollon's and Norris' frameworks are part of the field of critical discourse analysis called *mediated discourse analysis* (MDA). Mediated discourse analysis is not focused on the discourse in terms of talk and text alone, but rather on the point at which social practices converge and the role discourse plays in that convergence (Jones & Norris 2005). The unit of analysis in MDA is the *mediated action*, which is the point of 'tension' between the meditational means and the social parameters that give action meaning (Jones & Norris 2005, p. 5). The communicative actions that are associated with blogs leave artefacts: whether it is a post, a comment, or a reference to another action. Jones and Norris (2005, p. 6) describe the relationship between the mediated action and the tools used to produce them as a mutually transformative process: 'not only is the way we take action transformed by the tools we use, but these tools themselves are transformed by the actions they are appropriated to perform'.

Social identity is defined here as a 'construction in relation to others who may not be present at a given moment' (Norris 2005, p. 183). It is an acknowledgement of the role that perception plays in forming facets of our identity. Social identity can be explored by examining macro and micro modes of communication that are present in the weblog. The macro modes of analysis include the interplay between cultural projections and societal currents. Cultural projections are reflected in the response of bloggers to what they perceive are the opinions of their audience.[10] These can include discourses around prostitution, academia, parenthood, etc. Societal currents, in this study, are reflected in the media's response to the bloggers. The elements that make up these modes are then expressed through actions, or on the micro/blogger level. How these actions are foregrounded or backgrounded, i.e., the awareness paid to the actions, suggests claims of social identity.

Nexus analysis

In nexus analysis, as described by Scollon and Scollon (2004), individuals draw on available discourse systems to which they are, or have been, socialised. These systems teach individuals to act in ways that come together to either implicitly or explicitly construct and re-construct their social identity (Norris 2007; Scollon & Scollon 2004). This 'teaching' occurs in three cycles of discourse: engaging the nexus of practice, navigating the nexus of practice, and ultimately changing the nexus of practice (Scollon & Scollon 2004).

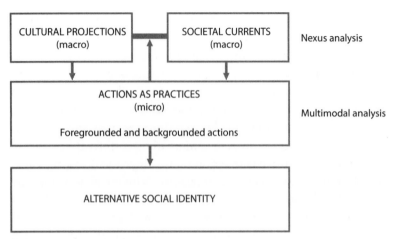

Figure 1. Adapted from Sigrid Norris' (2004) multimodal framework and Scollon and Scollon's (2004) nexus analysis.

In this case study, the relevant nexus of practice occurs between the competing, yet comparable, discourses that are based on a debate which periodically makes its way around the blogosphere: *Is blogging journalism?* Although many bloggers cringe with weariness at the question, the blogging format (i.e., push-button publishing) creates a cognitive blend of two related, yet separate spheres: diaries/journals and journalism (see Figure 2). Catchphrases that are attached to weblog platform brand names such as 'push-button publishing' and 'publishing for the people' are, in essence, statements by weblog platforms that the tool they are marketing straddles the line between self-expression and journalism. Weblog platform brand names such as MovableType and Wordpress, and the not-uncommon practice of bloggers receiving press passes to cover an event, stand in opposition to statistics that say that the majority of blogs are personal accounts (Herring et al. 2004). This also exemplifies the confusion between a blog as a journal and a blog as journalism. This blending, however, is not a new phenomenon, as journals and news accounts share a history in which they have had much in common, and the domains private/public and objectivity are grounded in both genres. Rosenberg (2009, p. 274) summarises the debate by stating that 'writing a blog neither qualified not disqualified you for the "journalist" label… *Blogger* and *journalist* ought to have served as simple names for straight-forward activities; too often they were used instead as badges of tribal fealty.' Allan (2006) also considers blogs to be an important addition to the media landscape in which *random acts of journalism* can occur. However, by demarcating the act of journalism, both Rosenberg and Allan separate the content from the platform – an important distinction that is often lost in the journalism versus blogging debate. As blogs have become an established medium of communication, discussions that attempt to define or pigeonhole blogging among bloggers and traditional media sources have brought this mixing of genres to the forefront. Despite, or possibly due to, the cultural projections discussed above, blogging incognito is an undesirable practice among mainstream bloggers. Belle de Jour (in Knight 2009), one of the bloggers examined in this study, comments on the desire to 'find out' in an article where she reveals her identity after six years of successfully keeping it hidden.

> Also, I started writing in 2003; I was one of the first bloggers to be anonymous. People weren't used to it. It was relatively easy for us to get our resources together and keep me anonymous. By the time other anonymous bloggers came along, people were looking out for them – they were under a lot more scrutiny (Knight 2009).

Norris suggests in her article (2007) on the micropolitics of identity that this type of behaviour may stem from deeply rooted assumptions that only one identity can be claimed at a time, and that the actions that the author chooses to focus upon are the only valid elements of identity. This cultural projection is reflected in the discourse of traditional and alternative media sources when writing about bloggers who write under a pseudonym, but also in these bloggers' responses to media accusations.

Multimodal analysis

According to Norris' (2005) theory on the construction of social identity, identity elements bind together and implicitly or explicitly ground themselves in discourse systems. Norris (2007, p. 658)

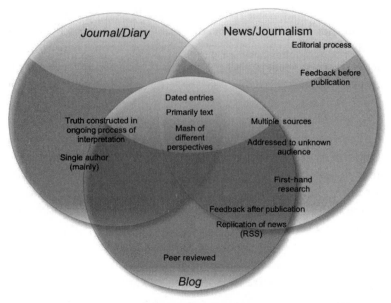

Figure 2. Attributes adapted from Prillinger's (2004) comparison of blogging and journalism of Journal/Diary, News/Journalism and Blog.

borrows Scollon and Scollon's notion of the discourse system, and claims that it is within such a system that social actors have been socialised to act in certain ways; ways that differentiate one discourse system from another. Norris relates this construction to Scollon and Scollon's (2004) theory of nexus analysis, which states that identity is continuously shaped on a micro level, but that identity is also claimed and contested against the 'histories and cultures of the individuals and the societies that they belong to' (Norris 2005, p. 183). The multimodal framework attempts to identify all communicative modes[11] at play during a communicative event (Norris 2004). This framework is most often applied to physical-world events, and as such there is an equal focus on actions and modes that would not leave digital artefacts on a blog; such as one's posture when sitting at the computer, the music that may be playing in the background, or where the blogging event takes place. Contextual information is an important part of Norris' framework as, according to him (2004), it is the interplay between the various actions and modes that allow identity to be performed (Norris 2004). Although contextual cues that do not leave digital traces are not fully accounted for in this study, identifiable communicative modes do include less explicit actions such as the layout of the blog or news site, and the blogger's awareness of a perceived audience.

Materials and methodology

Two bloggers who write under pseudonyms were chosen for close analysis: BitchPhD and Belle de Jour. These bloggers were chosen for their popularity within their communities of practice, for their appearance in traditional mass media debates, and for their ability to remain incognito.[12]

Both BitchPhD and Belle de Jour use the weblogging platform Blogger. This platform allows for attribution and social networking by default. Both bloggers posted regularly, and their newest posts were listed at the top of their pages. Both blogs were single-authored, although BitchPhD invited multiple authors to take part in her blog one year after it was posted online. However, BitchPhD remains the main voice on the blog, and the posts that were authored by the other authors are all attributed by name. As this study only uses the first month's posts of each blog, the other authors were not included in either sample. Feedbacks differ in the two blogs, as well. BitchPhD welcomes conversations, and, as will be shown in this study, she uses guidelines for her commentators as a way to negotiate her own social identity. Belle de Jour, on the other hand, closed her comment area, thereby removing the possibility for multiple authors to contribute to her blog – even minimally through the comment spaces.

BitchPhD

BitchPhD (http://bitchphd.blogspot.com) began blogging in 2004 as a discontented tenure-track academic.[13] Her personal life and professional life were at odds, and her relatively liberal view on issues such as open relationships, birth control, and academia – sprinkled with a mix of snarky remarks about co-workers – drew many readers. BitchPhD remains somewhat anonymous today, although the occasional speaking appearance has resulted in her identity becoming easily searchable without it being explicitly posted on her weblog.

In her second blog post, BitchPhD describes herself in the following way:

> I am busy trying to be the person my department and I have agreed to pretend I really am, so I want a space to try to figure it out (geographic discontent means leaving your therapist behind) without having to worry about adding 'indiscreet and self-sabotaging' to 'lazy and disorganized' as self-descriptors. Of course, by pretending, in real life, to be a person that I think no one really is I merely substitute 'hypocritical' for 'self- sabotaging.' Well, don't we all (BitchPhD, 6 July 2004).

Belle de Jour

Belle de Jour (http://belledejour-uk.blogspot.com) presents herself as a London-based call-girl who began blogging by recounting her interview for a call-girl job in 2003. Her explicit posts that cover the day-to-day happenings in the sex industry, and her witty, learned prose garnered her a large audience, quickly. Belle de Jour continues to blog, but more about daily life than about being a (now ex-) call-girl. There has been much speculation about the 'true identity' of Belle de Jour, but as Liz Miller, a contributing editor for Book-Slut,[14] writes:

> Suspicions persist that Belle is not a real person, but I believe her – if only because, aside from commenting on the fiction made of her life, she still writes candidly about her sexual experiences, drops updates on her other writing projects, and in general blogs about the same sort of trivialities one fills a personal blog with. I can see someone faking the blog of a prostitute – but the blog of an ex-prostitute? There have to be better ways to spend your time (Miller 2008).

Belle de Jour is now the author of three books: *The Intimate Adventures of a London Call Girl* (2005), *The Further Adventures of a Lon-*

don Call Girl (2006), and *Playing the Game* (2008). In addition, her memoirs have now been adapted for both TV[15] and film.

The first post was chosen for analysis in both cases in order to highlight the presentation of social identity in action. It is within these first few posts that both bloggers provide explanations for their choice to use a pseudonym. Excerpts from the actual posts are included in the analysis. From a close reading of the posts, higher- and lower-level actions were evaluated against cultural and societal currents (cf. Figure 1) as presented in news articles portraying both bloggers. The news items were concerned with the process of 'finding out' the physical-world's social identity counterpart to the online pseudonymous social identity. Both blogs were read over a course of four years; however, due to the scope of the research question, only the first month of posts from each blog has been examined further.

Analysis
BitchPhD

The popular, anonymous academic blogger, BitchPhD, begins her blog with a warning of anonymity. This 'warning' gives credibility to her posts, as she claims ownership of the ideas presented, but also shows an awareness of the taboo of blogging under a pseudonym by claiming the need to protect the *guilty* and the *innocent*. Her initial post states that:

> The events are real. The thoughts are my own. But the names have been changed to protect the guilty and the innocent (BitchPhD, 5 July 2004).

After this post, BitchPhD debates the elements of the discourse *anonymous blogger*, which are personally salient against her alternative lifestyle, leftist political views and position in a traditional, humanities tenure-track academic position. This debate is a running theme on BitchPhD's blog and, as will be shown later in the analysis, culminates in two key posts: a description on how to read and respond to her blog, as well as an academic article in which she reveals her physical-world identity while simultaneously analysing anonymity in blogging as a panellist at a scientific/academic conference:

> Which brings me to the question: why an anonymous blog? Well, because, like all academic types, I am paranoid. I am certain that everyone out there is as disorganized and lazy as I am, and I know that my own geographic discontent and frequent doubt as to whether I really want to be doing this are pretty common as well (Bitch-PhD, 5 July 2004).

> As I said in the comments, the question of anonymity is extremely troubling – and interesting – to me. I feel strongly that if we would all say publicly the things we say privately (on blogs, to our grad school friends, to our partners, whoever) about things like work/life balance, how much we *really* write during the summer, and so on, that academe would be a much better place (BitchPhD, 20 July 2004).

Two discourses are competing to be the foregrounded social identity. The first discourse, *pseudononymous blogger*, is constructed against the cultural projections of anonymity=deviancy, which is grounded in the elements of protection, fear, presumption, and attribution. You can see these elements at play in the excerpt below. BitchPhD underscores anonymity=deviancy when she states that now that she is becoming more well-known, her blogging practices have become more restrained. In fact, in the last sentence of the post below, BitchPhD states this explicitly.

> And now I have this feeling that, having gotten a couple trackbacks and gotten readers – which I'm very glad for – suddenly I'm 'on the radar' and even though I'm anonymous, I feel more constrained about the subject matter I can/should write about here. There are things that are on my mind that now I think don't 'belong' on an academic blog – another kind of blog, maybe. And yet, for solid professional reasons including my research area and the whole question of gender and academic identity, I know that these topics can and probably should be addressed; more to the point, I want to

write about them. So actually, it isn't I that thinks [sic] they don't belong on an academic blog; I think other people might think that. Cultural projection? I started an anonymous blog not just to bitch, but also to talk about these things, and yet now that people are reading the darn thing, I am nervous again. It's heinous

The private stuff that I fear is 'unacademic' is very much a part of my academic identity; the bitching about job stress is a personal and self-indulgent but no less important critique of academic culture. The fact of anonymous academic blogging is itself the object of study; this stuff doesn't belong in a locked diary somewhere, it belongs out there where people can think about it. That so many of us put it out there without our names on it might be perceived, not as a problem, but as a gift (BitchPhD, 20 July 2004).

The second competing discourse is the *attributed*[16] *academic*. Bitch-PhD comes from a formal humanities background that is steeped in traditions of attribution for written works. As her blog was started in order to discuss academia but later became more political, BitchPhD was unsure about whether or not to blog about personal matters. Discourses of politics, gender, and social geography – not strictly part of academia – are backgrounded as important to the construction of BitchPhD's social identity and her identification with elements of the discourse *attributed academic*.

The social taboos that BitchPhD feels driven to talk about, and mentions above as an important element in the construction of her academic identity, do not extend to the realm of the abstract. Instead, it is the potential personal ramifications of her opinions that keep BitchPhD anonymous. As can be seen in the post from 25 July, the blogger writes that she would publish written porn under her real name, as this is a socially accepted form of writing in her field.

Interestingly, however, I have been thinking about writing porn on the side, and that I would be willing to do under my real name: why not? Anyone who worked with me would 'know' that it's 'just writing' (BitchPhD, 25 July 2004).

However, when she writes about her everyday existence, BitchPhD takes great pains to keep her family and even location secret. This reinforces an awareness of the aforementioned cultural projection of anonymity=deviancy.

> To the person who asked about where I am/where I want to go: much as I long to go into great detail on that question, I am far, far too paranoid to be that specific. I will say only that I have moved from a large city to a small town, and there is NO WAY IN HELL I am staying here. Not. Gonna. Do. It (BitchPhD, 12 July 2004).

A year after BitchPhD began blogging, she posted a welcome message to her readers that explained the protocol for participating on her site. In this post, BitchPhD shows her awareness of the implicit rules of blogging, including that of identity disclosure. However, the post below foregrounds her own anonymity through foregrounding the readers. This is done while explaining the consequences for trolling[17] her comment sections. The reader's identity can never truly be anonymous. Even if they do not use any identifying marker to sign their comment (username, blog address, e-mail address), every comment is marked by an IP address, and that address can be blocked from further participation. Therefore, BitchPhD, not only acts as the hostess of the site, a role that is emphasised by her greeting in the post below, but also enjoys supreme control over the site, as she holds the power to steer conversation and banish those who break her rules.

> Hi. I hope you'll poke around the archives, hang out in the comment threads, meet the regulars, bookmark the site, and join in the discussions.
>
> A few explanations. This is, obviously, a feminist site; it is also leftist and, in the end, a personal site as well. If feminism pisses you off, or (after reading a couple of posts) you decide that I have my head irretrievably up my ass, it's pretty easy to go away and read something else, and that's what I expect you to do. The comments policy is right up there at the top of the first sidebar, so if you feel moved to leave a comment telling me I'm an idiot, or telling one

of the regulars that he or she is an idiot, expect your comment to be deleted and, if necessary, your ip to be banned. If you are condescending, insulting, don't know the difference between a blog and usenet, or are so self-centered that you think it's your god-given right to derail comment threads onto your pet issue, you can also expect your comments to be deleted: if you have some pet issue that needs airing, go right ahead and start your own blog like everyone else. ...

Basically it boils down to the importance of tone and community. If you can join in and argue as among friends, colleagues, and peers, then by all means grab a cup of coffee or a beer and pull up a chair. If you can't, though, or if you're the type of person who goes to a party and ends up joshing with the guys out back by the barbecue because you really have no interest in what the women have to say, then this isn't the place.

The regulars here are a hell of a great group, and I really value their contributions to the site. If you don't read the comment threads, you're missing half the value of the place--and as the blog owner and saloniste, it's my job to keep the conversation flowing and make sure no one breaks the furniture (BitchPhD, 25 July 2004).

BitchPhD has a large readership, according to blog trackers such as Technorati (http://www.technorati.com). However, her anonymity never fell under the same scrutiny as those bloggers who received book deals or otherwise benefited financially from their blogs. In fact, BitchPhD's anonymity was strongly defended after an irate former commenter threatened her after being banned from her site and another reader called his academic advisors to report her behaviour. While the reader who made the call to the commenter's advisors was publicly chastised, BitchPhD's right to remain anonymous was championed on many blog sites. News reports, too, such as the one cited below, presented BitchPhD by the topics commonly found in her blog – and did not mention her state of anonymity until she herself does in a quote.

Also on the morning of the 2nd, Deignan visited BitchPhD's blog about academe and politics where, by that time, the anonymous blogger had written about her distaste for President Bush's Supreme Court nominee, Samuel Alito Jr....

BitchPhD, said that she feels somewhat threatened by Deignan. 'I don't know if his attempts to track me down represent a real threat, either in terms of my identity or in terms of a physical threat,' she said via e-mail Wednesday. 'I don't know if what he's doing counts as cyberstalking. It's certainly upsetting' (*Online Quicksand* in Inside Higher Ed, 2005).

Why BitchPhD's anonymity is championed while other bloggers, such as WaiterRant[18] and Belle de Jour, are the objects of intense investigation may have something to do with the consistency of her performed identity. BitchPhD is explicit about her reasons for anonymity from the outset. Her need for anonymity is not to gain something, but rather a preventative measure in order to perform what she feels is her authentic identity – a contrast to the identity she is forced to perform in her professional life. The contrasting discourses are not something internal to her identity, but rather discourses that she is forced to perform and relate. This negotiation of contrasting discourses is an example of the negotiation between the cultural projection of being anonymous and the societal currents about the controversial topics in her blog, especially within the often traditional academe. Even the design of her webpage reinforces her performed alternative identity. While the blog is formatted as a typical weblog (a main posting area and a sidebar of links), the header of the blog contains a striking image of a little girl with a challenging look on her face. The girl is captured holding up her hand in a rude gesture while an older girl stares, mouth agape.

Belle de Jour

Belle de Jour presents herself through contrasting discourses – the *learned professional* and the *call-girl*. Belle opens her blog by describing the process of applying to be a call-girl. The language in the first post is subtle, and the only reference to her work is the use of the word *agency*. This subtle reference is somewhat contextualised by a distinct emphasis on the physical beauty of the interviewing manager. It is not until the last line of the second blog post that the reader begins to understand that the position for which Belle de Jour is applying is that of a call-girl. This becomes clear when she uses the explicit term, *punters* as a counterpoint to her manager's description, *domina*.

> Located what sounded like an excellent, small, discreet agency (word of mouth, as they say) (Belle de Jour, 24 October 2004).

> She had to take a few calls during lunch, where I learned she speaks fluent German and Arabic. More than a touch of the domina about her. God, the punters must love that (Belle de Jour, 25 October 2004).

> She looked hard at me. 'You›re bored? That›s terrible.'
> 'I was being ironic. Actually I›m not bored at all,' I said, cupping my own breast for the thirtieth time (Belle de Jour, 28 October 2004).

When Belle de Jour's posts are read in their entirety a pattern begins to emerge. They often begin with narratives that are characterised by their sophisticated vocabulary. It is often not until the end of her posts, however, that strongly sexual linguistic images are presented. In the post below, Belle de Jour narrates a conversation with her manager about recently taken portfolio pictures. It is not until the end of the post that the subtlety of the narrative becomes abrupt and explicit.

> 'Darling, the pictures, they are fabulous', the manager purred. I've noticed she never introduces herself on the phone but launches straight into conversation. Must be a graduate of the same charm school as my mother. 'Thank you, I was worried about not look-ing relaxed.' 'No, they are perfect. Can you do something for me? Can you write something about yourself for the portfolio? Most of the other girls, I write something for them, but you should do this very well.' Cripes. I am a tall, luscious... ah, no. Amusant, savoir faire? Save me. Self-motivated, works well in groups... perhaps

closer to the truth. Where are the CV clinics for whores? (Belle de Jour, 29 October 2004).

Belle de Jour's presentation of herself in her *The Intimate Adventures of a London Call Girl* (2005) is much more explicit then what can be found in her blog. In the introduction to her book, she states without hesitation that she is a whore. Choosing a harsh synonym for call-girl, Belle de Jour draws on the element *non-apology* for her chosen profession. There is no work-up to her profession; rather, Belle de Jour's use of the term *whore* underscores the cultural taboo by 'warning' the readers of what is to come.

> The first thing you should know is that I'm a whore. I don't mean that in a glib way. I'm not using the word as an analogy for working a desk job or toiling away in new media. Many of my friends will tell you how temping for a year or ending up in sales is equivalent to prostitution. It's not. I know this because I've been a temp and I've fucked for money, and they are in no way similar. Not even the same planet. Different solar systems altogether (Belle de Jour 2005).

In Belle de Jour's presentation of herself, there is a constant merging of contrasting discourses. Headlines in the mass media, however, present her as a puzzle to be solved – a search for the 'real' Belle de Jour rather than a figure who has written several books resulting in a highly successful TV adaptation. In the media's presentation of Belle de Jour, only one view seemed to be acceptable at a time – *blogger/author* or *call-girl*. When the mass media took up the story of Belle de Jour's publishing deal that made her popular blog into a book, their stories focused on either uncovering her identity or trying to prove why their guess at Belle de Jour's 'true' identity was legitimate (Bradberry & Wagner 2004). One theory put forward the idea that Belle de Jour was a 42-year-old man (Leitch 2005). An alternative theory, and one that received the most attention, was based on an investigation by forensic linguist Don Foster, who claimed that the linguistic markers found in Belle de Jour's blog were consistent with those of the writer Sarah Champion.[19]

Figure 3. Sarah Champion as 'Unmasked call-girl author' in *Times Online*,[21] 18 March 2004.

Language that reflects the discourses of deviancy, secrecy and conspiracy is present in the examples below. These discourses are further strengthened through the use of images such as that in Figure 3, which depicts a woman with a challenging facial expression dressed in a red Bionic Woman t-shirt.[20] The picture of Sarah Champion sneering at the camera was chosen to accompany an article in the *Times Online* (Coates 2004) entitled 'Internet "call-girl author" unmasked'. This picture was placed at the top of the article, before any text appeared, and it seems to have been a random shot unrelated to Champion's alleged Belle de Jour identity.

The academic, from Vassar College in New York, identified Sarah Champion using little more than common sense, the Internet and the vagaries of the English language. An initial reading of Belle's text gave him several clues. 'I immediately thought that Belle was English rather than American, Internet-savvy and probably lived outside London,' he said (Coates 2004).

The 'unmasked' author from the *Times Online* article above writes an article in response in *The Guardian Online*: 'I was branded a call girl'. In this article, language is used that reflects the discourses of deviancy (branded), secrecy (textual Ghostbuster) and conspiracy (conspiratorial), which serves to foreground the cultural projection of anonymity=deviancy.

> 'Can I just ask you, is this a work of fiction or are you a working call girl?' he concluded, with a conspiratorial whisper.
> A what? My heart missed more than one beat as reality hit, 'Oh fuck, this guy might be serious.... cause – Professor Don Foster, or 'Doctor Comma', as he quickly became known in my household. Daft as it sounds, merely to discover the identity of a blogger the paper had gone to the extremes of hiring a New York academic described as the world's number one 'textual Ghostbuster', an expert previously brought in to study Monica Lewinsky's writings (Champion 2004).

The elements of identity associated with Professor Don Foster, the person who allegedly 'unmasked' Champion, are important, yet backgrounded in the text. Whereas descriptors such as branded and unmasked were associated with Belle de Jour, Foster is described in terms of him being an 'academic from Vassar College'. There are also subtle statements that he was able to outfox Belle de Jour in mere minutes, using little more than Google and a little forensic linguistics. These backgrounded elements that are associated with Foster not only highlight the dichotomy between legitimate and illegitimate communicative online practices, but also allude to a dichotomy of power that is associated with these practices. Belle de Jour has built her online identity over time, and has garnered a substantial readership which seems to have accepted her identity make-up. However, she does seem to be easily unmasked by 'legitimate' communicative practices.

The construction of a social identity discourse is reflected in the following excerpt from the *Times Online* article 'Internet 'call-girl author' unmasked', where writing about sex and writing anonymously are expected to coincide. This conflation of a taboo topic and a taboo blogging style is drawn from the discourse of blog deviancy, and foregrounds Belle de Jour's identity as author/blogger:

> Belle is not the first anonymous sex columnist. Last year a teen-ager from Sicily became a sensation with a novel about her sexual adventures. It was pitched as a thinly veiled autobiography. The author, Melissa Panarello, initially tried to remain anonymous but the book's success forced her to reveal her identity. It has sold 500,000 copies and is being translated into English (Coates 2004).

Terms such as branded, unmasked, notorious, and conspiratorial in conjunction with the revealing of Belle de Jour further substantiate the implicit 'wrong-ness' of blogging under a false identity. Not only does Champion use this language in her response (see above), but it is also used by the editor to introduce her article:

> I was branded a call-girl blogger. Media speculation about the identity of the author behind an Internet diary of a London pros-titute fell upon one woman last week when she was unmasked in the Times. Here writer Sarah Champion gives an exclusive ac-count of how it feels to be mistaken for the notorious 'Belle de Jour' (Champion 2004).

Note that Sarah Champion (2004) felt the need to state clearly that she had never been a call-girl, thus negotiating cultural projections of prostitution and anonymity, which in this case both equal deviancy.

> She said that she was aware of the impact Belle de Jour had had and asked: 'How did you find my name? Give me a clue?' Later she sent an e-mail with the statement: 'I want to make clear that I have never been a call girl' (Champion 2004).

Concluding discussion

Through the use of words, images and links, weblogs not only represent the continuous deconstruction and reconstruction of the actual artefact, but also the author's online self (Serfaty 2004). Trust between the author and his or her public is formed over time, despite the fact that bloggers have no real way of identifying their readers. The continuous construction and regeneration of the blog through updating and posting creates a situation in which readers become invested and trust in the blogger's given identity – be it public or anonymous.

Cues as to how bloggers negotiate their social identity can be found using Norris' multimodal framework. Bloggers foreground and background aspects of their identity through the cultural projections of their perceived audience and the societal currents (in this study from media coverage) against the affordances of the weblog tool and the discourses that inform those affordances. Blogging is a practice in which one can commit acts of self-disclosure (diary-style), or acts of journalism. These two competing discourses bring with them strong practices of their own that they affect how identity is constructed within different blogging communities. In BitchPhD's (2007) presentation of her own pseudonymous blogging experiences at the 2006 Modern Languages Association conference, she stated that pseudonyms draw attention away from the name and place it on the author's role. She went on to say that 'pseudonyms mean something, and one of the things they mean is that the pseudonymous writer has a reason for pseudonymity... the genre entails risk, that publishing is risky' (BitchPhD 2007).

BitchPhD performed her social identity through the affordances of the weblog genre by foregrounding the discourse *attributed academic* against the societal currents of a traditional humanist academic background, and the cultural projections of gender, political correctness, and heteronormativity. Belle de Jour, on the other hand, performed her social identity, *professional call-girl*, through the affordances of the weblog genre by foregrounding the discourse *cultured professional* equally against the discourse of *call-girl*. By doing this she embraced the positively rewarding elements of the societal currents *professional* and *learned*, which were shown through linguistic choice and the professional process of performing 'call-girl', something simultaneously reinforced through articles in the media in order to restructure the call-girl discourse. While BitchPhD responded to the societal currents with anonymity due to fear of repercussions, Belle de Jour used such elements to reinforce the credibility of the call-girl discourse. As can be seen from the two cases presented here, blogging under a pseudonymous social identity can occur for different reasons. The affordances of the weblog, in combination with the cultural projections of the subject matter can provide rich opportunities to explore alternative identities. A multimodal analysis of their construction can identify elements that are important to the discourse, and which can uncover hidden or implicit cultural and societal projections that have an impact on the formation of identity. In the two cases presented here, anonymity is not equated with deviancy. The reasons for blogging with a pseudonymous social identity may be for protection, but also as a way to restructure societal currents. Identity becomes more than a name or a set of characteristics – blogging into existence a pseudonymous social identity involves building a reputation or credibility over time. It is through the foregrounding and backgrounding of different elements from competing discourses that one creates, plays and evolves social identity in action.

Notes

1 For a list of fictional blogs, see the fiction blog webring, http://fictionblogs2.blogspot.com/

2 The taboo-ness of blogging fictionally was expressed in discussions of fictional blogging at the weblog conference Blogher, in 2006, as well as in weblog discussions on my own research blog, The Sum of My Parts, in the same year. These discussions resulted in a commenter-generated 'contest' to find the identities of the subjects of this article, who were at the time of blogging anonymous. The commenters were unsuccessful.

3 Examples of weblog backlash against blogging as a fictional character can be found in the Kaycee Nicole case discussed later in this article, as well as in the discussion of resources dedicated to unmasking the physical identity of the bloggers in question.

4 This chapter is part of an ongoing Ph.D. project financed by the Knut and Alice Wallenberg Foundation and the Department of Language Studies at Umeå University. The aim of this project, 'Weblogs as mediators of virtual communities of practice', is to examine how virtual communities of practice emerge and are linguistically maintained from within larger online, networked communities. I would like to thank Annika Egan Sjölander, Jenny Gunnarsson Payne, Anders Steinvall, Kirk Sullivan, Chris Hudson and Patrik Svensson for valuable comments on this chapter. Additionally, I would like to thank my classmates on the course 'Perspectives on Discourse Analysis' for their valuable comments and their energy in creating an environment from which this chapter could emerge.

5 An early example of a punditry site is the Drudge Report. This is a conservative aggregator of editorialised links about news, entertainment and politics. The site was created in 1996 by Matt Drudge, who in his own words 'barely finished high school' (Allan 2006). The Drudge Report is most famous for having scooped the Clinton-Lewinsky scandal (Scott 2007). And while Rheingold (2003) considers the Drudge Report to be a cautionary tale about the idealisation of democratising publishing, Allan (2006, p. 44) considers it to be of 'major significance in the emergence of blogging as a citizen-based form of journalism'. While the journalistic ethics or intentions of the Drudge Report are hotly debated, it is clear that Matt Drudge's online activities led to a high-profile online identity.

6 The notion of truth is applied with the full acknowledgement that it is a relative term and always dependent on particular perspectives.

7 For more information about the Kaycee Nicole Swenson case, see the FAQ, http://rootnode.org/article.php?sid=26.

8 Andrew Orlowski, reporter for San Francisco's *The Register*.

9 Scollon and Scollon define a nexus as 'a link between two different ideas or objects which links them in a series or network' (2004, p. iii).

10 Audience perception can be determined by cues such as IP numbers, e-mail address and identifying information left in the comments, yet the blogger can only make assumptions on the audience based on their target audience, the outspoken audience, or their perceived audience (Viégas 2005).

11 Kress and Van Leeuwen (in Norris 2004, p. 101) define a communicative mode as a set of signs that have meanings and regularities attached.

12 However, it should be noted that both authors have now revealed their physical-world identities.

13 'Tenure-track' academic positions describe a senior research position in which the holder is granted the right to not be fired after a probationary period. Tenure is not usually granted upon hiring; rather, the professor must meet certain publishing and teaching standards before tenure is awarded.

14 BookSlut describes itself as 'a monthly web magazine and daily blog dedicated to those who love to read. We provide a constant supply of news, reviews, commentary, insight, and more than occasional opinions' (http://www.bookslut.com).

15 The TV adaptation of Belle's books is entitled *The Secret Diary of a Call Girl* and stars Billie Piper, formally the star of *Dr Who*. The series was aired first in September of 2007 in the UK. Currently, *Secret Diary* is in its third season and is internationally syndicated.

16 'Attributed' is used here to refer to the academic norms of citation and referencing as devices used to establish credibility.

17 According to the *Urban Dictionary Online*, trolling is the act of purposefully antagonising other people on the Internet, generally on message boards. (http://www.urbandictionary.com/define.php?term=trolling).

18 WaiterRant was the blog of a tell-all waiter describing the habits of restaurant patrons from two high-profile bistros in New York City. His blog also became a book, and like both the bloggers in this case study he revealed his own identity after four and a half years of blogging pseudonymously.

19 Belle de Jour's physical-world identity remained anonymous until she decided to 'out' herself in November of 2009.

20 The Bionic Woman is the star of a television show with the same name from the 1970s about a female tennis player turned superhero after receiving bionic implants.

21 Screenshot published with permission from *Times Online*.

References

Literature

Allan, S., 2006. *Online News: Journalism and the Internet.* Berkshire: Open University Press.

Anjewierden, A., Brussee, R. & Efimova, L. 2004. Shared Conceptualisations in Weblogs. In: BlogTalk 2.0, T.N. Burg (ed.), *The European Conference on Weblogs: Blogtalks 2.0. Vienna, Austria 5–6 July 2004.* Herstellung: Norderstedt, pp. 110–138.

Bell, A., 1984. Language Style as Audience Design. In: N. Coupland & A. Jaworski (eds), *Sociolinguistics: A Reader and Coursebook.* New York: St Mattin's Press In, pp. 240–50.

Belle de Jour, 2005. *The Intimate Adventures of a London Call Girl: Belle de Jour.* London: Weidenfeld & Nicolson.

Belle de Jour, 2006. *The Further Adventures of a London Call Girl.* London: Weidenfeld & Nicolson.

Belle de Jour, 2008. *Playing the Game.* London: Orion.

Berry, K., 2006. How to Unmask an Anonymous Blogger: The Company's Right to Know vs. the Anonymous Blogger's Right to Remain Unknown. *Law.com,* [Internet] 4 April. Available at: http://www.law.com/jsp/ihc/PubArticleIHC.jsp?id=1144067964387 [Accessed 18 June 2009].

Bishop, T., 2003. Microsoft Fires Worker over Weblog. *Seattlepi.com,* [Internet] 30 October. Available at: http://seattlepi.nwsource.com/business/146115_blogger30.html [Accessed 18 June 2009].

Blood, R., 2002. *The Weblog Handbook: Practical Advice on Creating and Maintaining Your Blog*. Cambridge: Perseus Publishing.

Chandler, D., 2004. Osobne web-stranice i stvaranje identiteta na webu (Personal Home Pages and the Construction of Identities on the Web, in Croatian). In: R. Senjkovic & I. Plese (eds), *Etnografije Interneta*. Zagreb: Institut za Etnologiuu i Folkloristiku Ibis Grafika, pp. 219–235.

Efimova, L., Hendrick, S., & Anjewierden, A., 2005. Finding 'The Life Between Buildings': An Approach for Defining a Weblog Community. Paper presented at Internet Research 6.0: Internet Generations, Chicago. Available at: https://doc. telin.nl/dscgi/ds.py/Get/File–55092/AOIR_blog_communities.pdf [Accessed 18 June 2009].

Efimova, L. & de Moor, A., 2005. Beyond Personal Webpublishing: An Exploratory Study of Conversational Blogging Practices. In: *Proceedings of the 38th Hawaii International Conference on System Sciences (HICSS'05)*. Los Alamitos: IEEE Press.

Fauconnier, G. & Turner, M., 2002. *The Way We Think: Conceptual Blending and the Mind's Hidden Complexities*. New York: Perseus Books Group.

Grant, T. & Baker, K., 2001. Identifying Reliable, Valid Markers of Authorship: A Response to Chaski. *Forensic Linguistics*, 8(1), pp. 66–79.

Geitgey, A., 2002. The Kaycee Nicole (Swenson) FAQ. In: R. Blood (ed.), *We've Got Blog: How Weblogs are Changing Our Culture*. Cambridge: Perseus Publishing, pp. 89–99.

Giddens, A., 1991. *Modernity and Self-Identity: Self and Society in the Late Modern Age*. Cambridge: Polity.

Hall, S., 2006. *The Blog Ahead: How Citizen-Generated Media is Radically Tilting the Communications Balance*. Garden City: Morgan James Publishing.

Herring, S., Kouper, I., Scheidt, L. & Wright, E., 2004. Women and Children Last: The Discursive Construction of Weblogs. In: L.J. Gurak, S. Antonijevic, L. Johnson, C. Ratliff & J. Reyman (eds), *Into the Blogosphere: Rhetoric, Community, and Culture of Weblogs*. [Internet]. Available at: http://blog.lib.umn.edu/ blogosphere/women_and_children.html [Accessed 18 June 2009].

Herring, S., Scheidt, L., Bonus, S. & Wright, W., 2004. Bridging the Gap: A Genre Analysis of Weblogs. *Proceedings of the 37th Hawaii International Conference on System Sciences*. (HICSS'04) – Track 4, p.40101.2, January 05-08. Available at: http://www.ics.uci.edu/~jpd/classes/ics234cw04/herring.pdf [Accessed 18 June 2009].

Huffaker, D., 2004. *Gender Similarities and Differences in Online Identity and Language Use among Teenage Bloggers*. (Diss.) Washington DC: Georgetown University. Available at: http://cct.georgetown.edu/thesis/DavidHuffaker.pdf [Accessed 18 June 2009].

Jones, R. & Norris, S. (eds), 2005. *Discourse in Action: Introducing Mediated Discourse Analysis*. New York: Routledge.

Lenhart, A. & Fox, S., 2006. Bloggers: A Portrait of the Internet's New Storytellers. Pew Internet and American Life Project. [Internet] Available at: http://www. pewInternet.org/Reports/2006/Bloggers.aspx?r=1 [Accessed 23 November 2009].

McIlvenny, P. & Raudaksoski, P., 2005. Mediating Discourses of Transnational

Adoption on the Internet. In: S. Norris & R. Jones (eds), *Discourse in Action: Introducing Mediated Discourse Analysis*. New York: Routledge, pp. 62–72.

Norris, S., 2004. Multimodal Discourse Analysis: A Conceptual Framework. In: P. Levine & R. Scollon (eds), *Discourse and Technology: Multimodal Discourse Analysis*. Washington DC: Georgetown University Press, pp. 101–115.

Norris, S., 2005. Habitus, Social Identity, the Perception of Male Domination – and Agency? In: S. Norris & R. Jones (eds), *Discourse in Action: Introducing Mediated Discourse Analysis*. New York: Routledge, pp. 183–196.

Norris, S., 2007. The Micropolitics of Personal, National and Ethnicity Identity. *Discourse & Society*, 18(5), pp. 653–674.

Prillinger, H., 2004. Are You Serious? In: BlogTalk 2.0, T.N. Burg (ed.), *The European Conference on Weblogs: BlogTalks 2.0. Vienna, Austria 5–6 July 2004*. Herstellung: Norderstedt, pp. 83–95.

Rheingold, H.R., 2003. Moblogs Seen as a Crystal Ball for a New Era in Online Journalism. *Online Journalism Review*, 9 July. [Internet] Available at: http://www.ojr.org/ojr/technology/1057780670.php [Accessed 23 November 2009].

Rosenberg, S., 2009. *Say Everything: How Blogging Began, What it is Becoming, and Why it Matters*. New York: Crown Publishers.

Scollon, R. & Scollon, S., 2004. *Nexus Analysis: Discourse and the Emerging Internet*. London & New York: Routledge, pp. xvi, 198.

Scott, D., 2007. Pundits in Muckrakers' Clothing. In: M. Tremayne (ed.), *Blogging, Citizenship, and the Future of Media*. New York: Routledge, pp. 39–57.

Serfty, V., 2004. *The Mirror and the Veil: An Overview of American Online Diaries and Blogs*. Amsterdam: Rodopi.

Thurlow, C., Lengel, L. & Tomic, A., 2004. *Computer Mediated Communication: Social Interaction and the Internet*. London: Sage Publishing.

van Dijck, J., 2004. Composing the Self: Of Diaries and Lifelogs. *Fibreculture: Internet – theory – criticism – research* [Internet]. 3, Available at: http://journal.fibreculture.org/issue3/issue3_vandijck.html [Accessed 18 June 2009].

Viégas, F., 2005. Bloggers' Expectations of Privacy and Accountability: An Initial Survey. *Journal of Computer-Mediated Communication* [Internet]. 10(3), article 12. Available at: http://jcmc.indiana.edu/vol10/issue3/viegas.html [Accessed 18 June 2009].

Walker Rettberg, J., 2008. *Blogging*. Cambridge: Polity Press.

Newspapers and magazines

Barkham, P., 2005. Blogger Sacked for Sounding off: Waterstone's Says Bookseller Brought Firm into Disrepute. *The Guardian* [Internet] 12 January. Available at: http://technology.guardian.co.uk/online/weblogs/story/0,14024,1388466,00.html [Accessed 18 June 2009].

Bradberry, G., Wagner, E., 2004. The Web Diary, the Book Deal and the Very Happy Hooker. *Times Online* [Internet] 10 March. Available at: http://www.timesonline.co.uk/tol/life_and_style/article1041521.ece [Accessed 18 June 2009].

Capriccioso, R., 2005. Online Quicksand. *Inside Higher Ed.* [Internet] 10 November. Available at: http://www.insidehighered.com/news/2005/11/10/bloggers [Accessed 18 June 2009].

Chase, R., 2005. Court Rules in Favor of Anonymous Blogger. *Breitbart.com.* [Internet] 6 October. No longer available online. http://www.breitbart.com/article.php?id=D8D2LHF06andshow_article=1

Champion, S., 2004. I was Branded a Call-Girl Blogger. *The Guardian* [Internet] 21 March. Available at: http://www.guardian.co.uk/technology/2004/mar/21/media.pressandpublishing [Accessed 18 June 2009].

Coates, S., 2004. Internet 'Call-Girl Author' Unmasked. *TimesOnline* [Internet] 18 March. Available at: http://www.timesonline.co.uk/tol/news/uk/article1048424.ece [Accessed 18 June 2009].

Dube, J., 2009. Why Bloggers Should Adopt Standards | CyberJournalist.net. *Cyberjournalist.net* [Internet] 21 January. http://www.cyberjournalist.net/why-bloggers-should-adopt-standards [Accessed 18 June 2009].

Knight, I., 2009. I'm Belle de Jour: Finally the Anonymous Sex Blogger from Diary of a London Call Girl Comes Clean to The Sunday Times. She's Dr. Brooke Magnanti. *Times Online* [Internet] 15 November. Available at: http://entertainment.timesonline.co.uk/tol/arts_and_entertainment/books/article6917495.ece [Accessed 23 November 2009].

Leitch, L., 2005. The Web's Belle de Jour. *London Evening Standard* [Internet] 15 November. Available at: http://www.thisislondon.co.uk/showbiz/article–17693582-the-webs-belle-de-jour.do [Accessed 23 November 2009].

Morris, S., 2005. An Anonymous Blogger Tells All. *This Is Not a Blog* [webzine] Spring. Available at: http://journalism.nyu.edu/pubzone/notablog/story/anonymous/ [Accessed 18 June 2009].

Rockwood, K., 2007. BlogStalker: BitchPhD. *Venuszine: Emerging Creativity,* [webzine] 24 September. Available at: http://www.venuszine.com/articles/art_and_culture/reads/271/blog_stalker_bitch_ph_d [Accessed 18 June 2009].

Vance, A., 2004. Did Register Staffer Mastermind 'Call-Girl Weblog' Conspiracy? *The Register,* [Internet] 21 March. Available at: http://www.theregister.co.uk/2004/03/21/did_register_staffer_mastermind_callgirl/. [Accessed 18 June 2009].

Woods, R. & Hellen, N., 2004. Focus: Who is 'Belle de Jour', the High-Class Hooker Whose Web Diary is Set to be a Literary Sensation? *Times Online* [Internet]14 March. Available at: http://www.timesonline.co.uk/tol/news/uk/article1045532.ece [Accessed 18 June 2009].

Online sources

BitchPhD, 2007. Academic Blogging Part II. *BitchPhD* [weblog] 28 January. Available at: http://bitchphd.blogspot.com/search?q=academic+blogging+part+II [Accessed 18 June 2009].

Fiction Blog Webring Homepage [Internet]. Available at: http://www.bowjamesbow.net/fictionbloggers.shtml [Accessed 18 June 2009].

Hendrick, S., 2006. Other Identity at Blogher. *The Sum of My Parts* [weblog] 6 July. Available at: http://sumofmyparts.org/blog/?p=803 [Accessed 18 June 2009].

Miller, L., 2008. Belle De Jour. *BookSlut* [weblog] 13 July. Available at: http://www.bookslut.com/hollywood_madam/2008_07_013122.php [Accessed 18 June 2009].

Zuckerman, E., 2005. A Technical Guide to Anonymous Blogging – A Very Early Draft. *GlobalVoices* [Internet] 13 April. Available at: http://www.globalvoicesonline.org/?p=125 [Accessed 18 June 2009].

CHAPTER 9

The Discursive Construction of a Responsible Corporate Self

Alon Lischinsky

What does it mean to speak of a corporation's 'identity'? In business communication, the term is traditionally understood in terms of branding and style: an organisation is identified by the logos and design schemes that make it recognisable (Knapp 2001). However, the question of what exactly is being recognised is open to discussion. Some scholars argue that 'essential' corporate identities are stocks of enduring, distinctive characteristics shared by members of an organisation (e.g., Balmer & Greyser 2002; Golden-Biddle & Rao 1997). On the other hand, the 'cultural turn' of organisational thinking since the early 1980s has shown that material devices and resources do not have an intrinsic meaning, but rather acquire meaning through discursive activity. The organisation and its different publics engage in 'interactions and interrelationships between insiders and outsiders' (Gioia et al. 2000, p. 70) that seek to make corporate activity meaningful through explanation, justification and description. Both the internal and external communicative endeavours of an institution, as well as their public responses and reinterpretations, are therefore seen as part of an ongoing dialogue between multiple, competing views of its identity (Humphreys & Brown 2002; Phillips & Hardy 1997; Taylor 1999).

This cultural shift is part of a renewed interest in the rhetorical and discursive aspects of organisational life. However, relatively little research has been carried out on the actual linguistic devices used to poster a given interpretation of organisational identity (but see Coupland & Brown 2004; Livesey 2001). In this chapter, I seek to partially redress this gap by examining choices in referential form in the self-presentation of corporate rhetors. Persons and institutions can be described in different ways, and choosing from the set of possible labels involves seeking those that are relevant to the specific communicative goals of the author and the interests and needs of the audience (Stivers 2007, p. 73). It is easy enough to figure out why Swedish energy giant Vattenfall, one of the companies in my sample, touts itself as 'number one for the environment'. Understanding why activists in Greenpeace prefer to call it 'number one in dirty energy' is no harder. But what about the less obvious, yet pervasive choices made by corporate report writers? Does 'the company' have a sustainability goal, or is it 'us'? Is 'managing personnel needs' the same as 'taking care of our workforce'? Who is the 'we' that claims to be 'a constructive partner in society'?

Previous research has highlighted the sophisticated way in which selections of referential form in conversation contribute to recipient design, tying them in with 'the demands of the larger social agendas' (Downing 1996, p. 95). I apply these insights to the study of corporate communication, where the complexities associated with multiple institutional roles make such selections maximally exploitable (Levinson 1988, p. 203). The data are drawn from a corpus of 50 Sustainability and Corporate Social Responsibility reports issued by large Swedish companies during 2009. A previous analysis (Lischinsky 2010) has shown that the construction of a committed, responsible corporate identity is a major concern in these reports. I aim to expand on that insight by focusing on how forms of self-reference are selected to further this goal, foregrounding ethical and prospective aspects of organisational identity.

From a theoretical point of view, the chapter is also intended as an illustration of the contribution that quantitative and qualitative linguistic analysis can make to the critical understanding of social issues. Usually labelled critical discourse analysis – a somewhat infelicitous moniker, for reasons discussed *infra* –, this form of inquiry seeks to identify the specific communicative and interactional features that guide the intersubjective construction of meaning. Unlike other approaches to discourse analysis, which take the abstract *configuration of meaning* in a discursive practice as their point of departure – such as the discourse theory of Ernesto Laclau and Chantal Mouffe, discussed at some length by Johansson in this volume–linguistically-informed discourse analysis focuses specifically on the *devices* used in this configuration and the *processes* in which it takes place.

The remainder of this chapter is structured as follows. In the following two sections, I present a broad outline of the theoretical outlook informing my research, both in general terms and specifically as regards the discursive analysis of identity construction. 'Referential choices in discourse' briefly reviews previous research on the forms and functions of self-reference. Finally, 'Self-reference in practice' provides an analysis of self-reference in the corpus. This is first discussed in terms of overall patterns and trends, and subsequently applied to the specific case of the referential shifts used to strategically influence the attribution of praise and blame for environmental and social responsibility.

Critical discourse analysis

In its broadest sense, critical discourse analysis (CDA) entails the use of linguistic theories and concepts to understand (and intervene in) how social relations are structured, especially when the structure leads to an unjustifiably unfair distribution of social goods: prestige, status, influence or, more generally, power.

This is, of course, far from a new endeavour. Principled critiques of the ambiguous role of language in human interaction – as a tool for rational argument, but also a resource to excite passion and prejudice – have accompanied Western culture since the time of Plato. However, while classical concerns about the use of language as a means of communication gave rise to disciplines such as rhetoric and dialectics, subsequent developments in scientific linguistics were ambivalent regarding these aspects. Both the structuralist school of Ferdinand de Saussure – with its focus on *langue*, the formal system of language considered separately from the less predictable aspects of production and comprehension – and the generative model of Noam Chomsky – interested in the universal, innate rules that govern the production of syntactic systems – deliberately ignored the variations in how language is actually used, and *a fortiori* the effects that such variations may have on social practices (Kress 2001, p. 33).

Interest in language as an instrument of social interaction remained in several Continental traditions in linguistics, such as the Prague and Copenhagen Schools, but also flourished rather independently in other disciplines. A strong tradition of linguistic anthropology in the United States, for example, investigated how language acquisition and competence are intimately tied to broader patterns of socialisation, while sociolinguists focused on how cultural norms about settings and roles affect the use and appraisal of language. Philosophical studies of natural language – as opposed to formal logical notation – provided materials for pragmatics through notions such as presupposition and implicature, while psycholinguistics tackled the empirical questions of language production and comprehension neglected by formalist theories.

It would seem a momentous task to subsume these multiple concerns under a single framework, and despite the increasing use of the CDA label over the past two decades, there is little theoretical and methodological unity to be found beyond a broadly constructivist tenet: that social entities are constructed and maintained by processes that are partly linguistic in nature. CDA is better understood as a problem-driven[1] interdisciplinary field sparked by the work of critical linguists Fowler, Hodge, Kress and Trew (1979), where different resources for analysing language-mediated interaction have been applied to the overarching goal of understanding how social inequality is enacted and reproduced in language (for further discussion of the historical and theoretical bases of CDA, see van Dijk 1993, p. 2001; Weiss & Wodak 2007; Wodak 2002; Wodak & Chilton 2005). This has led some scholars, especially Teun van Dijk, to advance the alternative label of 'critical discourse studies', in order to better reflect both the plurality in approaches and the fact that no method of analysis is inherently or exclusively critical. Instead, scholars focus on aspects of discourse that reveal, in a given time and setting, problems of inequality and unfairness.

My work in this chapter, for example, draws on a long-standing theme of pragmatics: the fact that the interpretation of certain linguistic expressions depends on the context in which they are uttered.

Terms such as 'here', 'in an hour', 'like this' or 'you' are called 'deictics' – from the Greek word for 'pointing out' – because they signal features of the context in which the utterance takes place, and their referent cannot be identified unless this contextual information – place, time, manner and the identity of the addressee, respectively – is known. However, it is not only these 'pure' deictics that index elements of the communicative situation. Sociolinguists and linguistic anthropologists speak of *non-referential* deictics to describe those communicative elements that do not change the referential value of an utterance, yet express important contextual variables that are relevant to the interactional goal.

Addressing someone as 'Sir' or 'Madam', for example, does not add to the reference of the sentence, but infuses the utterance with an additional level of pragmatic meaning: the speaker is showing deference towards the addressee in a way relevant to the immediate communicative purpose,[2] and thus providing information on their respective social roles, personal characteristics, and about the interactional setting, such as the expected level of formality (Silverstein 2003). In other words, most if not all linguistic elements can be seen as orienting to – i.e., making relevant to the ongoing interaction – the social and cultural features of the participants and their context.

As members of various discourse communities, we are intuitively aware of the existence of social deictics and, to some extent, of the relevant discourse patterns. Genres such as the etiquette book and the style guide are often attempts to formalise this intuitive knowledge in terms of general rules. However, such formalisations tend to fall flat, and not only because indexical elements do not function in isolation (they tend to cluster together, and their effect is a result of their combination rather than of any individual feature), but also because introspective native-speaker intuition is notoriously unreliable for understanding language. Stubbs (2001) points out that the cognitive frames and scripts we use to make sense of the social world are designed to represent a core model of routine, recurring situations, and hardly ever reflect the degree of variation and complexity that occurs in actual behaviour. Analogously, introspection can produce idealised linguistic prototypes, but is ill-equipped to accurately describe actual use (Stubbs 2007, p. 129).

One of the major contributions of corpus-oriented forms of linguistic analysis has been the development of technologies to record and compare empirical language use in volumes large enough to reliably reproduce such complex variations. The result is a view of language that is neither categorically deterministic nor in random variation, but rather probabilistic. While we cannot describe the linguistic system in terms of a finite, fixed, computable set of rules, we can use empirical data about the unequal likelihood of certain patterns to hypothesise about both the intentional process of discourse design by authors, and about their (largely unconscious) expectations about their readers' interpretations. Therefore, frequency in a representative corpus equals probability in the system of language (Halliday 1991, quoted in Stubbs 2007, p. 130). Even though each act of language use shifts the overall balance – with more or less force, on the grounds of basically extralinguistic factors, such as reach or personal prestige –, it can only become effective by honouring and realising the patterns established by prior use.

The management of discursive identity

A basic tenet in every form of discourse analysis is that language use is not simply making *statements*, true or false, about the world; it is rather an *interaction* between writer and reader, or speaker and audience,[3] and governed as much by the goals that they want to achieve as by the grammar of the language. It is with these in mind that writers conduct their self-presentation, positioning themselves vis-à-vis the reader by establishing their perspective, their affiliation and their place in the broader social world.

The construction of identities as the contingent product of particular historical circumstances at both a shared social and a local biographical level has received considerable attention in many branches of the social sciences. Carlbaum (this volume), for example, examines how the traditional identity of intellectuals as an elite, masculine group changes under the pressure of the growing number of women who continue into higher education due to the lack of suitable jobs. Lundgren (this volume) adopts a similar approach for discussing how political-economic changes have shifted the meaning and value we attribute to age labels such as 'older people'. However, critical discourse studies focus specifically on how this construction is taken up in every act of discourse, as when Lundgren's informant, Kerstin, calls herself a 'grumpy oldie'. This is an explicit signal that she acknowledges the cultural devaluation of old age, while also being ready to challenge it by setting up a competing discourse where her generation is portrayed as still energetic and healthy.

In this chapter, I intend to focus on a specific resource for the discursive construction of identity: the linguistic choices available to writers to refer to themselves. The most obvious means of self-reference (SR) is, of course, the use of personal pronouns. 'I' and its related forms – 'me', 'my', 'mine' – have the sole function of allowing participants in a communicative interaction to refer to themselves without the need for further specification. However, this seemingly straightforward device does not capture the complexity of the relationship between the empirical person who makes an utterance and their multiple social and institutional roles, which can be selectively highlighted by alternative forms of self-reference. In an influential essay, Goffman (1979, pp. 17–21) distinguished three roles conflated in the naïve concept of the writer: that of *animator*, the person who physically produces the utterance; that of *author*, the person who composes its linguistic realisation; and that of *principal*, the person who bears responsibility for the social act that the utterance performs. This echoes earlier work by Sacks (1992, 1, pp. 148–149), who had argued that, by choosing a specific form of self-reference, a writer can manifest the capacity in which they are acting, whether on their own behalf, that of a larger community, or even as animator of views not entirely their own (Land & Kitzinger 2007, p. 496).

In other words, pronominal (or 'deictic') reference does not make clear which of the multiple social roles and memberships relevant to an individual's self-characterisation are being oriented to in the specific interactional situation. Sometimes the context sufficiently restricts this ambiguity in discursive identity: by virtue of the genre conventions of academic writing, the 'I' in the paragraph above is to be read by reference to my identity as a linguist and a scholar, and sets a discursive position that could be occupied with little change by anyone else sharing these memberships. (Think of how differently the paragraph would read if I had written 'I personally' instead, explicitly defeating the default assumption.)

In other cases, ambiguity becomes an exploitable resource. Fetzer and Bull (2008) have looked at how politicians take advantage of the multiple possible meanings of pronominal reference to strategically shift the footing of their message from their own personal stance to broader and more relevant groups, such as their party, the entire national society, or all reasonable people. In addition, modal adjuncts, qualifiers and other similar resources can serve a disambiguating function when writers wish to explicitly negotiate their discursive identity. This is the case, for example, in regard to Susanne, an informant of Sjöstedt Landén (this volume), who shows the relevance of her countryside upbringing in her decision to move away from the capital by speaking of 'a chance for us *bumpkins* to get these very attractive jobs that otherwise wouldn't have become available' (my emphasis).

Referential choices in discourse

The growing literature on self-reference in discourse has made significant headway in identifying the functions typically attached to each linguistic form, even if some important difficulties remain. The main problematic point is that writers can choose *not* to mark their textual presence at all, and instead frame their communication as an entirely impersonal discourse on external facts. Benveniste (1966, p. 239) called this form of utterance *histoire*, as opposed to *discours*, where the relationship between writer and reader is openly recognised. Removing themselves from the text can be a strategy for authors to present the message as a direct reflection of natural or social fact (Calsamiglia Blancafort 1996, p. 66). This is typically the case in hard news, or in the natural sciences, where writers prefer to say that 'tests show' or 'results prove' rather than explicitly acknowledge the need for interpretation. In these cases, drawing attention to personal intervention 'makes the claim dependent on an individual, and thus fallible, human judgement' (Hyland 2000, p. 93).

But drawing the conclusion that overt authorial marking is always a hedging device is a gross simplification. Writing *histoire* is possible when genre conventions or other extralinguistic factors have already established authorial credibility (Lerman 1983, p. 100). In other cases, especially when coupled with other boosting devices, personal endorsement by means of explicit self-reference can actively strengthen the claims in the text. By overtly placing themselves behind their statements, authors can build on 'a personal ethos of competence and authority' (Hyland 1998, p. 236) and draw on the legitimacy associated with their social position to buttress their discourse.[4]

Reference to the author by means of the first-person plural (1PP) pronoun usually indexes the writer's role as a representative of a wider community (Calsamiglia Blancafort 1996, p. 68; Fetzer & Bull 2008, p. 279; Goffman 1979, p. 19). While certainly marked in the informal settings favoured by conversation analysts, 1PP is often the default choice in all forms of institutional communication. Messages from an official source, such as press releases or institutional documents, are designed to be read as if expressing the voice of a single 'corporate rhetor' (Cheney & McMillan 1990, p. 96). Whoever the empirical author of these documents, the identity assumed to stand behind them as principal is by default the corporate persona.

Speakers entitled to represent the organisation – either its specifically designated spokespeople or occupants of the top institutional echelons, such as managers and directors – can also exploit the ambiguities between their personal footing, that of the corporation as a whole, and even that of all organisational members. These shifts can obscure the complicated issues of representativeness and accountability in corporate communication; after all, official messages often say little about the decision processes within the organisation, and the possibility to reach the broader public through sanctioned channels is hardly evenly distributed among members. In a study of company magazines, Cheney (1983, p. 154) suggests:

> The assumed 'we' is both a subtle and powerful identification strategy because it often goes unnoticed. Uses of this strategy allow a corporation to present similarity and commonality among

organizational members as a taken-for-granted assumption. To the extent that employees accept this assumption and its corollaries unquestioningly, they identify with their corporate employer.

While the prototypical use of the pronoun highlights persistent membership in relevant social entities, such as organisations and disciplinary communities, Lerner and Kitzinger (2007, p. 527) note that membership can also be extended to transitory groups. Especially interesting is the pronoun's ability to strategically include the reader as principal of the utterance, in what has been called 'solidarity-building "we"'. As most Western languages do not distinguish inclusive from exclusive first-person pronouns, there are no markings to accompany the shift from a restricted interpretation of the pronoun to a broader one that encompasses the audience as well. This displacement presupposes, without the need for explicit assertion, that writer and audience are part of a group with common interests and goals. That is, the writer acts as animator for a 'reader-in-the-text' (Thompson & Thetela 1995, p. 104) who shares the writer's intentions, and fosters an affiliative reading rather than one oriented to challenge or disinterestedly assess them. Shifting between reference to a restricted, institutional 'we', and reference to imagined communities that include the reader, such as the public, works powerfully to gain legitimacy for the organisation's goals (Jacobs 1999, p. 226, and references therein).

Other devices can be used for this purpose as well. Sacks (1992, p. 166) noted that self-reference by means of 'you', prototypically used for the addressee, works to position both writer and audience as members of a universal community. Fairclough (1989, p. 180), Calsamiglia Blancafort (1996, p. 71) and especially Yates and Hiles (2010) discuss how this 'fourth person' functions to express impersonal principles and rules that are true for anyone in the same position. However, 'you' is normally regarded as too conversational, and 'one' too stilted, for corporate communication (see note 5).

Finally, writers can eschew pronominal reference altogether, and instead refer to themselves through forms typically used for third persons – either proper names or definite descriptions. In informal conversation, this is a highly marked resource, and usually intended to convey that the writer is animating 'the perspective of another' (Land & Kitzinger 2007, p. 494) – as when parents call themselves 'Mummy' or 'Daddy' when talking to their children. However, and precisely because of this detachment from the empirical person uttering the statement, third-person self-reference is a routine feature of institutional discourse, whenever writers seek to underscore that the topic of their statement and the principal of their views is not their private self, but the office they occupy and the larger community with whose representation they are entitled (Lerman 1983).

Self-reference in practice

In this section, I look at the overall patterns of self-reference by corporate rhetors with the specific goal of identifying how they serve to highlight the positive social and environmental results of their activity. The texts used are drawn from a purpose-built corpus. Reports containing the 2008 environmental and CSR results were requested from the 80 largest Swedish companies, whether government-owned or publicly traded on the Stockholm stock exchange. As not all companies produce such documents, the corpus comprises exactly 50 Sustainability and Corporate Social Responsibility reports with a total length of 721,322 word-tokens.

The choice of annual reports as the material for this study was motivated by them being 'the most publicized and visible document produced by publicly owned companies' (Henriques & Sadorsky 1999, p. 91). They possess the requisite uniformity in communicative function (Sinclair 2005, p. 1); they are the main voice for corporate beliefs about the role of the organisation in society, its mediate and immediate goals, its obligations and its interlocutors (Fiol 1989, p. 278); and, given the reports' engagement with sustainability and responsibility concerns, they are designed to address society as a whole rather than stockholders alone.

The documents were converted to plain text, ignoring all visual information and layout, but retaining textual elements such as charts and captions. All instances of the company's name were replaced by the string COMPANYNAME to allow global search and comparison.

The analysis of the material was performed using the corpus toolkit Antconc (Anthony 2005), which generates word lists, keyword-in-context concordances and collocation lists, as well as calculating statistical significance measures for collocates.

Institutional and affiliative voices

At the broadest level of generality, all reports employ both first-person (1P) pronouns and the company's proper names for self-reference, to the virtual exclusion of all other forms.[5] Consistent with prior research on corporate communication (e.g., Jacobs 1999; Rogers & Swales 1990; Swales & Rogers 1995), third-person self-reference (3PSR) by means of the company's full name is the most frequent choice, with 8,991 instances to 4,384 of pronominal usage, a ratio of 2.05:1.[6]

Although the ratios vary from document to document, in all cases writers alternate between what Lerman (1983) calls the 'institutional voice', that is, a strategy of 3PSR that highlights the role of the corporate principal in an apparently detached manner, and a more affiliative register in which the cooperative and personal aspects of institutional activity are emphasised. The 'larger social agendas' (Downing 1996, p. 95) of the issuing companies seem thus to require *both* the kind of impersonal legitimacy that is normally associated with the institutional voice, and the establishment of 'a group dynamic in terms of "*we*-ness"' (Rounds 1987, p. 25) that would support the company's claims to being a committed citizen (unless otherwise noted, all emphasis in the excerpts is mine):

(1)   a.   *COMPANYNAME* subscribes to externally developed charters and principles for sustainability management. They include the ICC Business Charter for Sustainable Development which *COMPANYNAME* signed in 1992, and ISO 14000 standards and technical reports.

            b.   *We* believe *we* are a constructive partner in society and therefore it is important for *us* to reflect the world around *us* and the markets *we* are active in.

Further evidence of the attempt to maintain both these claims can be found in the frequent pronominal shifts, where 1P pro-forms are used together with 3PSR antecedents. In contrast to the shifts discussed by Fetzer and Bull (2008), where speakers change their footing to address a potential discursive threat, the goal here is to simultaneously emphasise both the institutional and the affiliative dimensions:

(2)   a.   These calculations show that 95 per cent of the carbon dioxide emissions related to *COMPANYNAME* and *our* products are attributed to material extraction, suppliers, customer transportation and the use of products.

      b.   In accordance with the vision statement, *COMPANY-NAME* revisited and updated its Sustainability Agenda in 2008. The new agenda has three important elements: the desired future position for *COMPANYNAME, our* goals for 2020 and the actions to reach them.

The corporate rhetor as subject

However, the use of pronominal and proper-name reference does not remain constant across syntactic roles and rhetorical functions; that is, the authors' choices show distinctive patterns of usage, where specific alternatives tend to be preferred in specific settings. Table 1 presents the 30 most frequent verbs in finite clauses where the subject is the corporate rhetor. 1P and 3P self-reference are reported separately, together with a statistical measure (two-tailed Fisher's exact test) of the significance of the differences between the observed frequencies. A random sample of these clauses is offered as an illustration in Concordance 1, from which a number of patterns are readily apparent.

Concordance 1: Random sample of clauses with the corporate rhetor as grammatical subject (*n* = 8344).

1	ives to monitor and reduce environmental consequences.	COMPANYNAME	also offers environmental information, guidance and se
2	lected COMPANYNAME suppliers. Apart from funding,	COMPANYNAME	also supports the training centre by providing intern
3	ich have a reputation for reliability and durability.	COMPANYNAME	Aluminium was the initiator of a training project to
4	to develop their employees and team-building. In 2008	COMPANYNAME	conducted a course to prepare a group of middle-level
5	, as well as for its existing, employees. During 2008,	COMPANYNAME	continued to focus on offering a safe, healthy and div
6	ecrease in specific CO2 emissions per kWh in Germany.	COMPANYNAME	estimates that, once operating on a continuous basis,
7	For employees in Belgium, Norway, the UK and Germany,	COMPANYNAME	has defined-benefit plans as a complement to social in
8	ing Safety Week. As part of its environmental program	COMPANYNAME	helped local Brazilian agencies publish a children's
9	employees covered by collective bargaining agreements.	COMPANYNAME	implements collective bargaining agreements at a centr
10	o and Stockholm airports. Through COMPANYNAME Oil,	COMPANYNAME	is a minority owner of a number of smaller companies
11	ung potentials are active in the network. In addition,	COMPANYNAME	is also a member of a network organised by CSR Europe,
12	adapted, healthy and safe foods at competitive prices.	COMPANYNAME	is meeting this demand with a steadily growing range o
13	f a comprehensive hazardous waste management offering,	COMPANYNAME	is preparing to launch MediClean, a concept that has b
14	dy exist and are used in other applications. Currently	COMPANYNAME	is testing the technology in a new 30 MWth pilot plant
15	the year. Promoting early cancer detection Each year	COMPANYNAME	participates in a variety of activities and initiative
16	ars and will continue to be so in the future. In 2008	COMPANYNAME	redoubled its efforts by adopting a strategic directio
17	orations, governments and environmental organisations.	COMPANYNAME	rests assured that GHG is a reliable and thorough stan
18	power, biomass, waste and fossil fuels are also used.	COMPANYNAME	sells district heating and has a substantial volume of
19	milies, as well as culture and education. For example,	COMPANYNAME	supports Mobile University of South Alabama and has ma
20	managers and forest product producers to FSC standards	COMPANYNAME	supports the Forest Stewardship Council, and was one o
21	easing: this demands appropriate responses from us and	we	are driving changes forward with a new distribution st
22	ted part of the way COMPANYNAME is doing business.	We	believe in doing more with less, being humble by liste
23	ialogue even when we do not agree At COMPANYNAME,	we	believe that corporate responsibility must be integrat
24	rcent of our central food suppliers are IWAY approved.	We	believe that the goal of 100 a per cent IWAY- pproved s
25	to continually improve performance. "We must do what	we	can as individuals and as a company. It's our duty to
26	unities as well as challenges for all companies. Since	we	consider corporate responsibility to be a part of our
27	sed by biomass for energy generation. In November 2008	we	discussed the first draft of a Biomass Procurement Add
28	g steel from COMPANYNAME in some of its furniture "	We	do not do business with a supplier which fails to mee
29	atural gas heating combined with solar thermal energy.	We	grant subsidies for this at a level of EUR16.8 millio
30	has improved. As a result of this positive feedback,	we	have developed the pilot into a programme we call 'Ena
31	t was concentrated in our Swedwood units. Furthermore,	we	have seen that it takes a few years for new units to r
32	uing to work for an even better working environment. "	We	have worked extensively to create a safe workplace cha
33	still be ample demand for newsprint in the future. And	we	intend to go on playing a significant role on that mar
34	ift in behaviour; we need to reconsider how much space	we	need to be able to be productive, and how we use resou
35	also responsible for issues such as chemical handling.	We	note that this contributed to a high level of detectio
36	ees are covered by collective bargaining agreements.	We	strive for good relations with all our employees and t
37	age, gender and ethnicity is an asset to the company.	We	therefore strive for diversity at all job levels and a
38	l levels. We are not satisfied delivering a dumpster.	We	want our customers to be able to offer greater value t
39	is the theme of this corporate responsibility report.	WE	WANT TO INTEGRATE RESPONSIBILITY INTO ALL OUR ACTI
40	ommitment, such as health, ecology or the environment.	We	're also thinking about introducing a chat room in ord

Table 1: Most frequent verbs in clauses with the corporate rhetor as grammatical subject.

COMPANYNAME				**We**			
Main verb	*f*	**p-value**		**Main verb**	*f*	**p-value**	
be	753	≤ 0.001	***	be	311	≤ 0.001	***
have	364	0.012	*	have	252	0.012	*
work	124	0.196	*ns*	can	128	≤ 0.001	***
take	94	0.072	***	work	124	0.196	*ns*
support	81	≤ 0.001	**	do	99	≤ 0.001	***
conduct	80	0.004	***	believe	79	≤ 0.001	***
participate	77	≤ 0.001	*ns*	want	74	≤ 0.001	***
strive	75	0.079	***	make	72	≤ 0.001	***
offer	68	≤ 0.001	*ns*	use	66	0.043	*
operate	64	0.649	*ns*	develop	61	0.266	*ns*
develop	58	0.266	*ns*	aim	60	0.001	***
provide	55	0.081	*	take	59	0.072	*ns*
use	54	0.043	*ns*	operate	59	0.649	*ns*
continue	46	0.129	***	see	54	≤ 0.001	***
aim	44	0.001	***	continue	53	0.129	*ns*
make	43	≤ 0.001	*	strive	45	0.079	*ns*
carry	41	0.012	***	must	43	0.025	*
can	39	≤ 0.001	**	need	40	≤ 0.001	***
contribute	39	0.005	***	conduct	39	0.004	**
adopt	38	≤ 0.001	***	set	39	0.048	*
believe	36	≤ 0.001	*ns*	focus	36	0.040	*
report	36	0.802	*ns*	start	35	0.051	*ns*
invest	36	0.104	*	support	31	≤ 0.001	***
receive	35	0.020	***	provide	31	0.081	*ns*
apply	33	0.001	*	face	29	0.001	***
must	30	0.025	*ns*	report	28	0.802	*ns*
comply	29	0.092	*	identify	26	0.483	*ns*
follow	29	0.015	*	offer	24	≤ 0.001	***
set	28	0.048	*	consider	24	0.289	*ns*
decide	28	0.227	*ns*	reduce	23	0.043	***

Verbs showing a preference for 3PSR include SUPPORT, CONDUCT, PARTICIPATE and OFFER, together with others that relate to the actual business of the company and its involvement in industry initiatives. Rogers and Swales (1990, p. 303ff.) explain 1PP-avoidance as a way to avoid awkwardness when discussing ethics or profit; saying that 'the purpose of our company is to earn money' is less likely to antagonise the reader than the alternative 'our purpose'. The present corpus does not show such problems, and 3P preference seems to be related to emphasising the institutional dimension. On a purely lexical level, 3PSR matches the plethora of other organisations, initiatives and institutions mentioned as partners or beneficiaries; on a discursive level, the selection of this referential form can be interpreted as effectively highlighting the involvement of the institution as a whole, above and beyond the decision of any individual agent. As Cheney and McMillan (1990, p. 97) state, '[the] affiliated speaker in the industrialized world is accorded greater credibility and legitimacy than is the non-affiliated one'. Dwelling on institutional aspects emphasises the import and credibility of the report by framing it against a backdrop of industry standards and best practices.

Conversely, a preference for 1PSR is clear in verbs with an intrinsic ethical aspect, such as BELIEVE, WANT, or STRIVE. The affiliative aspect of pronominal reference is probably intended to maximise the affective impact by personifying the corporate rhetor. Speaking of 'we' makes it easier to suggest a distributive reading of ethical claims, where every individual member of the organisation is portrayed as personally committed to sustainable development and corporate responsibility.

This fosters a view of the organisation as a cooperative whole, while maintaining a level of generality that hampers criticism and falsification. It is hardly a coincidence that many of these verbs denote unfalsifiable orientation rather than provable action; they act as a creed that publicly defines the nature of good organisational members without necessarily being a faithful description of any individual one. The same rationale explains the greater preference for 1PSR with deontic modals, NEED or MUST.

The most frequent verbs, BE and HAVE, have little lexical content and do not show any global patterns of this sort, but the analysis of specific constructions shows parallel results. Looking at instances of copula BE shows that COMMITTED TO is a frequent predicate both for 1P and 3PSR, but beyond that they tend to diverge. The first person collocates mainly with ethical claims, while 3P is almost the exclusive choice for descriptions of the company as a LEADER, MEMBER or signatory.

In her analysis of the institutional voice, Lerman (1983) argues that 3PSR has the effect of immediately evoking a morality frame by downplaying the individual, with their own private interests and inclinations, in favour of the lasting, legitimate, respectable institution. This allows the speaker to appear dispassionate and objective, while claiming the greater authority accorded to supra-personal institutions. The evidence above suggests that this may not be the case for organisations whose claim to moral authority is more or less widely contested across the social domain, such as profit-oriented corporations. In their case, an inversion takes place: the 'discourse of power' still uses the 'language of morality', but this is not realised through an appeal to impersonal legitimacy. Rather, it is organisational members – as individuals engaged in a coopera-tive ethical project – that warrant the claim to morality, and readers are enjoined to take their identification with a common project for granted. The institutional aspect still features prominently in this discourse through enduring statements of the corporate creed, such as the COMPANYNAME CODE OF CONDUCT, but the desire for and the work towards the elusive goal of sustainability are attributed to *persons* rather than to roles within the corporate structure – persons with which the reader is invited to identify in terms of '*we*-ness'.

Possessive uses

A striking example of inversion of the global preference for 3PSR can be seen in the possessive forms, with 3,936 instances of 3P COMPANYNAME's[7] to 5,156 instances of 1P OUR, for a ratio of 0.76:1. Table 2 provides a list of the 25 noun phrases (NPs) most frequently prefixed with either form of the possessive, which shows that references to stakeholders (CUSTOMERS, EMPLOYEES, SUPPLI-ERS, STAKEHOLDERS, COLLEAGUES) tend to use the affiliative 1P and are rare with 3P. (Remarkably, references to the actual princi-pals of the reports, MANAGERS or MANAGEMENT, do not show this pattern.) 3PSR is more likely when speaking about organisational elements and documents (BOARD OF DIRECTORS, CODE OF CON-DUCT, ANNUAL REPORT), for which there seems to be no need to invoke an affective element.

Table 2: Most frequent NPs after self-referring possessive.

	COMPANYNAME			We	
f	MI	Collocate	f	MI	Collocate
114	2.400	operations	243	4.705	customers
109	2.040	sustainability	192	3.591	business
75	1.010	business	159	3.212	employees
69	2.270	code	142	3.913	suppliers
47	0.232	employees	123	3.232	products
38	0.152	work	115	3.634	operations
37	0.277	products	93	4.582	supply
35	3.729	website	87	3.826	code
29	2.810	forests	85	4.403	stakeholders
27	3.110	vision	70	3.287	corporate
23	-0.030	production	68	4.319	CR
67	2.451	responsibility	22	2.076	annual report
22	-0.517	management	63	4.442	review
22	0.019	customers	57	1.432	environmental
21	1.330	corporate responsibility	51	2.785	carbon
21	1.481	stores	49	2.282	production
21	−1.152	group	47	1.680	work
21	0.649	board	44	5.800	colleagues
20	1.898	values	43	3.753	approach
20	1.095	stakeholders	42	4.362	commitment
19	1.522	CSR	38	3.558	stores
18	1.723	goal	38	3.742	CSR
18	1.181	CR	37	3.983	goal
17	3.785	ambition	37	3.992	efforts
36	1.964	environment	16	2.086	mills

The specific example of the terms referring to the workforce provides a nuanced example of this rhetorical contrast. When offering statistics or describing aspects of the business process, the possessive determiner is likely to be in the third person; 1PSR is preferred whenever the discussion veers towards ethical matters of personal development, rights, values and feelings. This is independent of the label used: STAFF, PERSONNEL, PEOPLE and EMPLOYEES are described in largely identical ways. Generally speaking, references to stakeholders tend to prefer 1PSR to an often statistically significant extent, which is consistent with the verbal preferences shown in the previous section.

It is now generally accepted that evaluative meaning is not a fixed property of isolated terms; rather, words become 'coloured' with the connotational valence of other terms with which they co-occur in a given context (Stubbs 1995). Cognitively-oriented scholars argue that repeatedly encountering a lexical item in a given context *primes* readers to recognise and replicate said context in subsequent encounters (Hoey 2005). Given that 1PSR normally accompanies ethical claims in our corpus, it would naturally be the preferred choice for statements of responsibility and goodwill towards those who are more or less directly involved in the company's activities. The data in Concordance 2 bear out this hypothesis, showing that 1PSR habitually co-occurs with an emphasis on mutual care and support, while 3P is preferred for factual descriptions, especially in statistical terms, policy and procedure codes, and strategic planning.

Concordance 2: Random sample of possessive SR + stakeholder reference ($n = 999$).

rthquake victims and, in addition, COMPANYNAME's	colleagues	made personal contributions of CNY 230,000. Parts of
ated and refined, and ultimately sold to COMPANYNAME's	customers	, while others are deposited in tailings ponds or becom
y quality and partner outlets. COMPANYNAME Logistik's	customers	value the reliable delivery quality and the business r
, but only up to a certain level. For many COMPANYNAME	employees	this means a substantially lower income level of compe
made some acquisitions the total number of COMPANYNAME	employees	is 600 less than in 2007. Employee survey shows posit
s applies to all business partners and all COMPANYNAME	employees	that come into contact with business partners. Due t
itiatives and be self-sufficient. Several COMPANYNAME	employees	have been engaged as investors in the pilot project. W
bour rights Wherever in the world you see COMPANYNAME	people	at work, their tasks are guided by the same principles
loyee, SEKm Approximately two-thirds of COMPANYNAME	personnel	are employed in manufacturing at Group plants througho
bal financial crisis impacted both COMPANYNAME and our	personnel	. Unfortunately, workforce reductions could not be avoi
of the health profile results show that COMPANYNAME's	personnel	are generally in good health. Work Environment Day 20
. Shareholders, investors and analysts COMPANYNAME's	shareholders	expect the company to make effective use of its assets
unication and reporting has identified the COMPANYNAME	stakeholders	who affect or are affected by our operations. The dire
that being a good and attractive employer for all our	colleagues	and potential new employees is important for our futur
trate, many employee accidents are associated with our	contractors	, as the LTIF of our contractors is around twice that o
elated initiatives that are a cause for concern to our	customers	. These include environmentally friendly materials, the
rity that need to be addressed. We have always put our	customers	and their needs first, so I am convinced that this dev
is to provide affordable organic food products to our	customers	. PROGRESS IN 2008 UTZ certified coffee in all COMPAN
at we care. We show respect for each other and for our	customers	. We do not sell to just anyone: we do not, for example
for all employees are a common practice. They help our	employees	develop themselves, which in turn helps the Company to
on to their own safety. Our aim here is to support our	employees	and encourage them to pay more attention to their pers
seek high professionalism and make it possible for our	employees	to develop and assume responsibility. · We support di
ay, but it will also demand tremendous effort from our	people	. The business environment continues to be highly chall
ds our corporation and society as a whole--- to help our	people	balance work and family life in a positive way. Decrea
whole. One of our key values is that we care for our	people	and customers. Another key value is that we learn and
e newsletter, Wallpaper, to provide information to our	people	on our approach to CSR issues. In 2008 we published a
r competitiveness as well as for the well-being of our	personnel	, environmental and health and safety issues are – and
it. Our most prominent internal stakeholders, is our	personnel	. We maintain employer-employee relationships through
s, we have a particularly large responsibility, to our	shareholders	and society, to be clear about how we conduct our envi
nvironmental and social responsibility approach to our	stakeholders	, and how we work to address the environmental impacts

Referential shift

The previous sections have sought to explain the choice between 1P and 3PSR in terms of general patterns of lexical choice and their pragmatic force. This form of analysis can reveal probabilistic trends unnoticeable to the naked eye, but only at the expense of ignoring the effects that these choices have in specific textual contexts. Let us now discuss one such contextualised phenomenon and its effects: *referential shift*; the change in referential form, or in the contextually-determined referential scope of a given form, within a single stretch of discourse.

Some examples of such changes were shown *supra* in Excerpt (2), where the alternation of 1P and 3P forms illustrated the need to simultaneously maintain institutional and affiliative voices. In the following excerpts, however, referential shift serves a different purpose: to shift the attribution of responsibility or blame by means of *implicature*; the pragmatic meaning that is conveyed by a fully contextualised utterance, but neither explicitly expressed nor logically implied by the uttered sentence. Take, for example, the following statement from the report of an insurance company:

(3) *I* introduced last year's Sustainability Report with the question, 'How big a margin is big enough?' If it's about the greenhouse effect, it's important that *we* still have a margin for change available and that as many people as possible – preferably the governments and peoples of all the world – can agree on how this margin should be defined and used. ... Can *we* achieve the consensus on the climate problem that is indispensable if *we* are to overcome it? *I* am convinced *we* can, though *we* seem to be finding it hard to synchronise *our* clocks. And time is starting to run out. Today *we* are faced with two global crises, and the risks and consequences if *we* fail to stop them in their tracks are well-nigh unlimited. The financial crisis threatens the economic system by which *we* flourish; the climate crisis threatens the ecological system by which *we* are nourished.

This is part of the letter from the CEO, a finely crafted and impassioned plea for both environmental and economic reform. An especially interesting aspect is the subtle management of the discursive identity of the speaker. While the message is personally signed and clearly issued in his official capacity, most of the utterances are not anchored in this discursive identity. From the second sentence onwards, the referent of the 1P pronouns encompasses an unspecified social group that potentially includes 'the governments and peoples of all the world'. This is the broadest possible case of inclusive 'we', where species-wide solidarity is invoked to position the reader as principal of the utterance.

Such an appeal is unremarkable as a rhetorical choice when discussing a species-wide problem, such as climate change; the claim that every human being on the planet is dependent on the ecological system for sustenance is straightforward. However, it seems less apt when discussing economic arrangements. The NP 'the economic system by which we flourish' *presupposes* the belief that 'we flourish in the (current) economic system', in the technical sense that such a belief is necessary to correctly interpret the NP (Sbisà 1999). This may doubtlessly be a true belief if the 1PSR is interpreted as referring to the company, which has shown consistently positive results for its owner-policyholders, but it is far less likely under the broader referential scope sustained up to that point: not all 'the governments and peoples of all the world' flourish under modern capitalism.

In the terms of our analysis, the referent of the 1P pronoun *shifts* to a more restricted interpretation. However, there are no surface traces of such a shift; even the presupposition-bearing NP is unlikely to make it manifest in normal reading, given that the knowledge content of presupposed utterances is usually backgrounded in order to maintain the smooth flow of communication. The author has skilfully employed the polysemy of the referential form in order to support his arguments and maintain the elegant parallelism that forms the core of their structure.

There are few reasons to doubt this particular writer's sincerity, especially in light of the mutual nature of the company and its CEO's long track of public service in welfare and social affairs, but the resource is elsewhere used for more questionable purposes. Take the following example from an energy company:

(4)   Supporting educational projects is part of *our* broad-based understanding of responsibility at *COMPANY-NAME*. Alongside the issues of climate protection in *our own* power generation, access to energy, and security of supply, at *COMPANYNAME we* see *our* responsibility particularly in supporting customers and society to manage energy efficiently.

In the context of a corporate report, the natural assumption is to interpret this statement as the institutional voice. The repeated self-reference by means of the company name, as well as mentions of customers and the company business, immediately evoke the company itself as a provider of education in energy management through one of its organisational units. The initial framing of the project strategically identifies the principal of the action in institutional terms, thus implicating that any positive appraisal of this action should reflect on the company's ethics. However, such a reading is revealed as over-inclusive by an apparently parenthetical comment at the end of the following paragraph:

(4b)   all projects are supported by the voluntary involvement of *COMPANYNAME* employees

The reference here shifts to a specific group within the organisation, and is explicitly qualified to indicate that they are acting in a private capacity as volunteers. However, this is unlikely to cancel an implicature raised several sentences earlier and maintained throughout the entire subsection in the report. While in strictly semantic terms the company's statement cannot be claimed to be false, it nevertheless misleads the reader into apportioning responsibility for the actions to the corporate persona.

None of the utterances produces this result on its own: if the information contained in Excerpt (4b) had preceded that in (4), there would be no change in the formal truth values, but the argumentative effect on the reader would hardly be comparable and perhaps even the opposite. As it stands, the pragmatic meaning raised by the statement is the result of the shifting reference of the subject of 'support' – tacit in Excerpt (4), where the verb appears in non-finite form, but implicated by the prominent presence of the corporate rhetor.

A similar strategy of over-inclusion is used in the following extract from the report of a manufacturing company:

(5)   In 2009, the non-profit organization Water for All celebrates 25 years of dedicated work to provide clean drinking water to people in need. *We* are proud of the achievements and hope to have organizations in place in 25 countries before the end of 2009.

There is no antecedent for the 1P pronoun in this quotation, but its author is introduced in institutional terms as 'Vice President Public Affairs and Environment' – in itself a telling name for the office, lumping together environmental action and reputation management. Focusing on the organisational role again places emphasis on the institution, which becomes the default choice for interpretation of the 1P referential form. The ensuing assumption that both pride for the NGO's results and intent to expand its reach should be ascribed to the company is later belied by an explicit statement that

(5b)   *COMPANYNAME* employees run the local Water for All organization on a voluntary basis and largely in their own time

The company's sponsorship of the organisation hardly justifies the praise that it claims for the entirely voluntary activities of its members, and could have been more faithfully represented by a different phrasing. The issue lies not in the metonymical substitution of the company by its employees, but rather in the selective shift between referential strategies that leads the reader to incorrectly assume that the speaker is acting in an official capacity, and thus that the principal of their actions should be identified with the institution from which they derive their role.

Being essentially a pragmatic phenomenon, there is no reliable way to automatically identify such referential shifts. They are not raised by specific lexical items or referential forms, but rather triggered in each case by a constellation of inferential rules and contextual factors that may adopt very different realisations. Short of manually parsing the entire corpus, it is impossible to estimate how frequently this strategy is employed. However, it is attested in almost every report in the corpus, especially when accounting for corporate social involvement. The activities of employees are the most likely subject of such a transformation, but also donations by customers and associates are so expressed:

(6)   *COMPANYNAME Sweden* has worked with UNICEF since 2004, supporting its important work for the world's children. … *COMPANYNAME* and UNICEF initiated the Round Up campaign, which gave the customers the possibility to donate money by 'rounding up' the sum of their purchases. All in all, the activities generated a donation to UNICEF of more than 370,000 SEK.

(7)   Each year *COMPANYNAME* participates in a variety of activities and initiatives to raise awareness of various forms of cancer and help in their early detection … Three *COMPANYNAME* employees in the UK participated in a charity run to raise funds for the Kent Air Ambulance. One *COMPANYNAME* employee completed the London Marathon to raise funds for the Spinal Injuries Association.

(8)   For the sixth consecutive year, *COMPANYNAME* was the principal sponsor of the Pink Ribbon campaign to increase awareness of breast cancer and collect money for Swedish cancer research. … *COMPANYNAME* contributed just over SEK 6.8 million collected through the sale of pink products in *COMPANYNAME* stores and through donation inserts in the customer magazine.

Conclusions

In this chapter, I used both quantitative and qualitative linguistic methods to offer some insights into the construction of an ethical identity in corporate and CSR reports. Corpus techniques provide the means to approach general patterns of usage that are pervasive, yet undetectable to the naked eye, such as the correlation between verbs with ethical content and first-person pronominal forms. The qualitative analysis of pragmatic phenomena shows how these global choices are realised in specific settings in order to further the writers' arguments and to build evidence for what are sometimes questionable claims, such as praising the company for the unpaid volunteer work of employees. Used together, they provide an account of the strategic rhetorical choices that is firmly based on empirical materials, and flags critical points in the configuration of meaning in environmental discourse through the investigation of its dynamic construction in textually-mediated interaction.

I would argue that such an approach is especially important for researchers wishing to actively intervene in socially problematic questions. Understanding disagreements about environmental issues requires recognising that the various parties bring with them different implicit theories about what is relevant, appropriate and urgent about the issue. Some of these understandings are much more readily recoverable from textual patterns of behaviour than from abstract, streamlined theoretical summaries.

Interpretation is unavoidable in any discursive approach – which is, after all, concerned with how we make meaning out of the multiple, partial and sometimes contradictory accounts of the social world – and this is not a problem that could be solved simply by using more data. However, while it is impossible to definitely fixate meaning and determine the 'one true reading', there can be little doubt that not all meanings are equally probable (or provable). Remaining in constant dialogue with the empirical materials goes a long way towards controlling the biases and limitations of the researcher and their disciplinary culture.

Notes

1 That is, critical discourse scholars place more emphasis on solving specific (social) problems than in systematically accounting for all discursive structures and process through a parsimonious set of rules.

2 Of course, it is possible for such use to be ironic, but even in that case the rhetorical effect stems from the fact that certain forms of expression are conventionally deferential.

3 References to 'writers' and 'readers' throughout the text should be read as referring to both the written and spoken mode of communication, except where otherwise indicated. Although the differences between spoken and written interaction are by no means insignificant, a complete inventory of the relevant distinctions is outside the remit of this chapter.

4 The utterly context-bound function of self-reference is lost to researchers using mechanical, 'bag-of-words' techniques for the analysis of discourse, which leads them to inadequate assumptions and contradictory results. Cho et al. (2010) and Yuthas et al. (2002), for example, use dictionary-based software that takes *histoire* as its writing standard, and factors all self-references as indicators of decreased certainty on the part of the author. Contrarily, Merkl-Davies et al. (2010, p. 18) take the opposite stance, and consider that abstaining from self-reference indexes a wish of authors to '[distance] themselves from their stories and to avoid taking responsibility' for them. Needless to say, such decontextualised exercises in counting are unlikely to yield any meaningful results.

5 Instances of fourth-person you are scarce outside quotation, and fourth-person one is almost non-existent. First-person singular (1PS) pronouns, in turn, are restricted to verbatim quotations and messages from the CEO or President, which have a distinctive prosody and style (Hyland 1998).

6 An additional 819 instances mention the company, and 1,171 the group; if these are factored in, the ratio climbs to 2.50:1.

7 This figure includes 910 instances of ITS, manually identified as co-referring to an antecedent instance of COMPANYNAME.

References

Literature

Anthony, L., 2005. AntConc: A Learner and Classroom Friendly, Multi-Platform Corpus Analysis Toolkit. In: L. Anthony, S. Fujita & Y. Harada (eds), *Proceedings of IWLeL 2004: An Interactive Workshop on Language e-Learning.* Tokyo: Waseda University, pp. 7–13.

Balmer, J.M.T. & Greyser, S. A., 2002. Managing the Multiple Identities of the Corporation. *California Management Review,* 44(3), pp. 72–86.

Benveniste, E., 1966. *Problèmes de linguistique générale.* Paris: Gallimard.

Calsamiglia Blancafort, H., 1996. Multifaceted Dimensions of Self-Reference. *Links & Letters,* 3, pp. 61–76.

Cheney, G., 1983. The Rhetoric of Identification and the Study of Organizational Communication. *Quarterly Journal of Speech*, 69(2), pp. 143–158.

Cheney, G. & McMillan, J.J., 1990. Organizational Rhetoric and the Practice of Criticism. *Journal of Applied Communication Research*, 18(2), pp. 93–114.

Cho, C.H., Roberts, R.W. & Patten, D.M., 2010. The Language of US Corporate Environmental Disclosure. *Accounting, Organizations and Society*, 35(4), pp. 431–443.

Coupland, C. & Brown, A.D., 2004. Constructing Organizational Identities on the Web: A Case Study of Royal Dutch/Shell. *Journal of Management Studies*, 41(8), pp. 1325–1347.

Downing, P.A., 1996. Proper Names as a Referential Option in English Conversation. In: B.A. Fox (ed.), *Studies in Anaphora*. Amsterdam: John Benjamins, pp. 95–144.

Fairclough, N., 1989. *Language and Power*. London: Longman.

Fetzer, A. & Bull, P., 2008. 'Well, I Answer it by Simply Inviting You to Look at the Evidence': The Strategic Use of Pronouns in Political Interviews. *Journal of Language & Politics*, 7(2), pp. 271–289.

Fowler, R., Hodge, B., Kress, G. & Trew, T., 1979. *Language and Control*. London: Routledge.

Gioia, D.A., Schultz, M. & Corley, K.G., 2000. Organizational Identity, Image, and Adaptive Instability. *The Academy of Management Review*, 25(1), pp. 63–81.

Goffman, E., 1979. Footing. *Semiotica*, 25(1–2), pp. 1–30.

Golden-Biddle, K. & Rao, H., 1997. Breaches in the Boardroom: Organizational Identity and Conflicts of Commitment in a Nonprofit Organization. *Organization Science*, 8(6), pp. 593–611.

Hoey, M., 2005. *Lexical Priming: A New Theory of Words and Language*. London: Routledge.

Humphreys, M. & Brown, A.D., 2002. Narratives of Organizational Identity and Identification: A Case Study of Hegemony and Resistance. *Organization Studies*, 23(3), pp. 421–447.

Hyland, K., 1998. Exploring Corporate Rhetoric: Metadiscourse in the CEO's Letter. *Journal of Business Communication*, 35(2), pp. 224–245.

Hyland, K., 2000. *Disciplinary Discourses: Social Interactions in Academic Writing*. Harlow, Essex: Longman.

Jacobs, G., 1999. Self-Reference in Press Releases. *Journal of Pragmatics*, 31(2), pp. 219–242.

Knapp, P.M., 2001. *Designing Corporate Identity: Graphic Design as a Business Strategy*. Boston, MA: Rockport.

Kress, G., 2001. From Saussure to Critical Sociolinguistics: The Turn towards a Social View of Language. In: M. Wetherell, S. Taylor & S.J. Yates (eds), *Discourse Theory and Practice: A Reader*. London & Thousand Oaks, CA: Sage, pp. 29–38.

Land, V. & Kitzinger, C., 2007. Some Uses of Third-Person Reference Forms in Speaker Self-Reference. *Discourse Studies*, 9(4), pp. 493–525.

Lerman, C.L., 1983. Dominant Discourse: The Institutional Voice and Control of Topic. In: H. Davis & P. Walton (eds), *Language, Image, Media*. Oxford: Blackwell, pp. 75–103.

Lerner, G.H. & Kitzinger, C., 2007. Extraction and Aggregation in the Repair of Individual and Collective Self-Reference. *Discourse Studies*, 9(4), pp. 526–557.

Levinson, S.C., 1988. Putting Linguistics on a Proper Footing: Explorations in Goffman's Concepts of Participation. In: P. Drew & A. Wootton (eds), *Erving Goffman: Exploring the Interaction Order*. Cambridge: Polity Press, pp. 161–227.

Lischinsky, A., 2010. Elucidating Managerial Conceptions of Sustainable Development through Corpus Linguistics. Paper presented to the *International Association for Media and Communication Research Conference*. Braga.

Livesey, S.M., 2001. Eco-Identity as Discursive Struggle: Royal Dutch/Shell, Brent Spar, and Nigeria. *Journal of Business Communication*, 38(1), pp. 58–91.

Merkl-Davies, D.M., Brennan, N. & McLeay, S., 2010. Impression Management and Retrospective Sense-Making in Corporate Narratives: A Social Psychology Perspective. Working paper, Bangor University & University College Dublin.

Phillips, N. & Hardy, C., 1997. Managing Multiple Identities: Discourse, Legitimacy and Resources in the UK Refugee System. *Organization*, 4(2), pp. 159–185.

Rogers, P.S. & Swales, J.M., 1990. We the People? An Analysis of the Dana Corporation Policies Document. *Journal of Business Communication*, 27(3), pp. 293–313.

Rounds, P.L., 1987. Multifunctional Personal Pronoun use in an Educational Setting. *English for Specific Purposes*, 6(1), pp. 13–29.

Sacks, H., 1992. *Lectures on Conversation*. Oxford: Blackwell.

Sbisà, M., 1999. Presupposition, Implicature and Context in Text Understanding. In: P. Bouquet, L. Serafini, P. Brézillon, M. Benerecetti & F. Castellani (eds), *Modeling and Using Context: Proceedings of the Second International and Interdisciplinary Conference on Modeling and Using Context*. Berlin & Heidelberg & New York: Springer, pp. 324–338.

Silverstein, M., 2003. Indexical Order and the Dialectics of Sociolinguistic Life. *Language & Communication*, 23(3–4), pp. 193–229.

Stivers, T., 2007. Alternative Recognitionals in Person Reference. In: N. J. Enfield & T. Stivers (eds), *Person Reference in Interaction: Linguistic, Cultural, and Social Perspectives*. Cambridge: Cambridge University Press, pp. 73–96.

Stubbs, M., 1995. Collocations and Semantic Profiles: On the Cause of the Trouble with Quantitative Studies. *Functions of Language*, 2(1), pp. 23–55.

Stubbs, M., 2001. *Words and Phrases: Corpus Studies of Lexical Semantics*. Oxford: Blackwell.

Stubbs, M., 2007. On Texts, Corpora and Models. In: M. Hoey, M. Mahlberg, M. Stubbs & W. Teubert (eds), *Text, Discourse and Corpora: Theory and Analysis*. London: Continuum, pp. 127–161.

Swales, J.M. & Rogers, P.S., 1995. Discourse and the Projection of Corporate Culture: The Mission Statement. *Discourse & Society*, 6(2), pp. 223–242.

Taylor, J.R., 1999. What is 'Organizational Communication'? Communication as a Dialogic of Text and Conversation. *The Communication Review*, 3(1), pp. 21.

Thompson, G. & Thetela, P., 1995. The Sound of One Hand Clapping: The

Management of Interaction in Written Discourse. *Text-Interdisciplinary Journal for the Study of Discourse*, 15(1), pp. 103–128.

van Dijk, T.A., 1993. Principles of Critical Discourse Analysis. *Discourse & Society*, 4(2), pp. 249–283.

van Dijk, T.A., 2001. Critical Discourse Analysis. In: D. Tannen, D. Schiffrin & H. Hamilton (eds), *Handbook of Discourse Analysis*. Oxford: Blackwell, pp. 352–371.

Weiss, G. & Wodak, R., 2007. *Critical Discourse Analysis: Theory and Interdisciplinarity*. Basingstoke, Hampshire: Palgrave Macmillan.

Wodak, R., 2002. Aspects of Critical Discourse Analysis. *Zeitschrift für Angewandte Linguistik*, 36, pp. 5–31.

Wodak, R. & Chilton, P.A., 2005. *A New Agenda in (Critical) Discourse Analysis: Theory, Methodology, and Interdisciplinary*. Amsterdam: John Benjamins.

Yates, S. & Hiles, D., 2010. 'You Can't' but 'I do': Rules, Ethics and the Significance of Shifts in Pronominal Forms for Self-Positioning in Talk. *Discourse Studies*, 12(4), pp. 535–551.

Yuthas, K., Rogers, R. & Dillard, J.F., 2002. Communicative Action and Corporate Annual Reports. *Journal of Business Ethics*, 41(1/2), pp. 141–157.

CHAPTER 10

Exploring Ideological Fantasies on the Move

Angelika Sjöstedt Landén

This study engages with the extensive and somewhat abstract question of what could be made imaginable for subjects. It springs from the query of how possibilities become possibilities, not only in the past and present, but also in the form of *futures*. The empirical material that constitutes this study is drawn from interviews that were conducted with new recruits to a government agency[1] in Sweden in 2006. At this time, the agency was in the process of workplace relocation, which involved a move from Stockholm, the capital of Sweden, to Östersund, a relatively small town in the northern part of the country. The participants in the study had moved to Östersund in order to start working for the agency. In the interviews they talked about their visions of what a 'good life' should involve. These visions were often understood in relation to the socio-cultural imaginaries of the place to which they were moving, a place of which they had very little 'real life' experience. A point of departure in a critical explanation of the political and social role of fantasies about the future is taken from the exploration of fantasmatic logics as they are introduced by discourse theorists Jason Glynos and David Howarth (2007) in *Logics of Critical Explanation in Social and Political Theory*. Their framework will be combined with queer phenomenologist Sara Ahmed's (2004) feminist cultural-political theory of emotions.

This theoretical and practical base gave rise to three main questions: (1) Which fantasies constituted 'the good life' for the participants in this study? This question concerns the issue of which practices are seen as possible or impossible in the subjects' view of the future. (2) Why did particular ideas of the good life 'grip' subjects? The question draws attention to the reasons to why the participants in this study perceived particular practices as possible or impossible. The follow-up question to this particular question is: (3) Which gripping forces were involved? With this question I wanted to investigate what made certain possibilities 'stick' with the subjects, while others did not (and were instead, perhaps, understood as impossibilities).

In the analysis of the interviews it will be suggested that different explanations, motivations and ideas of 'the good life' could be understood within what I refer to as a *logic of centre and periphery*. This logic governs the perceived status relations between places and enforces the political implications of public sector relocation. The following section will present a brief background to the context in which public sector relocation has served a political tool.

The status of places

Cultural and social norms relate to geographical categorisations and influence how people 'make sense' of their (work) life choices. These norms have political implications for how geography becomes 'a practice of battles, over inclusion and exclusion, over the making of space and place, and over defining who constitutes a part of a group, a place, a region, or a nation' (Eriksson & Malmberg 2008, p. 1). Therefore, it is pivotal to pay attention to cultural and social norms that are 'taken for granted' within a particular context.

With approximately 60,000 inhabitants, Östersund constitutes the population centre in the county of Jämtland. The town is situated by Storsjön ('the Great Lake'), which is surrounded by agricultural landscape. The logging industry and water power plants has historically been important economic resources in the county (Johansson 2002). The mountains in the western part of the region constitute the border to Norway and contain one of the most well-known skiing resorts in Sweden, Åre. Jämtland is part of Norrland,[2] a region comprising five northern counties that cover a relatively large geographical area. In geographical terms Norrland encompasses about 60 per cent of the nation. The Norrlandic region has no administrative or formal responsibilities to the state, but it provides a powerful imaginary 'we'.

Norrland's inhabitants are thought to share common conditions of life that are distinct from the more urban centres which are associated with the south of Sweden, and especially Stockholm (Eriksson 2008). Mutually, Norrland constitutes a 'them' to those who do not identify with the supposed Norrlandic conditions of life. Today, Norrland is characterised by sparsely populated regions with long distances between its population centres. It is often understood as a region in need of financial support and as incapable of managing itself (Eriksson & Malmberg 2008). Even this very study is itself part of a research project that exists because of the denigration of sparsely populated regions in official discourses.[3]

Relocation politics

The acknowledgement of synonyms for the word relocation that have been used in the Swedish context could help to show that the practice of relocation is not 'neutral'. In fact, public sector relocation has to be regarded as a political practice that involves struggles over the distribution of resources and the determination of meanings associated with a certain place. Furthermore, the practice of relocation contributes to an understanding of how places can become 'affected', and these influences cannot be separated from the political (Ahmed 2004). This becomes clearer when thinking about words such as the Swedish *utlokalisering* (literally translated as 'out-locating') and *decentralisering*. These two synonyms for the relocation of public sector jobs presuppose a centre; that is, something 'original' where the workplace was located before it was *re*located to the periphery. These understandings of a centre and a related periphery create a dichotomy where the two opposites often become socially charged with different statuses: the centre is perceived as 'normal' and the periphery is identified as 'problematic' in different ways.

The relocation of government agencies has been regarded as a solution to a range of problems that have been identified as 'regional politics' since the end of the Second World War (Holm 1952; Statskontoret 1989; Pettersson 1980; Söderberg 1978; Hansen 1998; Rothstein 2002). The polarisation of regions against the capital Stockholm has a long history in Sweden. Hansen (1998, p. 190) argues that the state, which is often represented by a discourse about Stockholm as *the* governing centre, has provided a meaningful contrast in the construction of regional identities.[4] Such a construction of regional identities is inextricably linked to the construction of the welfare state. For example, the debate on the extensive relocations of government agencies during the 1970s was motivated by the 'Stockholm-argument'. This argument rested on the assumption that the capital region expanded at the expense of other parts of the country (Statskontoret 1989).

Norrland has been subjected to various demographic and economic crises in the past which have at times been followed up by help actions, such as relocations of public sector jobs. However, the reasons for these relocations were not only based on solidarity with the other regions. The argument of 'skyrocketing' site and building costs in Stockholm had been used as early as 1941 and thereafter to justify lower wage levels in more remote parts of the country (Statskontoret 1989). This argument is still used as a motivation for moving agencies 'out' from the most expanding region. The political problem of uneven economic growth in the country was going to be solved with a so-called politics of active localisation (*aktiv lokaliseringspolitik*); that is, strong regional politics. This meant that public and private sector corporations were going to be located in such a way that capital and labour force resources were fully utilised. Simultaneously, the increase in welfare was to be distributed in a way that people in all parts of the country were offered satisfactory social and cultural services (Söderberg 1978, p. 13). This type of regional politics constructs Stockholm as a dominant centre with governing ability and the powers to give something to the governed periphery. It implies that without the helping hand of 'the strong centre', the remote regions would not survive. This establishes a relationship, similar to the one between the coloniser and colonised, whereby the self-understanding of both parties is interdependent. This phenomenon has been called 'internal orientalism' (Eriksson 2008), which further enforces the unequal power relationship between the centre and the periphery (cf. Anna Sofia Lundgren's chapter in this book).

In order to link these social and political implications of public sector relocations with the specific interviews that constitute the core empirical data in this study, I will now turn to the notions of fantasmatic logics and emotions. The notion of fantasmatic logics provides us with theoretical tools for analysing the expressions of subjects' experience, while continuously situating such self-interpretations within their relevant political contexts.

Fantasmatic logics and emotions

Laclau and Mouffe (1985) introduced a concept of discourse which involves the idea that all objects and actions are meaningful. They put forward a theory in which discursive structures of meaning are constituted by the social and the political. Grounded in the work of Laclau and Mouffe, Glynos & Howarth (2007) claim that the notions of political and social *logics* are crucial for critical explanation. Social logics can be understood as the social rules that govern a particular practice at the moment of its empirical study. Political logics focus on how the practices under study are contested and/or transformed. In addition to these analytical concepts, Glynos & Howarth (2007) introduce *fantasmatic logics* as a third dimension of analysis, in order to explain change and continuity in social practices. This third layer of analysis concerns the very reasons *why* subjects consider particular practices to be possible or impossible. Fantasmatic logics not only enable explanations of political or social logics, but also explore why subjects 'invest' in certain logics. Hence, the notion of the fantasmatic proposes ways of linking together subjects' experiences with social and political logics. I find Glynos & Howarth's approach especially useful for the analysis of empirical data that is produced through qualitative methods such as ethnographic fieldwork and in-depth interviews. I believe that this approach is useful because the notion of fantasmatic logics provides us with theoretical tools that enable a focus on the expressions of subjects' experiences, while continuously situating the informants' self-interpretations within relevant political contexts. As the theoretical framework is inspired by psychoanalytical theory, the concept of fantasmatic logics forms an integral part of a tradition that is conceptually equipped to deal precisely with subjective experiences. The concept of fantasy is borrowed from psychoanalysis, but has been reworked from a clinical concept into a social concept (Glynos 2001, 2008; Glynos & Howarth 2007). The understanding of fantasy takes its point of departure in poststructuralist discourse theory, and attempts to conceptualise the ways in which subjects are enabled to identify with particular social rules; that is, so-called orders or ideology (Glynos & Howarth 2007, p. 145).

The concept of *identification* rejects the idea that identity should be read as an individual's innate natural features that are then cultivated throughout a person's life (Laclau 1994). Therefore, identification acknowledges that identity must be contingent, albeit acknowledging that the subject will try to keep contingency at bay, by erecting an ideological shield as protection from this radical undecidability. Glynos and Howarth propose that the ways in which subjects relate to contingency can be categorised into two different strands that are understood as the ideological and the ethical dimensions of fantasy. The first, the *ideological dimension* of fantasy, works to try and cover over or to veil contingency (Glynos & Howarth 2007, pp. 145–146). Therefore, the ideological dimension of fantasmatic logics provides a theoretical apparatus to analyse how subjects seek to keep contingency at bay. The second dimension is the *ethical dimension* of fantasmatic logics, which stands for openness to change and the contestation of the hegemonistion of ideals. Consequently, the ethical dimension refers to the moments where contingency is 'revealed' and made visible. 'The cynical subject' is brought up by Glynos (2008) as an example of such an ethical mode of subjectivity when contingency is revealed and destabilises identity. The question of how to identify and distinguish between the ethical and ideological modes will be addressed in the empirical analysis of this chapter. However, if subjects can take on different subject modes, how is it that certain modes become privileged over others? Glynos & Howarth suggest that the concept of fantasmatic logics can help us to account for how political and social logics 'grip' subjects. Glynos (2008) suggests that feelings like resentment, anger, guilt and blame could be viewed as possible 'gripping forces' that become meaningful in relation to how certain practices are made legitimate, while others are disregarded. Evidently, emotions could even operate as fuel for taking political action (Griggs & Howarth 2008).

In order to further explore the perspectives offered by Glynos and Howarth, a theory that specifically deals with emotions is necessary for this study. I will therefore introduce Sara Ahmed's (2004) *Cultural Politics of Emotions* into the analysis. According to Ahmed, emotions involve orientations and responses to others. She does not place feelings within individuals or treat emotions as essential interior states or features of a subject's character, but focuses on how the naming and meaning-making of different emotions can 'work' on subjects, 'grip' them as it were. Glynos & Howarth (2007) use the grip of ideology and the gripping forces on subjects in their analysis of identity formation and transformation. Ahmed is concerned with what sticks and the stickiness of emotions, meaning the symbolic sticking of signs to bodies. For example, the sign 'emotional' has traditionally female connotations. Within the parameters of the male/female dichotomy, 'emotionality' has been associated with female subjects, and in opposition to male-marked subjects. Emotions have also been 'stuck' with lower status because of the long-lived and uneven status relationship between notions of male and female. This view on emotions is included in the notion of 'stickiness' in Ahmed's (2004, p. 93) terms and points to 'how the signifier sticks to a signified in a chain of signifiers'.

It should also be noted that these two theoretical frameworks began their journey from slightly different positions. Whereas Ahmed positions emotions directly as a central aspect of her argument, Glynos & Howarth work their way towards the notion of emotions through the conceptual trio of political, social and fantasmatic logics. This essay is an opportunity to investigate how they nourish each other's arguments.

Ideological fantasies of 'the good life'

In this section I will address the three main questions in this study and discuss them in relation to the interviews that were conducted with the newly appointed employees of the organisation. The research questions partly overlap and will therefore be addressed as interdependent. The following analysis will focus on which fantasies constitute 'the good life' for the participants in this study, and try to identify why particular ideas of the so-called good life grip subjects. The discussion will then focus on how we can understand such 'gripping forces'. The findings will be summarised at the end of the chapter. In 2004, the Swedish government decided to relocate nine agencies that constituted 1,166 public sector jobs to Östersund, and this move is the reason why the interviewees in the study were offered jobs in the town (SOU 2004:15, p.10). The relocations were part of a programme that sought to compensate regions for earlier job losses, that were due to a reorganisation of the nation's military defence.

The government agency that features in this study consisted of 150 positions. The new recruits were not only accepting a new job, but also moving town, and this move apparently affected significant parts of their social worlds outside work Therefore, I was interested in how they dealt with the new situation. However, I was not especially interested in the social rules that governed the particular workplace practice. Instead, I was mainly concerned with the idea of work as part of life in a broader sense. A strong common theme in the participants' narratives was a desire or hope for 'the good life' as part of accepting the job in Östersund. At the time the interviews took place, the participants in the study were so recently employed that their narratives gave witness to very few actual experiences of the workplace itself. Instead, they were imagining what life could become, and therefore expressed how the move held a promise that their life situation would improve. If this improvement was not expressed in terms of a short-term perspective, it was expressed as a long-term perspective.

The fantasy of the successful woman

> And then we had a wish, me and my husband, that is to, eh… move from Stockholm because we had two little children, to have it all with work and housing and relative closeness to work and house… the six-year-old wanted to move to a house with a garden. And we moved to a house with a garden. And he wanted a red house and we moved to a red house.[5] (Katarina, 38)

As Katarina herself put it, to 'have it all' calls for a great many demands to be met. The move to Östersund became subject to the ideological fantasy of 'the good life' in her narrative and proposes that it would be possible to, as she formulates it, 'have it all'. This phrase involves the imaginary of the Swedish gender-equal and professionally successful woman. The fantasy combines her own career with a family life that includes raising children, intertwined with the small-town romantic image of the children playing in their prototypically red house with a garden of their own. She hopes the move will meet all these desires. Everything should be realisable simultaneously. Highly qualified work for the spouses, quality housing, quality childcare and quality leisure time, and everything within reasonable commuting distance. The logic of fantasy suggests that if the family moves to Östersund, these different demands could be fulfilled (cf. Glynos & Howarth 2007, p. 147).

This particular fantasy was also related to the broader context of the 'gendering' of work and profession. The Swedish public administration is 'feminised in the sense that women constitute the majority of all public employees' (Nexö Jensen 1998, p.160). The agency was no exception to this when it was located in Stockholm. When it moved to Östersund further possibilities were opened up to the large group of highly educated younger females, and the process of 'feminisation' at this workplace was extended. Once again, approximately 75 per cent of the workforce that were recruited by the organisation were women. The agency offered highly qualified positions where many recruits had at least a Master's degree and it was encouraged that new recruits even had Ph.D. degrees. As such, this agency was considered to be a high-status workplace, particularly when it was compared to other (feminised) parts of the public sector. When these highly qualified jobs were placed in Östersund and therefore situated in a lower-status region, an opportunity to enter the labour market was created for young female academics. The situation thus paved a way for the ideological fantasy of a successful woman flourishing in this new location.

The fantasy of the gender-equal man

As well as fitting into the fantasy of the successful woman, the fantasy of Norrland could become connected to the ideology of the equal man, which was the case for Erik. He and his wife and children were living in Stockholm before moving to Östersund. However, two circumstances seemed to intersect in his explanation of why he wanted to take up the new job. Firstly, he had the possibility of getting a permanent position at a place that provided qualified work. And secondly, he referred to the housing problem in Stockholm. The property market was described as a dominant force that could not be controlled unless the family moved to a place outside the city. Even though he and his wife had what he called 'proper jobs', the houses were so expensive in Stockholm that too much of the couple's wages went towards the house. Living outside the centre would demand several hours of commuting each day. Consequently, Östersund became an alternative future for Erik and his family, and presented the promise of 'the good life' in Norrland.

> So Stockholm has lots of advantages, but also disadvantages like housing and so on. But we had *proper jobs*, both of us. But you also need *proper capital* to borrow a large amount of money, and even if you borrow a horrendous amount of money you don't get the best-quality housing. In that case you need to buy something far out, so we had. I'm from [another county that is considered part of Norrland], so Norrland felt natural to me and also for my wife because she is also from there (Erik, 35, my emphasis).

When he moved from Stockholm, aspects of Erik's social orders were disrupted: a new workplace, a new house, new daycare for his children, and his wife left her job and did not know if she would get another one in the new town. In such a situation the search for identification opportunities could become urgent, and when order is needed, content could become a secondary consideration (Laclau 1996, p. 93). As mentioned earlier, Norrland is not an actual place, but a thought conglomeration of several counties in the northern part of Sweden. Even though Erik was not familiar with the physical place of Östersund itself, the fantasy of Norrland provided him with the opportunity to identify with the new location they moved to.[6] Therefore, the idea of Norrland constitutes a fantasmatic construction, and as such becomes part of the ideological fantasy which promised that 'the good life' could be achieved in Östersund. For Erik, the fantasy of Norrland was also intertwined with a promise that the ideology of the 'equal man' could be realised there. Erik talked about the difficulty in combining 'proper jobs' for both parents with the care of children and the possibility of obtaining quality housing in Stockholm. Compared to Östersund the social and economic structure of living as a family in Stockholm was presented as more difficult to combine with the ideology of gender equality. As Östersund was perceived as the opposite of Stockholm (in accordance with the logic of centre and periphery), Erik could argue that the ideology of the equal man was more practically probable when living in Östersund.

Being the Other

The next narrative further enforces how places could become 'affected' by emotions.

> *Susanne*: This move from Stockholm presents a chance for us bumpkins to get these very attractive jobs that otherwise wouldn't have become available if it had remained there. Because people had wanted to stay in their positions [a little laughter].
> *Angelika*: What do you mean by bumpkins? [a little laughter].
> *Susanne*: I mean it's us outside of Stockholm that are perceived as bumpkins, us people from other parts of Sweden that's not in Stockholm. (Susanne, 42)

Susanne's motivation for moving to Österund was a desire for the right to be 'different', and the possibility of an alternative identification which was not available to her in Stockholm. Östersund enabled identification for Susanne, as she perceives herself as the 'Other' and therefore the peripheral represents a promise of refuge. A form of relief was indicated by Susanne, as she was able to obtain a job like the one at the agency outside Stockholm that she experienced as a social straitjacket. In another part of the interview she tells me that when she was living in Stockholm she felt like being 'the first negro coming to a small northern inland village in the 1950s'. Susanne's statement highlights the 'affective quality' of becoming 'othered'. As Ahmed (2004, p. 94) argues with regard to feelings of disgust, to 'designate something as disgusting is also to create a distance from it'. By drawing on the coloniser/colonised discourse, Susanne relates her experience of Stockholm with a 'disgusting' colonial history. Therefore, Susanne's statement subverts the often negative attributes that are connected to the remote village as ethnocentric and conservative, and projects such values onto Stockholm instead. In other words, she used emotion to create distance to the 'disgusting' place, which in turn enabled identification with the 'non-disgusting' place (in this case identified as Östersund). Consequently, the idea of the new place was recreated in a dichotomised relationship with Stockholm.

The feeling of being the 'Other' in Stockholm enabled Susanne to identify herself with Östersund precisely *because* of its peripherality and perceived non-normality. This feeling distances the subject from the feeling of not being able to gain access to 'the good life' in the 'disgusting' place. In combination with an attractive job opportunity, this strategy worked as a justification for the investment of moving to Östersund. Ahmed (2004, p. 172) notes that as we remain invested in what we criticise, and therefore remain connected with it through 'affective quality', emotions may offer a way of understanding why transformations are so difficult. Emotions could also be of help for thinking about the possibilities of transformation. Susanne's statement is imbued with the hope of transformation and a 'desire that the future should not only repeat the past'. Her statement also involves a directed criticism towards the current order of the world (Ahmed 2004, pp. 183–184). Again, the logic of fantasy about a place could pose a range of possible promises for the stabilisation of identity.

The fantasy of the 'natural' life

You will now meet Ingrid, who, unlike the previously mentioned informants, wanted change as an end in and for its own sake. However, this did not mean that any change would do. At the age of 58,

Ingrid was afraid of becoming bored with her current work situation and beginning to long for her working life to end. Despite this, she could not picture herself in retirement at that point, and described both herself and her husband as driven by work – work being, for her, an important part of living 'the good life'. She incorporated the move to Östersund and the change of workplace in a package of change in her social life, and this change involved both work and non-work related activities. As part of that package, Ingrid identified a desire to nurture some of her personal interests, such as mountain hiking and skiing. She described these as possibilities that were offered in the Östersund region, which she characterised in terms of a symbiotic relationship with nature as well as in opposition to Stockholm. The effects of simultaneously moving town, house and work were positively foregrounded by Ingrid, but she never described the move from Stockholm as a definite break with her previous life there. She had left her adult children behind, which made it easy to go back and visit, and work in Östersund often required her to travel to Stockholm for shorter periods of time.

> So when I'm down there, so: 'Wow! It's so nice to live here in Stockholm.' And I stay downtown then; before I've lived outside town. But that has been so damn hard as well. I'm sick of these time-consuming journeys to and from work. So that's what I regard as a very positive change in the right direction for me, to be rid of these long journeys to and from work. Here I have a seven-minute walk, and I can control my way to work. But in Stockholm in winter time it normally takes fifty minutes, but it could be one and a half hours as well or more, and you never feel that you have control over that so it's… and now when I stay in Stockholm it's so much fun to have the time to stroll around in the city. (Ingrid, 58)

Ingrid constructed her understanding of Östersund in relation to her identification with Stockholm. She talked about how much she enjoyed the working conditions in the new place and how she was able to come back to Stockholm as a visitor and 'stroller'. In Östersund the pace was considered to be slow and controllable, with no traffic jams or long commuting distances. This statement was imbued with a desire for control. The imaginary of the controllable small town was contrasted with the heavily urbanised city that was signified by the time-consuming, uncontrollable and difficult traffic situation. The characterisation of the two places as differentiated from each other enabled them to exist in their respective particular (imaginary) forms. It was the social differentiation of the two places that made it possible to love and hate them both at the same time. Therefore, Ingrid's narrative illustrates how a desire for control is met by a fantasy about feeling in control. In other words, it poses a fantasmatic promise that helps her to justify her move to Östersund (cf. Glynos 2001).

Another interviewee, Katarina, drew on an ideological fantasy that included closeness to nature when she described Östersund as a space that was signified by mountains and possibilities of outdoor life.

> So even if I had never been to Östersund I didn't feel like… Well, it felt like one had been spending a lot of time in the mountains. And it's a shame that one doesn't have the possibilities to do that more often. (Katarina, 38)

Many of the new recruits who moved to work at the agency had access to the stereotyped travel guide image of the region. In both of the above statements, the character or the 'brand' of the region as a skier's paradise was established. Östersund and its hinterland were associated with nature and (as we shall see below) animals. In a sense the interviewees related to their new home town as tourists would, rather than inhabitants, because the ways in which they represented the place resembled the glossy tourist guide stereotypes.

Towards ethical dimensions

> Well, I didn't have a big problem with moving from Stockholm. First, I'm not, I didn't grow up there. But I think it was fun to live there a few years. But maybe I didn't want to live there any longer, so… it was almost only a plus for me that it was located in Östersund. Eh… because I had never been here, really, but I like outdoor life and animals and nature, so for me it was a bit exotic

that it was placed here, you know. It could have ended up closer to my home town, so that would have been good for me too. But this is a bit, to me it's sort of, yeah, well not a dream, but it's wonderful to live here. I don't know for how long I'm going to stay, but there was nothing negative to moving here. It was exciting. I get access to some important parts of my life here. (Sara, 33)

Earlier statements have presented us with the pros of moving to Östersund in a very convincing way: by presenting 'the good life' as achievable in Östersund and juxtaposing it to Stockholm. However, the ideological picture that Sara paints in her statements has instabilities that made me think that she is very much aware of how she 'should' present the picture of Östersund; that is, as a skier's paradise where dreams will come true. The ideal is present in her narrative: it was 'a plus' that the job was located in Östersund because Sara 'likes outdoor life and animals and nature' and it was 'exotic' to go and live there. This ideal was simultaneously disturbed by ambiguities that sneak into her narrative: 'it was *almost* only a plus', it was '*a bit* exotic', it is '*sort of not* a dream', '*don't know for how long*', she will stay; but there is '*nothing negative*' about moving to Östersund. These might seem to be minor markers in Sara's speech, but they do become significant because of their regular reoccurrence. Therefore, the promises presented by the fantasmatic ideology of Östersund did not seem to convince Sara in the same way as the other interviewees, who talked about their belief in the fulfilment of these imaginaries.

Questioning ideology

Sara's narrative suggests that there may be alternative ways of understanding the move to Östersund, because there are inbuilt ambiguities in her story. It is as if she is aware of the generalisation in her explanation, but still adopts the ideological fantasy in order to make her position graspable (or in the way that she thinks it will be graspable for me). This hesitancy destabilises the image of Östersund as a place where the need for closure of social contingency could be fulfilled. This moves us from ideological attachments to the logic of fantasy towards the ethical resistance and detachment from the same fantasy. In the following excerpt, Emma acknowledges that there is an ideal image, but one which she wishes to distance herself from.

> *Emma*: Yes, well, it's a little too sporty here! I don't do downhill skiing or cross–country skiing, I just don't do that! [laugh] A... and this is sort of the town of sports clothes.
> *Angelika*: [laugh].
> *Emma*: It's just like that and its unnoticeable that's the case and... and the reason to move to Jämtland from somewhere else is often because of the nature and so on. That's not the case for me at all. I understand from work that other people come here for work, but they also think there is something special about coming to live in Jämtland. (Emma, 28)

Emma openly criticised the glossy exoticism that characterised the former narratives. In this sense, she may be conceived as 'the post-modern subject' in Glynos' terms, which means that she has internalised the constant questioning of fixations of meaning which are typically associated with our postmodern times (Glynos 2001, p. 211). This mode of subjectivity destabilises Emma's ability to identify herself with Östersund and the 'ideal' social practices that are associated with the region, like outdoor life and particularly skiing. Emma told me about her experiences of Östersund in a funny way that problematised stereotypes in almost a stand-up comedian manner. We laughed about it, and as a native I could certainly identify with her sarcastic descriptions as well. On the other hand, the funny story was occasionally interrupted by experiences of non-belonging, and even feelings of exclusion. She told me that she had experienced some difficulties with the move, such as having a hard time feeling as if she was part of the social community outside work.

Simone was another interviewee, who addressed the move to Östersund in a similar way as Emma. In her narrative, the exotisation of Östersund was even manifested in expressions such as 'moving to Jämtland and leave... Sweden!' (Simone, 29). Simone looked for new opportunities of identification and told me that she was trying to create new social networks outside the context of the workplace. I asked her how she went about creating such social networks when she moved to the new town. Her responses were that she was thinking about joining some kind of study group and continued: 'something like that or maybe skiing lessons. I can't ski and that's what you're supposed to do in Östersund, right?' And then she laughed quietly. 'Do you feel like you have to ski?' I asked her as we laughed together. 'Yes! It's a bit like that, actually. Everybody wears sport clothes, one has to adjust!' In a similar fashion to Emma, Simone experienced difficulties 'fitting' in, other social networks outside the context of the workplace. The emphasis on sports, outdoor activities and skiing made alternative ways of social formation more or less invisible. It should thus be noted that 'the existence of a counter-argument does not necessarily imply the existence of a strategy of resistance in the strictest sense of the word, but it may imply the existence of a wish to rework the representations' (Eriksson 2008, p. 4).

When we discussed their difficulties, Emma and Simone expressed their thoughts through humour and laughter, and this behaviour leads to a relevant point concerning the role of affect and the 'concealment' of criticism. Emma's and Simone's critical voices called for a de-hegemonisation of the positive image of Östersund as a 'skier's paradise', but their laughter blurred the edge of the argument. The laughter may be a way for them to 'cover over' the harshness that they think I read into their statements, and this reaction may be related to the fact that they were both aware that I was from the region myself. Similarly, I laughed because I was anxious that they might think that they could not tell me what they 'really' thought of Östersund because they knew I lived there. My laughter, then, became a way for me to show them that I, too, can distance myself from regional romanticism. Consequently, the laughter became a 'double' concealing force that attempted to balance the critical statements. This reveals that ethical and ideological forces were at play *simultaneously*. It means that tending to the affective meaning of subjects' statements may be one way of engaging with the 'tricky methodological questions about how best to ascertain or grasp innovatively when subjects are (ideologically) attached to their fantasy; or, conversely, when they are (ethically) detached from their fantasy' (Glynos 2008, p. 293). Tending to the affective modes of practices could therefore help to identify how attachment to and detachment from fantasy interrelate in the interview situation.

A rational mode

It is nevertheless important to remember that the ways in which emotions are viewed are also already impregnated with cultural history and politics. As such, emotions are positioned in the middle of social systems of hierarchies and power relations. As mentioned earlier, showing signs of emotion has, in the tradition of Western thought, been perceived as an attribute of the 'soft' and 'feminised' body, while rationality and reason have been regarded as attributes of bodies marked as masculine (cf. Ahmed 2004, p. 4). Certain affective modes have therefore been made available for different subjects depending on whether the body was marked as feminine or masculine. Furthermore, these modes have been identified and sorted into a power relationship of domination and subordination. In the same way as emotions could stick to bodies and in that way sign status relationships, they (emotions) could also stick to places. The following extract shows that the rational mode of language becomes entangled with a desire to work and live in Stockholm. There is an imbalance in power relations, as feelings that stick to 'centrality' are imbued with high status and those that 'stick' to 'peripherality' with a lower status.

> One of the reasons I applied for this job was that I would probably not get a comparable job in Stockholm, especially under the circumstances of relocations during last spring. When the decision [to relocate several government agencies from Stockholm] was taken, one realises quite quickly that the people who have been working for these agencies are not going to move with the workplace. They are going to look for other jobs in Stockholm within this genre. And with their experience they will have an advantage in the recruitment processes, while I keep a place at the bottom of the food chain, strictly speaking... To put it shortly, because of changes in the labour market and difficulties in getting a job in Stockholm, one needs to eventually think in these directions, so that was one of the reasons. (Olov, 45)

There is a striking choice of language in Olov's statement. He identifies with the 'experts in Stockholm' and expresses that he wants to
become one of them, while simultaneously distancing himself from
them when he identifies himself as on the 'bottom of the food chain'
– as someone with less status because of his lack of work experience.
However, someone like him, who had lower status in the professional hierarchy, stood a better chance of making it in Östersund
than in Stockholm. He had 'no choice' but to move to Östersund
to gain the experience he needed to maximise his value on the
Stockholm job market. Again, this means that the non-normality
and peripherality of Östersund were used in a strategic way. Even
if Olov regarded moving there as a necessary evil, peripherality was
precisely what enabled him to see the possibilities with the move.
In that way he does not only articulate a relation of domination
and subordination that concerns himself as a professional, but also
one concerning place; place became affected by relations of domination and subordination. In this way, geographically oriented social
categorisation governed the possibilities for Olov to make sense of
his (work) life choices.

Olov presents a view of the future in words that tell us that he was
somehow 'deemed to choose' (Laclau 1990, p. 43). Olov argues that
under the circumstances he did not have much choice but to accept
this work opportunity because the current state of the labour market
made it impossible for him as a 'lower creature in the food chain'
to 'make it' in Stockholm. His understanding of his own situation
was described in a language that speaks to the rational, 'common
sense' way of perceiving the world as built on causal laws. Olov
could choose to stay in Stockholm and die (career-wise), but then
his investments in terms of education and several years of struggling
towards a 'good job' would never be rewarded. Therefore, he does
not have a choice. However, Östersund was just one of many other
possible locations that he had considered to get the work he was
interested in. He had been looking for suitable jobs all over Sweden,
and even though the relocation of the agency provided him with the
job opportunity, he was ambivalent about the relocation of public
sector jobs. He said it was 'stupid to move these workplaces from
Stockholm because that's my future workplace'. Olov identified

himself with Stockholm because he defined it as his future place of work. This constructs Östersund as a place that signifies a temporary solution and a stepping stone on the way to something better.

Notions of 'the good life'

I will now summarise how the 'good life' was characterised by the different participants in the study. I will also summarise the answer to the first question I posed in the introductory section of this article, namely: Which fantasies constituted 'the good life' for the participants in this study? I will then proceed to answer questions two and three and discuss emotions as gripping forces.

Firstly, what united all of the participants was that they were driven by work, which was also their primary incentive for moving to Östersund. Secondly, the normativity of work as the ideal for 'the good life' was intertwined with ideological fantasy of Östersund as a town in a sparsely populated region. This ideological fantasy could harbour a variety of desires. One example would be the ideal of 'the successful woman' who embodies the traits of having a successful career, being a wife and mother and living in a house in a setting where recreation activities that involved nature were always available (Katarina). Another example is the 'equal man', who, similarly to the idea of the successful woman, can combine qualified work with being an active father and husband (Erik). The differentiation and dichotomisation of places also enabled peripherality to provide a refuge for those who did not 'fit' in 'centred' contexts (Susanne). However, the move to work in Östersund could also be understood as a stepping stone towards something the subject 'really' desires; a 'necessary evil' on the way to the 'true' (centred) ideal (Olov). The primacy of work as a requirement for the good life could, however, create a conflict with an ideological fantasy of place. In those cases ideological images of place could become an excluding force instead of an inclusive one (Emma and Simone).

Many of the new employees discussed the desire for control as an important feature of 'the good life' and considered it to be reachable in Östersund. The desire for control could be said to constitute the drive that enabled Ingrid to identify with her ideological fantasy of

Östersund (as well as Stockholm). This leads us to the second question in focus for this study: why a certain ideology 'grips' subjects. In Glynos and Howarth's terms, the grip of ideology 'comprises a myriad of practices through which individuals are turned into subjects with an identity' (2007, p. 117). We could suppose, in line with Ahmed (2004), that there has to be a certain amount of 'affective quality' embodied by the subject for identification to 'stick'. Furthermore, these new acts of identification presuppose a subject that is already structured around certain fantasies (Glynos & Howarth 2007, p. 130). In relation to Ingrid, this means that some 'structuration' or 'embodiment' has taken place and provided her as a subject with access to historical narratives. According to Laclau, 'embodying' is the equivalent of giving something a name (Laclau 2005, p. 111) and the practice of naming can be understood as an attempt to fix identity. However, such attempts will always be susceptible to the possibility of failure; but this failure is the fuel that makes subjects want to invest in an ideological fantasy (Glynos 2008, p. 288) because the failure of the return of an investment extends that investment (Ahmed 2004, p. 131). This means that the subjects' former failures in engaging with fantasmatic structures will be of significance for how she or he interprets her or his possibilities of identification when subjected to the contingency of a social order.

Emotions as gripping forces?

I have addressed how different descriptions of the relation between ideological fantasies of place were related to ideas of the contents of a 'good life'. Furthermore, I have analysed why particular subjects were 'gripped' by ideology. These findings will now be related to my last question: Which were the 'gripping forces' in play in this specific case?

I was puzzled that some of the new recruits at the government agency in Östersund engaged with, or were 'gripped' by, the normative image of the town and region and that some treated it with suspicion or rejected it. However, all of the excerpts from the interviews are in one way or another emotional, and show that the participants were *moved*. The metaphor of movement is particularly fruitful in the study of people who move to a new place and workplace. The move was not only a 'physical' move that literally repositioned the participants' lives in a new location, but was also *emotionally moving*. The search for identification possibilities and attachment possibilities with place are a central feature in the analysis. Another way of expressing this is captured by Ahmed (2004, p. 11) when she states that 'what moves us is that which holds us in place'. Consequently, emotions comprise movement as well as attachment, or 'grip'. In terms of the findings of the study at hand, the subjects were united by the idea that *qualified work was a constitutive part of living 'the good life'.*[7] The ideology of work as part of the good life was then related to a logic of centre and periphery, the fantasy of place and the contexts of location. At this point, the subjects had constructed different meanings of what the good life could contain. Subjects took on different *modes* of 'getting to grips' with their situation. I asked them to talk about the move in a time of uncertainty. In their search for order, the logic of centre and periphery provided a discursive structure within which their decisions could become (re-)realisable. This logic rested on the idea of Östersund's 'otherness', which meant that the maximisation of social values was made practicable and the fantasy of a 'good life' could be imagined as possible to realise there. However, the same logic could also disable the possibilities for identification.

Nevertheless, there was no way of 'opting out' of the logic of centre and periphery.

All the subjects in the study related to the ideological image of Östersund, but in different ways. Glynos (2008, p. 288) argues that the subjects who succeed in identifying themselves with a fantasmatic content become very heavily invested in the fantasy. Identification, then, requires the investment of (emotional) 'capital', which, in turn, accumulates *affective quality* (Ahmed 2004, p.127). As the accumulated affective quality can act to cover contingency and acquire a sense of security, Glynos (2008, p. 288) acknowledges that large investments also comprise risks. To 'trust' an ideal very strongly is also to expose oneself to vulnerability. It is a risk that is involved in believing that moving to Östersund will deliver 'the whole package' intact. Heavily invested subjects could more easily be disappointed when they eventually become aware that their anticipations can never be fully realised. The subjects' insistent identification with an ideal inevitably becomes the way in which the subject realises that the fantasmatic ideology was 'only' a fantasy. Therefore, adopting a cynical or sceptical way of engagement with norms could be a way of safeguarding against disappointment. Consequently, Glynos (2008) argues that the cynical subject may be better armed to tackle change. Interestingly, in this particular case the subjects who were ready to invest in both the ideology of work as part of living the good life and the ideology of Östersund as a place and region seemed to come to terms more easily with the move. In that sense the ability to identify with a norm could also be a way of handling change.[8] This essay has explored the conceptualisation of fantasmatic logics, and empirically investigated how fantasy could relate to the normative or ethical dimensions of a practice (cf. Glynos 2008, p. 293). The analytical tools used in the study included a theorisation of emotions. Laclau (2005, p. 111) acknowledges that discursive formations would not be intelligible without the affective component. This study illustrates that analysing what the 'affective components' (emotional) do could highlight the dynamics of interaction between ideological and ethical dimensions. Here, the emphasis on *interaction* is of crucial importance. Drawing on the findings in this study, I would suggest that the ideological and ethical dimensions must imply some commitment to each other (cf. Glynos 2008). If we, as Ahmed argues, are always already part of what we critique, ethical dimensions will always emerge from 'inside' ideology. Furthermore, ideological dimensions are always dependent on the contingency of social relations that are constantly in need of something to 'cover over'. Indeed, to explore ideological fantasy requires a 'mobile gaze', because ideological fantasy is constantly on the move.

Notes

1 The data for this study consists of interviews with eight people who, at the time of the study, had recently been employed by the government agency (henceforth also referred to as the Institute). Interviews were conducted between June and November 2006. I was interested in the persons' background, in regard to education, former work experience, etc. I was also curious about

how they came to apply for the jobs at the agency and the nature of their future expectations in relation to their acceptance of them. The questions were asked in the light of a previous study that focused on the relocation and included interviews with employees, as well as observations at the workplaces in Stockholm and Östersund (Sjöstedt-Landén 2006). For reasons of confidentiality, all names have been altered, and ages have been changed by adding or subtracting up to five years. This article is part of my thesis work funded by the research council FORMAS and the Department of Culture and Media Studies at Umeå University, Sweden.

2 For a more extensive account of the history of Norrland, see Eriksson (2008). For further analysis of the meaning-making of the specificity of Norrlandic conditions of life for elderly people, see Lundgren in this volume.

3 The name of the research project is 'Decentralisation of government agencies, work force mobility and rural development'. It is financed by the Swedish research council FORMAS within a funding programme that is especially directed towards rural development. The project is led by Professor of Economics Olle Westerlund and conducted in cooperation between ethnologists and economists at Umeå University, Sweden. The results of the project will be fully reported in 2011.

4 The differentiation from Stockholm as a way of constructing regional identity, as in Norrland, can also be found in other regions. One such example is Skåne, in the very south of Sweden, where anticipations of empowerment and freedom from the state were expressed during the building of the bridge over Öresund to Denmark. Political efforts were exercised to shape a cross-country region, and the creation of identity became crucial for this project (Nilsson 1999). Place and identity within the Öresund region has also been written about by Falkheimer (2004), with a focus on the role of the mass media.

5 All interview extracts are translated by me from Swedish into English.

6 Norval (2000) refers to the conceptions of Laclau saying that the role of 'myth' is to re-establish closure where a social order has been dislocated. This is done though the construction of a new 'space of representation' (2000, p. 329). Norrland could here be viewed as one such space of representation.

7 Andersson (1999, 2003) has written about the norm of waged work as an important feature of becoming a proper citizen within the Swedish context.

8 The definition of *change* is in itself changeable. Investments in ideology that enabled these subjects to 'cope with the move' could also be what disable them to cope with other type types of changes. For example, if the agency was to be closed down, that event would probably force subjects to choose between attachment to place or to 'qualified' work. The reason for this choice would be the fact that Östersund and the ambient region cannot provide many comparable jobs to the ones at the agency.

References

Literature

Ahmed, S., 2004. *The Cultural Politics of Emotion.* New York: Routledge.

Andersson, M., 1999. Den diciplinerande arbetslösheten: lönearbetet som norm. In: G. Arvastsson (ed.), *Järnbur eller frigörelse? Studier i moderniseringen av Sverige.* Lund: Studentlitteratur.

Andersson, M., 2003. *Arbetslöshet och arbetsfrihet: moral makt och motstånd.* Uppsala universitet: Etnologiska avdelningen.

Eriksson, M., 2008. (Re)producing a 'Peripheral' Region – Northern Sweden in the News. In: *Geografiska Annaler: Series B. Human Geography* 90(4), pp. 1–20.

Eriksson, M. & Malmberg, G., 2008. *Spatial Otherness and Places of Others: Urban and Rural Imaginaries in Sweden.* Conference paper for the Spatial Injustice conference. Nanterre: Université Paris.

Falkheimer, J., 2004. *Att gestalta en region. Källornas strategier och mediernas föreställningar om Öresund.* Lunds universitet: Centrum för Danmarksstudier.

Glynos, J., 2001. The Grip of Ideology: A Lacanian Approach to the Theory of Ideology. In: *Journal of Political Ideologies* 6(2), pp. 191–214.

Glynos, J., 2008. Ideological Fantasy at Work. *Journal of Political ideologies* 13(3), pp. 275–296.

Glynos, J. & Howarth, D., 2007. *Logics of Critical Explanation in Social and Political Theory.* Oxon/New York: Routledge.

Griggs, S. & Howarth, D., 2008. Populism, Localism and Environment Politics: The Logic and Rhetoric of the Stop Stansted Expansion Campaign. *Planning Theory* (7), pp. 123–144.

Hansen, K., 1998. *Välfärdens motsträviga utkant. Lokal praktik och statlig styrning i efterkrigstidens nordsvenska inland.* Lund: Historiska Media.

Holm, P., 1952. *Näringslivets lokalisering. En sammanfattning med kommentarer och kompletteringar av lokaliseringsutredningens betänkande.* Stockholm: Tidens förlag.

Johansson, E., (ed.), 2002. *Periferins landskap. Historiska spår och nutida blickfält i svensk glesbygd.* Lund: Nordic Academic Press.

Laclau, E., 1990. *New Reflections on the Revolutions of our Time.* London & New York: Verso.

Laclau, E., 1994. *The Making of Political Identities.* London & New York: Verso.

Laclau, E., 1996. *Emancipation(s).* London & New York: Verso.

Laclau, E., 2005. *On Populist Reason.* London & New York: Verso.

Laclau, E. & Mouffe, C., 1985. *Hegemony and Socialist Strategy.* London & New York. Verso.

Nexö Jensen, H., 1998. Gender as the Dynamo: When Public Organisations have to Change. In: A. Jónasdóttir, D. von der Fehr & B. Rosenbeck (eds), *Is There a Nordic Feminism? Nordic Feminist Thought on Culture and Society.* London: Routledge.

Nilsson, F., 1999. *När en timme blir tio minuter. En studie av förväntan inför Öresundsbron.* Lund: Historiska Media.

Norval, A., 2000. *The Things we do with Words: Contemporary Approaches to the Analysis of Ideology. British Journal of Political Science*, vol. 30, no. 2, pp. 313–346.

Pettersson, R., 1980. *Omlokalisering av statlig verksamhet. Effekter på arbetsmarknaden i mottagande orter. Bilaga 8 till SOU 1980:6.* Göteborg: Kulturgeografiska institutionen, Göteborgs universitet.

Rothstein B., 2002. *Vad bör staten göra? Om välfärdsstatens moraliska och politiska logik.* Stockholm: SNS förlag.

Sjöstedt Landén, A., 2006. *Ställa in sig på omställning.* (Arbetslivsrapport 2006:40). Stockholm: Arbetslivsinstitutet.

Söderberg, B., 1978. *Omlokalisering av statlig verksamhet. En fallstudie.* Stockholm: Statsvetenskapliga institutionen, Stockholms universitet.

Statskontoret, 1989.*Omlokalisering av statlig verksamhet. Utvärdering av utflyttningen på 70-talet.* Huvudrapport 1989:8A. Stockholm: Statskontoret.

Official documents

SOU 2004:15. *Omlokalisering av statlig verksamhet, 2004.* Stockholm: Näringsdepartementet.

CHAPTER 11

Ageing in the Norrlandic Inland

Anna Sofia Lundgren

Ageing in marginal geographical areas has sometimes been described as particularly problematic, because of the low population density and the geographical distances involved (Keating & Phillips 2008). Working from the supposition that older adults are not passive recipients of such descriptions but act on the variety of notions that are connected to ageing and place, this text visualises how different discourses are used in stories of ageing and how different, but related, discursive systems are made meaningful in stories about growing old in the sparsely populated inland of northern Sweden. This area has often been seen as a forerunner of problems that are associated with the demographic process of population ageing, and it is therefore likely that older people who live in these areas have already been confronted with ideas and images associated with this process.

The initial aim was to describe the politicisation of old-age identities. As the analysis progressed, however, it became obvious that such a politicisation would be to presume too much. Therefore, the revised objective is to describe how agents relate to, and construct, a variety of 'enemies' – obstacles that are deemed responsible for the failure to fully attain a goal – and the discursive resources they thereby deploy in order to oppose, contest, or benefit from these enemies (cf. Howarth 2000, p. 105). The aim is also to empirically test Glynos & Howarth's logics approach (2007; see also Glynos 2008). My objective is to show how such an approach helps to make the workings of ideology[1] visible in people's stories of ageing in a sparsely populated area.

I follow the tradition of discourse theory that builds on Laclau and Mouffe's work from 1985, and take the concept of discourse to comprise the effects of articulatory practices (1985, p. 107). Discourse is thought to constitute the way a certain phenomenon is understood, and at the same time to define the limits of that understanding (Laclau & Mouffe 1990, p. 100). In this specific text, the concept will be used primarily to describe how a variety of articulations constitute certain topics or phenomena (cf. Foucault 2002; see also Mathias Sylwan's chapter).

The material on which the text is based consists of 20 telephone interviews that were carried out with the explicit aim of discussing older people's experiences of volunteer work.[2] The interviewees all had experiences of functioning as so-called 'class grandparents' (*skolmorfar/skolmormor*), and had volunteered in one way or another in children's schools. Another thing that some of the informants had in common was the experience of living in sparsely populated areas of the Swedish inland of Norrland. This geographical circumstance was often foregrounded in the conversations, and it was obvious that describing one's ideas of ageing was closely connected to notions of the specific place in which the ageing process took place.

I will begin by briefly presenting one of the interviewees whom I have chosen as a main 'case', and will refer to this interviewee as 'Kerstin'.[3] The content of this interview was of course not generalisable, but it touched upon most of the themes found in the material as a whole. I will then concisely describe the discourses that constituted the five dominating topics in Kerstin's story of ageing, and also include a number of brief examples of how these discourses are articulated in contemporary public texts; for example Swedish official reports and the Swedish news media on ageing and old age. The main reason for including and equating statements that were not in the interviews is not to point out the similarities and differences in order to define the character of the different sources, but to contextualise them and show how the discourses that were discernible in the interviews also existed elsewhere (cf. Wreder 2007). I then move on to discuss how the articulation of different discourses was made comprehensible through a few dominating logics, and, finally, will raise some self-critical questions concerning the ability of my approach to satisfyingly explain the material (cf. Howarth 2000, p. 140).

314

Growing older in a sparsely populated area of Sweden

Kerstin was 67 years old at the time of the interview. She was a widow of four years and had recently become an old-age pensioner who lived in a house on the outskirts of the same small community in the Norrlandic inland in which she had lived the major part of her life. In the nearby centre of the community was the home of her daughter and her three children. Her two sons had moved away from the community: one living in a city about 400 kilometres away, and the other in a community 50 kilometres away. The original reason for interviewing Kerstin was that she had been volunteering as a class grandparent. She had regularly visited a nearby school for a year and either helped the pupils in the classroom or, on occasion, helped them with their homework after school hours.

However, the focus of the interview was on ageing, and more specifically about what it meant to age in a sparsely populated rural area. Kerstin narrated how she had stayed at home as a housewife when the children were young and about the places where she had worked after her children had grown up. She also described her most recent transition from working part-time as an administrator at a smaller local company to retirement and being home most of her days. 'There are always those little things in the household that need to be done', Kerstin said, also mentioning a close friend with whom she used to talk, and how her dog was such great company and needed to be taken out for walks. However, she also expressed how her first year of retirement was filled with feelings of dissatisfaction. Engaging as a class grandparent meant a great deal to her, and she said she was now very content with her situation.

Kerstin's father had passed away over 15 years ago and her mother recently moved to a local geriatric care centre. She had an older brother who also lived in the same community, but it was Kerstin who took on the main responsibility of visiting her mother almost every day.

The initial story was of a rather enjoyable life, but this changed when she started to talk about her mother's situation. Talking about her mother's move seemed to make her think about her own position. Within the realm of the interview, Kerstin started to question her own story of contentment and well-being, and revealed a degree of indecision about her own future (cf. Glynos & Howarth 2007, p. 129). It seemed that when she talked about her mother she was not only confronted with her own frustration concerning her brother's lack of responsibility, and her worries about her mother's well-being, but also with the unsettling prospect of growing old herself. Kerstin began to talk about the problems associated with growing old in a sparsely populated area. Suddenly, she appeared to be a woman who worried a great deal about the future. In what follows I will present an account of how Kerstin described her situation, and how a specific number of discourses seemed to be particularly important for the structuring of that story.

Discourse on the depopulation of the Norrlandic inland

When the conversation touched upon living and ageing in a rural area, Kerstin almost immediately mentioned the problems associated with the ongoing depopulation of the inland.

> The question is how it's gonna be, you know, with the depopulation here. Young people don't want to stay where there's no work. But it's a pity, it is. They move, the young.

Depopulation was instantly connected to the lack of job opportunities. This was true for the majority of the interviewees – expressions like 'there are no jobs here' and '[people] have to make a living' were common when talking about depopulation. In the daily press, as well as in official reports, 'depopulation' was repeatedly articulated together with 'inter-regional migration' and the 'labour market'.

Kerstin's discussion of the effects of depopulation lingered on the ones who stayed behind. These problematic effects were very concretely described and were frequently repeated in the news media, which stated how 'The availability of different types of services is … becoming worse in rural areas.' (*Norrbottens-Kuriren*, 5 December 2008). Kerstin stated that 'You get more exposed to such things when you get older', and continually referred to the government as 'they': 'It's not like they're backing us'. Such a string of directed criticism was often present in the interview, and this criticism was often levelled at a power that was difficult to articulate precisely. Words like 'depopulation' and 'exploitation' were sometimes articulated together and used in terms of a threat to the inland identity.[4]

However, a counter discourse was also present and included the idea that the labour market was not the only influence on depopulation. Kerstin reflected on 'the youthful wish to look around' and to 'go somewhere to study', thus primarily associating migration with the characteristics of 'the young' and their attraction to 'the cities' (cf. Eriksson 2008). This counter-discourse, which was also visible for example in the 2000 official state report on regional policy (SOU 2000:87), seemed anxious to present an alternative image to the one that blamed the labour market and produced an image of the working population as victims who were forced to move against their will.

In the interviews, the discourse on depopulation of the Norrlandic inland pointed out clear subject positions. There were *the young people* and *the old people*: 'the young' were thought of as causing the depopulation by either moving away due to the job situation, or being youthful and wishing to 'see the world', whereas 'the old' were more often articulated through site-boundedness. However, Kerstin often used the pronoun *we*, which involved *all the people* who lived in the community, or in the Norrlandic inland as a whole. She then posited this 'we' with an unnamed other, a possible enemy, which was vaguely described as the state, the government, Stockholm, or even Brussels (cf. Sjölander 2004; Rönnblom 2002).

Kerstin repeated the discourse on depopulation in a similar way to how it existed in other public contexts. The effect was the combination of certain problems that older people were thought to be confronting in these areas, and an idea that the rural old were victims of political decisions that were made beyond their control.

There was a tendency to associate depopulation with a critique of a 'centre' in the material, and this resulted in a clear division between periphery and centre, and between the Norrlandic inland and the rest of Sweden. Whereas the young people's out-migration was described as a comprehensible phenomenon, the unappreciative centre of power was constituted in terms of an enemy that was responsible for the experienced 'failure' of fully constituting oneself (Laclau & Mouffe 1985, p. 125) in terms of a vital rural area. Had it not been for the cutbacks and out-migration 'we could have continued our lives here as normal', said Kerstin.

Discourse on population ageing

Intertwined with the discourse on depopulation was a discourse on population ageing. Kerstin used this discourse as a way of further emphasising her point: growing old in the Norrlandic inland meant having to confront real difficulties. The discourse on population ageing was not articulated as frequently as that on depopulation, but it seemed to have a common effect: it offered subject positions for older people as 'lonely' and as a possible 'burden' to society. Kerstin educated me on the topic as she articulated the discourses of 'depopulation' and 'population ageing' together:

> It's also this thing that we have fewer and fewer children. So we're getting older, you know, as a nation, and I think that means that it will be tougher to grow old in the future. And with the young moving away… there will be nobody left to care for the old.

Population ageing is a demographic fact that has attracted great attention in the West. In Swedish media the topic seems to have flourished since the 1990s (Abramsson 2005). Debates on this topic focus on anxieties about the costs involved as more and more people find themselves outside the labour market. Dramatic language is often used in the debate, as in the news article below where the ageing of the population is described as 'a ticking bomb':

> Too few children are born, people do not work long enough, the pension systems are not robust and budgets are too weak. All this strains finances and welfare systems and represents a demographic ticking bomb for the EU. Ageing, fewer children, mass retirement of baby-boomers, and a longer life expectancy lead to an impossible strain on finances. It is crucial to do something now, otherwise

catastrophic consequences are to be expected, cautions the EU Commission (*Dagens Nyheter*, 10 May 2009).

This economic perspective tends to offer passive subject positions for older people, and their increasing numbers are seen as problematic. The perspective has been criticised for excluding the aged population from the notion of 'society' and for ignoring how activities that are performed by older people *outside* the labour market have important economical and emotional values (cf. Narushima 2005; Warburton & McLaughlin 2005). Kerstin is, however, not interested in discussing her own volunteer work as a class grandparent in relation to this discourse, but emphasises a supposed lack of healthcare professionals in the future. She also mentioned value-laden stereotypes of older people:

> In the end there will be only older people left, especially here. And in today's society older people are not *appreciated*... the elderly aren't exactly seen as *resources*... we're only seen as grumpy oldies.

Since the breakthrough of the discourse on population ageing in public debate, such ageism (Butler 1969; Andersson 2008) has been widely recognised. The awareness is present in contemporary research on representations (Markström 2009), and in the official report *Äldrepolitik för framtiden* (Ageing policy for the future) it is stated that older people are often portrayed in relation to their healthcare needs and that society tends to ignore the elderly when dealing with issues of power, discrimination and development (SOU 2003:91, p. 21).

Articulating her own experienced situation with discourses on population ageing and depopulation of the inland provides Kerstin with relatively strong arguments for her fears for the future. Mentioning how society tends to stereotype older people also has the effect that quite vulnerable subject positions are once more constituted. However, her critique of these positions also reveals the possibility of reflexively distancing oneself from them.

Discourse on the dismantling
of the people's home of Sweden

A third discourse that is discernible in Kerstin's story describes how the specific period of Swedish socioeconomic history known as 'the people's home' era is about to be dismantled. When the idea of a people's home was introduced in the social democratic rhetoric of the late 1920s, it was the social and economic inequalities that were the primary targets when concepts like 'equality', 'cooperation' and 'helpfulness' came to signify an ideal Swedish social life (Dahlqvist 2002). In Kerstin's story 'the notion of a people's home' of Sweden is used to symbolise an equal society, but she rearticulates it to say something specifically about how *older* people are treated today.

> ... in the past things were more ordered and people cared for each other, for the elderly, took care of people that had worked all their lives. But today with the present government... no, the people's home era is definitely over. *Everything* is for sale. And you never know nowadays, do you? It's like *everything* is more insecure.

In Kerstin's story the past is comprised of better care and a higher level of state control, but also of nostalgic and more imprecise qualities such as 'honesty', 'safety' and 'social responsibility'. It is clear that this discourse is strongly connected to the long era of social democratic rule in Sweden, and the interviewees blame its dismantling partly on the politics of the present conservative-led government, and partly on an idea that the present is on the whole more insecure.

Kerstin mentions none of the critique that has been levelled against the people's home era (cf. Zaremba 2009; Runcis 1998). Instead, the notion of 'the people's home' functions as a *myth* (Laclau 1990, p. 61; Howarth 2000, p. 111) that brings together a multitude of positive but rather vague ideas connected to the past, and which inserts a paradoxical stability to the experienced present by stating its instability, incorporating it within a clear and coherent narrative. The myth states that once there was a specific culture in this country that meant that we took care of each other, did our share, respected authorities, trusted each other, and so on, and where responsibility was taken by a strong state. Zaremba, writing on the subject in *Dagens Nyheter*, points to how the myth also implies that those days are now gone and how this has been blamed on various and radically different phenomena, such as immigration or neo-liberalism, that ruined 'everything' (*Dagens Nyheter*, 10 May 2009). The myth thus has a describable content, but it represents something else and different from itself: 'the very principle of a fully achieved literality' (Laclau 1990, p. 63).

The notion of a lost people's home is only sparsely used within contemporary state investigations and reports. When used, it is often in order to make a contrastive point, as when a report on homelessness was entitled *Housing Wanted – an ESO-report on the homeless people in the people's home* (*Bostad sökes – en ESO-rapport om de hemlösa i folkhemmet*, Ds 1999:46). Such irony can also be found in the press in the shape of critical descriptions of a country that is unwilling to face the demands of a more globalised world. What is promoted is not the dismantling of the people's home welfare system, but its supposed inability to adapt to contemporary times. The tabloid *Expressen* (19 October 2008), one of the largest Swedish evening papers, states, 'When the wind blows, Sweden rather shuts the door to the people's home and buries its face in the pillow'.

In Kerstin's story, the myth of the people's home forms a distressing image of an insecure present, where 'vulnerable people' (i.e. the elderly), 'politicians', and indefinite 'present times' are articulated as the primary, but vaguely described agents. However, by representing the actual possibility of an alternative reality that is inspired by past values, the myth also opens up a subject position of a knowledgeable mediator between a mythical past and the present, and this is the position that older people can possibly fill, according to Kerstin. It was intimated by her that 'society' did not always offer this possibility and that it thereby missed out on the benefits possibly resulting from it; society thereby denied older people the possibility of taking up an acitve and positively charged position.

Discourse on the baby-boomers

> I think it will be a quite different thing to grow old for me than it was for my mother, for example. When she was my age, she was already old. There's a difference there. My generation, I think, is healthier, and I think … for me, growing old is something that will happen *later*, you know, maybe it's the case for all us baby-boomers of the forties [laughs].

The result of the discourses of depopulation, population ageing and the dismantling of 'the people's home', which positioned Kerstin in a somewhat victimised position, was to adopt what could be termed the discourse on the baby-boomers – the large generation that was born in the 1940s. This discourse made it possible for her to identify herself as 'different' from earlier generations; a qualitative difference that is often stressed as a unique feature of the baby-boomers, and which implies a rhetoric that probably has had an important impact on the boomers' self-perception. Kerstin pointed out 'health' as an important difference, and maybe health is also what makes it possible for her to think that 'growing old is something that will happen *later*' in her generation. A similar notion is aired in a state report where 'the old of tomorrow' are described as '[having] relatively good resources [covering] health, economy, social networks and levels of education' (SOU 2003:91, p. 20).

The notion of the baby-boomers as a qualitatively specific generation was also reflected in the media at the time. The retiring baby-boomers were portrayed as enviable, both by their predecessors and their successors.

> The baby-boomers were once frequenters of student clubs and class travellers in a Sweden where welfare grew. Subsequent generations will envy them. But also thank them: The first generation of older people who are healthy and cocky (*Sydsvenskan*, 2 June 2008).

The word 'cocky' reappears in many of the media representations. This is a generation that is believed to have high demands, and Kerstin echoes this with a sense of awareness of gender equality:

I also think that women of my generation… we are better prepared to demand things. We will not settle… so that's better, I think.

The baby-boomers are represented as a self-aware and demanding cohort. This is obvious in Swedish popular literature (cf. Lahger 2005) as well as in the press. The following was printed in one daily press editorial: 'They will never allow anyone to treat them as parasites. They will demand respect. Imagine the costs' (*Göteborgs Tidningen*, 5 October 2008).

Even though many media representations of the baby-boom generation do include a critical aspect, such as shutting younger generations out of the labour market, being self-righteous, or failing to understand or admit their privileged position, *generational conflict* is not a theme in Kerstin's nor the other informants' stories. Instead, the notion of the baby-boomers is primarily used to counter the stereotypical articulation between old age, helplessness and passivity. The articulation of one's experiences and imagined future, together with the specific qualities that are attributed to the baby-boomers, results in a subject position that is strongly associated with agency and individuality, and thus more valued in society.

It is, however, noteworthy that Kerstin, who lacks many of the experiences that are often associated with the baby-boomers, can so easily identify with a position within this discourse. Seen from the 'outside' she has no higher education, she has led a more traditional life as a housewife taking care of the children for many years, and has never left her village to live elsewhere. This reveals how there may be very different reasons why a person identifies with a discourse. Two aspects of identification seemed relevant: similar experiences, and co-identification with certain qualities and imagined possibilities.

Discourse on individual responsibility

Late modernity, or the postmodern world, is often characterised by references to an increased level of freedom. This freedom is sometimes strongly associated with notions of the neo-liberalisation of Western states, and with the possibility of re-inventing oneself through consumption. However, individual invention is also connected to ideas of individual responsibility. The responsibility to choose is said to bring about the possibility of guilt, stress, anxiety, and self-blame (cf. Bauman 2002; Giddens 1991; Beck 2002). Bonoli et al. (2000) have shown how the responsibility to provide for one's future economy as a pensioner has shifted: what used to be a responsibility of the state is now thought to be the responsibility of the individual (see also Jyrkämä & Haapamäki 2008). Such discourse on individual responsibility was present in Kerstin's story, but was approached ambivalently.

> It's also a question of how you plan. You have to 'feather your nest', so to speak, so… well, it's self-evident that you cannot rely on society anyway, isn't it [laughs]?

> Well, I don't know exactly, but I reckon it's mostly up to you, how you live your life, how you keep in contact with family and friends, if you keep healthy and take care of your body and exercise and eat right and so on. … But then it's not always easy to… it depends… some people… if you get ill or if you've had a physically demanding job… I mean, the GI diet doesn't fix everything [laughs]!

> I guess it's also a question of how you prepare yourself, by saving money and having a pension insurance. But of course, it depends on how much you've earned.

It is obvious that Kerstin's interpretation of today's individualised society is juxtaposed to, for example, the strong welfare state of the people's home. Individual responsibility was articulated together with ideas concerning planning, feathering one's nest, keeping in contact, keeping healthy, caring for one's body, and preparing by paying for private insurance. However, all these forms of pro-active action were articulated together with a certain amount of critique. As in almost all of the interviews this critique also included an ironic attitude towards the government or 'society', and an emphatic stance in favour of people who cannot live up to such demands.

Making discourse intelligible – a logics approach

In order to account for how the above-mentioned discourses made sense, I will try to describe them from a perspective of logics. Laclau understands logics as 'the type of relations between entities that makes possible the actual operation of [a] system of rules', or as 'the basic rules of the game' (2000, pp. 283–4). According to Glynos (2008, p. 277), these rules assist in describing and characterising practices, but they also seek to capture 'the various conditions which make [a] practice "work" or "tick"'. In order to further the understanding of the concept, Glynos & Howarth (2007) differentiate between social, political and fantasmatic logics.

'Social logics', according to Glynos, characterise practices by 'setting out the rules, norms, and self-understandings informing the practice' (2008, p. 278). They characterise the overall – and sedimented – pattern of a discursive practice that involves 'a system of rules drawing a horizon within which some objects are representable while others are excluded' (Laclau 2005, p. 117).

The term 'political logics' is used to diachronically describe the emergence of a practice, and focuses on how that practice is contingently constituted as an effect of different struggles. Political logics furnish us with 'a conceptual grammar with which to account for the dynamics of social change' (Glynos & Howarth 2007, p. 145).

Finally, 'fantasmatic logics' help to account for 'the way subjects are gripped by a practice' (Glynos 2008, p. 278). They try to answer questions such as *how* and *why* a certain practice makes sense to people. These different logics always work together (Glynos & Howarth 2007, p. 152). The following analysis is inspired by the work of Glynos & Howarth, but I have chosen a somewhat different approach from the one they suggest. I will not name certain logics as either social, political or fantasmatic, but instead try to analyse what I see as the dominant organising logics in the material from their social, political and fantasmatic *aspects*. I chose this approach because I wanted to be able to show how one logic could have different effects depending on how it was articulated. Two overall binary logics seemed strongly represented in the material: one logic of centre/periphery and one of past/present.[5]

The logic of centre and periphery

There is extensive research on *internal orientalism* (Schein 1997; Jansson 2003), which focuses on how nations identify their regions as culturally different. When it comes to Norrland, research on news representations has shown how the media make particular issues such as regional development policies, unemployment and migration 'synonymous with the entire region of Norrland regardless of actual local variation... [re-enacting] the role of the centre (Stockholm) as being in control of the distribution of resources' (Eriksson 2008, p. 384).

In the interview with Kerstin, and all the interviews that were carried out with people who lived in the inland, a logic prevailed that separated the centre from the periphery. This dichotomy influenced almost everything that was said about the inland. Symptomatically, the dichotomy was absent from all the interviews conducted with people who lived in larger cities; a pattern that confirms the unequal power relation where 'centre' was the privileged node.

Looking at the logic of centre/periphery as a *social logic* enables us to characterise a set of practices that constitute the 'periphery': longer distances, a more limited supply of goods and services and less diverse job opportunities, but also closeness to nature and a lower tempo. The discourses on depopulation, population ageing and the dismantling of the welfare state all rested heavily on a cultural knowledge about such geographical differences. This knowledge conditioned the understanding of growing old in the sparsely populated Norrlandic inland. It also provided the stories concerning the difficulties of ageing with an explanatory and legitimising context. Therefore, the social aspect of the centre/periphery dichotomy structured what was possible to say and what was expected to be said about ageing, and made the discourses on depopulation and population ageing comprehensible as contextualisations of ageing in the inland.

What is interesting about the logic of centre and periphery is that at the same time as it positioned the local population as peripheral and relatively underprivileged, it also seemed to offer a possibility to form a partly oppositional identity (Hansen 1998). This oppositional identity has a long and heterogeneous history. One well-known manifestation includes the popular catchphrase 'We won't move!' (*'Vi flytt' int'!'*) expressed in the Norrlandic dialect; one that was coined during the migration wave of the 1970s. The expression was used in a famous hit record from 1970[6] and in a written report from the same year (Öholm & Åberg 1970). In August 2011, an Internet search for the term 'Vi flytt' int'' gave 90,400 hits, and it is obvious that the contemporary usages of the expression in relation to Norrlanders have three distinct meanings: as a demeaning expression (a sign of conservatism), a self-expression of pride, and a reminder of an underprivileged social position.

In the latter sense the logic of centre and periphery is best viewed as a *political logic* that generates a two-dimensional matrix where a logic of equivalence between identities that are connected to the Norrlandic inland comes to predominate over a logic of difference. The Norrlandic identities become equivalent, as Glynos & Howarth (2007, p. 144) have put it, 'not insofar as they share a positive property (though empirically they *may* share something in common), but, crucially, insofar as they have a common enemy'. Consequently, internal differences are weakened. By positioning themselves in opposition to a series of others (Stockholm, the coastal cities, and, since Sweden joined the EU, also Brussels) it was possible for the interviewees to unite as Norrlanders and, *potentially*, forge a political frontier that challenges the subordination that in their view came with state politics. Thus they themselves contributed to the same internal orientalism that they used to criticise.[7]

Even though this construction of a social antagonism between centre and periphery did not seem to pose any serious threat to the social order, it did offer a model – a possibility of identifying oneself with rural life.

The logic of past and present

Being diachronic in character and focusing on the changes that have preceded the present situation, the logic of the past and present seemed to organise the meaning in the interviews in a slightly different way. By contrasting the present with ideas of the past and the hopes and fears for the future, this logic made visible the contingencies of the contemporary situation. Viewed as a *political logic*, the interviewees' frequent descriptions of the past undermined an understanding of the present as a natural and unproblematised condition.

The logic of past and present permeated all of the above-mentioned discourses; they all made sense of time in one way or another. Quite often the interviewees dealt with the notion of time in a nostalgic mode, either restoratively attempting to reconstruct a lost condition, or reflectively thriving in the distressing condition of longing itself (cf. Boym 2001). Therefore, nostalgia was a mode with bridging effects. By not always spelling out what was being yearned for, the interviewees could mediate the (lost) values of the sparsely populated areas without being specific as to exactly what these values were. Rather, the nostalgia that surrounded some of the statements in the interviews seemed to knit several 'losses' together: the loss of a sense of community (due to depopulation), and the loss of a functioning healthcare system (a symptom of a dismantled people's home). Furthermore, the loss of the open cultivated landscape was sometimes depicted as a manifest reminder of a time when everything was different. Angelika Sjöstedt Landén (in this book) states that there is something about affections that ties us to positions without us reflecting intellectually upon the content or character of that tie (from Ahmed 2004). Drawing on the 'ontology of lack', which implies that every system of meaning is constitutively incomplete (Glynos & Howarth 2007, pp. 14, 127), nostalgia seemed to fuel the 'inlander' identities and thus substituted the vague constitutive lack with a more comprehensible one.

Nostalgia also successfully helped to present 'the past' as an important period and – just as the myth of the people's home – made the position of knowledgeable mediators between the past and the present possible for older people to adopt. Such a positioning did not require 'success' within the late-modern discourse on individual responsibility, but foregrounded life experience and even place-boundedness. However, nostalgia was also an insidious mode, and when it was articulated with old age it risked producing culturally devalued retrogressive and anti-modern subject positions (cf. Lundgren 2010).

The dichotomic nodes that constitute the logics of past/present and centre/periphery offered the possibility of empty signifiers – signifiers that serve as surfaces of inscription for various political demands (Laclau 1996, p. 36). Even though the interviewees acknowledged the benefits of modernity ('nowadays') and city-dwelling ('centre'), the words 'nowadays' and 'centre' were constituted as vague threats, or 'enemies' to the possibility of an ageing identity in the inland of Norrland. Seen as enemies, 'nowadays' and 'centre' – or rather, identities and phenomena that are connected to the nodes of 'nowadays' and 'centre' – succeeded in privileging a dimension of equivalence within the heterogeneous totality of the rural periphery (cf. Laclau 1996, p. 39). Paradoxically, it was also possible to detect a simultaneous critique of the resultant connection of 'old age' to 'before' and 'periphery'. One interviewee stated that this articulation was at the core of ageist notions of older people.

As they were seen as political, the logics of centre/periphery and past/present made a critical position possible for the interviewees to adopt: they dealt with power relations by simplifying and politicising the social space and by transforming it into two opposite camps (cf. Glynos & Howarth 2007, p. 143). However, these two camps did not form a solid foundation for the constitution of clear-cut political frontiers (cf. Norval 2000).

Ideological fantasies

If the politico-economic system seems to drive people from living, working and ageing in sparsely populated areas, there must be a fantasmatic logic that constitutes a force behind the identifications that somehow make people (choose to) stay despite the difficulties (Glynos & Howarth 2007, p. 145). According to Glynos (2008, p. 283), fantasmatic logics are implicated in the subject's very being through the structuring of his or her desire with the Lacanian idea of a barrier: an obstacle that prevents the ideal from being fully realised. In the case presented here, the most prominent impediments consisted of concrete difficulties that were blamed on government politics, population changes and migrations. The interviewees seemed to think that if it were not for these difficulties, living and ageing in the inland would be perfect.

Taken together, these obstacles not only prevented the ideal from being realised, and thereby the necessary creation of new ideals and obstacles, but also constituted a superior Other, in relation to which the identity as an older Norrlander of the rural inland was made comprehensible as a subordinated identity and as paradoxically privileged. In comparison to city-dwellers, inland identities were articulated together with qualities such as closeness to nature and contact with one's inner self (cf. Sjöstedt Landén's chapter). This quite positive identity was inherently opposed to any idea of moving to the centre, but took pride in staying put.

The place-bound identity that was structured by the political logics of past/present and centre/periphery was also supported by counter-narratives that seemed to resist public official disclosure (Glynos & Howarth 2007, p. 148). The secret pleasure of being victimised by state politics, and the conviction that living in Norrland and outside the large cities somehow made one a more reliable person, are examples that indicate the presence of ideological fantasy in these informants' speech acts.[8] The *freedom* that came with the articulation of an oppositional identity and a peripheral location contributed to the feelings of *jouissance* that these sometimes politically incorrect fantasies evoked. This freedom was sometimes constituted as a value in itself, and associated with a closeness to nature and a freedom from control. However, freedom could also be articulated in relation to the victimised position and peripheral location as a real possibility for 'taking back' from the state what it presumably owed the sparsely populated areas (cf. Frykman & Hansen 2009).[9] Therefore, the state seemed to be constituted either as a (weakened) guarantee for welfare or as an unappreciative Other.

Glynos & Howarth (2007, p. 151) have described what they call an 'enjoyment of closure', and it is possible to see how the fantasmatic aspects of these logics functioned as driving forces in a partly joyful, partly defensive discursive closure; the closing off of the possibility to move to a place where ageing would supposedly be 'easier'. It was obvious that moving at this age (the interviewees were between 63 and 76) was constructed as a non-possibility, even though it was sometimes mentioned but just as quickly dismissed: 'I think that maybe there would be a better chance that they keep the geriatric centre in [the nearby community centre], so the smartest thing would of course be to move there now. But, you know, you don't just move, do you?'

However, attempting a cultural understanding of the practice of ageing in a place where ageing was described as more difficult than elsewhere seemed to call for an additional argument. Lurking in the interviews was also a logic within which human situatedness was constituted both as a right and as an ontological need; a logic that could be called *a logic of belonging*. What 'belonging' means here is the right to stay at the place that one somehow feels connected to, or even *own*. This logic made an aggressive defence against an imagined critique possible, and constituted both victim and hero identities.

It is easy to see how a logic of belonging organised the discourse on depopulation by legitimising the view on out-migration as a problem. The reason for viewing out-migration as a problem was not only because it results in a depopulated inland, but also because it goes against the experience of a sometimes nostalgic feeling, or even a moral conviction of what is right and good. The logic of belonging also helped to strengthen the discourse on the dismantling of the welfare state. By simply staying put it was made particularly visible how this dismantling process is materialised in sparsely populated areas. While organising the discourses on the baby-boomers and individual responsibility, this logic seemed to create either an antagonism between the modern baby-boomers and retrogressive place-bound identities, or emphasised how staying put was also a responsible choice for the future.

Therefore, there was a *beatific dimension* of the Norrlandic fantasy which stated that had 'things' not changed everything would have been better, or if only there was a change in state policy everything would be better, and the Norrlandic identities, nature and culture would prosper. There was also a *horrific dimension* stating that if politics – or the more vague capitalist market economy system of present times – does not change, nobody will be able to stay and the Norrlandic forms of life of past days will be forgotten forever (cf.

Glynos & Howarth 2007, p. 147; Glynos 2008, p. 283). Having closed off the radical contingency of social relations, these fantasies constituted a logic that implied comprehensible causal relations as well as stable identities.

Elusive emotions

All of the above-mentioned discourses and logics can be seen to offer a vocabulary to express, explain, legitimate and resist different conditions, feelings and choices. However, none of them seemed able to adequately explain the situation that the interviewees were living in. There were many other aspects loitering in the background that made the idea of moving preposterous: the long-term relations, the memories, the house that would be almost impossible to sell, the feelings, the sense of belonging. These things were almost never expanded upon in the telephone interviews, but were mentioned in passing.

It is possible that different kinds of interviews would have captured these feelings; a different conversation would have made it possible for the interviewees to reflect and expand on things that people seldom talk about because of their taken-for-grantedness. It is easy to imagine how an interview carried out in Kerstin's kitchen, in the midst of her everyday life, would have resulted in a different conversation, or how a repeated set of interviews would have resulted in different questions and a closer and more personal relationship between the interviewer and interviewee. I am not looking for something non-discursive, and I do not mean that a close relationship between the interviewer and interviewee would result in a conversation that is more authentic or *true*. The discourses and logics that were discernible in the interviews certainly have real effects, and they do help to constitute reality as Kerstin and the other interviewees experienced it. However, in order to understand the fullness of ideological fantasies, a telephone interview is methodologically speaking nowhere near perfect when it comes to talking about such things. This does not, however, mean that 'such things' do not exist, that they have no effects, or that they would be impossible to 'see'. Perhaps 'those things', difficult as they are to put into words, or to grasp discursively, constitute the really 'sticky' things of the so-called fantasmatic logics. This calls for research strategies (Howarth 2000, p. 133) that take the epistemological starting points of discourse theory (DT) seriously, and that find ways to handle materialisations into the everyday of movements, feelings and bodies. A sensitivity to this 'language' would no doubt help in the study of sedimented and culturally under-privileged logics.

The logics approach, as applied here, helps to elucidate how disparate and heterogeneous ongoing processes are connected (understood in terms of articulation). This discourse theoretical approach also sheds light on how these connections result in the constitution of potentially, but not necessarily politicised, old-age identities, and the way they are made meaningful to agents. It would therefore be of importance to carry out further investigation into how different research strategies are able to reach, or evoke, different aspects of how a practice exists in order to see how different modes of conversation, and different relations, make different articulations possible.

The initial objective – to discuss the interviews from the perspective of the politicisation of old–age identities – did not, however, work out the way I had thought. By relating to different discourses the interviewees certainly constituted subject positions to identify with, and these identities were equivalently organised by opposing themselves to a series of others. However, even though these identifications were voiced in the interviews and the 'foundation' of the social was sometimes questioned, it was unclear how visible this was in the interviewees' everyday lives. According to Laclau (1994, p. 4), political identities (as opposed to social identities) require visibility of the acts of identification. Such visibility is only obtained 'in so far as opposite forms of institution (of the social) are ... fought for in the historical arena', or when collective demands are articulated.

Although talking about ageing, the demands articulated by the interviewees were not united by *age* as an empty signifier (Laclau 2005, pp. ix, 95). If anything, they constructed a collective identity of Norrlanders. However, neither the identity as 'old' nor the identity as 'Norrlander', and the logics of equivalence that made these identities possible, seemed to constitute any clear-cut political frontiers.

Of the things that worked against the constitution of a collective political identity was perhaps that the demands did not seem important enough. There was no presence of floating signifiers that were strong enough to transform a logic of difference into an unequivocal logic of equivalence. Neither were the 'threats' antagonistic – they affected but did not prevent the existence of Norrlandic identities (Laclau & Mouffe 1985, p. 125).

What was problematic from the interviewees' point of view was that the two logics of centre/periphery and past/present risked colonising the whole field by correlating periphery with past and centre with present (and future). This fixation had implications for how the old-age position could be articulated. As old age was often connected to the past and the inland, it was not a position that was proposed as an important political identity. The identity, as well as the demands associated with it, also seemed to have been allotted a low status in the contemporary political landscape. The option seemed to be to articulate a modern baby-boomer identity, which made it more difficult to argue for the so-called 'Norrlandic values' that were so place-bound and related to tradition.

What further complicated the constitution was the fact that the positive qualities that were articulated with a Norrlandic identity were also part of the Swedish national self-image (cf. Frykman & Löfgren 1979). It was only in relation to Norrland that 'Sweden' became associated with opposite values. This made the Norrlandic identity both recognisable and likable, but also a difficult identity to claim because it in a sense belonged to everyone.

Aletta Norval (2000) has described how DT tends to privilege the moment of conflict, and asks for a distinction between the general logic of individuation, on the one hand, and the formation of political frontiers and the constitution of antagonistic forms of identity on the other. The case described here shows how logics of equivalence can help to constitute collective identities, but also how they can fail to constitute explicit political identities that are recognisable by others and themselves as antagonistically challenging and therefore a driving force for social change.

Notes

1 I take ideology to imply, as Žižek has put it, 'an (unconscious) fantasy structuring our social reality itself' (Žižek 1989, p. 30).

2 The initial project was called 'Making meaning in/of old age' and specifically focused on the identity production of older people that appeared to be privileged by the norms of ageing and old age in relation to health, activity and participation. The project was carried out within the Centre for Population Studies/Ageing and Living Conditions Programme (ALC), Umeå University, and mainly financed by the Swedish Research Council.

3 Glynos & Howarth argue that case studies as a research strategy provide important vehicles for 'critically explaining problematized phenomena by providing the contextually specific knowledge within which to link [the] more general logics together' (Glynos & Howarth 2007, p. 204). This strategy makes it possible to investigate the multiple ways that identities are represented, how 'individuals identify and disidentify with other groups, how one category is used to differentiate another in specific contexts, and how particular identities become salient or fore-grounded at particular moments' (Valentine 2007, p. 15).

4 This is true, for example, in descriptions of Storsjöyran, a very well-known and popular festival in Östersund. On the website it is stated that the festival existed as early as in the 1960s, as a manifestation against the exploitation and depopulation of the county (www.storsjoyran.se; see also *Dagens Nyheter,* 4 August 2008), and that it is sometimes called a 'Befrielsefest' (liberation party).

5 However, it is important to stress how the very naming of logics itself involves, as Glynos & Howarth have pointed out, a constitutive act and a critical judgement (2007, pp. 194, 186). In naming (articulating) logics we are, as they rightly remark, 'engaged in a hegemonic struggle' (2007, p. 196; see also Gunnarsson Payne 2006).

6 The song 'Vi flytt' int'!' was performed by Hasse Burman, and reached number one in the charts ('Svensktoppen') in 1970.

7 The concept internal orientalism is usually used to explain how national identity is constructed as privileged by othering an internal region of the state (Jansson 2003, p. 295). In this case the othering certainly involved the constitution of Sweden as modern, but paradoxically the (positive) characteristics attributed to Norrland can also constitute Swedishness, when Sweden is compared to other countries.

8 Another fantasy is the common idea in Kiruna (a city in the northernmost part of Sweden) that the Underground in Stockholm is built with steel from Kiruna, and implicitly that in the past the state had robbed Kiruna of its wealth (Nilsson 2010).

9 Frykman and Hansen (2009) have vividly described how exploiting the health insurance system can be understood as an act of resistance.

References
Literature

Abramsson, M., 2005. *Befolkningsfrågan i press och politik, 1995–2004*. Institutet för framtidsstudier, 2005:10.

Ahmed, S., 2004. *The Cultural Politics of Emotion*. New York: Routledge.

Andersson, H., 2008. *Ålderism*. Lund: Studentlitteratur.

Bonoli, G., George, V. & Taylor-Gooby, P., 2000. *European Welfare Futures*. Cambridge: Polity Press.

Bauman, Z., 2001. *The Individualized Society*. Cambridge. Polity Press.

Beck, U., 2002. *Individualization. Institutionalized Individualism and its Social and Political Consequences*. London: Sage.

Butler, R. N., 1969. Age-ism: Another Form of Bigotry. *Gerontologist*, 9, pp. 243–246.

Dahlqvist, H., 2002. Folkhemsbegreppet: Rudolf Kjellén vs Per Albin Hansson. *Historisk tidskrift*, no 3.

Eriksson, M., 2008. (Re)producing a 'Peripheral' Region – Northern Sweden in the News. *Geografiska Annaler: Series B, Human Geography*, 90(4), pp. 369–388.

Foucault, M., 2002. *The Archaeology of Knowledge*. London: Routledge.

Frykman, J. & Hansen, K., 2009. *I ohälsans tid: sjukskrivningar och kulturmönster i det samtida Sverige*. Stockholm: Carlssons.

Frykman, J. & Löfgren, O., 1979. *Den kultiverade människan*. Malmö: Gleerups.

Giddens, A., 1991. *Modernity and Self-identity*. Cambridge: Polity Press.

Glynos, J., 2008. Ideological Fantasy at Work. *Journal of Political Ideologies*, 13(3), pp. 275–296.

Glynos, J. & Howarth, D., 2007. *Logics of Critical Explanation in Social and Political Theory*. New York: Routledge.

Gunnarsson Payne, J., 2006. *Systerskapets logiker. En etnologisk studie av feministiska fanzines*. (Diss.) Umeå.

Hansen, K., 1998. *Välfärdens motsträviga utkant*. Lund: Historiska Media.

Howarth, D., 2000. *Discourse*. Buckingham: Open University Press.

Jansson, D. R., 2003. Internal Orientalism in America: W.J. Cash's The Mind of the South and the Spatial Construction of American National Identity. *Political Geography*, 22, pp. 293–316.

Jyrkämä, J. & Haapamäki, L., 2008. *Åldrande och alkohol*. NAD-publication nr 52.

Keating, N. & Phillips, J., 2008. A Critical Human Ecology Perspective on Rural Ageing. In: N. Keating (ed.), *Rural Ageing. A Good Place to Grow Old?* Bristol: Policy Press.

Laclau, E., 1990. *New Reflections on the Revolution of our Time*. London & New York: Verso.

Laclau, E., 1996. *Emancipation(s)*. London & New York: Verso.

Laclau, E., 2000. Constructing Universality. In: J. Butler, E. Laclau & S. Žižek (eds), *Contingency, Hegemony, Universality. Contemporary Dialogues on the Left*. London & New York: Verso.

Laclau, E. & Mouffe, C., 1985. *Hegemony and Socialist Strategy: Towards a Radical Democratic Politics*. London & New York: Verso.

Laclau, E. & Mouffe, C., 1990. Post-Marxism Without Apologies. In: E. Laclau (ed.), *New Reflections on the Revolution of our Time*. London: Verso, pp. 97–132.

Lahger, H., 2005. *Pensionär? – aldrig i livet! Elva 40-talister om sina liv och sin framtid.* Lidingö: Langenskiöld.

Lundgren, A.S., 2010. 'In the Good Old Days': Insidious Nostalgia and the Constitution of Old Age Identity. *Journal of Aging Studies,* 24:44, pp. 248–256.

Markström, C., 2009. *Vad fattas äldreomsorgen?* Umeå: Umeå universitet.

Narushima, M., 2005. 'Payback Time': Community Volunteering Among Older Adults as a Transformative Mechanism. *Ageing and Society,* 25, pp. 567–584.

Nilsson, B., 2010. *Kiruna. Staden som ideologi.* Umeå: Boréa.

Norval, A., 2000. Trajectories of Future Research in Discourse Theory. In: D. Howarth, A. Norval & Y. Stavrakakis (eds), *Discourse Theory and Political Analysis. Identities, Hegemonies and Social Change.* Manchester: Manchester University Press, pp. 219–236.

Öholm, S. & Åberg L., 1970. *Vi flytt' int': rapport från norrländsk ort.* Stockholm: Gebers.

Rönnblom, M., 2002. *Ett eget rum? Kvinnors organisering möter etablerad politik.* Umeå: Umeå universitet.

Rose, N., 1999. *Powers of Freedom: Reframing Political Thought.* Cambridge: Cambridge University Press.

Runcis, M., 1998. *Steriliseringar i folkhemmet.* Stockholm: Ordfront.

Schein, L., 1997. Gender and Internal Orientalism in China. *Modern China,* 23, 1, pp. 69–98.

Sjölander, A., 2004. *Kärnproblem. Opinionsbildning i kärnavfallsdiskursen i Malå.* Umeå: Umeå universitet.

Warburton, J. & McLaughlin, D., 2005. Lots of Little Kindnesses: Valuing the Role of Older Australians as Informal Volunteers in the Community. *Ageing and Society,* 25, pp. 715–730.

Wreder, M., 2007. Ovanliga analyser av vanliga material. In: M. Börjesson & E. Palmblad (eds), *Diskursanalys i praktiken.* Stockholm: Liber, pp. 28–51.

Zaremba, M., 2009. *De rena och de andra: om tvångssteriliseringar, rashygien och arvsynd.* Stockholm: Bokförlaget DN.

Žižek, S., 1989. *The Sublime Object of Ideology.* London: Verso.

Newspapers

Björklund, M., 2009. Åldrande befolkning hot mot EU-ländernas finanser. *Dagens Nyheter,* 10 May.

Boström, A., 2004. Storsjöyran ger Östersund ett lyft. *Dagens Nyheter,* 4 August.

Burell, H., 2006. Stopp för hyresrätter. *Göteborgs-Posten,* 3 November.

Dahlberg, A., 2008. Dags att vakna. *Expressen,* 19 October.

Editorial, 2008. Pigg som en pensionär. *Sydsvenskan,* 2 June.

Fredriksson, J., 2008. När äldre blev djur? *GöteborgsTidningen*, 5 October.
Hortin, P., 2005. Glesbygden blir allt mer avfolkad. *Norrbottens-Kuriren*, 5 December.
Zaremba, M., 2009. Vem äger flaggan? *Dagens Nyheter*, 10 May.

Official documents

Ds. 1999:46. *Bostad sökes – en ESO-rapport om de hemlösa i folkhemmet* (Final report from SENIOR 2005). Stockholm: Finansdepartementet.
SOU 2000:87. *Regionalpolitiska utredningens slutbetänkande* (Del A) (Final report from Regionalpolitiska utredningen). Stockholm: Näringsdepartementet.
SOU 2003:91. *Äldrepolitik för framtiden. 100 steg till trygghet och utveckling med en åldrande befolkning* (Final report from SENIOR 2005). Stockholm: Socialdepartementet.

Online sources

www.storsjoyran.se

Contributors

Sara Carlbaum is a Ph.D. student in political science at Umeå University. Her Ph.D. project is a deconstruction of Swedish upper secondary education policy from the 1970s to the present day, the aim of which is to provide a thorough understanding of the intersectional construction of citizenship in the context of Sweden. Her research interests include feminist and political theory, discourse analysis and education policy.

Annika Egan Sjölander is a senior lecturer in media and communication studies at Umeå University. Her thesis *Kärnproblem. Opinionsbildning i kärnavfallsdiskursen i Malå* (Core Issues. Opinion Formation in the Nuclear Waste Discourse in Malå) from 2004 is an application of Michel Foucault's discourse analytical perspective. In 2009 she was a visiting research fellow at the University of Lancaster, UK, and part of the Language-Ideology-Power group led by Professor Ruth Wodak. Several of her research projects have dealt with dimensions of democracy and the role of the media concerning environmental issues such as radioactive waste, chemicals and biofuels.

Stephanie Faye Hendrick is a Ph.D. student in English linguistics at Umeå University, where she is also affiliated with HUMlab. Her Ph.D. project examines the communicative affordances of the weblog as a media place. She is also a research assistant in two externally financed projects: YouTube as a performative arena (YAPA) and the role of the Internet as a surrogate social network in situations of domestic violence in the Swedish context (DVIS). Faye Hendrick's research interests include academic activism, web media, network theory, mediated discourse analysis, and sociolinguistics.

Jenny Gunnarsson Payne currently works as a lecturer and researcher in ethnology at Södertörn University, Stockholm. Her Ph.D. thesis was entitled *Systerskapets logiker. En etnologisk studie av feministiska fanzines* (The Logics of Sisterhood. An Ethnological Study of Feminist Zines, 2006). She has written extensively on feminist media. Her current research project is an investigation into cross-border reproductive care between Sweden and the Baltic States. Her research interests include discourse studies, feminist and gender theory, the study of political movements, alternative media production, and cultural and political perspectives on new reproductive technologies.

Joakim Isaksson is a senior lecturer at the Department of Social Work at Umeå University. His Ph.D. thesis was *Spänningen mellan normalitet och avvikelse. Om skolans insatser för elever i behov av särskilt stöd* (The Tension between Normality and Deviance. On Schools' support to Pupils with Special Educational Needs, 2009); an exploration of the tension between normality and deviance manifested in schools' work procedures for pupils with special educational needs, on both policy-, local (school level), as well as on an individual level (in terms of individual experiences). His current research interests include educational policy discourses on pupils' school difficulties and how the constituted meaning of pupil health activities in national policy documents is translated and put into practice at the local school level.

Anna Johansson is a lecturer and researcher at the Department of Culture and Media Studies, Umeå University and HUMlab. Her thesis *Self-harm: An Ethnological Study of Meaning and Identity in Accounts of Cutting* (2010) builds on post-Marxist discourse theory so as to provide an analysis of the construction of cutting and cutter identities, using material from Internet message boards as well as interviews. Her research and teaching interests include feminist approaches to gender and mental ill-health, media places and the hybridity of the physical and the digital, and girlhood studies.

Alon Lischinsky is a postdoctoral fellow at the Department of Media and Culture Studies, Umeå University. He earned his Ph.D.

in linguistics and communication from Universitat Pompeu Fabra, Barcelona, with a dissertation on the construction of expert knowledge in popular management books. His research interests focus on managerialism, the discursive construction of expert systems, and the use of corpus methods for critical discourse research. His first book, *Exploring Popular Management Discourse: A Discourse Approach*, will be published by Continuum in 2012.

David Payne is a Ph.D. student of political philosophy, and is part of the Ideology and Discourse Analysis programme at the University of Essex, UK. His thesis, *A Critique of Post-Emancipatory Reason: Political Possibility, Philosophical Visibility and the Question of Novelty*, is a defence of the importance of emancipatory ideas to politics in societies that would otherwise consign them to the pages of history. He teaches on the subject of children's rights at the Department of Children, Youth and Culture, Stockholm University. His research interests include contemporary French philosophy, Marxist theory (particularly Althusser), politics and social change, human and children's rights, as well as the philosophy of Kant.

Anna Sofia Lundgren is associate professor in ethnology and cultural analysis at Umeå University, and is also associated to the Ageing and Living Conditions Programme. She has previously published in the area of gender and sexuality in the education system. Currently, she is involved in a study of ageing and ageing identities.

Jonathan Ngeh completed his Ph.D. in sociology at Umeå University in the spring of 2011. His thesis, *Conflict, Marginalisation and Transformation: African Migrants in Sweden*, explored the challenges which African migrants experience in Sweden, how they respond to them and how they are affected. He is spending part of the autumn of 2011 at the Nordic Africa Institute in Uppsala as a visiting researcher.

Angelika Sjöstedt Landén is a Ph.D. student in ethnology at Umeå University. In her Ph.D. project she analyses the regional politics and practice of public sector relocation within the Swedish context.

In addition she studies healthcare plans and work life readjustment programmes for public sector employees. Her research involves a feminist and critical approach to the idea of work as a prerequisite for living 'the good life', where notions of place and centre and periphery are understood within a theoretical framework comprising affect and discourse theory.

Mathias Sylwan is a Ph.D. student at the Department of Culture and Media Studies, Umeå University, and an assistant lecturer at the Department of Media and Communication Studies, University of Gävle. His forthcoming thesis is entitled *The Mediated Family. Constructions of the Family and Parenthood in Swedish Public-Service Television News 1974–2006*. His main research interests lie in the fields of rhetorics and governmentality.